THE MENSHEVIKS
AFTER OCTOBER

And the Lord said unto Cain:
"Where is Abel, thy brother?"
And he said: "I know not: am
I my brother's keeper?" And
He said: "What hast thou done?"

Genesis 4:9–10

THE MENSHEVIKS AFTER OCTOBER

Socialist Opposition and the Rise of the Bolshevik Dictatorship

VLADIMIR N. BROVKIN

CORNELL UNIVERSITY PRESS

Ithaca and London

First published 1987 by Cornell University Press.

International Standard Book Number 0-8014-1858-5
Library of Congress Catalog Card Number 87-47952
Printed in the United States of America
Librarians: Library of Congress cataloging information
appears on the last page of the book.

The paper in this book is acid-free and meets the guidelines for permanence and durability of the Committee on Production Guidelines for Book Longevity of the Council on Library Resources.

To my teachers

Contents

PART III   THE SHOWDOWN,
MAY–OCTOBER 1918

Illustrations

TABLES

Acknowledgments

Research for this book has been done at the libraries of Princeton, Harvard, Columbia, Stanford, and Tübingen universities, Ruhr-University Bochum, and the University of California at Berkeley, and at the Library of Congress. Everywhere I was offered friendly assistance, and my thanks are due particularly to the Slavic bibliographers in these libraries.

I owe a great intellectual debt and deep gratitude to Stephen Cohen, my friend and teacher. Discussions with him over many years as my research progressed were of utmost importance in the writing of this book. I am also grateful to Richard Wortman for his critical scrutiny and advice as research went on.

Like so many others, I am obliged to the late Anna Bourgina for her guidance through the materials in the Boris I. Nikolaevsky Collection at the Hoover Institution on War, Revolution, and Peace. I am also thankful to the staff of the institution's library and archives. All of them were extremely helpful and forthcoming during my several research visits there.

My thanks are due to the DAAD (German Academic Exchange Service) for a remarkable opportunity to do research at the Institut für Osteuropäische Geschichte at the University of Tübingen. I owe a great deal to Dietrich Geyer, the institute's director. His patient advice and criticism were of inestimable value to me.

A Mellon postdoctoral fellowship from the Center for Slavic and East European Studies at the University of California, Berkeley, enabled me to prepare the manuscript of this book for publication. My sincere thanks go to Gail Lapidus, director of the center, and to Reginald Zelnik and Martin Malia, with whom I had many stimulating discussions there. I also thank Cyril Black and Abraham Ascher, who subsequently read the manuscript and made many useful comments.

I owe special gratitude to Susan Abel, who in the course of several years helped me immeasurably. She spent long hours discussing composition and style with me, she edited the manuscript, and she made numerous valuable suggestions.

The final stages of work on the manuscript were made possible by fellowships from the Social Science Research Council and the Russian Research Center of Harvard University. One could hardly wish for a more congenial and stimulating intellectual atmosphere than that of the Russian Research Center. I thank Adam Ulam, the center's director, and all my friends and colleagues for their support and encouragement.

Finally, I thank the editors of *Russian Review* for permission to present in somewhat altered form my article "The Mensheviks' Political Comeback: The Elections to the Provincial City Soviets in Spring 1918," *Russian Review* 42 (January 1983): 1–50, as Chapter 5 of this book.

My thanks are due also to the Institut zur Geschichte der Arbeiterbewegung at Ruhr-University Bochum for its kind permission to publish photographs of rare newspapers in its collection.

VLADIMIR N. BROVKIN

Cambridge, Massachusetts

Introduction

This book attempts to reconstruct the history of the Menshevik party during the first year of Bolshevik rule. It focuses on the ideas and actions of men and women who had united in a political party because of their shared understanding of Marxism, the workers' movement, and the goals of the Russian Revolution. The period I survey is the most critical in the party's history—a period when the Bolsheviks, the Mensheviks' primary socialist rivals, came to power and launched a socialist transformation of Russian society. During the turbulent months after October, the old arguments between those factions of a once united Social Democratic party were no longer confined to the pages of theoretical journals but were played out in earnest as the parties contended over policies, competed for voters, and struggled for power.

In the end, this struggle devastated the Menshevik party. In October 1917, both before and after the Bolsheviks seized power, the Mensheviks participated fully in negotiations to determine which party coalition would form Russia's next government. By October 1918 they had been expelled from the institutions of government, their local organizations had been decimated by arrests, some Mensheviks had been executed, and even Iulii Martov, the party leader—who with Lenin had helped to found the Russian Social Democratic Workers' party at the turn of the century—had to go into hiding. Worse still, the Menshevik party was split over the key question: How was the emerging Bolshevik dictatorship to be opposed?

One of the most important aspects of Menshevik party history is the impact of Bolshevik rule on Menshevik ideology. A core of values, beliefs, and attitudes unites individuals in a political party. After October 1917, the Mensheviks' primary tasks were to define what Bolshevism represented as a social, economic, and political phenomenon and to propose specific policies to counter the Bolshevik program. The Mensheviks had never spoken with a single voice, however, and they did not do so now. Their critique of Bolshevism changed several times during 1918, and their policies changed accordingly.

The internal debates over policy reflected an intermittent struggle for party leadership. At times this struggle precipitated crises that reduced the Mensheviks' capacity to act as an effective political force. In order to understand the political strength of the various factions within the Menshevik party, it is necessary to examine local organizations and their membership. This aspect of Menshevik party history is perhaps the most difficult to document, but I attempt here to follow the fluctuations in numerical strength of Menshevik party organizations, to characterize the party leaders and their followers in various parts of the country, and to interpret their political sympathies in light of the political conditions and needs they faced at the local level.

Despite the sharp differences between Menshevik organizations and their many disputes over policy, Mensheviks of all persuasions believed that their party had to oppose the Bolshevik government. The difficult issue was the kind of opposition they should offer: legal and parliamentary or extralegal and insurrectionist. Should they oppose Bolshevik policies or Bolshevik rule itself? In the period under consideration, then, the Mensheviks' relations with the Bolsheviks were shaped primarily by the Mensheviks' oppositionist stance. I explore this interaction on three levels: in the Central Executive Committee (CEC) of Soviets, in the local soviets, and in other workers' organizations throughout the country.

The Mensheviks' interaction with other opposition parties, especially the Socialist Revolutionaries (SRs), must also be considered. Though the two parties shared values and programs and often worked together as allies, they also had important differences. Sometimes dormant, these differences could emerge to place a serious strain on Menshevik-SR relations, as they did during the October 1917 crisis. In June 1918, they led to a break between the two erstwhile allies.

To explore the history of a political party is also to examine its interaction with the social groups whose grievances it seeks to articulate. In this sense, Menshevik party history is part of workers' political history. Since Menshevik political strength was directly related to worker support, I devote special attention to fluctuations in the extent of this support. What kinds of workers in which cities supported the

Mensheviks, and for what reasons? How did Menshevik party leaders and the workers who called themselves Mensheviks define their roles as members of an opposition workers' party in various places and at various times? The answers to these questions reveal the frictions within the Menshevik ranks on the one hand and the patterns of Menshevik confrontation with the Bolsheviks on the other.

During the months from October 1917 to October 1918, profound changes took place in Russia's political development. In October 1917, the moderate socialists and the Bolsheviks reversed political roles, and the political struggle between them entered a new phase. The Mensheviks and SRs, now the political opposition, had close to half of the delegates at the Second Congress of Soviets and they continued to hold leading positions in dozens of city soviets, dumas, zemstvos, unions, and economic agencies. The network of local Menshevik party organizations was as well developed as that of the Bolsheviks, and the SRs still had the strongest local base of all. The fall of 1917 was an exceptionally fluid period of multiparty electoral politics. The elections held to choose delegates to the soviets, dumas, and scores of other institutions were genuinely free. A free press debated every aspect of the political process. Indeed, when national elections to the Constituent Assembly were held in November, the outcome of the interparty struggle was far from clear.

Almost everything changed in the course of 1918. The Constitutional Democratic (Kadet) party was outlawed as early as November 1917. In January 1918 the new regime disbanded the Constituent Assembly, and throughout the winter and spring it abolished the popularly elected dumas. A multiparty electoral process survived, but the propertied classes and the nonsocialist political parties were now excluded from it. Working-class organizations, such as the soviets and the workers' independent assemblies, fared no better: dozens of these organizations were disbanded during the spring of 1918. Barely a year after the solemn proclamation of soviet power, that power remained soviet in name only. Political authority was firmly in the hands of appointed Bolshevik functionaries, and the country was in the midst of the Red Terror. New sets of governmental procedures emerged in 1918, accompanied by new attitudes toward political power, new habits, and a new ideology: as the vanguard of the proletariat, only the Communist party could represent the workers. In October 1917 the Bolsheviks had praised the will of the masses and the convocation of the Constituent Assembly; in October 1918 they suppressed all opposition and executed their political opponents en masse. In October 1917 the Mensheviks had walked out of the Second Congress of Soviets because they opposed the takeover of power by the soviets; in October 1918 the Mensheviks struggled to defend the soviets against the Bolshevik dictatorship. The transformation of Soviet politics in 1918 is a vast historical problem, and this book makes no claim to have resolved it. I focus on one aspect of this complex sociopolitical upheaval, the struggle between the Bolsheviks and the Mensheviks, for I believe that this struggle did much to shape the political system that had emerged by the fall of 1918.

The confrontation between the Mensheviks and the Bolsheviks passed through several stages in the course of 1918. At each stage the policies adopted by the key parties precipitated a new and more intense round of conflict. In the period after October and before the disbandment of the Constituent Assembly in January 1918, the Menshevik party was trying to play the role of mediator between the Bolsheviks and the SRs. It sought a negotiated settlement to the crisis of power. It was ready to participate in a government that included the Bolsheviks provided that government guaranteed the inviolability of the Constituent Assembly. After the Bolsheviks disbanded the Constituent Assembly, the character of the Mensheviks' opposition changed. Now they opposed not only specific Bolshevik policies, such as the Treaty of Brest-Litovsk and radical economic measures, but also the abolition of representative institutions based on universal suffrage. The Mensheviks strove to change the constitutional order by reconvening the Constituent Assembly—not by insurrection, as the Bolsheviks had done in October 1917, but by winning popular majorities in the existing soviet framework. This effort to compete with the Bolsheviks within the soviets unified Mensheviks of the right, center, and left, and united the Mensheviks and SRs as well.

In the pages that follow we shall explore the relationship between Bolshevik economic policies, which exacerbated the already chaotic situation in industry, and the growing popularity of the Mensheviks and SRs in the spring of 1918. Their stance on the independence of trade unions even under the dictatorship of the proletariat, their proposals in regard to food distribution, and their critique of Bolshevik local administrations won increasing popular support. The Bolsheviks perceived the impressive Menshevik-SR electoral victories as a threat. The Mensheviks rejected the idea of seizing power by violent means, as they were convinced that no minority government could effectively force a large population into submission. Their strategy was to apply peaceful pressure on the Bolsheviks through the soviets and other workers' organizations. They saw no need to change the rules of the political game when they were winning majorities in the soviets by those rules. With the electoral success of the Menshevik-SR bloc, however, the Bolsheviks themselves abandoned the rules. In the spring of 1918 they disbanded almost all of the newly elected soviets in which their socialist opponents had won majorities. A wave of strikes swept the country in May and June as workers turned against the Bolsheviks and peasants rebelled against the requisitioning of grain. Determined to hold on to power, the Bolsheviks shut down what was left of the opposition press, expelled the opposition parties from the CEC, suppressed independent workers' assemblies, and arrested local opposition leaders. In this crisis the Mensheviks had to find a new answer to the old question: How were they to oppose the Bolshevik dictatorship now? The Right Mensheviks saw no alternative to armed confrontation, but the center-left faction held firm in its opposition to violence, convinced that civil war would strengthen the extremists in the Communist party and that the ultimate beneficiaries would be the Whites. The two wings of the Menshevik party adopted contrary policies once again, and now only the Right Mensheviks maintained an alliance with the SRs. This alliance posed a genuine military threat to the Bolsheviks' survival and made it increasingly likely that the structure of political power would be imposed by military means. This book argues, in short, that the Bolshevik dictatorship emerged in the process of a struggle against the socialist opposition, which posed a challenge that was at first electoral and then military. The Bolsheviks resorted to dictatorial measures not because they were powerful but because they saw growing threats to their hold on power.

The period under consideration can be divided into three overlapping but distinct stages of political development. Each part of this book deals with one of those stages. Part I covers the crisis of Menshevism from October 1917 to March 1918. Part II examines the Menshevik political comeback in the spring of 1918. Part III deals with the period of confrontation and civil war, from June through October 1918.

Chapter 1 addresses the Mensheviks' contradictory record during the October struggle for power, the leadership crisis, and the emergence of new ideas in the course of that crisis. Chapter 2 examines the Menshevik critique of Bolshevik post-October policies and workers' political aspirations at this stage. Chapter 3 explores the concrete socioeconomic policies offered by the Bolsheviks and the Mensheviks as they interacted in the legislative institution (the CEC). Chapter 4 covers the first trials of Mensheviks on political charges for offenses committed by the Menshevik press. Chapter 5 examines patterns of local politics, taking into account such factors as the key issues at stake, the power settlement after the elections, and the consequences of these developments for political equilibrium as a whole. Chapter 6 follows the development of the Menshevik-led workers' assemblies, known as the *upolnomochennye*, from their beginnings early in the year to their final suppression in July. I here examine the triangular relationship of the workers, the Mensheviks, and the Bolsheviks to find answers to some puzzling questions: What were workers' political aspirations? Why did the Bolsheviks not fulfill them? Why did workers find the Menshevik political program attractive? And finally, what caused the downfall of the independent assemblies?

Chapter 7 discusses the process that led the Menshevik and SR parties to adopt contrary policies in June 1918. Chapter 8 reconstructs the Bolsheviks' attack on their socialist opponents, from the expulsion of the Mensheviks and SRs from the CEC in June to the Red Terror of September. Chapter 9 focuses on the Mensheviks' record in the civil war and attempts to discover why the center-left leadership remained neutral in this struggle even though this policy split the party, and why the winners of the struggle were determined to establish a one-party monopoly not only on government but on the press, unions, soviets, and political opinion, whereas the losers lost all possibility of ever again competing for political power.

The Menshevik party was one of the key players in the Soviet political process of 1917–18. Without an understanding of the parts, we cannot hope to understand the whole: unless we understand the part played by the socialist opposition in the soviets, we cannot properly understand the development of the Soviet system as we know it today.

Note on Transliteration and Dating Systems

The Library of Congress system of transliteration (without diacritical marks) is used in this study. The only exceptions are names that have become familiar in other forms or that were spelled otherwise by the persons themselves. In part I, dates are given according to the Julian calendar, which was in use in Russia at the time of the events discussed. In subsequent parts, dates are given according to the Gregorian calendar, which was in use in the West and was adopted in Russia early in 1918. The Julian calendar was thirteen days behind the Gregorian.

ABBREVIATIONS

CC	Central Committee
CEC	Central Executive Committee
CPC	Council of People's Commissars
EC	Executive Committee
Kadet	Constitutional Democrat
MRC	Military Revolutionary Committee
RSDWP	Russian Social Democratic Workers' Party
SD	Social Democrat
SR	Socialist Revolutionary

THE MENSHEVIKS
AFTER OCTOBER

Prologue:
The Road to October

The political struggle between the Mensheviks and the Bolsheviks in 1917 and 1918 marked a relatively late stage in the development of the social-democratic movement in Russia. Thus an understanding of the Bolsheviks' and Mensheviks' actions during that time requires a brief survey of the key divisions in the movement from 1903 until October 1917.

The very names Bolshevik and Menshevik were coined in the wake of a debate on party organization at the second congress of the Russian Social Democratic Workers' party in 1903. The followers of Vladimir Il'ich Lenin—who at that time were a majority and hence came to be known as Bolsheviks, from the Russian *bol'she*, "more"—advocated the creation of a tightly knit underground organization of professional revolutionaries. The followers of Iulii Martov, a minority—and hence Mensheviks, from the Russian *men'she*, "less"—argued for a large working-class party modeled on the German Social Democratic party.[1] In succeeding years the breach was widened by disagreements over many other aspects of revolutionary theory and practice. A central question was whether revolution in Russia, after ending tsarism and establishing a bourgeois-democratic republic, would then develop toward socialism. The Mensheviks continually denied the possibility of a socialist revolution in Russia.[2] They pointed out that, according to

1. For Menshevik critiques of Lenin's ideas on party organization, see Cherevanin, *Organizatsionnyi vopros*, and Martov, *Bor'ba s osadnym polozheniem*.
2. For a succinct summary of the evolution of Menshevik political theory, see Aksel'rod, *Kto izmenil sotsializmu?*

Marxist theory, such a revolution could take place only in a highly developed capitalist society. In their view, it was simply incorrect to speak of an imminent socialist revolution in such a backward country as Russia, where the working class was a tiny minority in a population that consisted largely of illiterate peasants. Most Bolsheviks agreed, in the days immediately after the fall of the tsar, that Russia was not yet ripe for a socialist revolution, but Lenin's return to Petrograd from exile brought about a shift in the Bolsheviks' position. Their goal now became to move on to the next stage of the revolution—the overthrow of the bourgeois-democratic order and of the capitalist mode of production and the establishment of a dictatorship of the proletariat, which would prepare the ground for the construction of socialism.[3]

The Mensheviks perceived themselves as orthodox Marxists. They firmly believed in Marx's stages of economic development. Socialist revolution could not succeed in a country where capitalism was still rudimentary; a premature revolution was bound to fail. This view was fortified by the Mensheviks' interpretation of the revolutions in recent European history. The tragic fate of the Paris Commune, which was discussed with unabated interest in socialist literature, convinced the Mensheviks that the Commune would have needed the support of the peasantry, at least part of the bourgeoisie, and the army in order to have had a chance of succeeding. In the Russian revolution of 1905, the army had remained loyal to the tsar; and the bourgeoisie, placated by the tsar's concessions and frightened by the radicalism of the masses, had withdrawn its support from the revolution, which thus failed. The lesson drawn was that in a future revolution, the socialists should strive only for what was achievable at the given historical stage of development; they must postpone socialist changes and concentrate instead on establishing a bourgeois-democratic order—a parliamentary republic and a democratic government elected by universal suffrage and responsible to the people.[4] Only afterward could the revolutionary government initiate some socialist measures, such as the eight-hour day, partial nationalization, and control over profits and wages. The socialists could not afford, however, to alienate the bourgeoisie. When revolution did break out in February 1917, the Mensheviks acted in accordance with these ideas.

In August 1914, when patriotic enthusiasm was sweeping through the European capitals, all European socialist parties were confronted with an urgent question: Should they support or oppose their country's war effort? Unlike the Social Democrats in the German Reichstag, both

---

3. For a discussion of Lenin's tactics, see Geyer, *Die russische Revolution*, pp. 81–92.
4. Dvinov, *Pervaia mirovaia voina*, p. 54.

the Mensheviks and the Bolsheviks in the Russian State Duma objected to the war credits.[5] Later in the war, these groups came to be known as Internationalists. Among the leading Menshevik Internationalists were Nikolai Chkheidze, the Menshevik leader in the State Duma and future chairman of the Petrograd soviet; Fedor Dan, the future chairman of the Central Executive Committee (CEC) of Soviets; Matvei Skobelev, the future minister of labor in the Provisional Government; Iraklii Tsereteli, the future architect of the successive cabinets of the Provisional Government; and Iulii Martov, one of the founders of the party and, with Dan, its cochairman after November 1917.

From the very beginning, though, there was a crucial difference between the Menshevik opponents of the war and Lenin. The mere struggle for peace was not enough for Lenin. He welcomed Russia's defeat in the war because it would mean the downfall of tsarism and would promote the cause of revolution in Russia. Lenin advocated turning the imperialist war, waged by the bourgeoisie of the belligerent countries, into a civil war, to be waged by the proletariat of each country against its bourgeoisie.[6] Martov's internationalism, on the other hand, was part of a pacifist trend in European socialist thought. The victory of one side over the other, he believed, would not advance the cause of socialism. On the contrary, it would exacerbate hostility between nations, encourage revanchism, and undermine workers' international solidarity. What was needed was not the defeat of Russia but a negotiated peace without annexations or indemnities. The socialist parties in all the belligerent countries must sponsor an international peace movement. The bourgeois governments must be forced by proletarian pressure to halt hostilities and negotiate a settlement.[7]

On the extreme right wing of the Russian Social Democratic movement, G. V. Plekhanov and his supporters rejected the Menshevik Internationalists' ideas as semi-Bolshevik and argued that, since Russia had been invaded by the Germans, the working class and the Social Democrats had to defend their country against the aggressors.[8] Aleksandr Potresov, another of the party's founders, did not go so far as Plekhanov did in his condemnation of the Internationalists' "defeatism," but he, too, believed in defense of the nation as an adjunct to the struggle for peace.[9] These Mensheviks came to be known as Defensists.

With the outbreak of the February 1917 revolution, a significant re-

5. For a description of the scene in the duma, see ibid., p. 22.
6. Lenin, *Sochineniia*, 4th ed., 35: 121–22.
7. Martov, *Proletariat i natsional'naia oborona*, p. 15.
8. Plekhanov, *God na rodine*, pp. 51–53, and Dvinov, *Pervaia mirovaia voina*, pp. 68–79.
9. On Potresov's position, see Dvinov, *Pervaia mirovaia voina*, pp. 23, 124–25.

alignment took place in the Menshevik party on the question of war and peace. Some of the Internationalists—Chkheidze, Tsereteli, and Dan (the latter two recently returned from exile in Siberia)—now called themselves Revolutionary Defensists.[10] They emphasized that the Russian Revolution had to be defended from domestic as well as foreign reaction. Russia would therefore wage a defensive war, but not an imperialist one. At their urging, the Petrograd soviet adopted the slogan "Peace without Annexations and Indemnities!" Thus the struggle for peace was to be combined with a defensive war. The position of the Revolutionary Defensists moved closer to that of Potresov's Defensists for the time being and reflected the views of the mainstream of the party. An Internationalist minority headed by Martov continued to insist that peace negotiations should be initiated immediately.

On questions of domestic politics, the Menshevik factions showed more unity. February 1917 was a time of exhilaration and hope for the future of Russian democracy. Since Russia was in the stage of bourgeois-democratic revolution, the socialists had to eschew governmental responsibility.[11] It may seem strange that the Mensheviks should pursue such a policy, given that the most powerful political organization to emerge in the first days of the revolution was the Petrograd Soviet of Workers' and Soldiers' Deputies, whose membership was overwhelmingly Menshevik and SR. Much has already been said about the Mensheviks' aversion to wielding power. One may look at their reluctance to assume governmental responsibility as evidence of weakness; it is also possible, however, to view it as stemming from a sober evaluation of Russia's political reality. The takeover of political power by the soviets would have disenfranchised all those groups that were not represented in the soviets. Such a step would have antagonized the propertied classes, accelerated social and political polarization, and led to civil war. This course was unacceptable to the Mensheviks.

The workers were a small minority in Russia, and that fact, according to the Mensheviks, required them to compromise with more powerful classes—numerically the peasants and financially the bourgeoisie. In the politics of 1917, the Mensheviks saw a need to come to an understanding with the Socialist Revolutionaries (SRs), whose constituency was primarily the peasantry, and with the Constitutional Democrats (Kadets). The Mensheviks' duty, as they saw it, was to represent workers' interests vis-à-vis other classes' interests, but without political polarization. Their social policy aimed at creating mechanisms for resolv-

10. On the formation of this group and its policy on war and peace, see Tsereteli, *Vospominaniia o fevral'skoi revoliutsii*, 1: 45–74.

11. "Rezoliutsiia Organizatsionnogo komiteta o koalitsionnom ministerstve," in L'vov-Rogachevskii, ed., *Sotsialisty o tekushchem momente*, pp. 96–97.

ing class conflicts by peaceful means. The Mensheviks did not want to repeat what they saw as the mistakes of 1905. The Petrograd soviet should not isolate itself from the rest of society, nor should it lay claim to political power. The soviets were to be mass political organizations, essentially defensive in character; their tasks were to safeguard the "democratic conquests of the revolution" and exert pressure on the Provisional Government.

Moreover, there was no need for the Petrograd soviet to strive for a formal takeover of political power: the leaders of the Provisional Government and the leaders of industry were quite willing to cooperate with the soviet, for they were well aware that any policy they pursued had to have the soviet's support. The system of "dual power" allowed the Menshevik leaders of the Petrograd soviet to exercise informal control over the overall policy of the government and play a de facto role in the governmental process.

The pace of the Russian Revolution, however, made the Mensheviks reconsider their policy. By the end of May they had concluded that it was no longer possible to shun formal participation in government. Under pressure from below, and after heated debates within the party, the Menshevik leaders decided to enter the Provisional Government.[12] Despite this change in policy, there was no change in the Mensheviks' goals. Within the government, the Mensheviks were determined to secure the cooperation of the bourgeoisie, which they believed was indispensable for the maintenance of industrial production and civil peace.

On the other hand, measures had to be undertaken to prevent reactionary elements from regrouping their forces and defeating the revolution. Since the army had traditionally been regarded as the main weapon in the hands of reaction, energetic efforts were made in the first days of the revolution to democratize the army. The authority of the officers was limited to purely military matters, and even their military orders had to be countersigned by the soldiers' elected representatives in the soviets and the army committees.

In the summer of 1917, elections of city and provincial governments (dumas and zemstvos) were held on the basis of universal suffrage. Scores of trade unions, mutual aid funds, and joint worker-management arbitration boards were set up. Menshevik social policy was intended to embrace as large a number of workers, soldiers, and peasants as possible in a variety of social and political organizations; this would be the first step toward improving their economic position and increasing their involvement in the political life of the country. In the long run, this schooling in social democracy would mold, so the Menshe-

12. "Krizis vlasti i koalitsionnoe ministerstvo," in ibid., pp. 190–95.

viks hoped, a mature and politically aware working class. In the short run, it was the best guarantee that, if counterrevolutionary elements tried to stage a coup d'état, they would be faced with a powerful general strike by an organized proletariat. The Mensheviks were utterly preoccupied with the right-wing threat to the democratic order, and General Lavr Kornilov's attempt to march on Petrograd at the end of August suggested that their fears were not unfounded. Yet the danger to universal suffrage would eventually arise from the left.

The Menshevik attempts at democratization backfired. The masses hardly needed any encouragement to make use of their liberty and resist authority. The workers' and soldiers' organizations were beginning to feel their strength, which then seemed to them boundless, and their demands grew correspondingly. Factory committees stepped up their pressure on the industrialists; peasants were unwilling to wait any longer for orderly and carefully worked-out agrarian reform; soldiers were desperate to get back home from the front. The Bolsheviks, who had initially been an insignificant minority in the soviets, capitalized on the rising expectations and made increasingly extravagant promises as they demanded the transfer of power to the soviets. General dissatisfaction with the government was mounting.

From May on, all successive cabinets included Menshevik ministers. Moreover, the Mensheviks were much more influential than their formal representation in the government might have indicated. A convincing case might be made that Iraklii Tsereteli played a more important role than Aleksandr Kerensky in the making of the last two cabinets and their policies. The institutions and organizations of the Provisional Government were the power base of the party's center-right wing, the Defensists, many of whom were Provisional Government commissars in the army, members of army committees, functionaries in the ministries, and specialists in the dumas.

But the Mensheviks were not only a government party; they were a soviet party as well. Until October 25, they were the leaders of the CEC. Although formally a public rather than a state organization, the CEC exercised immense political power. Indeed, the CEC before October had more power vis-à-vis the Provisional Government than it had after October vis-à-vis Lenin's government, even though the CEC officially became the supreme legislative institution after October. The CEC leaders Fedor Dan and Mark Liber, although not officially in the government, were in fact the leaders of the pre-October regime. The party center, the Revolutionary Defensists, embodied the link between the Provisional Government and the soviets. The party's left wing, the Internationalists, had its base in the soviets and trade unions and derived its strength from the leftward-drifting worker constituency, as workers abandoned the Revolutionary Defensists.

The Menshevik party as a whole thus reflected the contradictory nature of Russia's dual-power political system in 1917.[13] It was a government party and at the same time it embraced a growing minority that was opposed to the government. In the course of 1917, the Menshevik party unsuccessfully tried both to retain its soviet constituency and to participate in the Provisional Government. But by September 1917, it was becoming increasingly clear that the Menshevik-SR majorities in the soviets were waning; peace negotiations were stalled, inflation was rising, production was falling, and the Mensheviks' ability to create government coalitions had been exhausted.

From July on, Martov advocated a break with the Kadets, the creation of a purely socialist government, and the imposition of direct state controls on industry.[14] Market exchange had to be maintained, food prices controlled, and war profits and inflation curbed, not by persuasion, pressure, or coalition with the Kadets but by immediate and resolute action. The pace of agrarian reform had to be accelerated and foreign policy changed. The Allies had to be confronted with an ultimatum: either start peace negotiations immediately or consider Russia free of its obligations.[15] Perhaps Martov could have split his faction off from the Defensists over this policy and attracted many of the wavering Bolsheviks and left-wing SRs to a joint bloc at the Democratic State Conference in September, when all political parties and interest groups gathered to determine the composition of the government until the Constituent Assembly could be convened.[16] Nevertheless, Martov chose to remain in the United Menshevik party, primarily because the Internationalists were constantly winning new adherents and becoming a majority. Martov hoped to regain the leadership of the Menshevik party, and he was successful in doing so by late October. His choice, however, permitted the Bolsheviks to become the rallying center of the discontented masses.[17]

The Defensists—Potresov, Liber, and P. N. Kolokol'nikov—blamed the Internationalists and the Bolsheviks for the mounting problems.[18] It was the Internationalists' agitation at the front that had sown unrealistic expectations of speedy peace negotiations. The Internationalists' campaigns for fraternization at the front only played into the enemy's

13. For a discussion of the Mensheviks' role in this dual-power system, see Reisser, *Menschewismus und Revolution*, pp. 89–111.

14. "Martov Urges Soviet to Take Power," in Ascher, ed., *Mensheviks in the Russian Revolution*, pp. 101–2.

15. Getzler, *Martov*, p. 166; see also "Die Menschewiki zur Regierungsfrage," in *Texte der Menschewiki*, pp. 60–62.

16. Getzler, *Martov*, pp. 158, 162.

17. Ibid., pp. 164–66.

18. For Potresov's critique of Martov's proposals, see "Iskusstvo Generala Rennenkampfa," in Nikolaevsky, ed., *Potresov*, pp. 246–48.

hands and led to the disintegration of the army. The ultimatum to the Allies meant nothing other than a separate peace with Germany, which was unacceptable to all political parties. A break with the Kadets would antagonize the entire bourgeoisie and dangerously narrow the social base of the government. The Internationalists, argued the Defensists, were by their very nature incapable of enforcing discipline and strengthening the country's defense, even when one province after another was being overrun by the invader. The Defensists believed that Martov's policies would sharpen class conflict, further radicalize the masses, and thus play into the Bolsheviks' hands.[19] An increase in Bolshevik strength could lead to a formal transfer of power to the limited-franchise soviets, and this step, a realistic appraisal of the social forces in the country made clear, would provoke a civil war. The soviets must continue to be public organizations whose role was only to exercise pressure on the propertied classes. In effect, the Defensists were trying to maintain the status quo, a policy that, as it turned out, proved to be self-defeating. The government remained weak and ineffectual, and Bolshevik influence in the soviets began to acquire threatening proportions.

The decision by the center-right leadership to continue the coalition with the Kadets in September, when it was quite clear that the masses were becoming increasingly radical, intensified rivalry between the Menshevik factions, plunged the party into a crisis of leadership, and alienated the workers and pushed them further toward the Bolsheviks. Yet, because of their identification with the interests of the government, the Defensists believed that economic improvement could be achieved only by coalition with the Kadets. Those Mensheviks who worked in the government agencies, such as the Ministry of Labor, tended to see the solution to the mounting economic and political problems in alliances and compromises with the industrialists. Those Mensheviks who worked in the soviets, meanwhile, tended to support the demands of the radical workers. The party was internally divided in its identity and its policies.

In September the Internationalists demanded that the Menshevik ministers be recalled from the Provisional Government. They were not recalled, but on October 15 the Menshevik CC announced to the Menshevik ministers that they "must immediately leave the party."[20] Despite this manifestation of the Internationalists' ability to influence the decisions of the CC, until October 31 the leadership of the party re-

19. For a summary of the Defensist Menshevik critique, see "Perspektiven des rechten Fluegels der Menschewiki," in *Texte der Menschewiki*, pp. 57–59.

20. Leo Lande, "The Mensheviks and the Provisional Government," in Haimson, ed., *Mensheviks*, p. 33.

mained in the hands of the center-right bloc of Tsereteli, Liber, and Dan.

Tension between the Defensists and the Internationalists led to the formal breakup of some local organizations. In Petrograd, the Internationalists, who formed a majority in the city organization, refused to include the Defensists in the Constituent Assembly election slates. They violated no rules in doing so, because the majority in a local organization had the right to determine the names of the candidates in the elections. In response, the Defensists formed their own electoral committee, drew up their own separate election slates, and campaigned against the official party nominees. As the Party Committee on Elections to the Constituent Assembly reported later to the CC, "the natural result of the two election campaigns in the same place was, first, the formation of two parallel party organizations, and second, the defeat of both slates in the elections."[21]

A similar process of polarization and realignment of forces was going on within the SR party. In his commentaries on the proceedings in the SR CC, Viktor Chernov, the leader of the party's centrists, noted that in October the usual voting pattern was 6 for and 6 against, or 7 for and 7 abstaining, out of a total of 20 CC members.[22] The SR CC was paralyzed by its warring factions: the left and right wings were bitter political enemies. The divisions within the SRs were even more serious than those among the Mensheviks. Oliver Radkey has described the process of the breakup of the SR party.[23] The Left SRs, expelled en bloc by the center-Right leadership, had no alternative but to form their own party. According to Chernov, the SRs' right wing, grouped around Boris Savinkov, was involved in manipulating the slates of SR candidates in the Constituent Assembly elections.[24] Since the CC and provincial party organizations could fill in names on the party's list of candidates, the factionalists did all they could to exclude as many center-Left SRs as possible from the slates in areas where the electorate was likely to be conservative and, on the other hand, to combine the names of popular center-Left leaders with those of a few Right SRs in a joint list in areas where the electorate sympathized with the left, so that the center-Left SRs could carry with them as many Right SRs as possible. Radkey has called such practices "absurd bracketing," because Right and Left candidates were artificially combined in one election slate. Thus, in Petro-

---

21. "Iz zhizni RSDRP: Iz deiatel'nosti Tsentral'nogo Izbiratel'nogo Komiteta," *Novyi luch'* (newspaper of the Menshevik CC), 5 December 1917, p. 4.

22. Viktor Chernov, "Kommentarii k protokolam TsK PSR (sentiabr' 1917–fevral' 1918)," Nikolaevsky Collection no. 7, box 3, file 54, p. 40 (cited hereafter as Nik. Col.).

23. Radkey, *Sickle under the Hammer*, pp. 95–163, esp. pp. 105–7.

24. Chernov, "Kommentarii k protokolam TsK PSR," pp. 52–53.

grad, A. R. Gots, the organizer of an anti-Bolshevik uprising by military cadets on October 29, was placed on the list next to Boris Kamkov, the Left SR leader, and both were "balanced" by Chernov.[25] On the eve of the October Revolution, each of the Menshevik and SR party factions had its own journal and newspaper, gravitated toward a different institution, defended contrary policies, and campaigned against each other in elections. Both parties were in the throes of a crisis of internal development.

By late October, the relative strength of the Internationalists within the Menshevik party had grown to such an extent that they were able, with the aid of some wavering Revolutionary Defensists, to block Defensist policy decisions. At the eleventh hour, on October 24, Martov finally persuaded Dan and some others to join him in the so-called Left Bloc, a coalition of Menshevik Internationalists, Left SRs, and some Revolutionary Defensists in the Preparliament, the temporary legislative body created at the Democratic State Conference to govern until the convocation of the Constituent Assembly.[26] The Left Bloc demanded immediate transfer of land to the land committees and armistice at the fronts. The majority vote in support of this resolution amounted to a vote of no confidence in Kerensky's government.[27] Speaking about this vote at the December Menshevik party congress, Dan said: "No doubt we stood on the threshold of a government crisis, the resignation of Tereshchenko [the foreign minister], and the acceptance by the Provisional Government of our peace program."[28] But the Left Bloc had run out of time: the Bolshevik takeover was beginning.

For many years afterward, the Mensheviks were preoccupied with the question of what went wrong in 1917. The center-left Mensheviks contended that the timely adoption of their proposals for energetic implementation of peace and land reform could have arrested the radicalization of the masses and their flight to the Bolsheviks. The Defensists argued that the Provisional Government had done what it could to achieve an honorable peace and prepare for agrarian reform. They blamed the Internationalists for raising the expectations of the masses and thus driving them into the arms of the Bolsheviks. Yet perhaps Mensheviks of both persuasions tended to credit each other with more responsibility for the revolutionary processes of 1917 than they in fact had. In the face of the breakdown of state authority, neither a purely

25. Radkey, *Sickle under the Hammer*, p. 303.

26. For a good summary of Menshevik policies in the Preparliament and of Martov's initiative, see Kritchewsky, *Vers la catastrophe russe*, pp. 68–75.

27. "Debats au Conseil Provisoire et vote sur les ordres du jour," document no. 35B in Oldenbourg, ed., *Le Coup d'état bolcheviste*, p. 138. See also Fedor Dan, "Posledniaia popytka liderov TsIK," in Anin, *Revoliutsiia 1917 goda*, pp. 371–95.

28. "Materialy s"ezda," *Novyi luch'*, 3 December 1917, p. 3.

socialist Menshevik-SR government nor any other could have stopped the flood of desertions from the front, prevented seizures of land by the peasants, or induced the Allies or the Germans to conclude peace. The Menshevik debacle of 1917 was not attributable to either the Internationalists or the Defensists; it was a result of the revolutionary escalation, which was not under the control of any party. Still, the Mensheviks' position had been weakened by their effort to play two irreconcilable roles simultaneously: that of a government and that of an opposition. It was a dangerous course in a time of revolution and sharpening class antagonisms. In the event, the Mensheviks lost a large part of their constituency to the Bolsheviks and came close to a party breakup.

PART I

CATACLYSM AND READJUSTMENT

October 1917–March 1918

CHAPTER 1

The Mensheviks in October: From Government Party to Opposition

The dramatic events of late October 1917 marked the beginning of a new period in the history of Menshevism, a period of opposition to a triumphant Bolshevism. From the very first days after the Bolshevik seizure of power in Petrograd, however, the two factions of the Menshevik party clashed over the question of the kind of opposition the party could and should pursue.

All Mensheviks shared the view that the Bolshevik seizure of power represented a setback for the fledgling democratic, parliamentary republic. The Internationalists, however, emphasized the Bolsheviks' leftist extremism, which would, in their opinion, isolate the workers within society, push the bourgeoisie to the right, and thus provoke civil war. The possibility that the Bolsheviks would find it necessary to suppress even workers' protest was not anticipated at that time. Hence the Internationalists saw it as their task to moderate the Bolshevik program by means of a negotiated settlement. For the Defensists, the Bolshevik seizure of power brought to an abrupt end the government of which they had been a part. They emphasized the Bolsheviks' use of what was largely a soldiers' and sailors' rebellion for their own political ends. The Defensists' opposition to Bolshevism excluded negotiations, at least for the time being, and called for resistance to Bolshevik attempts to consolidate and spread their power.

The Search for a Negotiated Settlement

On October 25, 1917, the Menshevik leaders faced a twofold problem. On the one hand, the new center-left party majority had withdrawn its support from Kerensky's government in the Preparliament. On the other, the Bolsheviks had disbanded the Preparliament and were taking military actions against the Provisional Government. It was an awkward situation indeed. Should the Mensheviks back antigovernment action, or should they condemn it? If they supported it, they would impinge on the authority of the Second Congress of Soviets, which alone was empowered to take such action. If they opposed it, they ran the risk of being perceived as Kerensky's followers. Dan, the chairman of the CEC and the spokesman for the Menshevik CC, faced an additional dilemma. Some of his followers in the party upheld Martov's Left Bloc platform, which was quite similar to the Bolsheviks' public pronouncements. Dan had to find a way to endorse that Left Bloc platform while preventing the Bolsheviks from seizing power. The latter task became his priority, while resolving the power crisis by means of negotiations became the immediate objective of the Menshevik Internationalists.[1] The problem of what to do about the Bolshevik antigovernment offensive split the Internationalists and Revolutionary Defensists again.

The Second Congress of Soviets

Against this background, the Second Congress of Soviets opened on October 25. As Oskar Anweiler has pointed out, the Bolsheviks, even at the height of their success, had a very narrow margin of numerical strength over their opponents.[2] According to the Credentials Commission's figures, the combined strength of the 200 SR delegates and the 92 Menshevik delegates almost equaled the 300 Bolsheviks.[3]

The official breakdown of the political forces at the congress, however, did not correspond to the real alliances and antagonisms. The data from personal questionnaires give a somewhat more precise picture of the numbers in various factions. Of the 98 Mensheviks, according to this source, 62 were Martov's supporters, 14 backed the Menshevik Central Committee, and 22 belonged to the Defensists' faction.[4] These groups had fundamentally different political objectives. The SRs, the second largest faction at the congress, were also split. The Right SRs sided with the Defensist Mensheviks; the Left SRs were Martov's partners in the Left Bloc. The Bolsheviks, as is now well known,

---

1. "Ot Men'shevikov Internatsionalistov (27 oktiabria 1917 goda)," document no. 6 in Nikolaevsky, *Men'sheviki v dni Oktiabr'skogo perevorota*, p. 29.

2. Anweiler, *The Soviets*, app. B, pp. 260–61.

3. "Ot kommissii po proverke polnomochii Vtorogo S"ezda Sovetov," in *Vtoroi Vserossiiskii S"ezd Sovetov*, p. 26.

4. Ibid.

were divided as well, into radicals, led by Lenin and Lev Trotsky, and conciliatory Bolsheviks, led by Lev Kamenev and Grigorii Zinoviev. The political struggle at the congress developed on two planes: the leftist soviet parties—Bolsheviks, Menshevik Internationalists, and Left SRs—versus the rightist soviet parties—Right SRs and Defensist Mensheviks; and within the left wing itself, conciliatory Bolsheviks, Left SRs, and Menshevik Internationalists versus the extremist Bolsheviks.

As soon as the congress opened, Martov took the lead: "First of all, it is imperative to secure a peaceful resolution of the crisis. Blood is being shed in the streets of Petrograd! It is necessary to stop military actions on both sides. A peaceful resolution of the crisis can be reached by creating a political authority [*vlast'*] that would be recognized by all of Democracy."[5] This appeal was greeted by general applause. The Left SRs backed it immediately. After the dissolution of the Preparliament, the Left Bloc had reassembled at the Second Congress of Soviets. The combined strength of the Left SRs and Menshevik Internationalists was too impressive to ignore. Since the majority at the congress clearly favored creation of a socialist coalition government, the Bolshevik leaders authorized A. V. Lunacharskii to reply that the Bolshevik faction had "nothing against Martov's proposal." To the dismay of some and the surprise of others, it was accepted unanimously.

Immediately after the vote, though, the resolution was undermined by the Defensist Mensheviks and the extremist Bolsheviks. Lev Khinchuk, the official spokesman for the Menshevik CC, read a prepared statement:

> Taking into consideration that the military conspiracy has been perpetrated by the Bolshevik party in the name of the soviets and behind the backs of other parties and factions present at the congress, and bearing in mind that the conspiracy plunges the country into an internal war, menaces the Constituent Assembly, threatens to bring about a catastrophe on the front, and leads to the victory of counterrevolution, the party considers that the only possible solution to the current situation is to be found in negotiations with the Provisional Government to form a political authority [*vlast'*] that would derive its support from all of Democracy. The RSDWP (United) is leaving this assembly.[6]

The center-right Mensheviks maintained that the Military Revolutionary Committee (MRC), the Bolshevik organization that seized power in

---

5. Quoted in Sukhanov, *Zapiski o revoliutsii*, 7:193–94. In the Russian political vocabulary of 1917, "Democracy" or "Revolutionary Democracy" meant the socialist parties.

6. "Ukhod Men'shevikov," document no. 2 in Nikolaevsky, *Men'sheviki v dni Oktiabr'skogo perevorota*, p. 22.

Petrograd in the name of the soviets, had destroyed the authority of the congress by confronting it with a fait accompli,[7] and the Menshevik factions to the right of Martov walked out of the congress. Their departure angered the remaining delegates, who quite naturally had a stake in a successful outcome of the congress. It weakened the positions of both the extremist anti-Bolsheviks and the conciliatory Bolsheviks. There were hostile outbursts when Martov raised the issue of a negotiated settlement again.[8] Only at that point did Trotsky attack Martov and the proponents of a socialist coalition. Referring contemptuously to "conciliators," he made it sound as though anyone who sought to find grounds for agreement was compromising revolutionary principles: "To those who have left and to those who are making propositions we must say: You are pitifully alone! You are bankrupt! Your role is played out! And now you should go where you belong—to the trash bin of History!"[9] Martov retorted: "Then we are leaving!" N. N. Sukhanov, one of those at the extreme left of the SD party grouped around the newspaper *Novaia zhizn'*, recalled that during the immediately ensuing factional meeting, at which the walkout was debated, passions ran high.[10] Martov's view finally prevailed, although the minutes of the congress indicate that many Internationalists returned to the proceedings shortly thereafter.[11] They presented the following resolution to the congress:

> The only outcome of this situation which could still halt the escalation of the civil war would be an agreement between the insurrectionist part of Democracy and other democratic organizations in order to form a democratic government that would be recognized by all of Revolutionary Democracy and to which the Provisional Government could painlessly pass over political power. The Menshevik Internationalist faction suggests that the congress adopt a decision on the necessity of peacefully resolving the crisis by creating a joint democratic government.[12]

The Left SRs and the conciliatory Bolsheviks continued to support that principle. Even though Martov had left, Lev Kamenev tried to bring the issue to the attention of the congress:

7. "Reshenie TsIK pervogo sozyva," *Mira khleba svobody* (newspaper of the CEC of the first convocation after the Bolshevik seizure of power), 7 November 1917, p. 3.

8. N. N. Sukhanov, "Stsenki iz Vtorogo S"ezda Sovetov," in Anin, ed., *Revoliutsiia 1917 goda*, p. 405.

9. Quoted in Sukhanov, *Zapiski o revoliutsii*, 7:203.

10. Ibid., p. 216.

11. *Vtoroi Vserossiiskii S"ezd Sovetov*, p. 27.

12. "Deklaratsiia fraktsii Men'shevikov Internatsionalistov," document no. 3 in Nikolaevsky, *Men'sheviki v dni Oktiabr'skogo perevorota*, p. 24.

The congress has unanimously resolved to discuss as the first priority the question that has been put forward so insistently by the Menshevik Internationalists. But this unanimous decision of the congress has been impossible to carry out, only because the congress has been tied up all the time with extraordinary reports.[13]

The Left SR leader, Vladimir Karelin, warned the Bolsheviks that they did not have a majority and that an agreement was necessary. For the time being, the Left SRs turned down the Bolshevik offer to join the Council of People's Commissars (CPC). A purely Bolshevik government was formed and was entrusted by the congress to convene the Constituent Assembly as scheduled. Moreover, the Central Executive Committee of Soviets (CEC), which was proclaimed to be the supreme legislative institution until the convocation of the Constituent Assembly, was to be composed of representatives of all parties elected to the congress. Vacant seats on the CEC, in numbers proportionate to the numbers of Mensheviks and SRs at the congress, were reserved for them, should they decide to return to it.

The Committee to Save the Fatherland

After their departure from the congress, the members of the Menshevik CC, the Defensist groups, and the SR CC assembled in the Petrograd city duma to discuss the situation. The Menshevik CC newspaper reported:

After long debates on the subject, it was decided that a Committee to Save the Fatherland and the Revolution would be formed, to be composed of three representatives from each of the following organizations: the city duma, the CEC, the Executive Committee of the Peasant Congress, the factions that left the Second Congress of Soviets, the Trade Union of Railway Workers [Vikzhel], the SR CC, the SD CC, the Council of the Russian Republic [Preparliament], and the front-line organizations.[14]

One of the first acts of this committee was to publish a declaration, "To the Citizens of Russia," which said that, "to preserve the continuity of a single state power," the committee was "taking the initiative to recreate the Provisional Government, which will rely on the forces of Democracy and will lead the country to the Constituent As-

13. *Vtoroi Vserossiiskii S"ezd Sovetov*, p. 10.
14. *Rabochaia gazeta* (newspaper of the Menshevik CC), 27 October 1917, p. 1. See also the resolution of the Menshevik CC in support of the Committee to Save the Fatherland and the Revolution: "TsK o zakhvate vlasti Bol'shevikami," document no. 4 in Nikolaevsky, *Men'sheviki v dni oktiabr'skogo perevorota*, p. 26.

sembly."[15] The committee appealed to the population not to obey the orders of the Bolshevik MRC and demanded that government employees carry out only the committee's decisions. Thus the Bolshevik CPC and the Menshevik-SR Committee to Save the Fatherland and the Revolution each claimed to have created a governmental authority that would move toward the Constituent Assembly. The Menshevik CC appears to have given its support to the Committee to Save the Fatherland, declaring that "until the Bolshevik adventure is finally brought to a halt, no agreement with the Bolshevik party on the subject of joint organization of the government is possible."[16]

Oliver Radkey has shown that the Committee to Save the Fatherland was a very loose body. An ad hoc group of right-wing Socialists, primarily Abram Gots and Nikolai Avksent'ev of the SRs,[17] acted in its name. The committee desperately sought troops for Kerensky and organized an ill-fated uprising of military cadets in Petrograd on October 29. Radkey has rightly observed that the SRs threw in their lot with an armed force over which they would have had no control in the event of a victory.[18] This observation is applicable not only to the first armed clashes in late October but also to the SRs' greatest gamble, their effort to overthrow the Bolsheviks by force in the summer of 1918. The Right SRs' willingness to rely on the military officers was a source of friction between the Mensheviks and the SRs in those early days, and eventually it would lead to a break between the two allied parties.

The SR-backed cadet uprising brought yet another turn in the outlook of the Menshevik CC. Dan once again moved toward Martov and abandoned plans to oppose the Bolsheviks by force. The decision to change the CC policy was arrived at after a meeting with a delegation of Menshevik workers, which made an enormous impression on the CC members. The delegation told the CC that the workers understood the Kerensky-backed offensive on Petrograd by Cossack troops as a march against the Petrograd proletariat.[19] The unstable majority in the CC was inclined now to withdraw from the Committee to Save the Fatherland, to adopt Martov's policy, and to seek a negotiated settlement of the power struggle.

15. "K grazhdanam Rossii," in "Protokoly soveshchanii TsIK pervogo sozyva," *Krasnyi arkhiv*, 1925, no. 4:132.

16. "Rezoliutsiia TsK RSDRP (o)," document no. 10 in Nikolaevsky, *Men'sheviki v dni Oktiabr'skogo perevorota*, p. 40. Boris Nikolaevsky was a Menshevik who gained prominence particularly in the exile period, from the 1920s to the 1960s. The large collection of documents he assembled on the Russian Revolution is now in the Hoover Institution on War, Revolution, and Peace.

17. Radkey, *Sickle under the Hammer*, p. 34.

18. Ibid., pp. 60–61.

19. Nikolaevsky, *Men'sheviki v dni Oktiabr'skogo perevorota*, p. 6.

The Defensist Mensheviks, on the other hand, believed that they had a moral right to resist the Bolshevik military actions with arms. The joint Menshevik-SR newspaper, *Mira khleba svobody*, wrote:

> The Bolsheviks have taken up arms against everyone. They have trampled on everything. They would stop at nothing to achieve their goal. Now there is the question: Why couldn't others who consider themselves right return the Bolsheviks' blows? Clearly, the way to a peaceful solution was long ago destroyed by the Bolsheviks. The situation is absurd. Some are fighting and others are looking for peaceful solutions. That's not a bad idea. But the point is that instead of peace we get blows. Peace is a good thing. But how is it possible to keep peace when the other side is hitting mercilessly? No! To wait for the end of Bolshevik adventurism is a crime! We must struggle! We must cast away the old methods! In response to armed action there is only one alternative—to suppress it![20]

This article was probably a response to Martov's advocacy of a peaceful solution. The Defensist Mensheviks had decided to act on their own.

The Vikzhel Negotiations

Meanwhile, the central executive committee of the railway workers' union (Vserossiiskii Ispolnitel'nyi Komitet Zheleznodorozhnikov, or Vikzhel) declared its political neutrality and offered to mediate between the warring parties and to sponsor interparty negotiations to form a new government. Vikzhel's most powerful weapon was the threat, in the event that hostilities should continue, to declare a general strike on all the railroads of Russia. As bread supplies in the big cities were already extremely limited, this threat could not be ignored. For the time being, then, Vikzhel's offer was accepted by all sides. The strategic wish to gain time on the one hand and the political hope of saving what could still be saved on the other pulled the heterogeneous forces toward negotiations.

The negotiations opened on October 29 in the building of the Ministry of Transportation.[21] As a basis for discussion, the Vikzhel-sponsored formula was accepted: Resolved: to form a coalition government of all socialist parties, from the Bolsheviks to the People's Socialists.

The conciliatory Bolsheviks, led by Kamenev, favored the formation of such a government in principle. Kamenev had scored a major victory at a meeting of the Bolshevik CC earlier that day. With only three members absent—Lenin, Trotsky, and Zinoviev—the CC had unan-

20. "Nu a chto zhe dal'she," editorial in *Mira khleba svobody*, 7 November 1917, p. 1.
21. "Première réunion de la Conference sur le Compromis, dite Conference Vikzhel'," document no. 118 in Oldenbourg, ed., *Coup d'état bolcheviste*.

imously adopted a resolution in favor of negotiations to broaden the Soviet government to include those socialist parties that had walked out of the Second Congress of Soviets. The new government, said the resolution, was to be formed on the following principles: "1. recognition of the political program of the Second Congress of Soviets; 2. accountability of the new government to the soviets; 3. inclusion of all socialist parties, from the People's Socialists to the Bolsheviks."[22] Kamenev was convinced that the Bolsheviks had to join hands with left-of-center socialists in trying to persuade as many of the Defensists as possible to abandon armed struggle against the new regime. Certainly, the conciliatory Bolsheviks did not plan an accommodation with Kerensky and the Cossack commander Krasnov; rather, they wanted to strengthen their own camp by isolating Kerensky politically. The Bolshevik newspaper, *Izvestiia*, reported: "Without changing their viewpoint, the Bolsheviks readily accepted the railway workers' proposal to start negotiations aimed at broadening the Provisional Workers' and Peasants' government to include the representatives of the non-Bolshevik parties. A socialist coalition government is expected to be formed."[23] What remained unclear, though, was how much the Bolsheviks were willing to concede. At the Vikzhel session, Kamenev emphasized that, despite the departure of the socialist factions from the congress, their places in the CEC remained open and they were welcome to come back. Not everyone knew that Lenin and Trotsky saw the matter differently; but their view would have seemed irrelevant, anyway, because they were in the minority in the CC.

It appeared that there were no fundamental disagreements over principles, although Martov protested against the excesses of the MRC, the shootings without trials, and the closing down of the Socialist newspapers. He warned: "The split in the ranks of Russian Democracy will result in a horrifying civil war. . . . This is a matter of one or two weeks. The only solution that is still possible lies in courageous agreement between the two camps of Democracy."[24] Moreover, Dan said that Bolshevik participation in a joint socialist government would be desirable but that the Menshevik CC could not enter such a government unless the SRs were admitted as well.[25] The partners in the negotiations had to resolve a number of other difficulties as well: To what institution would the new government be accountable—to the CEC formed at the Second Congress of Soviets or to a larger and more representative body? How many seats in the new cabinet would the Bolsheviks, the center-left socialists, and the right socialists control? And finally, which polit-

22. "Zasedanie TsK," in *Protokoly TsK RSDRP (b)*, p. 122.
23. "Kakoi dolzhna byt' revoliutsionnaia vlast'," *Izvestiia*, 1 November 1917, p. 1.
24. Quoted in Vompe, *Dni oktiabr'skoi revoliutsii*, p. 31.
25. Ibid.

ical leaders of the participating parties would compose the new government?

The negotiations did progress, and the Menshevik CC took a further step toward Martov on October 31, when it adopted a resolution jointly proposed by Martov and Dan:

> Having discussed the current situation and having recognized that all other considerations must be moved to the background in the face of the necessity to prevent further bloodshed at any cost, the CC of the RSDWP (United) resolves to join in the attempt to organize a homogeneous government of all socialist parties, from the People's Socialists to the Bolsheviks.[26]

The Defensists' attitude toward this move was not hard to predict. They simply could not negotiate with what they considered to be the "Bolshevik usurpers." Ignoring the real constellation of forces, they doggedly insisted on continuing the armed struggle against the new regime.

> Every day of war and anarchy inevitably leads the country toward collapse. There is only one solution possible: immediate organization of a democratic government, but without the Bolsheviks! The only task of this government should be the immediate restoration of all the freedoms that have been trampled on, and the convocation of the Constituent Assembly without delay.[27]

Some Defensists supported the "legitimate government of Comrade Kerensky," others favored creation of a democratic government without Kerensky and/or without the Bolsheviks, and still others were inclined toward accommodation with the Bolsheviks but without inclusion of Lenin and Trotsky—the organizers of the coup d'état—in the government.

As the bargaining continued, a special multiparty commission managed to resolve the major differences. It was decided that the CEC elected at the Second Congress of Soviets would be reorganized into a "people's soviet" (*narodnyi sovet*).[28] This legislative body was to include representatives of the soviets, the dumas, the old and the new CEC, the Peasant Congress, and the main trade unions. It would be empowered to form a new cabinet, which would be accountable to it.

---

26. "Rezoliutsiia o peregovorakh s Bol'shevikami," document no. 11 in Nikolaevsky, *Men'sheviki v dni Oktiabr'skogo perevorota*, p. 42.
27. Editorial in *Mira khleba svobody*, 7 November 1917, p. 1.
28. Raphael Abramovitch, "Stranitsy istorii: Vikzhel' (noiabr' 1917)," *Sotsialisticheskii vestnik* (New York), no. 5 (May 1960), p. 119.

Even the list of new ministers was drawn up. Viktor Chernov would head the government. Lenin and Trotsky were not on the list of cabinet members.[29] The agreement was signed, and Kamenev promised that it would be published in all the major newspapers. At the heart of the agreement was an understanding among the conciliatory Bolsheviks, the Left SRs, and the Menshevik Internationalists, backed this time by the Menshevik CC. The agreement was considered final. *Izvestiia* announced:

> So among all factions an agreement has been reached in principle that the government should be composed of the representatives of all socialist parties that have deputies in the soviets of workers, soldiers, and peasants. This is exactly what the Bolsheviks have been advocating for a long time: political power must belong to Revolutionary Democracy, that is to say, to the soviets. But that means to the parties represented in the soviets. . . . Although the Right Mensheviks have refused to send their representatives to the new government, they have declared their readiness to support it fully. And finally, there seem to be no obstacles to the entry into the government of other internationalist groups, such as the Menshevik Internationalists and the United Internationalists.[30]

The *Izvestiia* report, however, did not hew closely to the actual agreement. *Izvestiia* failed to publish the list of the new Cabinet members, and it spoke of a "reorganization of soviet power," whereas the agreement had specified the inclusion of the dumas as well. On the surface, it was around this latter issue that the political struggle revolved in the next four days, but beneath it lay another factor. Lenin felt that Kamenev had yielded to the pressure of the non-Bolshevik participants in the negotiations and had conceded too much.

Turmoil within the Parties

Lenin and Trotsky struck back at a stormy meeting of the Bolshevik CC on the night of November 1. Their case against any coalition with the "petty-bourgeois" parties rested on the arguments that the cadets' uprising had been suppressed and that Kerensky had no chance of winning. "There can be no nonsoviet representation!" Lenin fulminated. "The Congress of Soviets has legitimated the principle of soviet power! It would be a capitulation to the petty-bourgeois parties to admit the dumas into the government! The Bolshevik slogan should be: 'A homogeneous government of the Bolsheviks!'" Lenin's speech was

29. L. Martov to P. Aksel'rod, 19 November 1917, Nik. Col. no. 17, box 1, file 1–2, p. 11.
30. "Kakoi dolzhna byt' revoliutsionnaia vlast'," *Izvestiia*, 1 November 1917, p. 1.

rather chaotic. He switched abruptly from one topic to another, bluster-
ing and making demands:

> Troops should be sent to Moscow immediately! [If we are] confronted with
> Vikzhel sabotage, their leaders must be arrested! Socialist revolution
> around the world will come to the aid of Soviet Russia! . . . Lunacharskii
> should be expelled from the party! . . . If there is a split, let there be one! If
> they have their majority, let them take power in the CEC and act, but we'll
> go to the sailors! . . . It is necessary to make arrests! And we will! And let
> them talk about the horrors of the dictatorship of the proletariat! Arrest
> Vikzhel, that's what we should do![31]

Lenin dismissed all ambiguities: there must be one-party rule, even at
the cost of splitting the Bolshevik party and of loosing terror if necessary. It is worthy of note that Lenin threatened to appeal not to the
Petrograd workers but to the Kronstadt sailors to safeguard the "proletarian" dictatorship.

Lunacharskii, in his reply to Lenin, cited objections to Lenin's position among the Bolsheviks:

> To give fifty seats to the dumas is not only legitimate, since they are
> elected by universal suffrage, but imperative. The new government would
> not be able to rule without the dumas and their administrative and techni-
> cal personnel. . . . The Bolsheviks can hold power only by reaching a
> compromise with other socialist parties. Why use terror when the same
> goals could be achieved peacefully? . . . The problem is that we have
> somehow begun to like warfare too much in our party, as though we are
> not workers but soldiers, as though we are a military party. . . . I am afraid
> that in the long run there will be just one man left—a dictator![32]

Lunacharskii's words were received with applause. Viktor Nogin continued the same line of reasoning, maintaining that a soviet system
without other soviet parties made no sense: "The SRs have left the
congress, the Mensheviks too. But that means that the soviets will
disintegrate. This state of things combined with the destruction in the
country will end with the collapse of our party in a short time."[33]

David Riazanov spoke in the same vein: "If we reject the agreement
today, we will be left without the Left SRs, without anything. We will
be faced with the fact that we deceived the masses when we promised
them a soviet government!"[34]

---

31. For an abridged and censored version of the proceedings of this session, see *Protokoly TsK RSDRP (b)*, pp. 124–30. For a somewhat more detailed version, see Trotsky,
ed., *Stalinskaia shkola fal'sifikatsii*, pp. 120–27 (Lenin's speech is cited on p. 119).
32. Trotsky, ed., *Stalinskaia shkola fal'sifikatsii*, p. 122.
33. Ibid., p. 128.
34. *Protokoly TsK RSDRP (b)*, p. 128.

Riazanov and Kamenev admitted in a conciliatory manner that the conditions to which the party had agreed should indeed be modified, but they insisted on continuing negotiations.

According to Lenin, the only purpose of the negotiations was to serve as a cover for military actions against Kerensky.[35] Trotsky believed that the Bolsheviks had nothing to gain by an alliance with the Mensheviks, for it would only put undue restraints on Bolshevik power.[36] Iakov Sverdlov, one of Lenin's closest allies, made an ominous suggestion: He urged his comrades not to break off the negotiations, but rather to create an incident that would disrupt them—by arresting some Vikzhel leaders, for example.[37]

The meeting ended inconclusively. Four CC members voted to break off the negotiations, ten to continue. At the same time, though, the CC adopted a resolution, drafted by Lenin, which stated that an agreement among the socialist parties was desirable, but only with seven reservations: (1) Any such agreement must be based on the acceptance of the soviet power principle. (2) It was necessary to wage a merciless struggle against the counterrevolutionary forces (Kerensky, Krasnov, Kornilov). (3) The Second Congress of Soviets was the only legitimate source of power. (4) The government must be responsible to the CEC. (5) Representation in the CEC must be denied to nonsoviet organizations. (6) Representatives of other socialist parties could be included in the CEC. (7) Lenin and Trotsky were to participate in any soviet government.[38] Points 1, 3, and particularly 5 were certain to be unacceptable to the Mensheviks and SRs. In order to save the negotiations, Kamenev had either to sway his party colleagues on the duma representation issue or persuade the Mensheviks and SRs to accept Lenin's reservations. Neither of these tasks would be easy. Still, the resolution did fall short of demanding one-party rule.

The Menshevik architects of the socialist coalition were faced with an equally determined opposition in their CC on the same night, November 1. A resolution to continue the negotiations had barely passed, 12 to 11, the day before.[39] The eleven CC members who were opposed had gathered separately that night and demanded that the debate continue the next day, since the resolution had been passed by such a small majority. They appealed to the CC:

> We, the undersigned members of the Central Committee of the RSDWP (United), find the decision of the CC concerning the negotiations with the

35. Ibid., p. 127.
36. Trotsky, *Stalinskaia shkola fal'sifikatsii*, pp. 124–27.
37. *Protokoly TsK RSDRP (b)*, p. 129.
38. Fedorov, *VTsIK v pervye gody sovetskoi vlasti*, p. 31.
39. Nikolaevsky, *Men'sheviki v dni oktiabr'skogo perevorota*, p. 8.

Bolsheviks on the subject of the creation of a new government with their participation to be ruinous for the cause of the working class, for the Revolution, and for our party, and we suggest that the CC immediately stop all negotiations with the Bolsheviks . . . and summon a general meeting of the CC tomorrow to reconsider this decision.

[CC members:] Liber, Baturskii, Gol'dman, Iudin, Gvozdev, Smirnov, Garvi, Ermolaev, Zaretskaia, Kolokol'nikov, Krokhmal'.

[CC candidate members:] Skobelev, Golikov, Bogdanov.[40]

On November 1, the debate was indeed resumed. The agreement with the conciliatory Bolsheviks and the Left SRs was already in hand, and the Martov-Dan majority was determined to defend its gains. The CC voted once more, with the same result: 12 in favor, 11 against. In this situation, the Defensist opposition decided to resign from the CC in protest. The conflict among the Menshevik leaders was exposed in all its virulence. The CC could no longer maneuver between the Internationalists and the Defensists.

Confronted with such strong resistance, the center-left leadership did make some concessions. The Martov-Dan majority continued to justify the agreement with the Bolsheviks but tried to mollify the opponents in the party. A CC resolution adopted on November 2 was simultaneously a response to both the Defensists' protests and the Bolsheviks' seven conditions. The CC put forward five conditions of its own. The first was that exclusion of the dumas and other democratic bodies from the government was unacceptable. By pressing this issue, Martov and Dan tried to win the wavering Defensists over to their side. This condition showed party members that the CC had not capitulated to Lenin's demands, which ran counter to the agreement of October 31. Just as the duma representation issue became a key point in Lenin's attack on the internal Bolshevik opposition, it also became a point of political honor for Martov and Dan. The other four Menshevik conditions were: liberation of all political prisoners arrested in the past few days; cessation of political terror, with the restoration of freedom of the press, assembly, unions, and strikes; a cease-fire in the confrontation with Krasnov's anti-Bolshevik troops; and transfer of some of the armed forces to the local city governments—the dumas—in order to combat pogroms and looting.[41]

All of these points were unacceptable to Lenin. He continued his attack the next day. The Bolshevik CC adopted another of his resolutions, even more implacable than the previous one.[42] Lenin wanted to

40. "Vykhod iz sostava TsK," document no. 12 in ibid., p. 43.

41. "Zaiavlenie TsK RSDRP (o) ot 2 noiabria, 1917," in Popov, ed., *Oktiabr'skii perevorot*, p. 407.

42. Ruban, *Oktiabr'skaia revoliutsiia i krakh Men'shevizma*, p. 340.

block the negotiations by making his terms unacceptable to the Mensheviks and SRs. He was very outspoken at the Bolshevik CC sessions, and he slowly expanded his demands publicly as well, without repudiating the core principle of the agreement.

The conciliatory Bolsheviks were losing ground in the Bolshevik CC, but Kamenev found an ingenious response. Again he took the initiative and managed to exploit fully the fact that the Bolshevik CC had voted for continuing negotiations whereas Lenin was trying to subvert them. Kamenev had to persuade the socialists to accept at least some of the Bolshevik reservations of November 1. To this end, Zinoviev, presumably fully aware of the impact it would produce, read Lenin's second resolution to the members of the CEC on November 2.[43] The Left SRs immediately issued a statement protesting "the establishment of the dictatorship of one political party."[44] At this point, Kamenev requested a recess on behalf of the Bolshevik faction in the CEC. When the members of the faction returned and introduced their resolution, it was accepted unanimously. It provided that the CEC was to be expanded to include representatives of the Peasant Congress, the army and navy, and the trade unions; fifty seats were to be given to the city dumas; the Bolsheviks were to control no less than 50 percent of all seats and head the ministries of Internal Affairs, Labor, and Foreign Affairs; and Lenin and Trotsky had to be included in any future government.[45] The CEC members knew the full scope of Lenin's demands, and that is why they hastened to accept Kamenev's compromise resolution, which they would not have approved otherwise.

This resolution of the CEC could not easily be ignored. All the Bolsheviks, Lenin included, had claimed that the CEC was the only legitimate legislative body. The resolution dealt a severe blow to Lenin's policies, and at the same time it was formulated in such a way that the major objections of the Bolshevik CC were satisfied. Would other members of the CC risk Bolshevik political isolation on the eve of the Constituent Assembly elections in order to avoid giving fifty seats to the dumas? The opposition obviously believed that they would not. On the other hand, since the duma representation issue was now resolved, Martov and Dan were expected to be satisfied.

Lenin was furious when he learned about the resolution, which he must have feared would find support among rank-and-file Bolsheviks. He summoned each Bolshevik CC member individually and suggested that he sign an ultimatum addressed to Lenin's opponents among the Bolsheviks:

43. *Protokoly TsK RSDRP (b)*, p. 275.
44. For the text of the statement, see Keep, ed., *The Debate on Soviet Power*, p. 61.
45. For the text of this resolution, see Popov, ed., *Oktiabr'skii perevorot*, p. 405.

Either the party must authorize the opposition to form a new government with those of its allies on whose behalf it is sabotaging our work (but then we would consider ourselves absolutely free in relation to this new government); or, and of this we have no doubt, the party will endorse the only possible revolutionary line, expressed in yesterday's CC decision, and then the party must decisively suggest that the representatives of the opposition transfer their disorganizational activity beyond the limits of our organization. . . . An honest and open split is certainly better than internal sabotage.[46]

Finally it was decided that the issue should be discussed in the lower party centers, the Moscow and Petrograd organizations. An extraordinary party congress was to be convened to determine the will of the Bolshevik party.

After the Defensists were outvoted in the Menshevik CC for the second time, they, too, demanded discussion of the issue at a larger party gathering of all Petrograd Menshevik organizations. An extraordinary congress was to be convened by the Mensheviks as well. The Defensist Committee on Elections to the Constituent Assembly launched a campaign against the Menshevik CC's resolution:

Both the negotiations and the decision of the CC on the nature of power are ruinous and treasonable to the interests of the Revolution and the proletariat. The Electoral Committee categorically demands immediate abolition of the fateful decision. If it does not abolish it, the Committee demands that all the Defensist CC members resign from its membership and, together with the rest of the party of Defensism, start a vigorous struggle against the CC policy, both inside and outside the party, unconstrained in this struggle by any formal obstacles.[47]

The Defensist press—the old CEC's *Mira khleba svobody*, Plekhanov's *Edinstvo*, Potresov's *Den'*, and other newspapers—virtually declared war on the CC. Martov's *Iskra*, Gorky and Sukhanov's *Novaia zhizn'*, and the CC's own *Rabochaia gazeta* responded by blaming the Defensists for the defeat of Menshevism, the loss of the soviets to the Bolsheviks, and the ineffectualness of all their policies. One of the Internationalists' columnists, Pavel Lapinskii, argued that the Bolshevik seizure of power had been carried out so easily because the Defensists' power lacked social support and "hung in the air." The coalition with the Kadets, he argued, should have been abandoned long ago.[48] Each

46. Lenin, "Ul'timatum bol'shinstva men'shinstvu," *Sochineniia*, 4th ed., 26:247–48. The entire episode is described in the editor's note to *Protokoly TsK RSDRP (b)*, p. 275.
47. "U Men'shevikov: Rezoliutsiia izbiratel'nogo komiteta Men'shevikov oborontsev," *Edinstvo*, 1 November 1917, p. 3.
48. S. Lapinskii, "Na rekakh Vavilonovykh," *Iskra* (newspaper of the Internationalists), 12 November 1917, p. 3. Pavel Levinson wrote under the name of Pavel Lapinskii or, as here, S. Lapinskii.

faction was determined to win a majority at a conference of the Petrograd Menshevik organizations which was held on November 3.

The Petrograd Conference

The crisis in the CC and the policy toward the Bolsheviks were the only two issues on the agenda. The break between the Internationalists and the Defensists had reached such proportions that they hardly seemed to belong to the same political party. Accusations of treason, calls to sabotage the decisions of the CC, and threats to split the party resounded from the Defensists' benches. In a conciliatory tone, Raphael Abramovitch presented the views of the left: The Defensists were just like the Bolsheviks. They wanted to answer Bolshevik violence with violence and to organize a conspiracy against the Bolshevik conspiracy. And yet, he continued, "the destruction of Bolshevism will lead to destruction of the Revolution. Unfortunately, the fate of the workers' revolution in Russia is closely tied to the fate of the Bolsheviks." Abramovitch concluded:

> The Bolsheviks' strength is underestimated and overestimated. Because it was underestimated, there were Kerensky's adventure and the cadets' uprising. Our understanding of the situation is that there is an equal alignment of forces. Hence a long and cruel civil war is starting all over the country. The consequences will be military and industrial devastation. Therefore, our slogan should be "Prevent the civil war through an agreement." . . .[49]

Abramovitch tried to limit his justification of the negotiations entirely to pragmatic considerations. His arguments only added more fuel to the fire. The CC member Sofiia Zaretskaia attempted to refute Abramovitch, and her forceful speech produced an enormous impression. "What are the goals of Menshevism?" she began. The main goal was to isolate the Bolsheviks politically. It was to expose their anti-Marxism, adventurism, and extremism, to denounce them as a clique acting in the name of the workers. To achieve these ends, all means were admissible, including armed struggle in alliance with all other democratic forces in the country. Zaretskaia rejected out of hand any coalition with the Bolsheviks:

> It would be disastrous for the Social Democrats to enter the Bolshevik government. In that case we will have to share responsibility for Bolshevik

---

49. "Zasedanie men'shevistskikh fraktsii," document no. 17 in Nikolaevsky, *Men'sheviki v dni Oktiabr'skogo perevorota*, p. 53.

policies and Bolshevik crimes. We must preserve the ideas of socialism so that when the fumes of Bolshevism disperse, the workers' movement will not perish, and so that the equation of Bolshevism with banditry does not discredit Social Democracy. Why on earth should the Social Democratic party be in the government at whatever cost? We will be the party of opposition![50]

Each of the party wings was convinced that it was the true bearer of Menshevism and that its course of action could save the Russian Revolution and Social Democracy.

Faced with such impressive opposition, Dan had to demonstrate that the new conciliatory policy would be successful, for only continued success could sway the hesitating Mensheviks. Dan reminded his audience of the Menshevik principle that "the government should be based on an alliance of all Democracy [i.e., including the dumas] and not only on the soviets. And that has already been agreed upon at Vikzhel." He then produced his trump card:

> The Bolsheviks are already splitting up, thanks to our tactics! . . . An agreement with the healthy elements in Bolshevism is necessary! When by means of this agreement we divert the healthy elements of the proletarian masses from the Bolsheviks, then conditions will be ripe for suppression of the soldiers' mob [*soldatchina*] grouped around Lenin and Trotsky.[51]

If the Menshevik CC policy could bring about a split in the Bolshevik CC and the isolation of Lenin and Trotsky together with their military "mob," then perhaps the coalition should be given a chance. Who had a better policy? These were the obvious implications of Dan's speech. S. L. Vainshtein, of the Committee to Save the Fatherland, argued that it was useless to seek an accommodation with the Bolsheviks; the civil war was already a fact of life. Dan's pragmatism would lead nowhere: "Bolshevism is isolated, and you want to galvanize it. You will not create any government with the Bolsheviks, but you will perish together with them. If Democracy does not suppress Bolshevism, even by armed force, this will be done by others; but along with the Bolsheviks, the Revolution and the proletariat will be smashed."[52] As will be shown, very similar arguments were advanced by the SRs and the Right Mensheviks later in 1918, when they rose up in arms against the Bolsheviks.

The debate intensified. Twenty-eight speakers requested the floor. Neither side, however, felt it had sufficient strength to secure the adop-

---

50. Ibid., pp. 54–55.
51. Ibid., pp. 56, 57.
52. Ibid., p. 56.

tion of its resolution. Zaretskaia countered Dan angrily: "Give us proof that the Bolsheviks' split is caused by the tactics of our CC! But the split among us is evident!"[53] The conference ended in a stalemate. The resolution that was adopted mildly reproached the CC and recommended a change in its policy, but it fell short of specifying in what ways the policy was to be amended, leaving room for maneuver.[54]

Lenin undertook further steps designed to disrupt the negotiations. The MRC kept arresting Socialists and closing their newspapers. According to a Soviet source, the old CEC's newspaper had to change its name nine times before the end of November, because of repeated closures, and it listed the successive titles: "*Golos soldata*, closed October 26; *Soldatskii golos*, closed October 27; *Soldatskii klich*: October 29–November 4; *Revoliutsionnyi nabat*, closed November 5; then appeared *Mira khleba svobody*; *Nabat revoliutsii*; *Za svobodu*; *Za svobodu naroda*; *Za svobodu i pravo*; *Za pravo naroda*."[55] In these conditions, the issue of greatest urgency was halting the repressions. Martov and Dan simply could not persuade the Mensheviks and the SRs to negotiate when their newspapers were being closed and their party comrades arrested. On November 4 the Menshevik CC sent an ultimatum to the Bolsheviks: unless the terror was stopped, the RSDWP (United) would no longer be able to participate in the negotiations.[56] The declaration was aimed at generating additional support for the CC. The party rank and file had to be convinced that advocating an understanding with the Bolsheviks did not mean appeasing Lenin. At the same time, Martov was signaling to Kamenev that repressions had to be stopped immediately; otherwise, the majority in the Menshevik CC might reject participation in the government with the Bolsheviks.

The next day, Kamenev's faction demanded that the MRC stop the terror campaign at once in order to allow the negotiations to continue in accordance with the previous decisions of the Bolshevik CC. The protest against the terror was indeed one of the dominant themes in a statement made by the conciliatory Bolsheviks:

> We stand for the necessity of creating a Socialist government of all Socialist parties. . . . We understand that there is only one alternative approach, that is the preservation of a purely Bolshevik government by means of political terror. This path has been chosen by the Council of People's Commissars. We cannot and do not want to take this path. We see that it

53. Ibid., p. 57.
54. Ibid., p. 58.
55. "Protokoly TsIK pervogo sozyva posle oktiabria," *Krasnyi arkhiv* 3, no. 10 (1925): 133.
56. "Rezoliutsiia TsK," document no. 16 in Nikolaevsky, *Men'sheviki v dni Oktiabr'skogo perevorota*, p. 51.

will lead to the isolation of the masses from the leadership of political life in the country and to the establishment of an irresponsible regime. It will lead to the destruction of the Revolution and the country. We cannot take the responsibility for these policies and therefore resign from the Council of People's Commissars and declare it to the CEC.

Nogin, Rykov, Miliutin, Teodorovich, Riazanov, Dervyshev, Arbuzov, Iurenev, Fedorov, Larin, Shliapnikov. November 5, 1917.[57]

In addition, Kamenev, Rykov, Zinoviev, Nogin, and Miliutin sent open letters to the Bolshevik CC, the party organizations, and the newspapers stating their views. The faction demanded that the party call an extraordinary party congress, as Lenin had threatened to do, and announced its intention to open its own newspaper. The resignations were submitted not out of despair or as an admission of defeat but as an act of public protest that would bring the issue before the Bolshevik constituency. Nevertheless, Lenin's Bolsheviks rejected the Menshevik ultimatum, and the Vikzhel negotiations were broken off. Once the threat (imaginary, as it turned out) of Kerensky's offensive disappeared, there was no longer any need to negotiate with the moderate socialists.

The record of the Menshevik leadership in the Vikzhel negotiations and in the October struggle for power was extremely inconsistent and contradictory. On October 24, a majority was building up in the CC for a vote of no confidence in Kerensky. But on October 25 the CC voted for resolute support of the Provisional Government; on October 26, to crush the Bolshevik coup; on October 28, for negotiations with the Bolsheviks; on October 31, for a coalition of the socialist parties, including the Bolsheviks; on November 4, for an ultimatum to the Bolsheviks on the subject of repressions. This record reflects the changing political weight of the Menshevik factions in the CC. Each faction followed its own policy, and the struggle among them defined the outlook of the CC. As a result, the CC alienated both sides because it supported neither. When Martov and Dan enjoyed a majority (by a margin of one vote), the CC had to reject an agreement with the Bolsheviks even on Kamenev's conditions if it wanted to avoid a breakup of the party. There is no doubt that the Defensists would have split the party if such an agreement had been signed. The SRs had no interest in coming to an understanding with the Bolsheviks, either. They took part in the negotiations only to win time and to let Kerensky assemble at the front as many troops as he could.

Thus in each of the three key parties, the opponents of a negotiated settlement prevailed. The result—the creation of a one-party Bolshevik government and the inability of the moderate socialists to mobilize any

---

57. "Zaiavlenie v TsK RSDRP (b)," in Popov, ed., *Oktiabr'skii perevorot*, p. 408.

Россійская Соціалъ-Демократическая Рабочая Партія.

Пролетаріи всѣхъ странъ соединяйтесь!

КОНТОРА „ИСКРЫ"
Обводный кан., 48, кв. 50.
Уголъ Лиговки.
Пріемъ отъ 11 до 5 час.

ЦѢНА ОТДѢЛЬНАГО НОМЕРА:
Въ Петроградѣ 20 к.
Въ провинціи 25 к.

Съ 26 сентября въ Петроградѣ выходитъ
„ИСКРА"
Органъ Меньшевиковъ-Интернаціоналистовъ.

№ 8. Воскресенье, 12-го Ноября 1917 г. № 8.

Органъ меньшевиковъ-интернаціоналистовъ.

ТОВАРИЩИ РАБОЧІЕ и СОЛДАТЫ!

Соглашеніе сорвано.

Большевики отказались передать захваченную ими власть Новому Правительству, которое состояло-бы изъ представителей всѣхъ демократическихъ партій.

Они отказались отъ ЕДИНСТВЕННАГО ИСХОДА, который еще могъ-бы СПАСТИ СТРАНУ ОТЪ АНАРХІИ, МЕЖДУ-УСОБІЙ, ГОЛОДА и РАЗВАЛА ФРОНТА.

Они отказались прекратить НАСИЛІЯ НАДЪ ПЕЧАТЬЮ, НАДЪ ПРАВОМЪ СОБРАНІЙ и СТАЧЕКЪ, выпустить изъ тюремъ ПОЛИТИЧЕСКИХЪ ЗАКЛЮЧЕНЫХЪ, принять ПЕРЕМИРІЕ на ВНУТРЕННЕМЪ ФРОНТѢ. Напротивъ, устами Ленина и Троцкаго они объявили, что терроръ и гражданская война должны продолжаться и усиливаться.

Часть большевиковъ возстала противъ этой непримиримости, открыто сказала, что Ленинъ и Троцкій ведутъ пролетаріатъ и революцію къ разгрому. Нѣсколько членовъ Совѣта народныхъ комиссаровъ сложили свои полномочія.

Новая власть явно разваливается.

Уходящихъ большевиковъ уже объявили измѣнниками революціи, какъ раньше объявили всѣ соціалистическія партіи. Отъ этого народу не станетъ легче.

Прокормить столицу и фронтъ, удержать страну отъ развала не станетъ легче, если всѣхъ кромѣ Ленина, Троцкаго и приставшихъ къ нимъ авантюристовъ признать единственными истинными соціалистами.

Сѣя ложь и клевету, объявляя „каледницами" всѣхъ другихъ соціалистовъ и натравливая на нихъ темныя массы, ленинцы продолжаютъ свое пагубное дѣло похоронъ русской революціи.

ТОВАРИЩИ! Спасайте свое собственное дѣло, вырвите его изъ рукъ обезумѣвшей кучки фанатиковъ!

Добивайтесь, во чтобы то ни стало, прекращенія диктатуры одной революціонной партіи. Требуйте созданія власти, которая была-бы признана всей демократіей всѣми соціалистическими партіями, которая могла-бы прочно опираясь на довѣріе демократіи, а не на силу штыковъ.

Да здравствуетъ перемиріе и соглашеніе. Довольно междуусобій, довольно крови, довольно убійствъ!

Долой царство кликъ и группъ!..

Да здравствуетъ власть всей демократіи!

Редакція „Искры"

Front page of the Menshevik Internationalists' newspaper *Iskra*, 12 November 1917 (Petrograd): "Comrades, Workers, and Soldiers! The agreement is broken. The Bolsheviks have refused to yield the political power they seized to a New Government that would have consisted of representatives of all democratic parties." Newspaper Collection, Institut zur Geschichte der Arbeiterbewegung, Ruhr-Universität Bochum, West Germany.

sizable anti-Bolshevik armed force—was fraught with weighty political consequences. For the time being, Lenin had a free hand to consolidate the Bolshevik position in the name of soviet power. From the very first days, however, the CPC issued dozens of decrees without even consulting what was supposed to be the supreme legislative institution, the CEC. The exclusion of the dumas from the CEC was followed by the Bolsheviks' disbandment of the dumas all over Russia.[58] In the following weeks, the Bolshevik CC was increasingly preoccupied with preparations for the disbandment of the Constituent Assembly as well.

The Bolshevik–Left SR Coalition

Within each of the three socialist parties, a realignment of political forces had taken place during the October crisis. The Menshevik party was left with a very unstable center-left margin of one vote in the CC, a state of affairs that effectively paralyzed the party's ability to act until the Extraordinary Party Congress in December. The split among the Bolsheviks did not last long; the conciliatory Bolsheviks returned to the party fold after an agreement with the Left SRs was worked out. They were in no position, though, to "engage in sabotage of party work," as Lenin had predicted they would do; they had no choice but to go along with Lenin's moves against the Constituent Assembly.

As for the SRs, the right wing, led by Avksent'ev and Gots, had not abandoned hope for the Bolsheviks' overthrow.[59] Chernov's centrist group sought in mid-November to create a "countergovernment" that would be backed by the Peasant Congress and the pro–Constituent Assembly army units.[60] Meanwhile, the Left SRs did everything they could to block any political initiative by the SRs, since their very identity depended on their distancing themselves from the SRs. On November 15 the Left SR part of the Peasant Congress split with the SRs and, to the jubilation of the Bolsheviks, agreed to join an expanded CEC. The demand by the conciliatory Bolsheviks and Left SRs that the social basis of the new regime be broadened was partly fulfilled. Moreover, the Left SRs were courted now by the de facto government, the CPC. Lenin abruptly altered his insistence on "all power to the Bolsheviks."

58. For a detailed account of the disbanding of both the dumas and the zemstvos in December 1917 and January 1918, see "Khronika likvidatsii zemstv," *Zemskii rabotnik* (journal of the All-Russian Union of Zemstvo Workers' Unions), no. 6–7 (March 1918), pp. 26–27; and "Soobshcheniia s mest," ibid., no. 4–5 (February 1918), pp. 24–31.

59. Viktor Chernov, "Kommentarii k protokolam TsK PSR (sentiabr' 1917–fevral' 1918)," Nik. Col. no. 7, box 3, file 54, p. 63.

60. For a detailed discussion, see Radkey, *Sickle under the Hammer*, pp. 73–91.

What must have changed his tactics was a new factor in the interparty struggle: the election returns for the Constituent Assembly. Since the SRs had won a majority, it was absolutely necessary to attract the Left SRs, who could also speak on behalf of the peasants, to the side of the new regime.

A comparison of the composition of the CEC before and after the Bolshevik-Left SR agreement of November 15 reveals how favorable to the Left SRs the conditions of the agreement were. On the eve of the agreement, the CEC consisted of 119 members: 77 Bolsheviks, 31 Left SRs, 6 SD Internationalists, 3 Ukrainian Socialists, 1 Maximalist, and 1 Polish Socialist. According to the provisions of the agreement, the CEC was to be expanded by 258 members, of whom 108 were to come from the Peasant Congress, 100 from the army and navy, and 50 from the trade unions. The delegates of the Peasant Congress were predominantly Left SR, while the delegates of the army and navy were likely to have a slight Bolshevik majority. Thus the conditions of the agreement made it possible for the Left SRs to outnumber the Bolsheviks. Indeed, immediately after the agreement, the Left SRs had a majority in the CEC. On November 19 the CEC consisted of 113 Left SRs, 92 Bolsheviks, 7 SD Internationalists, 4 SR Maximalists, 3 Ukrainian Socialists, 1 Anarchist, 1 Polish Socialist, and 6 others, for a total of 227 delegates.[61] The remaining new CEC delegates had not yet arrived in the capital. The Left SRs must have been convinced that time was working for them. The army and navy were soon going to be demobilized, and the peasant soviets would outnumber the worker-soldier soviets in the long run. The Left SRs could use the time to consolidate their provincial organizations and to wrest control of them from the SR party machine.

The expansion of the CEC had unpleasant surprises in store for the Left SRs, though. It created a precedent. In January 1918, Lenin would insist that other proletarian revolutionary organizations had to be represented in the CEC as well, and the organizations chosen were to be those that supported the Bolsheviks. The Left SRs would find themselves in the minority in the CEC again, since no criteria for CEC membership were formulated, beyond general phrases about the representation of all revolutionary and proletarian forces. Lenin is reported to have said to the Left SRs: "Don't you understand that we include organizations in the revolutionary Parliament not according to some formal criteria but according to their role and significance in the revolution?"[62]

Meanwhile, the Mensheviks, too, were invited to come back to the CEC. In a letter to Pavel Aksel'rod, Martov wrote on November 19:

61. Razgon, VTsIK Sovetov, pp. 31, 34.
62. Ibid., pp. 37, 35.

According to the agreement, the parties that walked out of the Second Congress [of Soviets] can enter this institution [the CEC] with a proportional number of representatives. According to [our] calculation, if all [representatives] entered, the Bolsheviks would have half the votes, all others the other half.[63]

The Menshevik center-left leadership continued to advocate the formation of a Socialist coalition government with the Bolsheviks. Yet the Mensheviks refused to enter either the Bolshevik-Left SR government or the CEC, at least in the role of a soviet opposition.

The anticipation of the coming struggle over the fate of the Constituent Assembly altered attitudes in the political parties again. In the Bolsheviks' case, it led them to seek a way out of their isolation, and thus mitigated their intransigence; in the Mensheviks' case, it hardened it. In the Defensists' view, there was no need to seek an accommodation with the Bolsheviks, especially now, when they had no majority in the Constituent Assembly. In the Internationalists' view, agreement with the Bolsheviks was possible only for the purpose of creating a caretaker government until the convocation of the Constituent Assembly. In late October this position had caused no problems, because the Bolsheviks not only pledged allegiance to the Constituent Assembly but actually justified their uprising on the ground that soviet power would provide the best guarantee for the Constituent Assembly's convocation. During November, however, the Bolsheviks dropped this argument, and it became increasingly obvious that they were preparing for a showdown with the Constituent Assembly. To enter the CEC in these conditions amounted in Martov's eyes to "our camouflaging the [Bolshevik] masquerade, because even now the real power is not in the hands of the CEC but in the hands of Lenin and Trotsky, who have reduced their own parliament to the role of the Bulygin Duma."[64]

Whether or not to join the CEC with the Left SRs became another explosive issue within the Menshevik party. The Defensists had no difficulty in determining their stance; their answer was an adamant no. The Internationalists split over the issue. On November 16–17, a conference of the Petrograd Internationalists voted in favor of joining, but the Central Bureau of the Internationalists overruled them. Sukhanov and some other Internationalists joined the CEC anyway, as representatives of the trade unions. Those who favored joining pointed out that Lenin's faction had had a very slim majority in the CEC on a number of very important votes; the Mensheviks could strengthen the opposition

---

63. Martov to Aksel'rod, 19 November 1917, Nik. Col. no. 17, box 1, file 1–2, p. 15.
64. Ibid. The Bulygin duma was the limited-franchise duma established in 1905 to play a consultative role under the tsar.

Россійская Соціалъ-Демократическая Рабочая Партія.

Пролетаріи всѣхъ странъ, соединяйтесь!

ИСКРА

Органъ меньшевиковъ-интернаціоналистовъ.

Съ 26 сентября въ Петроградѣ выходитъ
„ИСКРА"
Органъ Меньшевиковъ-Интернаціоналистовъ.

№ 10.   Понедѣльникъ, 20-го Ноября 1917 г.   № 10.

ВСЯ ВЛАСТЬ УЧРЕДИТЕЛЬНОМУ СОБРАНІЮ!

Въ настоящій моментъ Россія—безъ власти.

Да здравствуетъ Учредительное Собраніе!

Front page of the Menshevik Internationalists' newspaper *Iskra*, 20 November 1917 (Petrograd): "All Power to the Constituent Assembly!" The appeal, summarizing the Menshevik-Internationalist political position on the question of power, is notable for its reference to the Bolsheviks' threat to disband the Constituent Assembly. Newspaper Collection, Institut zur Geschichte der Arbeiterbewegung, Ruhr-Universität Bochum, West Germany.

to Lenin by acting jointly with the Left SRs.[65] Martov objected that this move would give Lenin a cloak of legitimacy, since he would then be speaking on behalf of a parliament that had united the three socialist parties against the "backers of Kerensky and Krasnov." The party's task, as Martov saw it, was to force the Bolsheviks to seek a peaceful compromise with the majority of the Constituent Assembly. He explained in a letter to Aksel'rod:

> That is why I thought it was necessary to put the question point-blank. If the new parliament declares that from the moment the Constituent Assembly is convoked, all power will be passed to it, we will enter this parliament, but only in this case. Because it is preferable that the Bolsheviks cannot say, in the event of a direct attack on the Constituent Assembly, that their "People's Soviet" unites all socialist currents.

It was not an easy decision for Martov. The same letter expressed his pain at hearing the reproaches of Menshevik workers, who were saying: "You were together with the Kadets in the Preparliament, but you don't want to be together with the Bolsheviks in the workers' parliament."[66] Yet Martov remained firm. At stake was the party's commitment to the Constituent Assembly.

The Extraordinary Party Congress

The Menshevik party was deeply divided on all major issues when its Extraordinary Congress opened in Petrograd on November 30. The authority of the CC had hit rock bottom, undermined by factionalism on the right and left. According to official documents, the party had more than 150,000 members.[67] Martov lamented, however, both in public pronouncements and in private letters, that many workers had left the party.[68] Moreover, the breakup of the party along factional lines was a realistic possibility. In some cities, such splits had already occurred. In the Constituent Assembly elections, the Defensists and the Internationalists in one-fifth of the electoral districts ran on separate slates, competing with each other. In Petrograd and Kharkov the Defensists had set up their own local organizations.[69] In addition, the elec-

---

65. "Men'sheviki Internatsionalisty i TsIK," document no. 29 in Nikolaevsky, *Men'sheviki v dni Oktiabr'skogo perevorota*, pp. 91–92.

66. Martov to Aksel'rod, 19 November 1917, Nik. Col. no. 17, box 1, file 1–2, pp. 16–17.

67. Reisser, "Menschewismus und Revolution," p. 143. See also "Polozhenie finansov partii," *Partiinye izvestiia*, no. 8 (20 January 1918), p. 22.

68. Martov to Aksel'rod, 30 December 1917, Nik. Col. no. 17, box 1, file 1–2, p. 1.

69. Znamenskii, *Vserossiiskoe Uchreditel'noe Sobranie*, p. 213. See also the report on the activities of the Petrograd Defensists, "Deiatel'nost' Petrogradskogo komiteta SD men'shevikov," *Nachalo*, 2 February 1918, p. 2.

Constituent Assembly election campaign poster of the Yaroslavl Social Democratic party organization, November 1917: "In the elections to the Constituent Assembly, vote for the United Social Democrats. Freedom—Peace—Land." The number 4 identifies the Social Democratic slate of candidates. Boris I. Nikolaevsky Collection, Hoover Institution Archives, box 200, file 5.

tions of delegates to the Extraordinary Party Congress were organized according to the principle of factional representation. The chosen delegates were instructed to defend at the congress the faction that had a majority in their local organization. Despite the Internationalists' growing strength within the party, Martov was not sure on December 1, the second day of the congress, whether the center-left bloc would have a majority.[70]

70. Martov to Aksel'rod, 1 December 1917, Nik. Col. no. 17, box 1, file 1–2, p. 3. On factional representation, see "Iz zhizni RSDRP," *Fakel*, 25 November 1917, p. 4.

In order to understand better the concerns that the delegates brought to the congress, it is necessary to take a closer look at the local organizations and at the changes that had taken place within the party since the last congress in August 1917. A comparison of the figures on the members registered at the two congresses reveals that overall the provincial party organizations remained fairly stable during this period (see table 1). Losses in some areas were offset by gains in others. The Moscow provincial organizations lost several thousand members, and a downward trend was also noticeable in Tula and Tver, but in Kostroma there was a slight increase, and in Vladimir and Yaroslavl the growth was dramatic. In the Central Industrial Region as a whole, the party lost slightly less than two thousand members. In the Black Earth Region, on the other hand, the Mensheviks gained several hundred new members. A small increase in membership was registered in the Upper Volga–Urals area. In Saratov and Viatka provinces, the Mensheviks lost members, but they gained in Nizhnii Novgorod, Ufa, and Perm. In the Lower Volga–Don area, the figures showed a substantial decline, from 13,150 to 6,000 members; however, since the Mensheviks had a majority in the Rostov soviet in October and December, and since they won the elections in March 1918, it is unlikely that these figures accurately reflected party membership in that area. It is more likely that only 6,000 Mensheviks from the area were represented at the congress because the area was virtually cut off from the central provinces by the fighting between the Bolshevik government and the troops under General Kaledin. In all northern provinces, Menshevik organizations became larger. The Petrograd organization grew by an impressive amount: more than 7,000 new members. Except in Mogilev, local organizations increased also in the western provinces: Smolensk, Vitebsk, and Minsk. In sum, the Menshevik provincial organizations in European Russia proper (that is to say, excluding the Ukraine, the Baltic, the Caucasus, Siberia, the Far East, and the army) for which data are available for both dates counted 88,717 members in August and 89,234 in December 1917.

Perhaps most surprising are the data on Menshevik party membership in the army during this period. To be sure, the Mensheviks' gains did not match those of the Bolsheviks; nevertheless, Menshevik organizations in the army continued to grow, especially on the southwestern front. In the Ukraine, on the other hand, the party lost considerable numbers of members in such provinces as Kiev, Kherson, and Poltava, although organizations in the important industrial areas of Kharkov and Ekaterinoslav held their own or showed a small increase in membership. In sum, even though the Mensheviks were losing voters, they were retaining their membership and perhaps even expanding it slightly.

TABLE 1

Number of members in local Menshevik organizations, August and December 1917, by area and subdivision

Area and subdivision	August	December
Central Industrial Region		
Moscow	15,645	11,000
Tver	1,050	500
Yaroslavl	1,420	4,432
Kostroma	981	1,080
Vladimir	400	1,200
Tula	4,200	3,500
All Central Industrial Region	23,696	21,712
Black Earth Region		
Tambov	988	1,600
Orel	1,765	1,700
Voronezh	560	740
All Black Earth Region	3,313	4,040
Upper Volga–Urals Region		
Saratov	5,028	4,500
Nizhnii Novgorod	1,500	1,900
Ufa	405	750
Viatka	2,500	1,300
Perm	6,750	10,000
Samara	3,095	1,000
All Upper Volga–Urals Region	19,278	19,450
Lower Volga–Don Region		
Rostov	13,150	6,000
Northern Region		
Arkhangelsk	700	800[a]
Petrograd	9,794	17,090
Pskov	900	932
Novgorod	2,460	4,000
All Northern Region	13,854	22,822
Western Region		
Smolensk	1,533	2,500[b]
Vitebsk	4,826	5,700
Minsk	3,760	5,570
Mogilev	5,307	1,440
All Western Region	15,426	15,210
All European Russia	88,717	89,234
Ukraine		
Kiev	7,378	3,000
Taurida	5,045	3,000
Kherson	7,102	2,500
Chernigov	3,134	3,350
Ekaterinoslav	14,620	15,803
Poltava	5,025	1,600
Kharkov	3,700	3,641
All Ukraine	46,004	32,894

TABLE 1 (*Continued*)

Area and subdivision	August	December
Army		
12th Army (including Rìga)	1,330	1,500
Western front	500	5,300
Southwestern front (incomplete)	1,558	10,000
Rumanian front (incomplete)	1,100	5,609
All army	4,488	22,409
All European Russia, Ukraine, and army	139,209c	144,537c

Source: B. I. Miller, "K voprosu o sostoianii partii Men'shevikov osen'iu 1917 goda," in I. I. Mints, ed., *Oktiabr'skoe vooruzhennoe vosstanie v Petrograde* (Moscow: Nauka, 1980), pp. 297–306.

aMore than 800.

bNot less than 2,500.

cOnly subdivisions for which data are available for both dates have been included. Because Miller did not observe that restriction, his totals differ somewhat. His total of 149,696 for August includes the following figures: Vologda, 585; Petrozavodsk, 500; Helsingfors, 150; Estonia, 150; Fifth Army, 500; Kursk, 500; Riazan, 390; Bessarabia, 200; Volyn, 3,010; Podolya, 927; Kuban, 1,080; Tersk, 624; Kazan, 500; Simbirsk, 500; Orenberg, 600. Miller's total of 143,037 for December excludes 2,500 members in the Smolensk organization but includes 1,000 party members in the North Caucasus.

The debates at the congress revolved around two key questions: What had gone wrong before October, and what was the party policy going to be in regard to the Bolsheviks now? O. A. Ermanskii put the party's problems in stark terms: "Can Menshevism be saved?"[71] For Martov, the Bolshevik rank and file, and particularly the workers who had voted for the Bolsheviks, were "mistaken" comrades on the left. They had been lured into simplistic and radical solutions, and in their naiveté they believed that once the proletariat came to power, all problems would be solved. The Mensheviks, as a workers' party, had to stand beside those workers, even when they were wrong.[72] Lenin was exploiting workers' radicalism and distorting the democratic potential of the workers' movement. The Mensheviks' role was to straighten out the course of the Russian Revolution. On the eve of the party congress, Martov wrote in a lead article in the party newspaper *Novyi luch'*:

> The task is to conceive and to carry out an effective policy that for the party of the proletariat issues from the very fact of the soldier-worker uprising, a policy that would enable this fact, which may become a starting point for the defeat of the Revolution, to become instead the starting point of its progressive development and strengthening.[73]

71. "Ekstrennyi Vserossiiskii S"ezd RSDRP," *Novyi luch'*, 6 December 1917, p. 3.

72. Martov to Aksel'rod, 19 November 1917, Nik. Col. no. 17, box 1, file 1–2, pp. 10 and 16.

73. Martov, "Iz zhizni RSDRP," *Novyi luch'*, 19 November 1917, p. 4.

The party's historic role at this stage of the revolution, as Martov saw it, lay, on the one hand, in opposing Bolshevik extremist, destructive, anarcho-syndicalist, and dictatorial policies, and on the other, in preventing the organization by the Right Socialists of armed struggle against the Bolsheviks. A historic compromise between the proletarian masses supporting the Bolsheviks and the peasant and petty-bourgeois classes who had voted for the SRs could prevent civil war in Russia by means of a peaceful power settlement between the Constituent Assembly and the Bolshevik-led soviets. If no such settlement were reached, Martov cautioned, civil war was inevitable, and the result would be the weakening of the proletariat and the democratic forces and the strengthening of the counterrevolutionary forces and the Bolshevik dictatorship. Martov's perception of the political situation proved to be remarkably accurate; he foresaw the course of Russia's political development in 1918. To a significant extent his ideas shaped the Menshevik CC policy toward the Bolshevik regime in 1918; at the party congress, he incorporated them, in somewhat altered form, in a draft resolution on the current situation.[74]

For Potresov, Liber, and P. N. Kolokol'nikov, all CC members, the Bolsheviks were no longer a party of Russian Democracy. They had broken with Democracy by organizing the uprising behind the back of the Congress of Soviets. During their short term in office, the Bolsheviks had shut down more socialist newspapers than the tsarist government had managed to close. They had declared the entire Kadet party and its legally elected delegates to the Constituent Assembly to be "counterrevolutionary." They had begun their rule by disbanding the city dumas, which had been elected on the basis of universal suffrage. To secure their party dictatorship they were now exploiting the wave of anarchy that had resulted from Russia's defeat in the war. The Defensist Mensheviks therefore rejected the application of the term "socialist" to what they believed was a process of disintegration provoked by the Bolsheviks.[75] There was nothing "socialist" about the seizure of land by peasants or the seizure of factories by workers. In an article titled "The Party of the Soldiers' Rebellion," Anatolii Diubua, a Defensist columnist, declared:

> The insurgent peasant masses used to be full of faith in the wonder-working capacity of the Revolution to bring about peace. . . . Thence stems their hatred, when it turned out that the Revolution could bring no peace, toward the now fallen gods and toward the parties of the Mensheviks and

74. "Iz materialov s"ezda: Proekty rezoliutsii po tekushchemu momentu: Rezoliutsiia Martova," *Novyi luch'*, 3 December 1917, p. 4.

75. A. N. Potresov, "Rokovye protivorechiia russkoi revoliutsii," in Nikolaevsky, ed., *Potresov*, pp. 238–40.

SRs, which had been at the helm. Thence also stems this blind and elemental attachment to the new master [*barin*], to the Bolsheviks.[76]

To the Defensists, the Bolsheviks were a destructive force, an irresponsible, adventuristic, extremist clique of party activists who had deceived the workers and betrayed Russian Democracy. The Defensists portrayed the Menshevik party as the party of the conscious proletariat, opposed to the destruction of the forces of production. Consequently, the Mensheviks should seek alliances with other democratic forces and not with the Bolsheviks.

Mark Liber reiterated these ideas in his speeches at the congress and in a draft resolution.[77] He accused the Bolsheviks of preparing an attack on the Constituent Assembly and argued that it was therefore imperative to "refuse recognition to the party which had seized power . . . and to mobilize the forces of the working class, together with all of Democracy, for . . . a struggle with the usurpers under the rallying cry of the Constituent Assembly." Agreement with the Bolsheviks was impermissible, even criminal, and would lead the party to catastrophe. The Mensheviks' historic task was to struggle for Democracy: "We need to draw the workers away from the Bolsheviks. But first of all we must draw away from the Bolsheviks ourselves. We must recognize the people's right to rise up against the Bolsheviks . . . for Freedom, for universal suffrage, for local self-government, for the All-Russian Constituent Assembly!"[78]

Potresov's speech was similar, but was couched in more categorical terms. The Bolsheviks represented, he said, not a part of the proletariat but only the interests of the disillusioned, violent, hungry hordes of exhausted soldiers. For this reason, Martov's slogan, "Peace within the ranks of Revolutionary Democracy!" made no sense. Social Democracy stood on the brink of great national calamities: the disintegration of Russia, disaster at the peace negotiations, anarchy, civil war.[79] The victories of the February revolution were being destroyed by the Bolshevik counterrevolution. The Social Democrats had to do their patriotic duty and join together with all democratic forces against the Bolsheviks.

Four draft resolutions were presented to the congress. Potresov's received 10 votes, Liber's 13, Dan's 26, and Martov's 50, out of a total of 120 votes.[80] Even if Dan had decided to form a bloc with everyone to

76. Anatolii Diubua, "Partiia soldatskogo bunta," *Novyi luch'*, 10 December 1917, p. 2.
77. "Rezoliutsiia Libera," *Novyi luch'*, 3 December 1917, p. 4.
78. Quoted in Aronson, *K istorii pravogo techeniia*, pp. 38, 40.
79. "Tezisy po dokladu Potresova o voine i peremirii," *Novyi luch'*, 5 December 1917, p. 4.
80. "Rezoliutsii po tekushchemu momentu," *Novyi luch'*, 6 December 1917, p. 3.

the right of him, it would not have had enough votes to defeat Martov. Dan supported Martov on issues concerning the party's future policy, but he vigorously defended the party's record in 1917. In a letter to Aksel'rod, Martov later wrote that the center-left victory would have been even more impressive had the Georgian delegation of thirty to forty members managed to reach the congress, but it could not because of war conditions.[81]

After some amendments, Martov's resolution was voted upon again and this time received 57 votes to 28 against and 2 abstentions.[82] Of the 28 nays, 23 were probably cast by Potresov's and Liber's supporters. Dan's Revolutionary Defensist faction split: 5 evidently joined the right opposition; 7 joined Martov; the others did not vote. The cornerstone of the understanding between the Internationalists and a segment of the Revolutionary Defensists was their shared view that the Menshevik party had to oppose Lenin's design to disband the Constituent Assembly and at the same time seek an accommodation with the "democratic elements" in Bolshevism. In terms of practical policy, the new center-left bloc determined not to enter the CEC, in order to dissociate itself from any possible attack on the Constituent Assembly; at the same time, it did not rule out returning to the CEC at a later date in the role of an opposition.

In his discussion of the decisions of the December congress, Haimson has suggested that the Mensheviks displayed "a lack of enthusiasm" for the Constituent Assembly, "whatever their protestations," because they knew that its political composition would be far to the right of the political platform just adopted and because their own delegation at the assembly was so small.[83] There is no evidence to substantiate that view. Mensheviks of all persuasions were committed to the principle of universal suffrage and to the convocation of the Constituent Assembly. It was the Bolsheviks' determination to attack the Constituent Assembly that forced the CC's decision not to join the CEC, even though the conditions were very favorable.

Some Internationalists again tried to persuade the party to join the CEC without delay. Ermanskii, for example, reasoned that the Mensheviks had "to recognize the fact that there were times when Lenin had a majority [in the CEC] of only one vote. A sufficiently strong opposition could have forced Lenin to reckon with it."[84] Even though

81. Martov to Aksel'rod, 30 December 1917, Nik. Col. no. 17, box 1, file 1–2, p. 2.

82. "Vechernee zasedanie 4 dekabria," *Novyi luch'*, 7 December 1917, p. 4.

83. Haimson, "Mensheviks after the October Revolution," pt. 1, p. 472, and pt. 2, p. 206.

84. "Rech' Ermanskogo: Vechernee zasedanie 6 dekabria," *Novyi luch'*, 10 December 1917, p. 4.

Lenin did not, as it turned out, take any heed of the opposition in the CEC, this view was not entirely unfounded. The Left SRs were reluctant until the very last moment to go along with the disbandment of the Constituent Assembly. The Bolshevik faction in the assembly was also in favor of a compromise settlement. Thus a majority vote in the CEC against disbandment would have brought additional pressure to bear on Lenin to accept a compromise solution. The Right Mensheviks were categorically opposed to joining the CEC, though. Liber and others even advocated walking out of the soviets and boycotting them. Kolokol'-nikov explained that "to participate in the soviets would be to sanction the Bolshevik seizure [of power]. We must support the Constituent Assembly and the organs of local self-government. . . . I am decidedly against participation in the soviets, which in the Bolsheviks' hands have become instruments of struggle against the conquests of democracy."[85] Zaretskaia added: "If there is an agreement [with the Bolsheviks] we will be cursed, along with the Bolsheviks, as traitors to democracy!"[86]

Some Defensists were nevertheless inclined to accept the decision of the congress. According to a newspaper report, one of them, S. Telia, "while remaining a Defensist, voted for [Martov's] resolution because in agreement with the Bolsheviks he sees a means of preventing a civil war. And to this end he is ready to agree not only with the Bolsheviks but also with the devil and his grandmother."[87] There was no question of entering the CEC; the new majority had to defend even the party's willingness to remain in the soviets, which in itself was too much for the right wing. Potresov, according to a recent study, considered splitting off from the party and tried to persuade Liber to follow.[88] Liber refused, but he declared that any agreement with the Bolsheviks would cause him to change his mind, and many of his supporters would follow him out of the party.[89] For the time being, they would "carry on a decisive struggle within the party against the decisions of the congress."[90]

Such declarations brought to the fore the problem of factionalism, or, as it was euphemistically called, the problem of party unity. Martov's speech on the subject revealed a new approach: "It is clear," he said, "that striving to ensure unity at any cost may bring more harm than

85. "Zakliuchitel'naia rech' Kolokol'nikova," ibid., p. 4.

86. Aronson, *K istorii pravogo techeniia*, p. 41.

87. "Vechernee zasedanie 4 dekabria," *Novyi luch'*, 7 December 1917, p. 4.

88. Reisser, *Menschewismus und Revolution*, p. 146.

89. Aronson, *K istorii pravogo techeniia*, p. 41.

90. "V Sotsial Demokraticheskoi partii (ob'edinennoi)" (typed document copied from an article in the newspaper *Den'* and labeled "around December 15, 1917, Petrograd"), T. S. Russia Collection, Hoover Institution Archives.

good now. . . . The party is restricted in all its actions because neither of the factions considers itself answerable to party discipline. In point of fact, this is drawing the party out of the political arena."[91] The Defensists should thus either submit to party discipline or leave the party. The current situation was intolerable. The party had to have a clearly defined program, not an indecisive hodgepodge of irreconcilable statements. Martov wrote to Aksel'rod that he thought that the Defensists would leave the party.[92] At the congress, P. Golikov, an ardent Defensist, finished his speech with the words "Long live the split!" Zaretskaia announced that she was "not going to keep hanging on to the door handle [of the party]"; she would act according to her convictions.[93]

It is hard to estimate how many Defensists left the party in protest over the congress's decisions. Certainly the majority stayed. No matter how unpalatable Martov's position was to them, most did not want to break away from the party. A resolution on party unity recognized the right of the opposition to criticize the CC within party organizations and in the party press. Such criticism outside the party—that is, in such multiparty organizations as the soviets—was forbidden, however.[94] To demonstrate their objection to this new stricture, the eleven members of the old CC who had resigned on November 1 and then returned now refused to participate in the new CC, to which Internationalists and Revolutionary Defensists were elected.[95]

What held the Menshevik factions together, Leopold Haimson has suggested, was the perilous condition of the party after its poor showing in the Constituent Assembly elections.[96] Two other facts, however, were much more instrumental in uniting them: the new party majority was based on a consensus and the crisis of leadership had been overcome.

91. "Edinstvo partii," *Novyi luch'*, 6 December 1917, p. 3.

92. Martov to Aksel'rod, 1 December 1917, Nik. Col. no. 17, box 1, file 1–2, p. 4.

93. "Ekstrennyi Vserossiiskii S"ezd RSDRP," *Novyi luch'*, 6 December 1917, p. 4.

94. "Iz materialov s"ezda: Rezoliutsiia s"ezda o edinstve partii," *Novyi luch'*, 6 December 1917, p. 4.

95. Martov to Aksel'rod, 30 December 1917, Nik. Col. no. 17, box 1, file 1–2, p. 2.

96. Haimson, "Mensheviks after the October Revolution," pt. 1, p. 472.

CHAPTER 2

The Mensheviks Confront
the Bolshevik Challenge

In the fall of 1917, the Mensheviks faced a twofold political challenge. First, their Marxist rivals on the left had come to power and embarked upon what they believed was a socialist transformation of society: transfer of power to the soviets, inauguration of workers' control, and nationalization of the banks. In Soviet historiography this period is described as that of the "overthrow of the bourgeoisie" and the "establishment of the dictatorship of the proletariat."[1] Second, the majority of Russian workers and soldiers had lost patience with the Menshevik policy of national consensus, compromise, and negotiations with the bourgeoisie. The Menshevik insistence on "consciousness," by which they meant the moderation of workers' "excessive demands," led workers to support the Bolsheviks, who promised to fulfill those demands. Excited by the popular slogan "Bread, Peace, and Land," the masses supported a course that seemed to promise quick and easy solutions: destroying the power of the bourgeoisie and the landlords. The peasants were seizing the land. The soldiers were seizing the trains and ammunition in their flight from the front line. Workers' committees were taking over the management of factories. The socioeconomic order was being transformed. The country was close to anarchy.[2] November and December 1917 witnessed the frag-

---

1. Sobolev, ed., *The Great October Socialist Revolution*, esp. pp. 240–347.
2. For vivid descriptions of the scene, see Miliukov, *Rossiia na perelome*, p. 95; F. Dan, "Voprosy voiny i mira," in Martov, ed., *Za god*, p. 12; "Po Rossii: V sotsialisticheskom tsarstve," *Nash vek* (Kadet newspaper), 20 December 1917, p. 4.

mentation of political authority among a myriad of organizations. For the first time since the Pugachev uprising, whole provinces were no longer governed from the capital, or were not governed at all. Dumas, soviets, councils of people's commissars, and military revolutionary committees competed for power.

The Attack on the Bourgeoisie

The first legislative acts of the Bolshevik government aimed at preserving the loyalty of the revolutionary masses, on the one hand, and undermining the political and economic power of the bourgeoisie, on the other. The Bolshevik decrees on peace, land, and workers' control brought them popularity. Trying to consolidate and augment this popularity, the Bolsheviks promised to take apartments away from the bourgeoisie and give them to the proletariat.[3] Mocking the Menshevik slogan "Peace without annexations and indemnities," the Bolsheviks declared in the Moscow soviet: "What we need is annexations from the landlords and indemnities from the bourgeoisie."[4] A campaign to impose indemnities on the overthrown class enemy was indeed begun in many cities of European Russia. A wave of "requisitions," "socializations," and "nationalizations" of property of all kinds rolled across the country, sometimes to brutal effect. It was often unclear how the requisitioned property was disposed of and by whom, but in any case it is estimated that 739 million rubles were raised in this fashion. The Bolsheviks called upon the workers to take the factories into their own hands; some hated plant administrators were physically ejected, to the jubilation of the workers. Many of these measures put additional strains on the already disrupted economy of the country. But what mattered most for the Bolsheviks at this stage was the effort to enhance the political and economic power of the organizations under their leadership. For the moment, the Bolshevik-led factory committees were given great authority, even though they were hardly prepared to take over the management of the factories.[5] In order to put an end to the economic power of the bourgeoisie, the Bolshevik government also decided to nationalize the banks. Countless editorials in the Bolshevik press reiterated that it was not enough to seize political power; to win the historic battle against the bourgeoisie, one had to take over the

---

3. Potekhin, *Pervyi sovet*, p. 161.
4. "Sredi rabochikh," *Nash vek*, 9 December 1917, p. 4.
5. Scheibert, *Lenin an der Macht*, p. 193. For a detailed discussion of "localism" in workers' control, see Rosenberg, "Russian Labor and Bolshevik Power," p. 218.

capitalists' most powerful weapon—the banks. The decree in December on the nationalization of the banks was a step in this direction.

During the first months after October, the Bolsheviks made a concerted effort to wrest control over provincial administration from the zemstvos and dumas, most of which had been elected on the basis of universal suffrage earlier in 1917. In almost all cities of European Russia, Mensheviks and SRs headed the city dumas. These bodies were now disbanded, even though the Bolsheviks, by their own admission, had no qualified personnel with which to organize a functioning administration.[6]

These policies were known at the time as "the Red Guards' attack on the bourgeoisie." They were designed, whatever the rhetoric, to undermine the political and economic power of the Bolsheviks' opponents— the Kadets, the SRs, and the Mensheviks. In the short run, they contributed to Bolshevik consolidation of power, but in the long run they were bound to lead to a drastic deterioration in the economic situation, which in turn would become a weapon in the hands of the opposition.

All Mensheviks agreed that Bolshevik economic policies were leading to economic catastrophe and civil war.[7] Even according to Martov, not to mention Liber and Potresov, the soviets were ill equipped to take over the running of local governments. As political organizations of the working class, the soviets were a valuable asset, but as surrogate dumas, they were worthless. Furthermore, they were much less democratic than the dumas, because the elections to the soviets were not based on a direct, equal, and secret ballot.[8] The task of the soviets was to represent workers' interests in society, not to provide community services. The Mensheviks reiterated their demand that political power be vested in the institutions based on universal suffrage: the Constituent Assembly and the dumas.[9]

The Mensheviks criticized with equal vigor the Bolsheviks' implementation of workers' control.[10] The brunt of their argument was that the

---

6. That this was the case was attested to by both the Bolsheviks and their opponents; see Mints, *Istoriia velikogo oktiabria*, pp. 700–701 (where the disbanded dumas are listed), and "Polozhenie partii SR v Rossii," Nik. Col. no. 7, box 2, file 45.

7. The view that Bolshevik policies were bound to lead to civil war has also recently been expressed by Sheila Fitzpatrick in "The Civil War as a Formative Experience," in Gleason, Kenez, and Stites, eds., *Bolshevik Culture*, p. 59.

8. "Rech' Martova: Zasedanie 25 ianvaria" (speech at the Third Congress of Soviets), *Petrogradskii golos*, 16 January 1918 (old calendar), p. 3.

9. "Deklaratsiia SD fraktsii Uchreditel'nogo Sobraniia," *Novyi luch'*, 6 January 1918, p. 1.

10. "Men'sheviki oborontsy o rabochem kontrole," *Fakel*, 25 November 1917, p. 4; see also "Rezoliutsiia o rabochem kontrole" (resolution offered at the December party congress), *Novyi luch'*, 6 December 1917, p. 4. For discussions of the negative results of the introduction of workers' control, see N. Cherevanin, "Revoliutsiia pered zadachei regu-

Bolsheviks were distorting the socialist notion of workers' control, which the Mensheviks understood to mean a certain degree of supervision over the financial operations of the factories for purposes of increased worker participation in management and a more just distribution of profits. Under the Provisional Government, argued the Mensheviks, the workers had had more actual control over the operation of the factories than they had under workers' control as practiced by the Bolsheviks. Previously, as a result of the energetic intervention of the Ministry of Labor, the workers had indeed exercised considerable authority in bargaining over wages, in the work of the Conflict Settlement Boards and management boards, and in profit-sharing arrangements.[11] The Menshevik critics reiterated over and over that Russia was a backward country, that it was not ready for socialist experiments, that Russian workers understood the Bolshevik slogan "Worker! Take the factory!" too literally and had begun to regard the factories as their own property. Analyzing the underlying causes of workers' behavior, some Menshevik authors wrote that the alienation of labor about which Marx had written manifested itself in Russian conditions in a revolt not only against the bourgeoisie but also against the factories, machinery, and work as such. The coming of socialism was often taken to mean freedom not to work; now, with the victory of the proletariat, it was the turn of the bourgeoisie to work. "The socialization of industry," wrote David Dallin, soon to be a CC member, "was a means for the workers to liquidate industry painlessly."[12]

Other Menshevik commentators saw in this movement the effects of what they referred to as the peasant takeover of the Russian working class. The tremendous influx of peasants into the Russian labor force during the war had overwhelmed the small contingent of workers who had identified themselves with the interests of industrial production:

> The relations of production in the capitalist order are beyond the grasp of a factory worker with the psychology of a peasant. Having socialized the landlord's land, he is striving for only one thing: to increase the indemnity from the factory. In vain would you try to convince such a worker that he is destroying industry. He cannot understand it; his aspirations are in the village.[13]

It was the unskilled peasant laborers that proved to be most radical and "Bolshevik" in the assault on "capitalism." According to the Men-

---

lirovaniia ekonomicheskoi zhizni," *Rabochii internatsional*, no. 1, 1918, p. 29; and V. Epifanov, "V strane skazok," in *Nash golos: Sotsial Demokraticheskii sbornik* (Moscow [late 1917]), pp. 17–19.

11. For a recent treatment of this question, see Hogan, "Conciliation Boards."

12. David Dallin, "Narodnoe khoziaistvo i 'sotsializm,'" in Martov, ed., *Za god*, p. 61.

13. V. Makarov, "Derevnia i fabrika," *Novaia zaria*, 10 June 1918, pp. 29–30. Recent research confirms the Menshevik observations on the expansion and composition of the

sheviks, workers' control degenerated in Russian conditions into anarcho-syndicalism, which was fraught with grave consequences: "The
Bolshevik experiments with workers' control, in the event of their consistent implementation, must end in a disgraceful fiasco, in the total
collapse of industry, in unemployment, and in the discrediting of the
very idea of socialism in the eyes of the masses for many years."[14]

The Mensheviks objected to the nationalization of the banks as well.
The gist of their critique was that, while in principle the establishment
of government control over the banks in order to coordinate overall
investment policy was a good idea, the means that the Bolsheviks had
used were destructive. If the government had taken over the operations
of the major banks without disrupting their functioning, the result
could have been advantageous. By simply seizing their assets, the Bolsheviks dealt a death blow to the system of credit and deprived both the
capitalists and themselves of a functioning system of monetary circulation.[15] Private capital no longer flowed back into investment, but instead accumulated in the hands of the remaining private holders. The
money supply was drying up, and the Bolsheviks would soon face the
need to replenish it by issuing more paper money. The resultant inflation would add to the number of industrial bankruptcies and to the
ranks of the unemployed.

One Menshevik analyst, Semen Zagorskii, argued that it was a combination of political expediency and ideological commitment that
drove Lenin to nationalize the banks. His objective was to break the
resistance of the bourgeoisie by "picking their pockets," by seizing
their deposits or forbidding withdrawals. At the same time, by merging
all the banks into one state bank, he thought he could create a unified,
centralized system for funding "socialist" industry. The Bolsheviks
partly achieved their political objectives—the bourgeoisie was financially ruined—but with it, argued Zagorskii, Russian industry was
ruined, too.[16] The Bolsheviks' actions were to have other devastating
effects as well. Russian peasants would not sell their grain for worthless paper money, and the urban population would stand on the threshold of famine in the spring of 1918.

The Bolsheviks claimed that the nationalization of the banks and the
establishment of workers' control were measures aimed at introducing
"socialism now." In the Mensheviks' judgment, these measures led to a

---

labor force, at least in Petrograd; see S. A. Smith, *Red Petrograd*, p. 21, and Rosenberg,
"Russian Labor and Bolshevik Power," pp. 222–23.

14. "Rezoliutsiia o rabochem kontrole," *Novyi luch'*, 6 December 1917, p. 4.

15. For a discussion of the economic consequences of the nationalization of the banks,
see Spektator, "Bol'shevistskii perevorot i khoziaistvennoe polozhenie Rossii," *Rabochii
internatsional*, no. 1 (1918), pp. 42–46, esp. 43.

16. Semen Zagorskii, "Natsionalizatsiia bankov i razrushenie narodnogo khoziaistva,"
Delo, 21 April 1918, pp. 8–9.

wasteful, petty-bourgeois redivision of national wealth which was going to ruin the Russian economy.

During November and December 1917, the Menshevik critique of the Bolshevik policies was not on the whole favorably received by the masses. The Mensheviks were fully aware that they had lost a substantial part of their constituency to the Bolsheviks. Commenting on the results of the elections for the Constituent Assembly, Martov wrote to Aksel'rod that in the major cities the Mensheviks had received only 5 to 10 percent of the vote—the "upper layer of the working class," as he put it—and that the masses were backing the Bolsheviks, SRs, and Kadets. The only consolation, he wrote later, was that "we are no longer hated."[17] Yet Martov believed that the Mensheviks had to continue in their repudiation of the Bolshevik travesty of socialism.[18] When the Bolshevik experiments backfired on the workers, the Menshevik warnings would be remembered.

First Signs of Worker Dissatisfaction

The workers' vote for the Bolsheviks in October did not necessarily imply support for Lenin's political objectives. The vote was an expression of support for a variety of policies: for the Bolshevik guarantee of a speedy convocation of the Constituent Assembly (which had supposedly been sabotaged by the propertied classes); for the creation of a caretaker worker-peasant government of socialist parties, with the participation of the dumas and soviets; and for a transfer of power to the soviets, either permanently or until the convocation of the Constituent Assembly. Support for these objectives did not necessarily indicate support for the establishment of Bolshevik one-party rule. It appears that even some of the workers who fought for the Bolshevik cause in the streets of Moscow in early November were fighting not for a Bolshevik government but for the convocation of the Constituent Assembly and to forestall a possible victory of the military and other supporters of Ke-

17. Martov to Aksel'rod, 19 November and 30 December 1917, Nik. Col. no. 17, box 1, file 1–2.

18. For years to come, Martov would be preoccupied with the task of presenting a Marxist critique of Bolshevik socialism. For his most important contributions in 1918, see "Diktatura i demokratiia," in Martov, ed., *Za god*, pp. 19–38, and the essay "Marks i problema diktatury proletariata," which was published in a French translation in Dan and Martov, eds., *La Dictature du proletariat*, pp. 37–48. Together with two other essays written in 1919, "The Ideology of Sovietism" and "The Conquest of the State," it also appeared in English under the title *The State and the Socialist Revolution*. For the most recent edition in English, see *The New International Review*, Winter and Summer 1977, pp. 11–39, and Winter 1978, pp. 41–60.

rensky. The majority of Moscow workers did not actively support the Bolsheviks' bid for power, but rather remained neutral, giving at most tacit support to the Bolsheviks.[19] Similarly, recent studies of the Petrograd workers show that they hoped for soviet power, not for a one-party dictatorship, and that the workers in the large plants that formed the core of the Petrograd metal industry were swept up by the Bolshevik tide rather late.[20]

The soldiers' vote for the Bolsheviks in November 1917 was not a vote for the dictatorship of the Bolshevik party, either, nor was it a mandate for the construction of socialism. Rather, it was first and foremost a vote for the party that promised immediate peace. As we shall see, the soldiers' "Bolshevism" would dissipate with the first orders of the Bolshevik government to resume military action at the time of the German offensive in February 1918.

The Bolshevik honeymoon with the workers, too, was relatively brief. As early as December 1917, sporadic conflicts broke out. The Bolsheviks had promised too much, and they were increasingly running the risk of being unable to deliver. Several types of disputes can be distinguished at this stage.[21] The most common type arose out of what the Bolsheviks themselves described as the "unreasonable demands" of the workers. The demobilized soldiers who before the war had worked at the plant that produced paper money, for example, demanded that the workers currently employed there, mostly women, be fired and that their old jobs be returned to them. When the authorities stalled, the soldiers threatened to storm the plant and seize it by force of arms.[22] It must have been difficult to settle this conflict in view of the calls to workers to "take the factory!" Other demobilized soldiers who returned to their factories demanded back pay for a month or two, or half a year, or in some cases for the entire duration of the war, on the ground that it had been harder to be a soldier with virtually no pay than a worker receiving relatively high wages throughout those years. According to the Bolshevik Commissariat of Labor, "the number of demands by soldiers that they be paid for the duration of their service at the front was particularly high."[23] According to a Menshevik source,

19. Koenker, *Moscow Workers*, pp. 334, 342–44.

20. Mandel, *The Petrograd Workers and the Soviet Seizure of Power*, pp. 299, 324, 327.

21. Detailed statistics on labor conflicts in the early months of Bolshevik rule are provided in *Biulleten' Narodnogo Kommissariata Truda*, nos. 1–4 (August–September 1918), pp. 49–55.

22. "Rabochaia zhizn'," *Nash vek*, 19 December 1917, p. 4, and "Rabochaia zhizn'," *Novyi luch'*, 19 December 1917, p. 4.

23. "Doklad zaveduiushchego konfliktnym otdeleniem otdela vzaimootnoshenii," *Biulleten' Narodnogo Kommissariata Truda*, nos. 1–4 (August–September 1918), pp. 53–54.

the demand was made at a meeting of the Petrograd garrison that every demobilized soldier be given 250 rubles. A Menshevik writer said that at many regimental meetings, the soldiers decided to divide up the regiment's property and ammunition and go home.[24] This comment implies that the Bolsheviks now had to deal with the problem of military discipline which had earlier bedeviled the Provisional Government. In those days, however, any attempt to restore discipline had been attacked by the Bolsheviks as "counterrevolutionary."

After seizing power in October, the Bolsheviks promised the workers an immediate improvement in their situation at the expense of the bourgeoisie. The unemployed, for example, would receive compensation equal to the average wage of an unskilled worker.[25] What counted was not the economic feasibility of this measure but its political effect. Such promises only stimulated workers' demands, however, and as a result, some of the early disputes involving "unreasonable demands" ended with political threats to the Bolshevik government. In early December, a spokesman for the unskilled workers demanded that the wages of unskilled workers be made equal to those of skilled workers, and he warned the Bolsheviks: "You welcomed the establishment of equal rights for officers and soldiers, and now the unskilled workers want a material situation equal to the skilled workers'. If the demands of the Petrograd unskilled workers are not met, the government of the people's commissars will fall, just as the governments of Romanov and Kerensky did."[26]

According to the Commissariat of Labor, the largest number of labor conflicts in the first months of Bolshevik rule involved workers' demands for higher wages.[27] Other conflicts arose out of complaints about decisions of commissars, factory administrators, or other officials. In Moscow alone, the Conflict Commission of the Commissariat of Labor was processing thirty conflicts on the average daily, which involved forty-five enterprises at any given time.[28] A Menshevik correspondent reported that at a workers' rally in Okulovka, "the workers succeeded in passing a pay scale that increased their wages by more than 100

24. A. Nikitskii, "Finansovoe polozhenie Rossii," *Rabochii internatsional*, no. 2 [n.d., presumably February or March 1918], p. 38.

25. "Proekt strakhovaniia na sluchai bezrabotitsy," *Izvestiia* (Petrograd), 14 November 1917, p. 6.

26. "Rabochaia zhizn'," *Novyi luch'*, 5 December 1917, p. 4.

27. "Doklad zaveduiushchego konfliktnym otdeleniem otdela vzaimootnoshenii," *Biulleten' Narodnogo Kommissariata Truda*, nos. 1–4 (August–September 1918), pp. 53–55.

28. "Kratkii otchet o deiatel'nosti Kommissariata Truda Moskovskoi promyshlennoi oblasti so dnia ego obrazovaniia (po mai 1918 goda)," ibid., p. 19.

percent."[29] The demands for higher pay multiplied with every "victory over the bourgeoisie."

In December 1917 the workers at four plants in Petrograd were stunned when a pay raise they had been promised was withdrawn. The Bolsheviks at one of the plants had campaigned before October for a 50 percent pay raise, retroactive to the previous May. This demand had made them very popular at the expense of the Mensheviks. When the Bolsheviks came to power, the pay raise was granted, to the jubilation of the workers. When the raise was withdrawn in December, the pro-Bolshevik mood withered away overnight, and the workers passed a resolution calling for support of the Constituent Assembly: "The Constituent Assembly will give us the pay raise," read the resolution. The Bolshevik candidates for the factory committee were overwhelmingly defeated.[30]

In most disputes over wages, the Bolshevik government encountered the same problems that had plagued the Menshevik Ministry of Labor. Realizing how quickly popular support would dissipate, the Bolsheviks chose not to apply the brakes to these demands for a while, since their political fortunes were far from secure in those hectic days just before the opening of the Constituent Assembly. They chose instead to continue the policy of the Provisional Government—that is, to satisfy the workers' demands and to print more money to cover the mounting deficits.

The introduction of workers' control, however, generated new problems that the Provisional Government had not had to face: conflicts among the workers of a given plant, the factory committee or factory administration, and the state economic agency. The "Bolshevik" factory committees at seized plants tended to act like the new owners of the plant and jealously guarded "their" plant from the intrusion of the state commissars. The high-handed ways of some of these factory committee members provoked bitterness among the workers, who felt that the committee was running the factory in their name but without their consent.[31] According to the Conflict Commission at the Commissariat of Labor, several hundred conflicts involving 388,814 workers were registered by May 1918.[32]

29. "Rabochaia zhizn'," *Novyi luch'*, 5 December 1917, p. 4.

30. "Sredi rabochikh," *Nashe edinstvo*, 20 December 1917, p. 3; "Otdai nazad: Patron-nyi zavod," *Novyi luch'*, 19 December 1917, p. 4. G. Strumilo described a similar situation in "Iz zapisok rabochego: Na Trubochnom," *Zaria* (Berlin), 31 May 1922, p. 79.

31. "Po Rossii: V sotsialisticheskom tsarstve," *Nash vek*, 20 December 1917, p. 4. See also S. A. Smith, *Red Petrograd*, pp. 208, 251.

32. "Doklad zaveduiushchego konfliktnym otdeleniem otdela vzaimootnoshenii," *Biulleten' Narodnogo Kommissariata Truda*, 1918, no. 1–4:54.

In December 1917, workers at the Orudiinyi plant voted to withhold monetary contributions to the Petrograd soviet, and a few days later they recalled their Bolshevik deputies.[33] On December 20, a newspaper reported, the workers at the Lesner plant, "after a speech by a Menshevik comrade, refused to listen to a Bolshevik speaker." Around the same time, the workers at the Tube plant adopted a resolution demanding the "resignation of the Council of People's Commissars and a guarantee of [the convocation of] the Constituent Assembly."[34] A Kadet newspaper, no friend of the Mensheviks and SRs, noted that "the wave of Bolshevism is beginning to subside in the workers' neighborhoods. At many factories and plants new elections [of deputies] to the Petrograd soviet have started. And what is noteworthy is that the new delegates are no longer Bolsheviks."[35]

The dramatic worsening of the economic situation in January 1918 exacerbated the workers' dissatisfaction with the Bolshevik government. Numerous plants in the metal industry, many of which had greatly expanded their work force during the war, were now closing down or curtailing production and laying off workers. The Rosenkrants copper plant, for example, had employed 4,000 workers in 1917; by March 1918, only 900 remained. The Parviainen factory, which produced mines, shells, and other war-related products, had employed 7,000 workers; by March 1918, the works were shut down and only 200 manual workers and 350 office employees remained. It was ironic that the largest number of closings happened to be in the Vyborg district of Petrograd, known in 1917 as staunchly pro-Bolshevik.[36]

The immediate cause of the closings was the government decree of December 23 on the conversion of war industry to peacetime production. But war production had been lagging for some time. Between 1914 and 1917, the number of metal workers in Petrograd increased by 400 percent. Mounting difficulties with supplies, transport, management, and organization throughout 1917 reduced production by 40 percent from February to July alone. The contraction of the defense industry was, as a recent study shows, to a certain extent inevitable.[37] Neither the Provisional nor the Bolshevik government could control this process. Before October 25, 1917, the Bolsheviks, as an opposition party, were the beneficiaries of the worsening situation; after October, as the

33. "Sredi rabochikh," *Nash vek*, 9 December 1917, p. 4; "Poslednie izvestiia," ibid., 15 December 1917, p. 1.

34. "Zavod Lesner" and "Sobranie Trubochnogo zavoda," *Nashe edinstvo*, 29 December 1917, p. 4.

35. "Poslednie izvestiia," *Nash vek*, 15 December 1917, p. 1.

36. "Po fabrikam i zavodam," *Novaia zhizn'*, 20 March 1918, p. 4; "Po fabrikam i zavodam," ibid., 28 March 1918, p. 4; and "Zakrytie zavodov," ibid., 6 January 1918, p. 4.

37. Rosenberg, "Russian Labor and Bolshevik Power," pp. 216, 220.

governing party, they had to take the brunt of workers' discontent. Political preferences changed very quickly. Many factories that had been voting for the Mensheviks and SRs in August, then for the Bolsheviks and the transfer of power to the soviets in October, in December voted for the Mensheviks and SRs again and demanded the convocation of the Constituent Assembly. The post-October conflicts between workers and soldiers and the Bolsheviks show how volatile and transitory popular support was. The overall pattern of popular allegiance manifested itself in a large-scale defection of the revolutionary masses from one party to another.

Disbandment of the Constituent Assembly

On January 5, 1918, the Bolsheviks disbanded the Constituent Assembly. This action marked a turning point in their relations with the Petrograd workers. Red Guards shot at a peaceful, unarmed procession in defense of the assembly and burned the demonstrators' banners in street fires.[38] Compared to the Red Terror that was to follow, it was a minor incident; twenty-one people were killed.[39] Before that day, however, the Bolsheviks had been known as the party that had assailed Kerensky for daring to consider restoring the death penalty for desertion at the front, the party that had accused the Kadets, the Mensheviks, and the SRs of postponing and sabotaging the convocation of the Constituent Assembly. On November 11, on the eve of the elections to the Constituent Assembly, the Bolshevik newspapers had printed large headlines proclaiming that only the Bolsheviks' accession to power had made possible the convocation of the Constituent Assembly. The Bolsheviks' image had been that of a radical, uncompromising, revolutionary, and democratic party. This image was badly tarnished by the events of January 5.

In the fall of 1917, when the Bolsheviks were winning majorities in the city soviets, Lenin had demanded that the workers be given the right to recall their delegates from the soviet at any time, without waiting for the expiration of their term. This right, argued the Bolsheviks at that time, would make the soviets truly reflect the "revolutionary mood" of the masses. After January 5, the right of recall began to work against the Bolsheviks. The workers were still convinced that the Bol-

38. For detailed descriptions of the event, see Lev Deich, "Rasstrel mirnykh manifestantov," *Nashe edinstvo*, 11 January 1918, p. 2, and "Pervye stolknoveniia," *Novaia zhizn'*, 9 January 1918, p. 3.

39. This figure was given by Sverdlov at the Third Congress of Soviets; see "Tretii S"ezd Sovetov," *Petrogradskii golos*, 12 January 1918, p. 3.

sheviks, as "honest comrades," would not obstruct the recall of delegates. One of the workers' protest resolutions declared:

> We, the workers and employees of the Main Rail Car and Locomotive works at the Nikolaevskaia railroad, having assembled at a general meeting on January 8 (4,000 people), and having discussed the firing by the Soviet government on the demonstration in which we took part in defense of the Constituent Assembly, have decided: (1) to protest against these actions and against the policy of "not sparing the bullets" [patronov ne zhalet']; (2) to recall our representatives from the city soviet; (3) to render firm support to the Constituent Assembly and come to its defense; (4) to consider the day of January 5 a day of mourning and grief, like January 9, 1905; (5) to charge the newly elected delegates to read this resolution in the Petrograd soviet; (6) as soon as the Constituent Assembly meets, all political power must belong to the Constituent Assembly and not to the government [vlast'] that shot at the people.[40]

The Bolsheviks were now perceived as having deceived the workers. This was the predominant mood at a rally of the Obukhov plant workers, who had taken part in the demonstration in support of the Constituent Assembly. According to a report in an SR paper, the Bolshevik speakers at the rally read from Pravda, the Bolshevik paper, a description of the events which roused a storm of indignation. The speech of A. A. Troianovskii, a candidate member of the Menshevik CC, was greeted by applause. The rally voted to condemn the shooting, to send a special delegation to other factories and plants to rouse the workers, and to recall the plant's Bolshevik delegates from the soviet and replace them with Mensheviks and SRs. Of the 8,000 in attendance, only 100 voted against the resolution.[41] Commenting on the sudden change in workers' attitudes toward the Bolsheviks, Chernov wrote:

> It has gotten to the point where the Bolsheviks have started to worry about their continued dominance of the Petrograd soviet. In order to keep their majority from melting away, they have had to forbid the recall [of deputies] before their term has expired and to forbid elections to the soviet from separate plants under the pretense that they are preparing new general elections of the entire Petrograd soviet, to take place soon.[42]

At a rally at the Cartridge plant, attended by 2,500 workers, the Menshevik and SR speakers were again applauded. A protest resolution,

40. "Sredi rabochikh," Nashe edinstvo, 11 January 1918, p. 4. On January 9, 1905, troops of the tsarist government had fired on a peaceful demonstration at the Palace Square in Petersburg, sparking the first Russian revolution.
41. Ibid.
42. Viktor Chernov, "Kommentarii k protokolam TsK PSR (sentiabr' 1917–fevral' 1918)," Nik. Col. no. 7, box 3, file 54, p. 82.

sponsored by the Mensheviks and SRs, was adopted, expressing "profound indignation" at the actions of the peoples' commissars and calling for immediate election of new delegates to represent the plant in the Petrograd soviet. Similar resolutions were adopted at the Semiannikovskii plant, the Aleksandrovskii Rail Car plant, and others.[43] Some workers' protests led to confrontations with the Bolsheviks. The workers of the Siemens-Schuckert plant decided to recall their Red Guards, since they acted like "the old gendarmes." The Red Guards refused to abide by the resolution of the plant's general meeting, however, and arrested a member of the Petrograd soviet from the plant, one Pavlov, an SR.[44] Workers increasingly sent delegations to other plants and factories in order to coordinate actions and share information. These delegations, elected in an ad hoc manner for the specific purpose of coordinating protest efforts, formed the nucleus of the future Extraordinary Assembly of Workers' Representatives from the Petrograd Factories and Plants, which would play an important role in the opposition movement in the spring and summer of 1918.

The Bolshevik disbandment of the Constituent Assembly had the effect of rallying center-Left and Right Mensheviks in a common cause. This is not to say that there were no differences in reaction among the Menshevik factions. The Defensists felt that they had been proved right. They had warned that attempts to find an accommodation with the Bolsheviks were doomed to failure. The party should now abandon its illusions about the Bolsheviks. The myth that the Bolsheviks were a party of democracy had been exploded by the Bolsheviks themselves. The attitude of the Right Mensheviks was summarized in these words: "From the point of view of the Socialists who have remained faithful to the understanding of socialism which all of Social Democracy used to share, there are at present no more rabid enemies of socialism than the gentlemen from Smolnyi [the Bolshevik headquarters]."[45] Unlike the Defensists, the Internationalists had been in close touch with the maneuvering in the CEC (in fact, some of them had entered the CEC, as mentioned earlier, despite the party boycott), and so they had been aware that the Bolsheviks were preparing to disband the Constituent Assembly. What was particularly shocking to them was the Bolsheviks' cynical violation of the laws and principles they had pledged to support only two months earlier.

The CPC decree on the dissolution of the Constituent Assembly was

43. "Na Patronnom zavode" and "Na fabrikakh i zavodakh," *Novaia zhizn'*, 9 January 1918, p. 2.
44. "Krasnogvardeitsy i rabochie," *Novaia zhizn'*, 17 January 1918, p. 3.
45. Vera Zasulich, "Sotsializm Smol'nogo," *Nachalo* (Right Menshevik newspaper, Petrograd), 2 February 1918, p. 2.

debated at a special session of the CEC on January 6—that is, the day after the assembly had been disbanded. Not only the Internationalists Boris Moiseev, Nikolai Sukhanov, and Boris Avilov but also the Bolshevik Riazanov pointed out in their speeches that the government was again confronting the CEC, the supreme legislative institution, with a fait accompli, even though the government had no right to act without the consent and approval of the CEC. Second, they all stressed, the CEC had been entrusted by the Second Congress of Soviets to convene the Constituent Assembly. The Bolshevik government was therefore violating the will of the congress and of the Russian people. The Bolsheviks interrupted the speakers with catcalls and shouts of "Down with them!" and "Traitors!" When the CPC decree was finally approved by the Bolshevik majority in the CEC, Boris Moiseev declared: "Remember that you will yet regret that you have committed this crime today. The country will never forgive you this!"[46]

All of the newspapers that had started to print the procedures of the Constituent Assembly were closed, and the already printed issues were confiscated and burned on the streets by the Red Guards.[47] The SRs claimed that the Bolsheviks were trying to prevent the peasants from learning that the Constituent Assembly had passed laws on the socialization and distribution of land.

The Bolsheviks convened the Third Congress of Soviets (10–18 January) as a counterweight to the Constituent Assembly, to demonstrate that the masses still supported them. The small Menshevik faction (fifty members) at that hastily assembled congress called it a mockery, a ploy designed to cover up the Bolshevik crime with a cloak of legitimacy. The congress had no say about the fortunes of the Constituent Assembly, and the disbandment was not even debated. Representatives of the opposition parties were not admitted to the credentials commission.[48] Both the Mensheviks and the SRs claimed that many delegates from the provinces who belonged to their parties were arbitrarily refused admittance to the congress itself.[49] The Bolshevik government did not account to the congress for its policies since October. Instead, orchestras played revolutionary songs, and Bolsheviks delivered speeches on the inevitability of world revolution.

Even Ermanskii, who had been on the extreme left of the Menshevik Internationalists and in December had urged the party to enter the CEC,

---

46. "Vo VTsIK sovetov," *Nash vek*, 9 January 1918, p. 1.
47. "Sredi rabochikh," *Nashe edinstvo*, 11 January 1918, p. 4.
48. "Iz deiatel'nosti TsK RSDRP i ego biuro (8 dekabria 1917–1 marta 1918)," *Partiinye izvestiia* (journal of the Menshevik CC), nos. 1–2 (1918), pp. 15–16.
49. O. A. Ermanskii, "Politicheskie otkliki," *Rabochii internatsional*, no. 1 (1918), pp. 58–59.

now published an article condemning the Bolshevik machinations. More than any other single political event, the disbandment of the Constituent Assembly opened the eyes of the Internationalists about the Bolsheviks' intentions. It was clear now that the post-October Menshevik platform, which had called for the creation of a socialist coalition government with the Bolsheviks, was outdated. The party had to revise its policy objectives once again.

To assess the new political situation, a conference of Menshevik organizations of the Central Industrial Region met in Moscow in mid-January. Reports from the provincial capitals described conditions of growing unemployment and the beginning of famine. The numbers of soldiers and workers in the cities was diminishing considerably, and the exodus to the countryside was reducing membership in local organizations. The party was in dire financial straits. Nevertheless, the documents of the conference show that it was the unanimous opinion of all those present that "a sharp turnaround is noticeable in the mood of the working masses." The workers were beginning to "grow disillusioned with Bolshevik 'socialism.'" This situation, a conference resolution stated, opened up new possibilities for the Menshevik party, possibilities of winning back majorities in the local soviets. In some areas this process had already begun; almost everywhere that new elections had taken place, the Bolsheviks were defeated.[50]

Domestic Repercussions of the War and the Peace Negotiations

Hardly had the storm over the disbandment of the Constituent Assembly quieted down than new clouds began to gather. The Menshevik leaders were following with the utmost attention the moves of the Bolshevik government in the unfolding drama of the peace negotiations at Brest-Litovsk. As in their critique of Bolshevik domestic policy, they pointed out that Bolshevik foreign policy was bound to do more harm than good. An appeal to the masses of the belligerent countries over the heads of the bourgeois governments might win the acclaim of the war-weary soldiers of Russia but would hardly induce either the Germans or the Allies to negotiate for general peace. The Bolsheviks had tried to drag out the negotiations with the Germans, threatened revolutionary war and then unilateral disarmament, and urged fraternization at the front in order to win time and delay the denouement as long as possi-

---

50. "Oblastnaia konferentsiia v Moskve," *Partiinye izvestiia*, nos. 1–2 (5 March 1918), p. 24. The workers' flight from the cities is discussed in Koenker, "Urbanization and Deurbanization."

ble. By late January, all these moves had been played out. Russia had either to continue the war or to sign a separate peace treaty. All the opposition political parties, as well as a part of the Bolshevik party, rejected the German conditions. A German offensive was imminent. This was the setting for the events at the end of February.

The crisis that ensued had a profound effect on Russia's internal politics. It caused yet another realignment of forces within the socialist parties, which resulted in a breakup of the Bolshevik–Left SR coalition. Along with the breakdown of the Vikzhel negotiations and the disbandment of the Constituent Assembly, the peace-treaty negotiations were a landmark in the series of events that shaped Russia's political development in 1918. The Bolshevik government and the Menshevik/SR opposition emerged from this crisis with new commitments and new ideas concerning their future policy.

As soon as the Germans opened their offensive, the panic-stricken soldiers abandoned their positions and weapons and fled. The situation was vividly described by the Committee for the Defense of the Revolution: "As a result of the events taking place at the front, a massive flow of soldiers is to be observed running from the enemy and jamming the railroads. According to reports from the railroad agents, the soldiers are seizing trains, plundering, and threatening with arms all who resist."[51] In a speech to the Petrograd soviet on February 26, V. Volodarskii, commissar for agitation and propaganda, sharply criticized the soldiers of the Petrograd garrison: they did not want to fight, did not want to go to the front, and were only playing balalaikas.[52] Even the paper of the Left Communists, who stood for revolutionary war, admitted that "the majority of the soldiers do not want to take part in the cause of creating a new army. The soviet power must firmly say to such soldiers that if they do not want to use their weapons for the defense of the revolution, then they do not need these weapons at all. Then their place is behind the plow."[53]

In early October, when the Provisional Government had attempted to transfer some regiments of the Petrograd garrison to the front, the soldiers, then backed by the Bolsheviks, had refused to abandon "the revolutionary capital." Now that they themselves were the government, the Bolsheviks encountered the same problem. The soldiers still preferred the barracks in the capital to the trenches at the front. The situation was embarrassing and dangerous for the four-month-old govern-

51. "Prikaz Komiteta Revoliutsionnoi Oborony," *Izvestiia Omskogo Oblastnogo Ispolnitel'nogo Komiteta*, 3 March 1918, p. 2.
52. "Zasedanie petrogradskogo soveta 26 fevralia," *Vecherniaia zvezda*, 27 February 1918, p. 7.
53. "Politicheskoe obozrenie: Razoruzhenie polkov," *Kommunist*, 19 March 1918, p. 2.

ment. Suddenly it became clear that the soldiers and sailors, who had appeared to be a bastion of Bolshevik strength, were in fact unwilling to fight for the Bolsheviks or for the "socialist fatherland." The Bolsheviks, who had been bragging about their "triumphal march" and their victories over the bourgeoisie, overnight were revealed to be defenseless and vulnerable. The socialist fatherland was declared to be in danger. Lenin decided to accept the German conditions.

The Mensheviks blamed the government for the catastrophic situation at the front. The Bolsheviks' revolutionary diplomacy, Dan concluded, was achieving no better results than the diplomacy of the Provisional Government. Trotsky's diplomacy was mere bravado, with no real force to back it, because the Bolshevik government was in a sense a hostage of the demoralized soldiers.[54] A Menshevik CC proclamation stressed the point that the current crisis was a logical consequence of the Bolshevik policy of demoralizing the army.[55] Throughout 1917, Bolshevik propaganda had been undermining the soldiers' morale and discipline, calling on them to drive their bayonets into the ground and go home (*shtyki v zemliu i po domam*). They had sown the wind and must now reap the whirlwind. The Bolshevik government responded by shutting down all opposition papers in the capital.

The Mensheviks' position was that Russia had no option but to fight a defensive war against Germany. The Left SRs and the Left Communists also advocated war, but with a significant difference: theirs was to be a revolutionary war. The Mensheviks and the SRs believed that the bargaining position of a Russian government vis-à-vis the Germans would be stronger if a legitimate government formed by the Constituent Assembly were in power. Only a government based on a national consensus, argued the Mensheviks, could wind down the civil war and resist German expansionism.[56] The Menshevik reasoning here can be seen as another instance of Dan's general effort to save what could be saved. The Bolshevik government could not get decent peace terms from Germany, wrote Dan, because the Germans knew very well that the Bolsheviks' priority was to secure their shaky power against the attacks of their domestic opponents.[57] Perceptive politicians, Martov and Dan had concluded as early as January that Lenin would rather

---

54. Fedor Dan, "Na prusskuiu dorogu," *Rabochii internatsional*, no. 2 (1918), p. 33. An identical view was expressed by Abramovitch; see "Rech' Abramovicha," *Novyi luch'*, 3 December 1917, p. 4.

55. TsK RSDRP, "Protiv podpisaniia mirnogo dogovora," 22 February 1918, Nik. Col. no. 6, box 1, file 2.

56. Ibid.

57. Dan, "Na prusskuiu dorogu," p. 28; see also A. Martynov, "Likvidatsiia i vozrozhdenie," *Rabochii internatsional*, no. 2 (1918), pp. 4–10.

Распродажа фронтового имущества.
(Рисунокъ Ли).

Солдатъ. Почемъ дашь за пушку?
Нѣмецъ. Рубль двадцать да фунтъ подсолнуховъ.
Солдатъ. По рукамъ, товарищъ!

A cartoon in the Samara provincial satirical journal *Gorchichnik*, March 1918, on the Bolshevik-led campaign to encourage fraternization at the front, which led to the signing of the Treaty of Brest-Litovsk: "Selling army property at the front." Soldier: "How much will you give for the gun?" German: "One ruble twenty and a pound of sunflower seeds." Soldier: "It's a deal, comrade!" Russian Serials Collection, Hoover Institution Archives.

deal with the Germans over territories than with the Constituent Assembly over power. He would rather engage the country's meager fighting forces against General Kaledin's troops than against the German armies. Potresov saw the situation in the same terms: "What is more important for the well-being of Soviet power? To attack Rostov [the stronghold of the anti-Bolshevik Cossacks] or to defend Dvinsk [from the Germans]? To defeat [the anti-Bolshevik general] Alekseev or to defend [the country] against Hindenburg?"[58] Like Potresov, Dan concluded that the Bolsheviks were betraying Russia's national interests

58. A. N. Potresov, "Rossiia i sovety," *Novyi den'*, 21 February 1918, p. 1.

and the ideals of internationalism for the sake of staying in power: "Preservation of Soviet power, that is, the preservation of power in the hands of Lenin & Co.—this is the point of departure for all the political considerations of the chairman of the CPC."[59]

The rejection of a capitulationist treaty by the Left SRs and a part of the Bolshevik party itself put Lenin in a precarious position: as in early November, the majority was now opposed to his policy. His opponents demanded the recall of the Soviet delegation from Brest and a continuation of the revolutionary war against Germany. The Menshevik leaders believed that a defensive war offered a remarkable opportunity to halt the escalation of civil strife in Russia and to mobilize support for national unity and for the Constituent Assembly. In Lenin's view, the revolutionary war advocated by the Left Communists would lead at best to a sharing of power and at worst to their losing it altogether. Leonard Schapiro has commented:

> Whatever other considerations swayed them [the Bolsheviks], it is clear that they realized that this course would mean the end of their precarious hold on the country. The only units of the army where the morale was good were anti-Bolshevik, and in the patriotic upsurge created by the resumption of hostilities the defeatist Bolsheviks would soon be swept away. (The Germans had foreseen that this factor would be the decisive one, as the German Foreign Office appreciation at the time reveals.)[60]

Lenin fully realized what catastrophic consequences for his party the continuation of the war was likely to unleash. In his articles "On the Revolutionary Phrase," "An Unhappy Peace," and others, he ridiculed his opponents and repeated that the Bolshevik government needed a breathing spell (*peredyshka*), however brief and whatever the cost.[61] If the Germans wanted to overthrow the Bolshevik government, then the Bolsheviks would have to fight; otherwise, the Bolsheviks would have to sign the peace treaty. Lenin had his way.

The opposition continued to argue its case at the Fourth Extraordinary Congress of Soviets, which was summoned to ratify the treaty. Boris Kamkov of the Left SRs denounced the treaty as a betrayal of the Ukrainian workers and peasants and a capitulation to German imperialism. The Left SRs resigned from the CPC in protest. Continuing the attack on the treaty on behalf of the Menshevik faction, Martov countered Lenin's arguments one by one and focused on four major questions: who was responsible for the flight of the army from the front? Were the terms

---

59. Dan, "Na prusskuiu dorogu," p. 28.
60. Schapiro, *Communist Party*, p. 186.
61. Lenin, "O revoliutsionnoi fraze," in *Polnoe sobranie sochinenii*, 35:343–53; "Neschastnyi mir," in ibid., pp. 243–52.

signed by the Bolsheviks indeed the only terms that could have been obtained? Would the treaty in fact provide the breathing spell for which Lenin was ready to pay so dearly? And finally, was there any alternative, in the present circumstances, to the Bolshevik policy?[62] Having referred to Lenin's own admission that the army had fled in panic, Martov demanded that the congress appoint "a commission to investigate the circumstances under which an order of unilateral demobilization was given. . . . Trotsky was saying recently that if Germany refused to sign a democratic peace, we would declare a holy war. Where is that war?!" Martov was thus attacking as well Trotsky's policy of "no war, no peace, and send the army home." The Germans had resumed their offensive after the front had been exposed by Trotsky's actions. The Bolshevik policy had completely destroyed the morale even of the units that were still capable of fighting.

Switching to a critique of the treaty itself, Martov exclaimed: "Comrades! We are being asked to ratify a treaty whose text we have not seen! Do you know what you are signing?"[63] The text of the treaty had indeed not even been distributed to the delegates. Why were the Bolsheviks, who in October had been shouting about open diplomacy and condemning secret clauses, unwilling now to reveal their treaty with the Germans? "Where are the borders between Russia and Germany?" asked Martov; "between Russia and the Ukraine? between Russia and Finland?"[64] Actually, the treaty did not define the borders, and this lapse would permit the Germans to increase their demands and annex new territories. Lenin's breathing spell would turn into a slow capitulation. But the treaty was the price Lenin had to pay to retain the support of the soldiers who had helped him to seize power in the name of peace at any price. The CPC had wrecked the Russian army and mishandled the negotiations. "We demand the immediate resignation of the Council of People's Commissars," concluded Martov, "and the convocation of the Constituent Assembly!"[65]

Martov's speech was well received, but his call for the resignation of the CPC and the convocation of the Constituent Assembly reminded the Bolsheviks of the deep divisions among the treaty's opponents. The final vote on the treaty was 724 in favor and 276 against, with 118 abstentions. The formation of a majority had not been an easy matter, since all non-Bolshevik political parties and part of the Bolshevik party opposed the treaty. Of the roughly 1,000 delegates registered on the first day of the congress, 623 were Bolsheviks, 219 Left SRs, 80 Mensheviks,

62. "Chrezvychainyi s"ezd: Rech' Martova," Vecherniaia zvezda, 16 March 1918, p. 4.
63. Ascher, ed., Mensheviks in the Russian Revolution, document no. 28, "The Treaty of Brest-Litovsk," p. 110.
64. "Vpechatleniia: Lenin i Martov," Vecherniaia zvezda, 16 March 1918, p. 1.
65. "Chrezvychainyi s"ezd: Rech' Martova," ibid., p. 4.

A cartoon on the front page of the Samara provincial satirical journal *Gorchichnik*, March 1918. The head reads: "Weekly. Satire and Humor. Peace without annexations." The text at the bottom reads: "As the German busies himself with the head, the Japanese wastes no time and saws off Russia's legs. It seems that only the stomach will be left, and an empty stomach at that." Lenin clutches a "peacetime accord" as he strides over Russia's prostrate body. Russian Serials Collection, Hoover Institution Archives.

38 SRs, 2 People's Socialists, 13 Anarchists, and 20 without party affil-iation.[66] In violation of the procedural rules, the Mensheviks and SRs were not permitted to sit on the credentials committee, and many of the opposition parties' delegates were simply rejected. The Menshevik CC sent a vehement protest to the Bolshevik CC, but to no avail.[67] The machinery for convoking and managing the congress was controlled by the Bolsheviks.

Even then, however, Lenin had to make sure that the Bolshevik dele-gates from the provinces voted in support of the treaty. Many of them were newcomers to the party and were not willing to conform to the party line. In Saratov, for example, the local Bolshevik leader V. P. Antonov and the majority of the local Bolshevik organization vehe-mently opposed the treaty. In the last days of February and the first two weeks of March, not a single article in favor of the treaty appeared in the Saratov Izvestiia. (After the treaty was ratified, Izvestiia avoided the topic altogether. For the duration of the crisis, the first two pages of the paper were filled with advertisements.) The Left Communists pub-lished the results of a survey that had been taken on attitudes toward the treaty among the city soviets, which showed that, "out of twenty-four replies sent by large cities, only two were in favor of concluding peace."[68]

Without access to Soviet archives, it is very difficult, if not impossi-ble, to reconstruct precisely how the majority was formed. Some details that appeared in the Menshevik and the Left Communist press, how-ever, shed light on part of the process.

According to the electoral rules, each delegate was to represent 25,000 voters. As approximately 1,000 delegates arrived at the con-gress, ostensibly 25 million voters were represented. But, as a Men-shevik observer pointed out, this simply could not be true, as an exam-ination of the data on particular provinces revealed. Vladimir province, for example, was recorded as having sent thirty-eight delegates, which meant that they must have been elected by about one million voters; but the entire population of the province was only two million people, so there could not possibly have been enough eligible voters to send such a large delegation. On the other hand, Petrograd province had only twenty-two delegates at the congress, fewer than tiny Vladimir and no more than Novgorod. The delegates, concluded this observer,

66. "V Moskve na s'ezde," Vechernii chas, 18 March 1918, pp. 1–2.
67. "Fraktsiia RSDRP na Chetvertom S"ezde Sovetov," Partiinye izvestiia, 20 May 1918, pp. 15–17.
68. "Politika ustupok i proletariat," Kommunist, 19 March 1918, p. 2. For a discussion of this survey, see Schapiro, Origin of the Communist Autocracy, p. 100.

must have been chosen in an arbitrary fashion and in violation of the electoral rules.[69] According to the Left Communists' newspaper, the Petrograd Bolshevik organization had voted at a city conference on March 1 against the signing of the peace treaty; yet at the Fourth Congress of Soviets, the Petrograd delegation somehow voted in favor of ratification.[70] According to Menshevik sources, the discrepancies in the numbers of delegates from various provinces reflected the Bolsheviks' attempts to make sure that the opposition was outnumbered.[71]

The key lesson that Lenin drew from the crisis over the peace treaty was that Bolshevik economic policy had to be changed. The threat of German occupation had made it all too obvious that the army had to be rebuilt and industrial production restored. The "Red Guards' attack on the bourgeoisie" had to be restrained. In the spring of 1918 the Bolsheviks did attempt to moderate their policies, pursuing what was known at the time as the "New Course."

The acceptance of the peace treaty of Brest-Litovsk by the Bolshevik government, and especially the methods employed to achieve the majority for its ratification, made the leaders of the opposition draw some conclusions of their own. From the Menshevik point of view, the Bolsheviks had demonstrated that their top priority was the survival of their party dictatorship, not the defense of Russia. The Bolsheviks had again shown themselves willing to disregard their own Soviet laws. Their actions could no longer be regarded as merely mistaken. Dan described the resultant change in the Mensheviks' perception of the Bolsheviks:

> For us, the Social Democrats, it was clear from the very beginning [of the peace-treaty crisis] that if earlier it was possible to talk about honest delusion, about illusions about the facts, and about the self-deception of the Bolshevik government, now, after Brest, in the conditions that have been created, all this talk about the strengthening of socialism is nothing but charlatanism of the first order, deliberate deception of the laboring masses.[72]

69. "Chernaia tysiacha," *Severnaia zaria*, 23 March 1918, p. 2.

70. "Otvet protestantam," *Kommunist*, 14 March 1918, p. 1. The data published by the Left Communists in "S"ezd Sovetov," ibid., p. 3, on the representation of various provinces at the congress jibe with the Menshevik allegations. According to *Kommunist*, the numbers of members in the provincial delegations were: Arkhangelsk, 5; Vladimir, 38; Viatka, 16; Vologda, 16; Vitebsk, 22; Voronezh, 33; Ekaterinoslav, 29; Kaluga, 16; Kostroma, 15; Kazan, 4; Kursk, 19; Moscow, 55; Petrograd, 23; Nizhnii Novgorod, 21; Poltava, 4; Novgorod, 26; Pskov, 13; Riazan, 24; Orel, 27; Olonetsk, 3; Samara, 4; Saratov, 11; Penza, 13; Tambov, 24; Smolensk, 18; Chernigov, 5; Tver, 41; Mogilev, 1; Tiflis, 1; Baku, 1; Turkestan, 1; Finland, 1; Latvia, 9.

71. P. Iur'ev, "Tragicheskii tupik," *Vecherniaia zvezda*, 18 March 1918, p. 3.

72. Fedor Dan, "Bol'shevistskii bonapartizm," *Novaia zaria*, 20 May 1918, pp. 12–13.

The Menshevik critique of Bolshevik foreign policy marked the beginning of a change in the attitudes particularly of the center-left Mensheviks toward the Bolsheviks. The prevailing earlier tone of sensible and reasonable criticism of the mistakes of comrades who had gone too far along the wrong path was now giving way to an impassioned condemnation of "Bolshevik treason." This was the keynote of the pronouncements at a joint session of the Menshevik CC, the Moscow party committee, the Menshevik delegation at the Fourth Congress of Soviets, and the editorial board of Vpered in mid-March. The Mensheviks had to struggle for the support of the masses: they had to explain to the Soviet electorate why they believed the Bolshevik policies were ruinous. The party had to regain the majorities in those soviets that had been lost to the Bolsheviks in October. The time of boycotts and walk-outs was over. The Mensheviks had to plunge into the workers' midst, in the trade unions, factory committees, and soviets. They had to establish new workers' organizations that would be independent of government control.[73] The party's goals now were to work for reconvocation of the Constituent Assembly and to drive the Bolsheviks out of office by winning elections to the soviets and by exerting peaceful pressure on the government from below. All the Menshevik factions rallied behind these goals, and the spring of 1918 was a period of rapprochement among them. The shock of the October days, the bitter recriminations over the mistakes of 1917, and the helpless astonishment at what the Bolsheviks were doing were now behind them. As the workers began to cool toward the Bolsheviks, the Mensheviks believed time was working for them.

As a part of the new approach, the Mensheviks dropped their boycott of the CEC, which had been in effect since October, and their delegation, along with that of the SRs, returned to the legislative body after elections to the Fourth Congress of Soviets. The Mensheviks received four seats, a number that bore no relation to the strength of the party in the local soviets. It should be recalled that in December 1917, the Mensheviks, and SRs, and Left SRs had been offered much more favorable conditions: their representation would have been proportional to their strength at the Second Congress of Soviets, so that half of the seats on the CEC would have been occupied by non-Bolsheviks. The only way to increase the size of the Menshevik delegation now was to wait until the next congress of soviets and hope to seat a delegation proportionate to the party's strength in the local soviets then. The Bolsheviks' motive for admitting their staunchest opponents to the CEC was the desire to appear as legitimate as possible after the disbandment of the Constitu-

73. "O rabote v sovetskikh organizatsiiakh," Partiinye izvestiia, 20 May 1918, p. 16.

ent Assembly. To bar the Mensheviks and SRs from CEC membership completely would have been a gross violation of soviet laws, since those parties had a substantial number of supporters in the local soviets. The Bolshevik leadership was in no position to undertake such drastic action in February and March 1918. The Bolshevik–Left SR coalition was sharply divided over the Treaty of Brest-Litovsk. The Bolshevik party itself was in the grip of factional struggle. If the Left SRs and the Left Communists could advocate revolutionary war as a normal, legal political activity, why could the Mensheviks and SRs not advocate it as well? Preoccupied with internal dissension and the government crisis, Lenin must have decided that it would be safer to have the Mensheviks and SRs as an opposition within the system of soviets rather than outside it. As long as the Mensheviks were unable to outvote the Bolsheviks, their opposition could be tolerated.

PART II

ELECTORAL POLITICS

March–May 1918

CHAPTER 3

The Politics of
the "New Course"

The period between March and June 1918 is generally known in
Soviet history as *peredyshka*—a breathing spell, the short interlude
between the signing of the Treaty of Brest-Litovsk and the eruption of
full-fledged civil war. It was a unique period in Soviet history. The
government publicly debated its policies with the opposition in a legislative and deliberative institution, the Central Executive Committee.
The opposition parties and the independent press were active, despite
a mounting attack on them by the Cheka. Dozens of Menshevik and SR
dailies and weeklies openly discussed every step of the Bolshevik government. The courts continued to work with a certain degree of impar-
tiality. Elections to the city soviets, despite disbandments and arrests,
continued to be held, bringing victories to the Menshevik-SR bloc.
Independent workers' organizations openly challenged the Bolshevik
claim to represent the workers.

In the early summer of 1918, the Bolsheviks abandoned their attempt
at moderation in economic policy and reverted to a class-war approach.
The battles in the courts between government and opposition were now
replaced by summary executions without trials. Electoral politics in the
soviets gave way to the imposition of martial law in many cities, and
the independent workers' organizations were suppressed.

The debates between the Bolshevik government and the Menshevik
opposition on the floor of the CEC and in the press that spring revealed
the conflicts between Bolshevik economic policies and Menshevik alternative proposals. The debates are of particular interest because both

sides espoused the same economic doctrine, generally referred to as "state capitalism." The differences between them revolved around the roles of the state, entrepreneurs, and workers' organizations in such a politicoeconomic system. The legislative session of the CEC of the Fourth Convocation, which took place from March to July 1918, was one of the last in Soviet history where the Bolshevik government debated policy with a non-Bolshevik opposition. These deliberations, though outwardly similar to debates in other parliamentary assemblies, actually bore little resemblance to democratic procedures. The rights and prerogatives of the CEC, nominally the supreme legislative institution, were ill defined, and the CPC could and often did legislate by decree without even consulting the CEC. The CEC's membership was constantly changing to suit the political needs of the Bolshevik party. The votes on proposed legislation were not very important for the legislative process in the CEC, since the Bolshevik party had a built-in majority, due, the opposition claimed, to machinations during the elections to the Fourth Congress of Soviets. Thus, once a bill was put to a vote, its passage was guaranteed.

The debates over policy matters in the CEC ought not to be viewed as simply an exercise in futility, however. Much attention was paid to shaping bills before they came to a vote. The party factions engaged in public and private debates, agreements, attacks, and deals, in the course of which they made commitments, defined proposals, and inaugurated policies. The minutes of the proceedings were published in full, and abridged versions were printed in both the Bolshevik and the opposition press.[1] Positions on issues were defined and explained and were reported to the local soviets by party representatives during vigorous election campaigns in most provincial capitals of European Russia. At this time the Soviet political system was still based on the principle that the party that obtained a majority at the Congress of Soviets would also have a majority in the CEC, and so in effect would form a government. It was on that principle that the Bolsheviks based their claim to legitimacy, since theirs had been the largest single group at the Second Congress of Soviets. It has already been seen that the Bolsheviks sabotaged this principle, even at that early date, by altering the norms of representation for the Fourth Congress of Soviets in order to secure a majority for themselves. Yet the doctrine that only one party, the "vanguard of the proletariat," should be permitted to exist

1. See *Protokoly zasedanii Vserossiiskogo Tsentral'nogo Ispolnitel'nogo Komiteta, chetvertogo sozyva* (hereafter cited as *Protokoly TsIK*); and the newspapers *Izvestiia* (Bolshevik), *Vpered* (Menshevik), *Delo naroda* (SR), and *Znamia bor'by* (Left SR) during the period in question. For the CEC debates at the end of 1917 and in early 1918, see the excellent annotated edition of Keep, ed., *Debate on Soviet Power*.

had not yet been officially proclaimed. The Bolshevik manipulations did not deter the opposition parties from striving to regain a majority at the Fifth Congress of Soviets.

Defining State Capitalism

On March 29, 1918, Commissar of Education A. V. Lunacharskii granted an interview to a Menshevik center-left newspaper, *Novaia zhizn'*. This interview generated a long controversy in the CEC and in the press on the nature of the "New Course" of the Bolshevik government. The CPC, Lunacharskii said, was contemplating measures that would drastically alter its domestic economic policy. The government was ready to halt its attacks on private capital and take steps to secure the cooperation of "creative elements" in the business community. Soviet power was now so strong, said Lunacharskii, that coercive measures were no longer productive.[2]

Coming after a wave of Bolshevik nationalizations and confiscations, these pronouncements sounded conciliatory, albeit general and vague. The correspondent asked Lunacharskii what specific measures the government had in mind, but Lunacharskii gave no definite answer, merely hinting that the reforms would be in such crucial areas as industrial management, banking, and financial policy. The government was determined to put an end to anarchy and slackness. "A general and overall turnabout" of policy was being prepared, concluded Lunacharskii: "We cannot engage in purely socialist construction. This would lead us to a catastrophe."[3]

An avalanche of questions surged forth from the pages of the Menshevik press. Was Lunacharskii implying that the chaos and anarchy of requisitions in the preceding months were supposed to have been a form of Bolshevik socialist construction? Was the New Course to be a step toward socialism or a return to capitalism? Were the Bolshevik slogans "Stifle the bourgeoisie!" and "Loot the looters!" to be withdrawn?[4] Lunacharskii's interview, which was published and republished in some form in all the major newspapers of the two capitals, created strong political reverberations and added to the anxiety in the debate on the "true meaning" of the New Course.

2. "Perspektivy sovetskoi vlasti: Beseda s A. Lunacharskim," *Novaia zhizn'*, 29 March 1918, p. 2. See also "Otkroveniia liberal'nogo ministra," *Den'*, 30 March 1918, p. 1; and "Novaia orientatsiia," *Delo* (a Right Menshevik journal), 7 April 1918, p. 14.

3. I. Kubikov, "Nozhki ot komoda," *Den'*, 31 March 1918, p. 3.

4. See, for example, A. N. Potresov, "Osadi nazad," *Den'*, 2 April 1918, p. 2; and E. A. Stalinskii, "Bol'shevistskii povorot," *Za rodinu* (SR journal), 20 April 1918, pp. 4–7.

In the weeks following the interview, Lenin clarified the nature of the projected reforms. He defined the goal as the establishment of a system of state capitalism during a long stage of historical development which he called "the transition to socialism." State capitalism, he said, "would be our salvation; if we had it in Russia, the transition to full socialism would be easy, would be within our grasp, because state capitalism is something centralized, calculated, controlled, and socialized, and that is exactly what we lack."[5]

Throughout March and April, Lenin's language was moderate. He called for restoration of the authority of technical personnel and for large increases in their salaries.[6] He advocated inviting foreign, particularly American, engineers to work in Russian industry.[7] He urged his colleagues to borrow the most advanced methods of industrial organization from the West. Equal pay had to be abolished. A wage differential modeled on Frederick Taylor's system was to be introduced and engineers would be invited to return to the managerial boards. No longer were they considered parasites and traitors.[8] Lenin began to use such terms as "business people," "specialists," and "merchants": "And we say, let him be a thoroughpaced rascal even, but if he has organized a trust, if he is a merchant who has dealt with the organization of production and distribution for millions and tens of millions, if he has acquired experience—we must learn from him."[9] Campaigns that had been started earlier under such slogans as "Seize the bourgeoisie by the throat!" were to be halted. Moreover, attempts to find a modus vivendi with the industrialists were to be made, in order to make cooperation between the state and the private sector possible. Nationalizations were to be ended; the time had come to start producing.[10]

It is hard to judge whether Lenin's program of state capitalism represented an attempt to adjust to reality or a new tack in his course toward implementation of his ideology. One thing is obvious, though: the program was a significant departure from Lenin's earlier statements and actions. It was not the first time that he had drastically altered his

5. Lenin, "Report on the Immediate Tasks of Soviet Government," in Collected Works, 27:294.

6. Lenin, "Zakliuchitel'noe slovo po dokladu ob ocherednykh zadachakh sovetskoi vlasti: Zasedanie TsIK 29 aprelia 1918 goda," in Polnoe sobranie sochinenii, 36:273.

7. Lenin, "Vystuplenie na zasedanii prezidiuma VTsNKh, 1 aprelia 1918 goda," in ibid., 36:212.

8. Lenin, "Shest' tezisov ob ocherednykh zadachakh sovetskoi vlasti," in ibid., 36:279.

9. Lenin, Collected Works, 27:297.

10. Lenin, "Zasedanie TsIK 29 aprelia 1918 goda," in Polnoe sobranie sochinenii, 36:271.

whole policy. Nor was it the first time that he had had trouble bringing his own party along with him. His words cannot be attributed to a change of heart toward the Kadets or toward what he called the bourgeoisie. Once the political and economic power of the industrialists had been seriously weakened, Lenin, a pragmatist, must have felt he could afford to invite his political opponents to take part in the economic life of the country—on his terms.

Lenin's package of reforms contained some proposals that the Mensheviks welcomed and others that they eventually rejected. The thrust of the reforms, however, was not clear immediately. Only in the process of debating policy and putting it into practice did the actual direction of the New Course become discernible. The Mensheviks of both the right and the center-left considered the ostensible return to moderation to be a step in the right direction. The arguments in the Menshevik press focused on the extent of the promised reforms and on the specific forms that state capitalism could take in Russia. The Right Mensheviks, who had always regarded Bolshevik undertakings with suspicion, expressed doubts as to whether the Bolsheviks were capable of abandoning their "illusory chase after socialism."[11] The country had gone through the squalls of requisitions, nationalizations, and indemnities; now it needed normal conditions for commercial and industrial activity, and mere state capitalism—that is, a state-regulated capitalism—was not enough. In an article titled "Our Call to Capitalism," A. N. Potresov reiterated what may be recognized as a classic Menshevik statement: Russia was not ready for socialism. Socialism could emerge only after a prolonged industrial and capitalist development. To speak of socialism in Russia in 1918, he insisted, one had to be either blind or mad. Such beginnings of large-scale industrial production as had existed in Russia before the war, Potresov went on, were now destroyed. The Bolshevik "socialism" of the first months after October had amounted to nothing more than a state takeover of bankrupt industries. In Potresov's view, "socialism now" was a premature and hasty parody of West European socialism, and Lenin's state capitalism was, though a step in the right direction, a step undertaken only after economic reality had proved the utter futility of the Bolshevik experiments. To Potresov, the only way out lay through a return to free-market enterprise, based on freedom of competition, nonintervention of the state in commercial activity, and freedom from state control for both the industrialists' and the workers' organizations.[12]

The Menshevik center-left party leaders, Martov and Dan, responded

---

11. See, for example, A. Fishgendler, " 'Na vsekh parakh k sotsializmu,' " *Nash golos: Sotsial Demokraticheskii sbornik* (Moscow [1918]), pp. 19–25.
12. A. N. Potresov, "Nash prizyv k kapitalizmu," *Novyi den'*, 7 April 1918, p. 1.

quite differently to the New Course. They saw Lenin's latest turnabout as natural, logical, and sensible, a policy that was basically social-democratic, and the only one possible in the "tragic conditions" of Russia. Dan wrote:

> The policy of Bolshevik Communism has suffered a collapse, and the Bolsheviks are going over to an openly bourgeois-capitalist policy with such techniques of state intervention and regulation of economic life as are practiced under the influence of the war experience, to a greater or lesser degree, in countries that did not have the "fortune" to live under Soviet power. This change in itself the proletariat can only welcome.[13]

Dan objected, however, to the notion that the new policy was some kind of return to capitalism. In reality, except in Lenin's fantasy, capitalism had not ceased to exist for a single day in Russia. Heavy industry, transport, and the banks were dying, but private petty-bourgeois entrepreneurship was thriving. The whole country was busy dividing and redividing confiscated and requisitioned property. The slogan "Loot the looters!" had led to a wave of robberies, Dan went on, and created a host of private entrepreneurs and traders.[14] As a Menshevik economist put it, "where there is socialism, there is no production, and where there is production, there is bourgeois enterprise."[15] The system that then existed, Dan concluded, was the worst kind of capitalism—a petty-bourgeois, anarchic perversion of Western capitalism which caricatured the ideas of socialism. That, Dan explained, was why the Mensheviks, a socialist party, welcomed the policy of state capitalism, which amounted to no more than a return to normality after the chaos of requisitions and indemnities. Other Mensheviks wrote that under the Bolsheviks, "the beginnings of planned intervention in economic life which had existed earlier had been destroyed, and chaos had set in";[16] that the New Course was a "decisive turn toward a realistic policy, which in many respects coincided with the policy that, under the present circumstances, any bourgeois democratic government would have had to follow";[17] and that the New Course was a break with the "socialism now" policy of the first months and a return to a Social Democratic policy—without the socialists.

13. Fedor Dan, "Bolshevistskii bonapartizm," *Novaia zaria*, 20 May 1918, pp. 12–18.
14. Ibid.
15. David Dallin, "Narodnoe khoziaistvo i 'sotsializm,'" in Martov, ed., *Za god*, p. 65.
16. N. Cherevanin, "Revoliutsiia pered zadachei regulirovaniia ekonomicheskoi zhizni," *Rabochii internatsional*, February 1918:1 p. 30.
17. S. Lapinskii, "Ministerializm pod vidom diktatury," *Vecherniaia zvezda*, 30 March 1918, p. 3.

In repudiating their own program, the Bolsheviks repudiate the things that distinguished them from other parties. They cease to be Bolsheviks in the real sense of the word. They simply turn into a party that wants to stay in power at any cost. In this, only in this, lies the essence of their current program.[18]

In short, the Mensheviks felt that they had been proved right in their prediction of the inevitable collapse of industry as a result of the "socialism now" policy. As Solomon Shvarts said, "We Social Democrats have warned from the very beginning that any attempt to end the capitalist system in Russia now would lead to the collapse not of capitalism but of industry, to mass unemployment and hardship for the working class."[19]

Some left-of-center Mensheviks, however, were quite enthusiastic about the New Course. Many of them worked in the economic section of the Moscow Soviet or in other economic agencies. The New Course offered them an opportunity to work within the Soviet institutions for policies that they had long been advocating. One of them, Vladimir Bazarov, conveyed that spirit of optimism when he wrote, "A truly new step forward would be the introduction here of the most advanced forms of capitalism, which would be regulated by a democratic state and adjusted by powerful working-class organizations that have a direct interest in the development of the country's production."[20] These Mensheviks opposed Potresov's ideas on free-enterprise capitalism. In their minds, this type of capitalism was just as hazardous as Lenin's experiments.[21] In their view, the best system for Russia was one based on a partnership between the state, the workers, and the industrialists.

Thus the Mensheviks, to varying degrees, welcomed in principle Lenin's call for the establishment of a system of state capitalism. In practice, however, their definition of that system quickly brought them into conflict with Lenin's government. When joint boards of management, consisting of representatives of the owners, the trade unions, and state agencies, were slated to be re-established, the Mensheviks praised the measure, for they considered it to be a part of their own pre-October program.[22] They tried to infuse the new policy of state regulation of industry with their own ideas. According to a Soviet historian, Men-

18. E. A. Stalinskii, "Bol'shevistskii povorot," *Za rodinu*, 20 April 1918, pp. 4–7.

19. Solomon Shvarts, "Kapitalizm i sotsializm," *Delo*, 7 April 1918, pp. 4–5. See also Semen Zagorskii, "Pozdnee raskaianie," *Novyi den'*, 17 April 1918, p. 1.

20. Quoted in Anatolii Diubua, "Novaia orientatsiia profsoiuzov," *Delo*, 14 April 1918, p. 4.

21. See the debate "Po povodu odnoi programmy," *Delo*, 14 April 1918, pp. 15–16.

22. Semen Zagorskii, "Vozrozhdenie ili dodushenie," *Novyi den'*, 9 April 1918, p. 1.

sheviks played an important role in the work of the economic section of the Moscow Soviet and put forward a number of economic proposals.[23] An editorial in a Menshevik newspaper suggested that "industrial recovery requires the creation of special, mixed agencies in all major branches of industry, to consist of representatives of the workers and democracy [i.e., socialist parties], to regulate the economic activity in those industries."[24] Aleksandr Martynov cautioned that excessive zeal in regulating industry could "kill private initiative."[25] The Social Democrats should encourage state intervention only in those areas where private capital could not do a better job. State capitalism had to be based on a mixed economy. Vladimir Kantorovich commented that it was a good thing Lenin finally realized that Russia needed engineers, managers, and industrialists, because "cooperation" at gunpoint did not work; "many will want to serve Russia," he added, "but there are few volunteers to serve communism."[26] How was it possible, asked A. N. Potresov, to talk seriously about cooperation with the bourgeoisie when "Stifle the bourgeoisie!" remained an official slogan of the Bolshevik party?[27] How was it possible to establish state capitalism without capitalists? Under the New Course, the political rights of all classes had to be guaranteed. Were the Bolsheviks willing to recognize the political rights of their opponents? Taking advantage of the favorable climate, the Mensheviks demanded further steps in the direction of "normalization": they pressed for guarantees of an independent press, independent trade unions, and fair elections.

For many Bolsheviks, this was going too far. At the end of April, Lenin reassured his colleagues that state capitalism would not turn into Menshevik capitalism. In speeches before the Moscow Soviet and the CEC, he revealed what, in practical terms, the New Course had in store. Lenin admitted that the October seizures had led to anarcho-syndicalism, theft of merchandise, inflated wages, and lack of accountability among local Bolshevik leaders.[28] The result was mass unemployment and famine.[29] Lenin no longer urged workers to "take the factory," for workers' control had led to today's "ferment and total disarray."[30] He rejected, however, Menshevik allegations that the Bolshevik tactic of

23. Soboleva, *Oktiabr'skaia revoliutsiia*, p. 255.

24. "Vozrozhdenie strany," *Novaia zhizn'*, 31 March 1918, p. 1.

25. Aleksandr Martynov, "Puti k ekonomicheskomu vozrozhdeniiu," *Vpered*, 16 April 1918, p. 1.

26. Vladimir Kantorovich, "Komu sluzhit'?" *Novyi den'*, 1 May 1918, p. 2.

27. A. N. Potresov, "Osadi nazad," *Den'*, 2 April 1918, p. 2.

28. Lenin, "Ocherednye zadachi sovetskoi vlasti," in *Polnoe sobranie sochinenii*, 36:200–201.

29. Lenin, "Rech v Moskovskom sovete 23 aprelia 1918 goda," in ibid., 36:235.

30. Lenin, "Variant stat'i ocherednye zadachi sovetskoi vlasti," in ibid., 36:154.

"looting the looters" had in any way distorted the "proletarian principle." In his view, there was nothing wrong with that slogan: "With the words 'Loot the looters,' there begins a differentiation between the bourgeois revolution and the proletarian revolution, which now says: 'Count what you have looted; and don't let anyone steal it; and if someone tries to steal it, directly or indirectly, then those violators should be shot.' "[31] Lenin scorned what he called the petty-bourgeois instincts that discredited the ideal of "proletarian self-rule." Lenin's solution lay in obedience, discipline, and centralization.[32] He demanded "subordination of the will of thousands to the single will," and dreamed of "iron battalions of the proletariat" marching toward socialism.[33] In practical terms, he meant no strikes, hard work, and sacrifice.

But if Lenin himself was beginning to condemn anarcho-syndicalism, it appeared that the positions of the Communists and the Social Democrats might not be so far apart. Indeed, some Menshevik analysts continued to believe for a while that Lenin's appeal to the workers to restore discipline, stop looting, and prepare for sacrifice differed little from similar appeals by M. I. Skobelev, the Menshevik minister of labor in the Provisional Government.[34] At the CEC session of April 29, Martov was still trying to sound an optimistic and conciliatory note, mitigating his usual criticism with cautious approval of some of Lenin's measures: "We must welcome Lenin's words that after destruction there must follow positive and creative work, but we must also criticize this program."[35] His criticism focused on Lenin's plan to bring industry under the direct control of the state. Lenin was going from one extreme to the other: from complete decentralization, anarchy, and hectic worker self-rule in the first months to "militarist, bureaucratic centralization."[36] This was a very dangerous trend, Martov warned. It threatened to take away the independence of workers' organizations from the state.

By the end of April, Martov had become more apprehensive of Lenin's new policy. He condemned Lenin's call to the workers "not to demand higher wages, to accept the piece-rate system, to abandon the eight-hour day for the sake of the workers' state." Even though Lenin's government called itself a "workers' and peasants' government," Martov went on, the interests of workers had to be guarded by legal guarantees of the eight-hour day and of freedom of organization, and the trade

31. Lenin, "Zasedanie TsIK 29 aprelia 1918 goda," in ibid., 36:270.
32. Lenin, "O 'levom' rebiachestve i o melkoburzhuaznosti," in ibid., 36:298.
33. Lenin, "Ocherednye zadachi sovetskoi vlasti," in ibid., 36:200.
34. "Dve bol'shie raznitsy i odno bol'shoe skhodstvo," *Novyi den'*, 5 April 1918.
35. "Zasedanie TsIK," *Novyi den'*, 1 May 1918, p. 3.
36. Martov, "Demokratiia i revoliutsiia," in Martov, ed., *Za god*, p. 27.

unions had to continue to protect the economic interests of the workers vis-à-vis the employer, whether he be a private entrepreneur or "the socialist state."[37] This was a key Menshevik premise, elaborated upon in numerous articles, speeches, and trade union congresses in 1918.[38]

Lenin ridiculed Martov's calls for independent trade unions: "This view, which has been supported by the Mensheviks, is utterly wrong, because the defense of workers' interests was the task of the unions under capitalism, but since power has passed to the hands of the proletariat, the state itself, in its essence the workers' state, defends the workers' interests."[39]

In response, Martov argued that Lenin simply identified the workers' interests with the interests of his party. In reality, those interests diverged, and if conflict arose, the party-state would be omnipotent, the workers defenseless. That was why Martov insisted that the Mensheviks had to oppose state control of the unions. In the ensuing debates in the CEC, the Mensheviks tried to defend the New Course against both renewed pressure to continue "stifling the bourgeoisie," and increased reliance on a dictatorial approach to economic problems.

The Debate over Indemnities

A debate on the state budget and banking policy opened on April 15, at a CEC session devoted to a special report of the deputy commissar of finance, I. E. Gukovskii.[40] A moderate Bolshevik, Gukovskii was known to advocate denationalization of the banks. Only a few days after Lunacharskii's interview, he was promoted to deputy under Commissar V. R. Menzhinskii.[41] The government and the opposition discussed the significance of this appointment, the extent of the expected reforms, and the constellation of forces in the CEC. In his report, Gukovskii frankly described the dimensions of the financial catastrophe: he estimated the state's expenses for the first six months of 1918 at 20 billion rubles, with net revenues not to exceed 3 billion rubles, for a deficit of 17 billion rubles. Gukovskii pointed to several factors that had produced this distressing situation. Workers' wages had risen constantly throughout 1917 and the beginning of 1918, whereas productivity had

37. Martov, "Leninskoe novoe slovo," Vpered, 26 April 1918, p. 2.
38. See, for example, "Protests against the Soviet Trade Union Policy," in Bunyan and Fisher, eds., Bolshevik Revolution, p. 645.
39. Lenin, "Variant stat'i ocherednye zadachi sovetskoi vlasti," in Polnoe sobranie sochinenii, 36:160.
40. "Zasedanie TsIK," Vecherniaia zvezda, 16 April 1918, p. 1.
41. "V kommissariate finansov," Vecherniaia zvezda, 2 April 1918, p. 1.

fallen. Railroad transport was no longer centrally controlled; every local soviet was doing what it pleased with the goods that passed through its territory. The peasants had seized the nobles' land but were paying no taxes. The local soviets imposed huge indemnities on the bourgeoisie, but these funds never reached the treasury. And finally, concluded Gukovskii, the nationalization of the banks had destroyed credit, and "how can there be any exchange of goods without credit?" Gukovskii considered it imperative to reduce state expenditures, insist on the accountability of local governments, and restore healthy monetary circulation. Most important, the local soviets had to stop imposing indemnities on the bourgeoisie.[42]

Gukovskii's report was received with consternation on the Bolshevik benches and with applause from the opposition. The general picture of financial bankruptcy he painted and the measures he proposed differed little from those presented by the Social Democrats.[43] The Left SRs, however, vigorously criticized Gukovskii's propo . V. E. Trutovskii and V. A. Karelin urged continuation of the Red G rds' attack on the bourgeoisie and spoke of the widening of the social revolution. Behind the facade of this revolutionary rhetoric, the true concern of the Left SRs was the taxation of the peasantry: they did not want the Bolshevik government to make the peasants carry the financial burden for the "transition to socialism."[44]

The sharpest attack on Gukovskii's program came from the Left Communists. N. I. Bukharin said: "The speaker forgets that we are in the process of destroying capitalism. He proceeds from the ridiculous assumption that the capitalist order must be restored."[45] Therefore, the right of the local soviets to impose indemnities should not be abolished. The Left Communists took their stand on ideological ground: the class struggle had to go on.

The Mensheviks supported Gukovskii's plan. Their spokesman, S. A. Lozovskii, expressed concern that the main burden of taxes was being carried by the workers. The SDs were all in favor of energetic measures to restore the system of taxing the peasantry. Much more was needed than mere abolition of the right to levy indemnities. The restoration of normal economic life in the country was inconceivable without the restoration of democratically elected local governments.[46]

---

42. "Sovety: TsIK, zasedanie 15 aprelia," Vpered, 16 April 1918, p. 3. See also Protokoly TsIK, pp. 130–33.

43. For the Menshevik program of banking reform, see N. A. Rozhkov, "Zadachi bankovoi politiki," Rabochii internatsional, no. 2 (1918), pp. 48–54.

44. "Zasedanie TsIK," Vecherniaia zvezda, 16 April 1918, p. 1.

45. Ibid.

46. "TsIK, zasedanie 18 aprelia," Vpered, 19 April 1918, p. 3; see also Protokoly TsIK, p. 134.

Lenin did not back Gukovskii unequivocally: "Comrade Gukovskii has proposed a plan to us here. Whether it is a good plan or a bad one I shall not discuss now. What is clear to me, though, is that even the best possible plan . . . cannot be carried out now, because in fact we have not organized the apparatus that would carry out that plan."[47] The chief reason for this failure, Lenin believed, was that the local soviets were often in the hands of armed groups, who were often at war with the revolutionary committees. One of the government's numerous decrees on this subject, signed by Lenin, said: "Provincial authorities still continue to issue their own laws and decrees, which often contradict the decrees of the central authorities, thus bringing chaos and confusion into the general legislative work of the Soviet republic."[48]

Martov described the situation in very similar terms: "We do not have a unified, national state power that can act on the basis of clearly defined laws and be accountable to the people." Nevertheless, there was an unmistakable difference of emphasis between the head of the government and the leader of the opposition. In those cities where the soviets were controlled by the Bolsheviks, Martov asserted, power in the sense of government had ceased to exist. The soviets there were run by all kinds of revolutionary *troiki*, whose main source of power was a machine gun: "In reality, in real life, the soviet power had degenerated into irresponsible, uncontrollable, unjust, tyrannical, and expensive rule by commissars, committees, headquarters, and armed gangs." All those feuding bands, calling themselves Bolsheviks or some other kind of revolutionary communists, were at the root of the problem. They were disbanding the dumas and any opposition-led soviets, thereby undermining and wrecking the local economy and the systems of supply and taxation. In principle, Martov welcomed Lenin's call to put an end to the refractoriness of the local Bolshevik zealots. In fact, however, the Bolshevik government was incapable of doing so, because "those who imagined that they were ruling found themselves in actuality under the control of those who had been conducting campaigns of violence—that is, the owners of bayonets and machine guns, and their commanders."[49] Normality would return only when the election results were recognized—in other words, when authority was restored to the disbanded dumas and soviets. Unfortunately, Martov concluded,

47. Lenin, "Rech' po finansovomu voprosu na zasedanii TsIK 18 aprelia," in *Polnoe sobranie sochinenii*, 36:226.

48. "Postanovlenie Soveta . . . o tochnom i bystrom ispolnenii rasporiazhenii tsentral'noi vlasti i ustranenii kantseliarskoi volokity," in *Iz istorii grazhdanskoi voiny*, 1:222.

49. Martov, "Rabochie i gosudarstvennaia vlast'," *Novaia zaria*, 21 April 1918, pp. 14–16.

the Bolsheviks did not want to restore their authority, at least in the provinces, because to do so would be to recognize the democratic process and the recent electoral defeat of the Bolsheviks (see chapter 5).

Thus Lenin and Martov arrived at very different solutions to the problem. Lenin was preoccupied with building a centralized apparatus; Martov fought for the recognition of the newly elected soviets. Lenin's problem was that his October constituency had served well in seizing power but was now proving unruly, impeding the governing of the country. Martov's problem was that it was not enough to regain popular support when the dumas and soviets on which the Mensheviks and SRs won a majority were simply disbanded.

Gukovskii's report generated a storm of attacks on him personally and on his proposals, especially the proposed ban on indemnities.[50] Some Bolsheviks accused him of conciliating the bourgeoisie, others of secretly being a Menshevik. He defended himself at a CEC session on April 18: "I am criticized for the fact that my report was applauded by the CEC members on the right. But we should concern ourselves not with what side the applause comes from, but rather with accounting for our expenditures."[51] But the Menshevik applause was not the sole reason for the harsh attack on Gukovskii. More important, apparently, was that Gukovskii's report destroyed the illusion that the "iron battalions of the proletariat" were marching toward socialism. Although— or perhaps because—it addressed the problem in prosaic terms, it opened a Pandora's box.

The Mensheviks repeatedly pointed out that they had warned the Bolshevik government about the catastrophic consequences of nationalizations and confiscations. Sukhanov and Abramovitch demanded a full accounting of the expenditures by the local and central authorities during their term in office.[52] On what projects was the Bolshevik government spending 20 billion rubles? How much was being allocated for the Red Army? What did the Red Guards cost? How much had the government spent on the January offensive in the Ukraine? And finally, how and by whom had the millions of rubles raised by the indemnities from the bourgeoisie in the provinces been disposed of if, as Gukovskii now claimed, those funds had never reached the treasury? Abramovitch and Sukhanov were deprived of the floor to prevent further questioning. Martov wrote angrily that even Stolypin's duma had had more rights to debate the state budget than Lenin's so-called workers' parliament. "The opposition's participation in the debates on

50. David Dallin, "Finansovoe bankrotstvo," Vpered, 19 April 1918, p. 2.
51. "TsIK, zasedanie 18 aprelia," Vpered, 19 April 1918, p. 3.
52. Ibid.

the state budget and finances," he went on, "is the most important guarantee of the fruitfulness of these debates, because the main goal of an open parliamentary discussion of state finances is the establishment of actual accountability in the national economy."[53]

Since the Bolshevik government refused to give an accounting, declared a Menshevik editorial, the opposition economists would make their own calculations. According to conservative estimates, the total sum of indemnities extracted by force from the bourgeoisie exceeded 340 million rubles.[54] The indemnities were collected in fifty-one cities and reached their height in March and April 1918, when they averaged 38 million rubles a week. Most of these funds, asserted the Mensheviks, were spent on the local Bolshevik apparatus, the Red Guards, the Red Army, and bankrupt enterprises under workers' control; but in many cities the funds were divided up by the local Bolshevik commissars for their personal use.[55] Since taxes could not be collected and the indemnities had been used up or misused, the government was, for all practical purposes, bankrupt. Its chief recourse was to print more money. The opposition did not say it could cure all these ills, but they did believe they could do a better job than the Bolsheviks had done:

> Could [financial catastrophe] be averted if, after six months of Bolshevik rule, they were replaced by others? It is not easy to answer that question. However, it is beyond any doubt that economic life cannot be made livelier and healthier under the Bolshevik regime; and a new one would mitigate the horrors of the approaching catastrophe.[56]

Gukovskii's opponents in the Bolshevik party must have felt somewhat satisfied with such a hail of Menshevik questions and demands, since it put Gukovskii in such a weak position. According to Martov, Gukovskii was ostracized, having been discredited behind the scenes.[57] His Bolshevik opponents managed to soften, if not nullify, a CEC resolution prohibiting the imposition of indemnities on the bourgeoisie. An amendment stipulated that the ban was not a law but merely a recommendation of the CEC.[58] The debate on the matter was ended, since it had proved to be too embarrassing for the Bolshevik government.

One is struck by the fact that these deliberations in the spring of 1918

53. Martov, "Plokhie finansy khoroshei revoliutsii," *Vpered*, 20 April 1918, p. 1.
54. Semen Zagorskii, "Natsionalizatsiia bankov i razrushenie narodnogo khoziaistva," *Delo*, 21 April 1918, pp. 8–9; "Statistika kontributsii," *Vpered*, 1 April 1918.
55. On this last point, see, for example, the testimony of a Rostov Menshevik: Lockerman, *Bolcheviks à l'oeuvre*.
56. Dallin, "Finansovoe bankrotstvo," p. 2.
57. Martov, "Plokhie finansy khoroshei revoliutsii," *Vpered*, 20 April 1918, p. 1.
58. "Postanovlenie prezidiuma TsIK," *Dekrety sovetskoi vlasti*, 2:71.

dealt with such mundane matters. The members of the CEC were debating the nation's budget, taxation, and the prerogatives of local governments. They differed from other such deliberations only in their "socialist" rhetoric. But the ideological phraseology cannot hide the aspirations of the various party factions. When we consider who benefited from what kind of policies, it becomes clear that an end to requisitions and indemnities would have hurt the local extremists most. Conversely, the restoration of normal taxation and banking operations would have benefited most the moderate socialist intelligentsia in the provinces, who were the backbone of the administrations earlier disbanded by the Bolsheviks. The recognition of the election results and a return to normality would in fact have meant coming to some kind of understanding with the moderate elements: in political terms, with the Mensheviks, SRs, and Kadets. The next debate, on the problems of the railroads, revealed the Bolsheviks' refusal to do so, as well as their ever-growing reliance on dictatorial methods in dealing with economic problems.

The Railroad Decree

In January 1918, Lenin finally managed to disband Vikzhel, the Menshevik-SR-led railroad workers' union, and replaced it with a Bolshevik-controlled union, known as Vikzheldor.[59] The Mensheviks and SRs refused to comply with the orders of the appointed commissars, and as a result, those workers and engineers who supported them were removed from the management boards of the railroads. Authority over the railroads was divided between the new union and the local Bolshevik soviets, so that the union never acquired a degree of power comparable to that of its Menshevik predecessor. Meanwhile, as the Mensheviks pointed out and as Lenin himself recognized, the local Bolshevik leaders were using the railroads to satisfy their own rather than the nation's needs. Both Lenin and Gukovskii cited a number of cases in which local soviets imposed tolls on goods in transit.[60]

Two other problems imperiled the functioning of the railroads, as both the government and the opposition acknowledged: the deterioration of tracks and rolling stock, and unpaid travel by hordes of so-called bagmen (meshochniki). A new decree on the railroads was proposed to remedy these problems.[61]

59. Lenin's Soviet editors say that the Mensheviks still had enormous influence in Vikzheldor; see Lenin, Polnoe sobranie sochinenii, 36:592.
60. "Zasedanie TsIK," Vecherniaia zvezda, 16 April 1918, p. 1.
61. For the final text of the decree, see "O tsentralizatsii upravleniia, okhrane dorog i povyshenii ikh provozosposobnosti," Dekrety sovetskoi vlasti, 2:18–20.

By October 1917, the mass flight of soldiers from the front had made the railroads virtually incapable of sustaining regular traffic. The deserters were seizing trains by force of arms and of course not paying for the ride. Once home, the soldiers often had no land at their disposal or means to establish a household. They knew, however, that food was bringing high prices in urban areas, so many of them began to make a living by buying grain in the villages and transporting it in bags to the cities, where they sold it at a profit. Since they offered the peasants higher prices than the government's food-supply agencies were paying, the peasants preferred to sell to them. As the former soldiers were well armed and still wore their uniforms, they continued to ride the railroads without paying. They were soon joined by others who had never worn a uniform. The cars, the platforms between the cars, and even the car roofs were packed with nonpaying travelers and their sacks of grain.

From the point of view of the Bolshevik government, these "bagmen" were marauders, anarchists, and speculators who were exploiting for their own gain the price differential between the capitals and the provinces and subverting the government's fixed prices for grain.[62] The government placed so-called antiprofiteering detachments (*zagraditel'nye otriady*) at the railway stations and other strategic points, and in other ways fought against the bagmen's activities.

Menshevik economists, many of whom worked in the food-supply agencies of the dumas and soviets, discussed the problem of dealing with the bagmen in the party press.[63] It was true, they agreed, that the bagmen were speculators and that they undermined efforts to control prices. It was also true, though, that most of them were former Bolsheviks or at least October Bolshevik sympathizers.[64] One Menshevik who had personal experience with the situation pointed out, however, that the bagmen were not a homogeneous group. Some of them were indeed ex-soldiers and had even organized themselves in a military fashion, with their own commanders and guards armed with machine guns, who sometimes skirmished with representatives of the local soviets or with Cheka detachments that tried to confiscate their goods. Others were simple peasants, bringing two or three sacks of foodstuffs to the city market. In any case, the bagmen had in effect created underground grain-selling companies.[65]

Thus, from the Menshevik point of view, the government's measures against the bagmen were cruel, expensive, and inefficacious. If the mar-

---

62. For an expression of the present-day Soviet view of the bagmen, see Osipova, "Razvitie sotsialisticheskoi revoliutsii v derevne," p. 54.

63. "Bor'ba s meshochnikami," *Vecherniaia zvezda*, 7 March 1918, p. 2.

64. I. Nakatov, "Meshochniki," *Petrogradskoe ekho*, 29 May 1918.

65. "Bor'ba s meshochnikami," *Vecherniaia zvezda*, 7 March 1918, p. 2.

ket price was higher than the fixed price, that simply indicated a lagging supply. Some Menshevik food-supply specialists reported that
negotiations with the bagmen had brought fruitful results: the bagmen
agreed to sell their grain to the food-supply agent at a price that was
higher than the fixed price but lower than the free-market price. Some
bagmen were even hired by the food-supply agents to provide armed
escort for the grain being transported to the cities.[66] On the basis of
such accounts, Menshevik politicians argued that a policy of competitive pricing could be effective in bringing grain to the cities. Capitalism
was functioning, and, at least in food supply, the private sector was
proving a formidable competitor for the governmental agencies.

At times Lenin seemed to find these views consistent with the spirit
of the New Course. "When I see a merchant who tells me . . . that on
such-and-such a railroad there is a noticeable improvement," he said at
one point, "I value such praise a million times more than twenty resolutions of Communists or any others, and more than all kinds of
speeches."[67] The new railroad decree was evidently supposed to provide incentives for private trade within the framework of state capitalism. When Lenin also began to talk of restoring the authority of experts
and specialists and of raising their salaries, it seemed that he was going
to follow at least some of his opponents' suggestions. These expectations proved to be illusory.

In addition to the measures welcomed by the opposition, the railroad
decree contained one provision that caused an uproar among all parties
and factions in the CEC: special commissars with unlimited "dictatorial" authority were to be appointed on the main railroad lines.
These commissars were to be empowered to undertake at their discre-
tion any measures they deemed necessary to restore order, including
execution. Both Martov and Bukharin flatly rejected this provision,
holding it to be a violation of the principles of democracy and soviet
power. Lenin denied that there was any "contradiction in principle
between Soviet—that is, socialist—democracy and the application of
dictatorial power by single individuals."[68] Martov responded that this
measure not only would not normalize the situation but would lead to
unprecedented despotism. The whole point of the reform was to restore
accountability and responsibility; such measures would thwart those
efforts.

The Left Communists and Left SRs joined the Mensheviks and SRs in
protesting this provision. Apparently they, too, feared the power of the

---

66. Ibid.
67. Lenin, "Zasedanie TsIK 29 aprelia," in *Polnoe sobranie sochinenii*, 36:271.
68. Lenin, "Ocherednye zadachi sovetskoi vlasti," in ibid., 36:199.

new commissars. Nevertheless, Lenin was adamant: "Both Comrade Bukharin and Comrade Martov have mounted their hobbyhorse, the railroad decree, and . . . talk about the dictatorship of Napoleon III, Julius Caesar, etc. . . . But without the railroads not only will there be no socialism, but everyone will die of starvation while bread is nearby."[69] Despite the respect implied by his use of the term "comrade," Lenin's insistence on the appointment of commissars presented the New Course in a new light. Lenin's earlier pronouncements had been seen as an indication of a genuine desire to solve the problems of the railroads through cooperation with the merchants and the technical intelligentsia; the appointment of officials with dictatorial power destroyed these hopes. Further, the Mensheviks suspected that the dictatorial approach was designed to prevent them from regaining leadership of the railroad union. Lenin, it appeared, merely wanted to use opposition specialists to pacify the opposition workers, without giving anything in return.

Dan commented that "the proletarian character of the Caesar-like dictatorship is manifested only in the fact that all openings for all bureaucrats and policemen of all ranks will be filled with Bolsheviks, amidst the complete destruction of democratic statehood." The workers needed a legal guarantee of freedom to organize and to engage in political action, not an opportunity to be petty despots. The system as it was evolving, Dan asserted, had as little to do with state capitalism as the previous one had had with socialism. Bureaucratic appointees were to run a centralized economy with the help of gun-waving commissars recruited among the workers. This, concluded Dan, was Lenin's version of the transition to "socialism."[70] Another Menshevik, summing up the key changes in the Soviet regime since October, wrote:

> We are witnessing an inevitable process, in the course of which the dictatorship of the [working] class is replaced by the dictatorship of the soldiers, and the dictatorship of the soldiers by the dictatorship of separate groups of usurpers or a single usurper. However, where there is dictatorship of the class, there can be no dictatorship of a single individual; in other words, the dictatorship of single individuals dooms the dictatorship of the class.[71]

Analyzing the factors that accounted for such a distortion of the original promise of the New Course, Martov explained that the problem with the Bolshevik party was that, like Don Quixote, it went to ex-

69. Lenin, "Zasedanie TsIK 29 aprelia," in ibid., 36:271.
70. Dan, "Bol'shevistskii bonapartizm," *Novaia zaria*, 20 May 1918, pp. 16–17.
71. Stepan Ivanovich, "Konets diktatury," *Novyi den'*, 1 May 1918, p. 1.

tremes in everything it did. Many Bolsheviks meant well; they genuinely wanted to improve the situation; but in the end the excesses (*peregiby*) of these gallant warriors for socialism defeated their good intentions.[72]

The struggle over the railroad decree again revealed the discord between Mensheviks and Bolsheviks over methods. The Mensheviks advocated economic approaches, notably competitive pricing, to deal with the problem of the bagmen and to bring about cooperation among the interested parties in managing the railroads. The Bolsheviks were determined to fight the bagmen and assert control over the railroads by naked force. This was Lenin's way out of a dilemma: how to restore rail service without augmenting the opposition parties' share of authority. The Mensheviks' proposals were more attuned to the spirit of the New Course than the government's policies. In the end Lenin had his way. His decision, taken ostensibly for the success of state capitalism, led to the strengthening of the Cheka.

The Cheka, or Extraordinary Commission, created in December 1917 to deal with cases of sabotage and speculation, had slowly grown into a political police enforcing the government's economic policies. Now its sphere of competence was further widened to include control over the railroads. As a result, the return to moderation never came, and the gulf between the government and the opposition widened. This trend was revealed with utmost clarity during yet another policy struggle in May 1918—this time, the debate over the requisitioning of grain.

The Problem of Food Supplies

At the end of April 1918, all the political parties agreed that Russia was facing widespread famine. Food supplies in the big cities were running out. The state food-supply agencies were unable to deliver enough grain. The bagmen's supplies, despite the antiprofiteering detachments, were almost the sole source of grain in the cities.[73] The food-supply policy became another major issue in the debates between the government and the opposition.

The Menshevik and SR economists pointed to three factors that had brought the country to this pass. First, soon after the Bolsheviks seized power, they moved to do away with the zemstvos' and dumas' food-supply agencies, since in the main they were in the hands of Men-

---

72. "Zasedanie TsIK," ibid., p. 3. See also *Protokoly TsIK*, p. 224, and "Iu. O. Martov i F. Dan v TsIK," in *Martov i ego blizkie*, pp. 155–67.

73. Nakatov, "Meshochniki." For a detailed treatment of the food-supply crisis, see Lih, "Bread and Authority."

sheviks and SRs.[74] The irony of the situation, wrote I. Zorin, a Menshevik analyst, was that the Bolsheviks themselves thereby dealt a death blow to the state grain monopoly, which was based on the system of fixed prices; the passing of the state monopoly cleared the way for the bagmen.[75] Zagorskii elaborated:

> The very principle on which the Bolsheviks have based their food-supply organizations can produce only anarchy. When the task of food supply is withdrawn from the authority of the food-supply agencies and entrusted to the local soviets, it is obvious that a system of organized, coordinated, and united actions, based on an overall plan, simply cannot exist.[76]

Not only did the local soviets not take over the task of food supply; on the contrary, they actually slowed or cut off the flow of food to the cities by imposing their own tolls and tributes. In place of a system of food supply, there was "disintegration of the local food-supply organizations, total disregard for national interests on the part of the local Bolshevik soviets, and an absence of any central organization."[77]

The second reason for the decrease in food supplies, argued the Menshevik and SR critics, was the Treaty of Brest-Litovsk, which had cut off the grain-rich Ukraine from Russia. Finally, and most important, the October land seizures kept the peasants from producing as much grain as they could have produced otherwise.[78] The Bolsheviks had interrupted the slow but orderly process of land reform which had been going on under the Provisional Government. For political ends, wrote Aleksandr Martynov, "they appealed with their demagoguery not to the peasants' reason but to their prejudices, kindled the flame of peasant anarchy, incited the peasants to chaotic seizures of land, and inflamed them with the slogan 'Loot the looters!' "[79] Potresov wrote that October had been no more than a peasant revolt for the redivision of land: "The communism of the existing regime is merely the culmination of the

74. For data on the Menshevik and SR proportions of membership in the dumas and zemstvos in early 1918, see "Chastnoe soveshchanie predstavitelei zemstv i gorodov," Zemskii rabotnik (journal of the All-Russian Union of Zemstvo Employees), no. 2–3 (January 1918), p. 23. For a Soviet source, see S. Loginova, "Bor'ba Bol'shevikov s sabotazhem chinovnikov starykh prodovol'stvennykh organov v pervye mesiatsy sovetskoi vlasti (noiabr' 1917–ianvar' 1918)," Vestnik Leningradskogo universiteta, History, Language, and Literature Series, 1958, 20:34–48.

75. I. Zorin, "Sovetskaia vlast' i golod v Rossii," Nashe edinstvo, 20 December 1917, pp. 1–2.

76. Semen Zagorskii, "Bor'ba s golodom," Novyi den', 19 February 1918, p. 1.

77. G. Shub, "Prodovol'stvennaia katastrofa," Novaia zaria, 10 June 1918, p. 29.

78. A. Kin, "V derevne," Vpered, 3 May 1918, p. 1; Nicolas Roussanoff, "Les Bolsheviks et la question agraire," Echos de Russie (joint Menshevik-SR journal published in French in Stockholm), nos. 18–19 (1 August 1918), pp. 1–11.

79. Aleksandr Martynov, "V tupike," Vpered, 25 April 1918, p. 1.

essence [*stikhiia*] of our revolution of 1917, which realized, by the soldiers' bayonets, the innately Russian, primordial idea of land repartition."[80] Potresov, Martynov, and Chernov wrote about the bloody rebellion of the Russian peasants, their destructive instincts and their ruthlessness, the pseudo-socialist character of their looting in October, and their strong drive for personal enrichment. These writers and others described what they saw as the Russian intelligentsia's sentimental perceptions of the Russian people. Destructiveness and greed, which the intelligentsia had so long ignored, were part of the age-old psychological makeup of the Russian peasants. They could be ruthless and kind, lazy and hard-working, generous and stingy at the same time. One could hardly blame them for the anarchic land seizures or for the desire to get a better price for grain. The blame lay rather with the Bolsheviks, who had incited the peasants to seize and loot.[81]

Although the Mensheviks attributed the deterioration of the economic situation to the government's policies, as opposition parties generally do, it is implicit in their analysis that those policies were not the sole cause of the catastrophe. The tremendous social upheaval of the peasant rebellion in its destructive and anarchic Russian form had destroyed the social and economic fabric of society. But still more important for the debate on agrarian policy in May 1918 was the Mensheviks' explicit advocacy of an economic policy that would satisfy the peasants. Violence in the countryside had already led to famine; further violence would have incalculable consequences.

Lenin's perception of the causes of the food-supply crisis was in some respects very similar to Martov's. Lenin was not blind to the fact that the local soviets were impeding the shipment of supplies, and he recognized the necessity of getting opposition specialists back on the job. Furthermore, his thinking on the nature of the October seizures underwent serious changes in the spring of 1918. He became increasingly preoccupied with the petty-bourgeois element of the Russian Revolution. In defending his program of state capitalism against attacks by Bukharin and others, Lenin said:

> How can they regard state capitalism as the chief enemy? They should not forget that in the transition from capitalism to socialism our chief enemy is the petty bourgeoisie, its habits and customs, its economic position. The petty proprietor fears state capitalism above all, because he has only one

---

80. A. N. Potresov, "Nash prizyv k kapitalizmu," *Novyi den'*, 7 April 1918, p. 1.

81. A. N. Potresov, "Rokovye protivorechiia v russkoi revoliutsii," in Nikolaevsky, ed., *Potresov*, pp. 230–43; Martynov, "V tupike"; Chernov, *Rozhdenie revoliutsionnoi Rossii*, chap. 2, esp. p. 31. On Chernov's views on the destructiveness of Russian peasants, see also Viacheslav Polonskii, "Zametki," *Vecherniaia zvezda*, 8 April 1918, p. 2.

desire—to grab, to get as much as possible for himself, to ruin and smash the big landowners, the big exploiters. In this the petty proprietor eagerly supports us. Here he is more revolutionary than the workers, because he is more embittered and more indignant, and therefore he readily marches forward to smash the bourgeoisie—but not as the socialist does.[82]

Here Lenin inadvertently repeated what was essentially a Menshevik argument: that a large segment of the "revolutionary masses" who seized and looted in October had supported the Bolsheviks for reasons that had little to do with socialism. Still another similarity between Lenin's and Martov's views lay in their support for state capitalism, though they supported it for different reasons.

Despite these similarities, there was a subtle yet crucial difference between the views of the two men. Lenin, unlike his opponent, considered the petty proprietor to be the main enemy now. He believed that the hope for personal enrichment was the main obstacle to realization of his plans for state capitalism. Throughout March and April, he talked constantly about huge trusts, a gigantic centralized state bank, and a large-scale railroad network; but Russia's reality turned his mind to the hordes of bagmen, the factories plagued by theft, and the local soviets' expropriations of supplies.

From this difference arose two different approaches to the resolution of the food-supply crisis. Lenin interpreted the refusal of peasants to sell grain at fixed prices as a manifestation of their petty-bourgeois consciousness. That was sabotage, and he could not tolerate it. The Mensheviks maintained that the fixed prices had to be raised, competitive pricing introduced, and the efficiency of the procurement agencies restored, so that peasants would have incentives to sell and the bagmen would eventually be driven out of business by economic pressure. The Mensheviks viewed with apprehension the Bolsheviks' stubborn resistance to raising prices and their creation of the Cheka-run antiprofiteering detachments. These differences concerning methods soon escalated into a confrontation over the principles underlying the respective social policies.

A decision to use extraordinary measures against the "petty bourgeoisie" in the villages evidently crystallized sometime between April 30 and May 9. In a speech to the CEC on April 29, Lenin made no mention of such a decision, but the CEC session of May 9 was devoted to a debate on it. The decision was probably influenced by the political situation in Kiev. There, the Rada, or legislature, which had been dominated by SRs and Mensheviks, was dissolved by the German occupa-

---

82. "Session of the All-Russian CEC, April 29, 1918," in Lenin, *Collected Works,* 27:294.

tion forces, and General P. P. Skoropadskii was proclaimed hetman (leader) of the Ukraine at a congress of Ukrainian graingrowers. Skoropadskii promised to disband the revolutionary committees and to defend private ownership of land. These events filled the Bolsheviks in Moscow with consternation.[83] The peasants in Tambov, Orel, and Samara were also demanding an unequivocal commitment by the government to private ownership of land and free trade.

In this tense atmosphere, the debate on food-supply policy opened with the report of the commissar for supplies, A. D. Tsiurupa, on May 9. His description of the situation differed little from the picture painted by the opposition: "The abolition of the grain monopoly and a struggle against fixed prices on the part of the local authorities and congresses, requisitioning of provisions en route by anyone who feels like it—these are some typical manifestations of this disintegration."[84] A new element in his speech, though, was that the blame for this situation was placed squarely on the petty bourgeoisie, which was "conspiring against the soviet power." Hence it was imperative to grant extraordinary authority to the Commissariat of Supplies. The key provision of the proposed decree on the establishment of a food-supply dictatorship aroused stormy protests from the opposition benches. It called for "the use of armed force in the struggle against the peasant bourgeoisie or any other element in the event of resistance to the confiscation of surplus grain or any other foodstuffs and to the organization of food-supply detachments in all localities."[85]

The proposed decree intertwined new strands with old. Armed struggle against the bourgeoisie was of course an old slogan, but its application to the peasantry was something new. The antiprofiteering detachments had been deployed against the bagmen, not against the peasants in the villages. The decree stated that anyone who refused to sell surplus grain at the fixed price would be considered an "enemy of the people." Volunteers who informed the authorities about those who were hiding grain would be "entitled to fair compensation."[86] These measures were referred to as extraordinary and temporary, intended to enforce grain procurement on the basis of fixed prices.

Opposition speakers immediately pointed up the contradictions in the bill. Its methods of requisition amounted to plain robbery, Dan said,

83. For a description of the impact of Skoropadskii's coup on the Mensheviks and the Bolsheviks in Moscow, see George Denicke, "From the Dissolution of the Constituent Assembly to the Outbreak of the Civil War," in Haimson, ed., Mensheviks, pp. 140–41.

84. "V TsIK," Znamia truda (Moscow), 10 May 1918, p. 3; see also Protokoly TsIK, pp. 241–51.

85. Znamia truda (Moscow), 10 May 1918, p. 3; identical wording is found in Protokoly TsIK, p. 252.

86. Znamia truda (Moscow), 10 May 1918, p. 3; Protokoly TsIK, p. 251.

and were precisely what had led to the food-supply crisis in the first place. It was ludicrous to try to solve the problem by more robbery. Such actions, he warned, would spark civil war in the countryside and would drive a wedge between the peasants and the workers. The system of fixed prices, about which the Bolsheviks were ostensibly so worried, would be wrecked altogether. The peasants would stop selling to the state agencies, and grain speculation would run rampant. What was needed, Dan insisted, was the cultivation of trust and confidence between the government and the peasants and the restoration of reliable, democratic procurement agencies that could improve the grain supply through a competitive pricing policy.[87]

The Left SRs attacked the bill in scarcely milder terms: "How will you distinguish between the village bourgeoisie and the peasantry?" asked Karelin. "The proposed measures for armed expropriation of grain would degenerate into throat-slitting among the peasants!"[88] The session adjourned with the bill still unapproved.

The Mensheviks and the Left SRs, together with the SRs, launched a furious campaign against the Bolsheviks' proposal in the factories and soviets, on the boards of food-supply agencies and cooperatives, and of course in the press. A number of food-supply agencies in which Mensheviks and Bolsheviks were working together, notably such important ones as the Northern Food Board and the Moscow Food-Supply Committee, under the leadership of the Menshevik specialists V. G. Groman and M. Shefler, respectively, passed resolutions condemning the bill. They called armed requisitioning a "fruitless measure" that would paralyze the procurement process.[89] Even after the adoption of the decree, the Petrograd Food Board continued to lobby for higher fixed prices.[90] Many moderate Bolsheviks, particularly those who worked in economic agencies, defended the alternative proposals of Groman and other Menshevik supply specialists. A. I. Rykov, for example, put his signature next to Groman's on a document urging the CPC to drop grain requisitioning, improve trade between the countryside and the cities, change the structure of the procurement agencies, encourage the efforts of the cooperatives and of private capital, and raise the fixed prices.[91]

87. "Moskva, po telefonu: Zasedanie TsIK," *Znamia bor'by* (Petrograd), 11 May 1918, p. 3.
88. "V TsIK," *Znamia truda* (Moscow), 10 May 1918, p. 3.
89. Strizhkov cites the TsGANKh archive in his *Prodovol'stvennye otriady*, p. 59.
90. See the resolutions in "Otdel prodovol'stviia: Zagotovka khlebov i tverdye tseny," *Izvestiia Petrogradskogo gorodskogo obshchestvennogo samoupravleniia*, 22 June 1918, p. 3.
91. Strizhkov, *Prodovol'stvennye otriady*, p. 59.

These proposals had of course to be defended against the attack of the more militant Bolsheviks.[92]

In the middle of May, a decree on the food-supply system was passed in the CEC, with only the Bolsheviks voting for it.[93] But the struggle over policy was just beginning. During the next stage, the Bolsheviks' ideological justification of their policy emerged. At the CEC session on May 20, Sverdlov declared that the class struggle against the bourgeoisie had to be directed now against the peasant bourgeoisie.[94] The proletariat in the cities and the poorest peasantry in the countryside were to be the Bolshevik army against the bourgeoisie of all kinds. No longer were the measures to be taken described as "extraordinary"; the struggle with the peasant bourgeoisie was now hailed as the central task of soviet power. Sukhanov and Martov ridiculed the Bolsheviks' "self-deception." The Bolsheviks, they said, needed a hysterical campaign against the "village bourgeoisie" in order to blame the latter for their own ruinous policies and to deflect the rising rage of the workers from the Bolsheviks themselves to the peasants.[95] One observer, who later became a well-known Soviet writer, described the dramatic scene:

> All of a sudden, the audience gave a start. I did not understand immediately what had happened. From the podium thundered Martov's voice, shaking the walls. Rage bubbled in it. Pieces of his notes, shredded and scattered, were falling, whirling like snowflakes on the front rows. Martov was shaking his fists and shouting, gasping for breath: "Treason! You have made up this decree in order to remove all discontented workers—the flower of the proletariat—from Petrograd and Moscow! And in this way to stifle the healthy protest of the working class!" After a short pause, all jumped to their feet. A storm of shouts rippled across the hall. Cries rang out: "Down from the podium!"; "Traitor!"; "Bravo, Martov!"; "How dare he?"; "If the shoe fits, wear it!" Sverdlov was frantically ringing his bell, calling Martov to order. But Martov continued to shout even more furiously than before. Sverdlov deprived Martov of the floor, but he continued to speak. Sverdlov suspended him from the CEC for three sessions, but Martov only waved him away and continued to throw forth accusations, one sharper than the other.[96]

The Bolsheviks were determined to go ahead with grain requisitioning regardless of the opposition. Such terms as "business people" and

92. "O golodnom dvizhenii: Postanovlenie Moskovskogo biuro tsentral'noi oblasti RSDRP 28 maia 1918 goda," *Novaia zaria*, 10 June 1918, pp. 42–44.
93. For the text of the decree, see *Dekrety sovetskoi vlasti*, 2:266.
94. "TsIK: Plenum 20 maia," *Znamia truda* (Moscow), 21 May 1918, p. 3.
95. "Zasedanie TsIK: Doklad Sverdlova," *Novaia zhizn'*, 22 May 1918, p. 1. See also *Protokoly TsIK*, pp. 298–301.
96. Paustovskii, *Povest' o zhizni*, 3:629–30.

"merchants" disappeared from their vocabulary. The moves against the petty proprietors had acquired an ideological foundation, and they now escalated into a new wave of terror against the bourgeoisie, then the village bourgeoisie, and finally the "lackeys of the bourgeoisie"—the Mensheviks and SRs. The portrayal of the opposition parties as defenders of the bourgeoisie was a tactical move calculated to discredit the Bolsheviks' opponents.

Lenin was well aware that the Menshevik food-supply proposals were very close to some of the moderate pronouncements he had made himself only a short time before. Nevertheless, he now condemned them as counterrevolutionary:

> I will take the liberty of briefly quoting from the report of the recent [party] conference of the Mensheviks. This report appeared in the newspaper Zhizn'. From this report . . . we learn that Cherevanin, who made a report on economic policy, criticized the policy of the Soviet government and proposed a compromise solution to the problem—to enlist the services of representatives of merchant capital, as practical businessmen, to act as commission agents on terms that would be very favorable to them. We learn from that report that the chairman of the Northern Food Board, [Uprava] Groman, who was present at the conference, announced the following conclusions, which he had arrived at, so that report states, on the basis of a vast store of personal and all sorts of other observations—observations, I would add, made entirely in bourgeois circles. "Two methods," he said, "must be adopted: the first is that the current prices [of grain] must be raised; the second, that a special reward must be offered for prompt deliveries of grain, etc."

"What's wrong with that?" someone called out to Lenin from the audience.

Lenin, citing the petty-bourgeois danger, class struggle in the village, and a hidden counterrevolution, again lashed out at Menshevik moderation. In a key passage he said: "When they tell us about other methods, we reply as we did at the CEC session. When they talked about other methods, we said: 'Go to Skoropadskii, to the bourgeoisie. Teach them your methods, such as raising grain prices, or forming a bloc with the kulaks. There you will find willing ears.' "[97]

The decision to send armed detachments to requisition grain necessitated the restructuring of many political institutions of the new regime, and the third and last stage in the debate on food-supply policy revolved around these fundamental changes. At the CEC session on May 27, a Bolshevik speaker, Aleksei Sviderskii, presented a new bill grant-

---

97. "Ob"edinennoe zasedanie TsIK, Moskovskogo soveta i professional'nykh soiuzov," in Lenin, *Polnoe sobranie sochinenii*, 36:403, 408.

ing "unlimited dictatorial authority" to the government-appointed commissars. The commissars were even to have the power to disband local soviets that failed to implement the measures of the food-supply authorities.[98]

The Mensheviks, the SRs, and the Left SRs fiercely attacked the new bill. Martov pointed out that in granting their commissars the right to do what they had in fact been doing—disbanding the opposition soviets—the Bolsheviks had stopped pretending that they were a government responsible to the soviets.[99] I. Z. Shteinberg of the Left SRs declared the bill "absolutely unacceptable" because it completely contradicted the very principle of soviet power.[100] The Left SRs had every reason to fight the bill as vigorously as the Mensheviks and the SRs did, because many of the local soviets, especially in rural areas, were in their hands. The bill was passed, however, again by the votes of the Bolsheviks alone. Such legislation left little room for multiparty competition and paved the way for the confrontations of the summer of 1918.

During the debates on industry, finance, transport, and food supply, the parties and factions defined their positions. Control of the economy had to be taken over by the party, according to Lenin; but according to Martov, it had to be based on a partnership of government, labor, and industrialists. The trade unions were to be the agents of the state, according to Lenin, but according to Martov they were to be independent workers' organizations. The Mensheviks welcomed state regulation of industry but opposed the centralization and bureaucratization sought by the Bolsheviks; they approved action to curb anarcho-syndicalism but rejected total submission of the workers to the dictatorial commissars. The Mensheviks encouraged cooperation with the specialists but rejected mere use of them, without true partnership.

The Mensheviks demanded that the government account for its financial dealings during its time in office; they favored partial denationalization of the banks to stimulate the economy and supported Gukovskii's proposals to ban the imposition of indemnities on the bourgeoisie. The Bolsheviks refused to make an accounting, rejected partial denationalization of the banks, and stopped short of forbidding requisitions from the bourgeoisie. On food-supply policy, the Mensheviks advocated raising the fixed prices and offering other economic incentives to induce the peasants to sell. The policy adopted by the Bolsheviks called for grain requisitioning by force.

These differences should not obscure the fact that during the debates, the Mensheviks and SRs found much common ground not only with

98. "TsIK," *Znamia truda* (Moscow), 29 May 1918, p. 3; *Protokoly TsIK*, pp. 321, 325.
99. "TsIK," *Znamia bor'by* (Petrograd), 29 May 1918, p. 3.
100. "TsIK," *Znamia truda* (Moscow), 29 May 1918, p. 3.

the Left SRs but even with various Bolshevik factions. Political opinion within the Bolshevik party was not monolithic. It would thus be misleading to group the factions in the CEC according to an unvarying right-left dichotomy. On issues of war and peace, the "right" factions in the CEC, the Mensheviks and the SRs, supported the revolutionary war policy advocated by the "left" factions, the Left Communists and the Left SRs. The same coalition opposed the appointment of special commissars with unlimited authority on the railroads. On issues of banking and food policy, however, the "right" factions joined hands with the "right" Bolsheviks and with the Left SRs. The Menshevik-SR bloc was usually in agreement with the Left SRs, but not on the issues of banking policy and indemnities from the bourgeoisie.

The Mensheviks' critique of Bolshevik economic policy indicates that they still perceived their role as that of a parliamentary opposition. They criticized the government, offered alternative solutions, tried to mobilize public support for their proposals, and sought agreement, not confrontation, with the Bolsheviks. Even though the Mensheviks and SRs could not outvote their opponents in the CEC, they could and did outvote them, as we shall see, in a number of elections to local soviets during the spring and early summer of 1918.

The Bolsheviks' rejection of moderate economic policies might have been motivated in part by their realization that the adoption of competitive food prices would have enhanced the influence of the moderate food-supply agencies and led to reliance on the "village bourgeoisie," who were suspicious of the Bolsheviks and tended to vote for the SRs. Restoration of the responsibility and accountability of local government would have meant an end to the rule of the various Bolshevik "headquarters" and a partial transfer of power to the newly elected Menshevik-SR soviets.

The practice of partnership in industry, which would have been consistent with the principles of state capitalism, likewise would have required recognition of independent workers' organizations, a step that would have strengthened the Mensheviks and SRs, who were often their leaders. The Bolshevik government chose instead to rely on dictatorial methods, which in the end scuttled state capitalism. Lenin wanted to practice economic moderation, but by radical methods and without the moderate parties. In the end, the Cheka's fight against the bagmen, the speculators, and the "lackeys of the bourgeoisie," supposedly to ensure the success of the New Course, changed the institutions, attitudes, and ideology to such an extent that any talk of moderation became outdated. Practices that had been introduced as temporary, extraordinary measures were later discovered to have represented the intended policy from the very beginning.

CHAPTER 4

The Beleaguered Press

The effectiveness of any criticism of government policy depends on the ability of the opposition parties to communicate it to the electorate. Thus the fortunes of the independent Russian press deserve close attention. Two court battles set off by critical articles in the Menshevik press highlighted the development of political institutions generally, for the arguments presented at the trials concerned not only the press but also the relationship of individual politicians to their political parties and the status of the courts vis-à-vis the ruling party, the opposition, and the state. These trials provide a glimpse at the overlapping personal relationships of the leading politicians and the effect of these relationships on the individuals' fulfillment of their state duties.

Bolshevik Policy toward the Opposition Press

It is well known that the Bolshevik government, from the very first days of its existence, consistently harassed the non-Bolshevik press. It is useful to distinguish at least three sets of tactics employed by the government in the period from October 1917 to June 1918. At each stage, the policy change necessitated a restructuring of political institutions which had far-reaching consequences for the Bolshevik government and the Menshevik-SR opposition.

According to a report of the Menshevik CC to the Second International in June 1918, the socialist parties, the SDs and the SRs, had been publishing several hundred periodicals in Russia before the October overturn, more than two dozen in Petrograd and Moscow alone. All provincial capitals and most smaller towns had at least one Menshevik or SR paper.[1]

After the Bolsheviks seized power, they attacked primarily what they called the "bourgeois press." Even then, however, they attempted also to close down several publications of the opposition socialist parties: the *Rabochaia gazeta*, the newspaper of the Menshevik CC; the *Den'*, edited by Potresov; *Edinstvo*, edited by Plekhanov; and others published by the SRs. As we saw in chapter 1, these closures contributed to the breakdown of the Vikzhel negotiations. But efforts to destroy the opposition press did not always succeed: editors often ignored orders to shut down. To enforce their ban, the people's commissars would send detachments of sailors, who would burn the already published issues and perhaps destroy the printing shop. Sometimes, however, the sailors, contrary to their orders, would leave after the raid.[2] To frustrate these efforts, the newspapers changed names and locations almost daily. Thus in November 1917 the Menshevik *Rabochaia gazeta* appeared as *Molniia, Molot, Zaria, Luch'*, and finally *Novyi Luch'*.

Little by little, this guerrilla-style warfare against the opposition press gave way to a more conventional approach, based on court action and CPC decrees. Although these decrees were draconian from the socialists' point of view, they nevertheless provided some legal basis for continued publication. The opposition press was given the right to exist and to criticize the Bolshevik government. This change of policy should not be seen as some kind of weakening of pressure, however; closures of the newspapers continued, albeit on a smaller scale.

In December 1917, a decree prohibited the publication of announcements and advertisements in all newspapers, thus striking at the financial sources of papers that received no state subsidy.[3] Another decree ordered all papers to publish all edicts (*rasporiazheniia*) of the Soviet government on the first page. The papers had to be registered with the Commissariat of the Press and have a permit to publish. The same month saw the first attempt to introduce censorship. Editors were required to submit all materials selected for publication to the Commissariat of the Press. The editors of all the opposition papers in the capitals refused to obey the order, and as a result these papers were

---

1. *Rabochii klass pod bol'shevistskoi diktaturoi: Doklad Vtoromu Internatsionalu*, Nik. Col. no. 6, box 1, file 12, p. 16.

2. Ibid., pp. 9–10.

3. A. Iurko, "Likvidatsiia burzhuaznoi pechati v pervyi period sovetskoi vlasti (oktiabr' 1917–iiul' 1918)," *Uchenye zapiski AON pri TsK KPSS*, no. 45 (1958), pp. 108–41; Okorokov, *Oktiabr' i krakh russkoi burzhuaznoi pressy*, p. 216.

Россійская Соціалъ-Демократическая Рабочая Партія.

Пролетаріи всѣхъ странъ соединитесь!

ИСКРА

Органъ меньшевиковъ-интернаціоналистовъ.

КОНТОРА „ИСКРЫ"
Обводный кан., 48, кв. 53.
Уголъ Лиговки.
Пріемъ отъ 11 до 5 час.
Цѣна отдѣльнаго номера:
Въ Петроградѣ 20 к.
Въ провинціи 25 к.

Съ 26 сентября въ Петроградѣ выходитъ
„ИСКРА"
Органъ Меньшевиковъ-Интернаціоналистовъ.

№ 9. Пятница, 17-го Ноября 1917 г. № 9.

ТОВАРИЩИ
СОЛДАТЫ и РАБОЧІЕ!

Большевики задушили свободу печати.

Они отняли у народа его самое драгоцѣнное достояніе. БОЛЬШЕВИКИ СДѢЛАЛИ ПЕЧАТНОЕ СЛОВО СВОЕЙ ИСКЛЮЧИТЕЛЬНОЙ ПРИВИЛЛЕГІЕЙ. Только та ПЕЧАТЬ, что ПОДПѢВАЕТЪ большевикамъ имѣетъ возможность безпрепятственно выходить.

Большевики лгутъ, когда утверждаютъ, что ими преслѣдуется только буржуазная печать. Они громятъ всѣ газеты, несогласныя съ ними.

Большевики закрываютъ, конфискуютъ, разоряютъ какъ буржуазную, такъ и соціалистическую небольшевистскую печать.

Большевики вернули печать въ тѣ условія, въ которыхъ печатное слово жило при царскомъ режимѣ.

Революція лишена независимаго слова.

Свободой слова пользуются только подхалимы. Ни одна газета, несвязанная съ большевиками общностью преступленій противъ Россіи и революціи, не увѣрена въ завтрашнемъ днѣ.

РАБОЧІЕ!

ВСЯ ПЕЧАТЬ должна быть СВОБОДНА. Свобода печати для всѣхъ добыта кровью всего русскаго народа. БЕРЕГИТЕ СВОБОДУ ПЕЧАТИ! Въ демократической республикѣ ни какія гоненія на печать недопустимы. Всякій гражданинъ, всякая партія должна имѣть право свободно выражать свои взгляды. Потому что каждый гражданинъ, каждая партія должна имѣть возможность вліять на народъ, добиваться того, чтобы убѣдить его въ правильности своихъ взглядовъ. Каждый долженъ пользоваться свободой говорить то, что онъ считаетъ правдой, и изобличать то, что считаетъ неправдой. Поэтому, даже врагамъ пролетаріата должна быть предоставлена полная свобода слова. Нѣтъ соціалиста въ Европѣ, который считалъ-бы возможнымъ подавлять насиліемъ печать другихъ партій.

КРАСНОГВАРДЕЙЦЫ!

Заявите БОЛЬШЕВИКАМЪ, что они не имѣютъ права примѣнять ВАСЪ, честныхъ пролетаріевъ, для исполненія грязныхъ полицейскихъ обязанностей по удушенію печати. Пусть Военно-Революціонный Комитетъ навербуетъ для этого отряды изъ бывшихъ жандармовъ и полицейскихъ. Они охотно пойдутъ на службу къ новымъ самодержцамъ.

Рабочіе и Солдаты! Вмѣстѣ съ нами издайте кличъ
Да здравствуетъ свобода печати!

Front page of the Menshevik Internationalist newspaper *Iskra*, 17 November 1917 (Petrograd): "Comrades, Workers, and Soldiers! The Bolsheviks have strangled freedom of the press." Russian Serials Collection, Hoover Institution Archives.

ordered shut down. Shortly afterward, though, both the censorship regulation and the ban were lifted. The numerous Bolshevik ad hoc rules and decrees governing the status of the press were codified in the Provisional Rules for the Press, published on February 2, 1918: editors were to be held personally responsible for the political content of the materials they published, and were liable to arrest and trial for publishing "slanderous information discrediting the Soviet power."[4] A Revolutionary Tribunal for the Press, set up by a CPC decree of January 28, was empowered to deal with "crimes against the people perpetrated by means of the press."[5]

From the outset, the Revolutionary Tribunal for the Press was swamped with work. In the weeks preceding its establishment, dozens of papers had been ordered to close down for protesting the disbandment of the Constituent Assembly. In Petrograd, two SR papers, *Volia strany* and *Delo naroda*, were temporarily closed, as were, again, *Luch'* and *Edinstvo*. Klivanskii, co-editor of *Den'*, was arrested and confined for a month, and in Moscow, *Vpered*, an SD publication, the SRs' *Vlast' naroda*, and other papers were also closed temporarily.[6] Some editors forwarded complaints and protests to the Revolutionary Tribunal for the Press, and numerous trials ensued.

The Menshevik report to the Second International pointed out that closures fell off noticeably in February. In all probability, the slacking off was part of a Bolshevik concession to the Left SRs, who were then partners in the ruling coalition and one of whom, I. Z. Shteinberg, headed the Commissariat of Justice. Shteinberg's energetic measures to replace arbitrary raids with judicial procedures must have contributed to the relative normalization of publishing activity. In addition, the Bolshevik party was apparently preoccupied with the peace-treaty negotiations. The opponents of the treaty, among them the Left Communists, themselves started publishing attacks on Lenin's foreign policy.

The editors of the Menshevik and SR papers responded favorably to the more tolerant climate and complied, on the whole, with the Provisional Rules. The defiant tone of many papers softened somewhat. Materials unfavorable to the government were presented with little commentary. Commentary might provoke legal charges; the publication of

---

4. Okorokov, *Oktiabr' i krakh russkoi burzhuaznoi pressy*, p. 255; see also Peter Kenez, "Lenin and the Freedom of the Press," in Gleason, Kenez, and Stites, eds., *Bolshevik Culture*, p. 152.

5. E. A. Finn, "Antisovetskaia pechat' na skam'e podsudimykh (zametki sovremennika o tribunalakh po delam pechati)," *Sovetskoe gosudarstvo i pravo*, no. 2 (February 1967), pp. 71–72.

6. *Rabochii klass pod bol'shevistskoi diktaturoi*, p. 12.

the bare facts made it difficult to charge the editors with slander. Meanwhile, the editors gradually grew used to periodic closures of limited duration and to occasional fines and court trials.

The breathing spell lasted until March, when the Treaty of Brest-Litovsk had been signed and ratified. According to the Menshevik report to the Second International, forty-seven opposition papers were closed during March alone, fines totaling 278,000 rubles were imposed on seventeen papers, and the editors of fourteen dailies were put on trial. By May, more than twenty slander cases involving socialist and "bourgeois" dailies were awaiting trial in Petrograd.[7]

In the course of the spring of 1918, press trials took place in Odessa, Kaluga, Kharkov, Rostov, Yaroslavl, Saratov, and many other cities. Most of these trials either never ended officially or led to the acquittal of the accused, as in the trial of the editorial board of *Iuzhnyi rabochii,* a Menshevik paper in Odessa. In Rostov and Kharkov, too, the Bolsheviks' efforts to try the Mensheviks for treason and anti-Soviet propaganda ended in a fiasco.[8]

The failure to convict the Mensheviks at these trials is partly explained by the Mensheviks' well-organized defense. Their knowledge of the law, brilliant argumentation, and convincing evidence bewildered the Bolshevik prosecutors. More important, and perhaps decisive in some cases, was the strong popular support for the opposition party. The Mensheviks consistently sought to turn the deliberations on their articles into investigations of the truth of their reports. The relevant facts in the case often discredited the local Bolshevik authorities. The Menshevik CC told the Second International that "the attempts to try journalists always led to the triumph of the accused, and bit by bit, the authorities gave up on trying their political opponents. More and more often they practiced administrative reprisals [*rasprava*]."[9] Perhaps because the trials of the opposition leaders in provincial cities almost always intensified anti-Bolshevik sentiment without getting any Mensheviks convicted, the judicial approach was abandoned earlier there than in the capitals. The Bolsheviks in the provinces reverted to the tactics of staging raids on the opposition papers, but now by an organized force, the Cheka. Confiscations of printed issues, arrests, and ambushes of editors became regular practices in the Cheka war on the opposition press in the provinces. April 1918, a month of Menshevik

7. Ibid., p. 14.
8. On the trials in Kaluga, Yaroslavl', Saratov, and Rostov, see chap. 5. The most complete source on the trial in Odessa is Odessa Menshevik Committee, *Protsess "Iuzhnogo rabochego."*
9. *Rabochii klass pod bol'shevistskoi diktaturoi,* p. 17.

and SR victories in provincial soviet elections, saw the highest number
of closings of newspapers and arrests of editors.[10] By May the stage of
court battles was drawing to an end in the provinces.

In the capitals, voices proposing the abolition of the Revolutionary
Tribunal for the Press were heard as early as March. Gorelik, a functionary in the tribunal, wrote a memo to that effect to the higher Bolshevik
authorities. This memo, according to a contemporary Soviet historian,
was leaked to the Mensheviks by the Left SRs and published in *Novaia
Zhizn'*, to the great displeasure of the Bolsheviks.[11] Gorelik argued that
the proceedings in the tribunal discredited the Soviet government. The
Mensheviks' and SRs' skillful presentation of evidence, their experienced lawyers, and the wide publicity given to the trials usually led to
mild sentences or even the outright victory of the representatives of the
opposition press. Gorelik recommended that the tribunal be abolished
and that the Commissariat of the Press be empowered to deal with the
opposition press in an "administrative manner"—that is, without trial.
If this recommendation were to be followed, the court battles in Moscow would give way to such practices as were already in use in the
provinces.

The Dispute between Martov and Stalin

One of the most significant court cases concerning the press grew out
of an article by Martov titled "Artillery Fire," which was published in
Vpered on March 31, 1918. Though the complaint against Martov
seemed minor, the case snowballed, eventually involving political
leaders in a court battle that had a profound impact on the shaping of
judicial and political institutions. It is also of interest that the complaint was brought by one Iosif Dzhugashvili, who used the name Stalin.

The first hearing on the case was held before the Revolutionary Tribunal for the Press on April 5.[12] Stalin claimed that Martov's article
contained a slanderous statement concerning his (Stalin's) revolutionary past. In the article, which criticized the Brest treaty, Martov touched
upon the precarious position of Georgia, which was threatened by the
Turks from the south. Martov asserted that the provision in the treaty

10. Ibid., pp. 14–15.
11. Finn, "Antisovetskaia pechat'," p. 75.
12. On the opening of the case, see "Martov-Stalin," *Vechernie ogni*, 4 April 1918, p. 2;
and Wolfe, *Three Who Made a Revolution*, p. 471. The most extensive coverage of the
proceedings at that session is in "Tribunal pechati: Delo Martova," *Rannee utro*, 6 April
1918, p. 4.

Законопроэкты.

(Ленинъ). Упразднимъ, товарищъ, гласный судъ? (Троцкій). По боку, его, товарищъ! (продолж. см. на 7-й стр.).

A cartoon from the Samara provincial satirical journal *Gorchichnik*, January 1918. The head reads: "Lawmaking projects." Lenin: "Comrade, shall we do away with public trial?" Trotsky: "Down with it, comrade!" Russian Serials Collection, Hoover Institution Archives.

that allowed the Turks to occupy Batum (now Batumi) amounted to a sellout of the Caucasus to the Turkish invaders, who were slaughtering the Armenian population. Stalin was mentioned only in passing: reviewing the history of the SD party in the Caucasus, Martov mentioned that Stalin, who was now the commissar of nationalities, had been expelled from the SD party in 1908 for his participation in several "expropriations" and bank robberies, though such actions had been explicitly banned by the party's rules.

The session of the Revolutionary Tribunal attracted large crowds. The chairman, Pechak, opened the proceedings: "Who wants to accuse Martov?" "I, Iosif Dzhugashvili, Stalin." Stalin was represented not by an attorney but by Lev Sosnovskii, a prominent Bolshevik, a member of the CEC and of the editorial board of *Pravda*. Martov's defense team consisted of Lapinskii and Aleksandrov. Stalin himself declared from the podium that Martov's allegation was a slanderous lie. Martov was asked to explain his position and comment on his statement in the article, but he refused to do so. Instead, he argued that Stalin's complaint against him could not be brought before the Revolutionary Tribunal because, under the decree that established it, only "crimes against the people, through the medium of the press," fell under its jurisdiction. "Up until now," he said, "I have not heard that Stalin personified the people."[13]

The chairman rejected Martov's objection on the ground that any statements in the press could be considered by the tribunal. Martov was ordered to offer testimony on the substance of his allegations against Stalin. Having conferred with his defense team, Martov declared to the tribunal that Stalin had taken part in the expropriation of funds on the steamship *Nicholas I* in Baku and that this case had been brought before a party disciplinary court in 1908.[14] Martov suggested that the tribunal summon as witnesses a former member of the First Duma, Isidor Ramishvili, since he had chaired the proceedings that resulted in Stalin's expulsion; the head of the Georgian Menshevik government, Noi Zhordaniia; a Bolshevik leader in the Caucasus, Stepan Shaumian; and Isidor Gukovskii, currently deputy commissar of finance in the Bolshevik government, who might be able to enlighten the tribunal on Stalin's assassination attempt on the worker Zharinov, who had disclosed the facts of Stalin's participation in the robberies.

According to the newspaper report, Stalin shouted that Martov was "a dishonest slanderer" and that "no witnesses should be summoned."

13. "Tribunal pechati," *Rannee utro*, 6 April 1918, p. 4.
14. Ibid. Martov returned to this point a few years later in his article "Tainstvennyi neznakomets," *Sotsialisticheskii vestnik*, 16 August 1922, p. 8. See also E. E. Smith, *Young Stalin*, pp. 207–10.

Martov retorted that no one had ever called him a slanderer during all his years in the revolutionary movement. Amid this stormy exchange, the chairman called a recess, leaving the chambers in consternation for consultations. The audience gave Martov an ovation.[15]

Upon resumption of the proceedings, the chairman ruled in Stalin's favor. Witnesses would not be summoned; the case was to be resolved in one session, without delay. Martov's defense lawyers raised objections. The chairman said that the witnesses from Georgia could not be summoned because of wartime conditions. "That's not true!" Martov cried out. "What about the witness in Moscow? Stalin is afraid to speak about his past!" A volunteer among the spectators offered to set out for Georgia immediately and bring back written statements by the witnesses named by Martov. The questions and demands from the floor could no longer be subdued. The chairman called in the Red Guards. Amid a general uproar, they cleared the spectators out by force.[16]

The situation was now almost the reverse of what it had been at the outset. Now Martov was the accuser, and he asserted "the right to affirm that Stalin's past is the past of an expropriator." Sosnovskii, Stalin's lawyer, who had worked with him in the Caucasus in 1908, admitted reluctantly that rumors that Stalin had participated in expropriations had circulated at the time, but, he added, they "were only rumors." Apparently seeking a compromise, Sosnovskii proposed that the hearing be postponed for a week, so that the witnesses could be summoned to the tribunal, as Martov insisted. Stalin, however, abruptly changed his position: "Let Martov declare that he has no evidence against me, and I will withdraw my complaint." Martov refused to make any such statement and insisted on continuing with the trial. The tribunal, after a long consultation, issued a decision to "postpone the hearing by a week, trying in the meantime all means to obtain testimony from the witnesses named by Martov."[17]

The issue was debated extensively in the press, and the affair threatened to turn into a political scandal damaging to the Bolsheviks. The questioning of the witnesses, however, never took place. By a special decree of the CPC, the Revolutionary Tribunal for the Press was abolished within a week after the case had begun.[18] Many details of the episode remain obscure. A contemporary Soviet historian has written that the archives may yet yield documents that will make it possible "to

15. "Tribunal pechati," *Rannee utro*, 6 April 1918, p. 4.
16. Ibid.
17. Ibid.
18. Martov, "Narod eto ia! V Moskovskii revoliutsionnyi tribunal: Zaiavlenie," *Vpered*, 14 April 1918, p. 3.

highlight the problem from all sides."[19] Meanwhile, it does not seem farfetched to suggest that Stalin had a hand in the tribunal's abolition. His complaint was forwarded to the Revolutionary Tribunal of the city of Moscow.

The opposition press launched a stormy campaign of protests: Why do courts that rule in favor of the opposition get disbanded in Soviet Russia? Why, after the Revolutionary Tribunal for the Press had been abolished, was Stalin's complaint forwarded to the Revolutionary Tribunal of the city of Moscow, instead of to a regular people's court? Martov saw here the result of Stalin's behind-the-scenes machinations.[20] The Moscow Revolutionary Tribunal, he wrote, had no jurisdiction over the case. It had been set up to consider crimes against the state, such as treason, plotting to overthrow the government, and preparation of uprisings. None of these crimes could be imputed to him simply because he had insulted Stalin.[21] On the one hand, Martov wanted a continuation of the trial to prove that what he said was true. On the other, he considered it politically detrimental to go ahead with it at the Revolutionary Tribunal of Moscow, for such a step might set a dangerous precedent. If public criticism of a highly placed Bolshevik could be equated with a crime against the state, the consequences could be catastrophic. He demanded that the transfer of the case to the Moscow Revolutionary Tribunal be revoked.

The April 16 session of the Moscow Revolutionary Tribunal opened with a tempestuous debate over the issue of jurisdiction.[22] Correspondents of major newspapers, leaders of political parties, and even larger crowds than before had assembled at the entrance. The Red Guards admitted only those with permits. In the center of the dais sat the chairman of the proceedings, the lawyer A. M. Diakonov, flanked on one side by Stalin and Sosnovskii and on the other by Martov, Abramovitch (a member of the Menshevik CC), and A. A. Pleskov, a lawyer and long-time Menshevik (later to become a CC member). Martov appealed to the tribunal:

> "I have the right to demand that no privileges be created in the Soviet republic for separate individuals, even for those in power, and since according to the decree this case does not fall under the jurisdiction of this tribunal, the people's commissar, Stalin, must be the first to comply, es-

19. Finn, "Antisovetskaia pechat'," p. 75. One witness Martov wanted to call, Noi Zhordaniia, in fact gave his testimony in written form eighteen years later, in an article in *Ekho bor'by*; manuscript copy in Nik. Col. no. 90, file 2.

20. Martov, "Ia udovletvoren," *Vpered*, 26 April 1918, p. 2.

21. Martov, "Narod eto ia!" p. 3.

22. "Delo Martova," *Den'*, 17 April 1918, p. 3.

pecially since at the time I was writing about in my article, Stalin was not yet a commissar, but merely a simple expropriator."

The chairman asked Martov to be more tactful toward his opponent. Martov was unyielding: Stalin should bring his complaint before a regular district people's court. Sosnovskii parried Martov's objections by saying that the matter had already been settled by the Revolutionary Tribunal for the Press, and Martov was wasting his time on this futile debate. The chairman overruled him, however, asserting that this tribunal could not be bound by the decisions of one that no longer existed. This was another unexpected turn for Stalin and Sosnovskii. Again assuming a conciliatory tone, Stalin repeated that Martov was only trying to drag out the trial, without having any evidence. After three hours of consultations, Diakonov announced that Stalin's complaint against Martov was not within the tribunal's jurisdiction. Martov's objection had been upheld.[23]

The chairman was not about to let Martov walk out in triumph, however. He put forward new charges. "In that same article of Martov's," he observed, were the words " 'the government in the Caucasus [i.e., the Georgian Menshevik government] fighting the Turks would not degrade itself like some petty government of Lenin-Trotsky, or Wilhelm-Hindenburg.' " These words were "insulting to the Soviet government and undermine its prestige."[24] Martov was furious: "These new charges, made with no preliminary investigation . . . , are being brought as compensation to those persons whose attempt to give me short shrift for the sake of Bolshevism has come to nothing." He went on:

"It is your right to want to gag me. But I do not envy the kind of federal republic where the authorities can try people for political criticism and for their judgment of events. . . . I have always considered that the Council of People's Commissars violated the interests of the people and had no right to sign either the Brest treaty or the provision about the Caucasus . . . because the Bolsheviks took it upon themselves to act in accord with Germany in clearing the Caucasus area for its [Germany's] ally."

Pleskov and Abramovitch declared that they were in complete agreement with Martov's statement and that by the same logic the tribunal could bring charges against the entire CC of the Social Democratic party, as well as all rank-and-file members who supported Martov's

---

23. "Delo Stalina priznano nepodsudnym tribunalu," *Rannee utro,* 17 April 1918, p. 3. This is probably the most complete account of the proceedings of this session.
24. "V revoliutsionnom tribunale," *Zaria Rossii,* 17 April 1918.

denunciation of the Brest treaty. Was the tribunal prepared to try an entire political party for criticism of the government's policy? Martov had to make himself heard over the uproar in the room: "And when the Bolsheviks stifle the press that points to their mistakes, I affirm, I have shouted, and I will shout, even from prison if you are going to shut me up there, that you are committing an act of treason."[25]

After this fiery speech, the tribunal again retired for an hour-long recess. Finally the chairman announced that Martov's article had been "intended to undermine the people's trust in the workers' and peasants' government. For a use of the press [that was] frivolous for a political leader, and for careless disrespect to the people," the tribunal found it necessary to censure Martov.[26] Both cases, Stalin's complaint and Martov's insult to the Soviet government, were closed.

The chairman of the tribunal was clearly seeking a compromise. By reprimanding Martov for an insult to the entire government, rather than to Stalin personally, he glossed over the impression that he had upheld Martov's views on the limits of jurisdiction. Neither Martov nor Stalin, however, was satisfied with the verdict.[27] Stalin had not been vindicated, but since the case was closed, he was in the awkward position of having to pursue the matter in another court, which might permit the testimony of witnesses. That was something Stalin clearly preferred to avoid, yet he was unwilling to let Martov have the last say. Over the next week he used his influence to try to reverse the verdict of the Moscow tribunal.

Martov and Dan launched a campaign in the press, raising questions the Bolsheviks did not want to discuss publicly. Why had the witnesses named by Martov never been summoned? Would Stalin forward his complaint to the people's court, and would the witnesses finally testify? Was it not a matter of honor for the people's commissar to go ahead with the case? The affair had by now turned into a political scandal. In an article, "The Right to 'Undermine Trust,'" Martov questioned the legitimacy of the charges against him. Only a monarchy ruling by divine right, he argued, could try its opponents for undermining public trust in it. The very essence of the political process in a democratic system lay in the right to undermine the people's trust in the government: "Without the right to undermine trust in a government that derives its power from the people's trust, there is no freedom of political struggle. Without such a right, power ceases to be democratic

25. "Delo Stalina," *Rannee utro*, 17 April 1918, p. 3.
26. "V revoliutsionnom tribunale," *Zaria Rossii*, 17 April 1918; see also "Delo Martova," *Novyi den'*, 17 April 1918, p. 3.
27. Pleskov sent a protest to the Commissariat of Justice; see "K delu Martova," *Vpered*, 25 April 1918, p. 3.

and becomes tyrannical." Were the Bolsheviks prepared to recognize, asked Martov, that their power, which they claimed they had received from the soviets, was founded on the trust of the people? If the people withdrew their trust, would the Bolshevik government have the decency to resign?[28]

Stalin must have been lobbying behind the scenes for the top Bolshevik leaders' support for the annulment of the Moscow tribunal's verdict. The newspapers carried reports that some highly placed Bolsheviks were critical of the verdict, whereas others were reluctant to bring the matter to the floor of the CEC.[29] Stalin demanded that an end be put to the Menshevik slander and appealed to the CEC to reconsider the verdict. A mere reprimand was not enough. Was it not clear to everyone that Martov and his Mensheviks were slandering every aspect of Bolshevik policy? They should be taught a lesson.

The case was finally brought before the CEC on April 25. Some leading Bolsheviks who usually attended the sessions were absent—perhaps, as the opposition believed, because they wanted nothing to do with Stalin's action against Martov. In contrast to the previous hearings, no discussion of the matter took place on the floor of the CEC. Sverdlov, the chairman, hurriedly read a prepared resolution to the effect that the verdict of the Revolutionary Tribunal on the complaint of Stalin against Martov was annulled, and without letting anyone speak, he brought the resolution to a vote. The Bolshevik majority passed it without debate. The Menshevik faction had not expected such a gross violation of procedural rules. Martov rushed from his seat to the podium, demanding the floor. Sverdlov refused. "I demand the floor! Have the decency to let the accused speak!" shouted Martov. Clamor and whistles were heard from the Bolshevik benches. "Coward! Abject coward!" roared Martov, evidently at Stalin. Sverdlov rang his bell for order and declared to Martov, "I deprive you of the floor! I deprive you of the right to attend this assembly for three sessions!" Dan rushed to the podium and tried to speak, but his words could not be heard. Sukhanov, Abramovitch, and others from the opposition benches vehemently objected. The Menshevik faction walked out in protest.[30]

The turbulent session ended with a decision to try Martov again. Stalin must have felt satisfied. It appeared as though he and his supporters were finally in a good position to render a crushing blow to the Mensheviks. Curiously, however, Stalin's case against Martov was never retried.

---

28. Martov, "Pravo na 'podryv very,'" *Vpered*, 21 April 1918, p. 1.

29. "Delo Martova," *Vpered*, 21 April 1918, p. 2.

30. For the Bolshevik account of the proceedings, see *Protokoly TsIK*, pp. 196–97; for the Menshevik account (much more complete), see "TsIK: Delo Martova," *Vpered*, 26 April 1918, p. 2.

The Case of the Newspaper *Vpered*

A second major court battle between the Bolshevik government and the Menshevik opposition was getting under way at about the same time. It had no official connection with the dispute between Martov and Stalin, but the two cases together manifested a well-orchestrated attack on the Menshevik press.

This second case grew out of articles that had been published in *Vpered*, the central newspaper of the Menshevik party after the transfer of the capital to Moscow in March 1918. One of these articles, Dan's "Murder Will Out," criticized the Brest treaty in strong and sarcastic terms.[31] Dan wrote that the Bolshevik government was aiding German imperialism in its conquest of the Ukraine, and in return Lenin had been granted the "most august permission of the Kaiser" to rule over the remnants of Russia. Another article in the same issue, by E. Kaplan, accused the officials of the Soviet government of "shooting the workers, bribing counterrevolutionary elements, persecuting revolutionary organizations, executing with or without trial, and falsifying the voice of the electorate, just like the leaders of the Old Regime."[32] This time, the entire editorial board of the paper was charged with slander.

Even though Dan's article, like Martov's, had focused primarily on the Brest treaty, the court trial that followed avoided that issue almost entirely. Just as the charges against Martov concentrated on his derogatory remarks about Stalin, those against Dan took issue with his attacks on Bolshevik domestic policy.[33] The Bolshevik government could not easily strike out at critics of the Brest treaty, for there were too many of them, and they included the Left SRs and a part of the Bolshevik party itself, the Left Communists. The question of how to deal with the Menshevik critics was inevitably linked, therefore, with the factional struggles within the Bolshevik party. On the issue of the peace treaty, as we have seen, the Left Communists advocated war, as the Mensheviks did, although for different reasons. On the issue of the New Course in economic policy, however, the Left Communists were far removed from the Mensheviks, whose position was closer to that of the Right Bolsheviks. This complex framework of positions, attitudes, and aspirations partly explains the fluctuations and zigzags in the development of the two trials.

31. Dan, "Shila v meshke ne utaish'," *Vpered*, 3 April 1918, p. 2. The title of the article is actually a Russian proverb whose literal translation is "You can't hide an awl in a sack" (because it will poke through).

32. E. Kaplan, "Ukreplenie sovetskoi vlasti," *Vpered*, 3 April 1918, p. 2.

33. "Delo gazety *Vpered*," *Vpered*, 19 April 1918, p. 2.

The attack on *Vpered* was evidently intended to deflect attention from the Martov-Stalin affair, to demonstrate that it was not the defense of an individual that was paramount, but rather the defense of Bolshevik policies and of the government's prestige. The embarrassing twist in the Martov-Stalin case at the first and only session of the Revolutionary Tribunal for the Press put the Bolsheviks on the defensive. As a step toward recovery, the Commissariat of Justice—now headed by a Bolshevik, P. Stuchka, after the resignation of Shteinberg in the aftermath of the Left SRs' departure from the government in protest against the Brest treaty—ordered that, "for libelous agitation against the Soviet power," the editors of *Vpered* "be arrested immediately, that the paper be closed, if possible today, and that measures be undertaken to prevent its publication in the future under a different name."[34] This was the first time since the order for the arrest of Iraklii Tsereteli and Viktor Chernov in December 1917 that an agency of the Bolshevik government had called for the arrest of opposition leaders.

On April 18, just two days after Martov's moral victory, the members of the editorial board of *Vpered* (Dan, S. S. Kats, and Semenovich) were informed that a public hearing on the charges against them would be held on April 20.[35] The Mensheviks were convinced that the new drive against them was directed by those who felt themselves to have been humiliated by Martov. A trial of the top Menshevik leaders for libel against the Bolshevik government as a whole would have demonstrated that Stalin had been right when he asserted that the point was not only to defend his personal reputation.

The editorial board of *Vpered* also initiated a full-scale self-defense campaign.[36] Workers' rallies were held in various cities, and the charges against *Vpered* were circulated to generate public support.[37] Groups of workers sent petitions to the Revolutionary Tribunal asking to be put on trial as well, since they shared *Vpered*'s views.[38] Local Menshevik newspapers, entire local party organizations, and rank-and-file supporters all pledged solidarity with the newspaper's editorial board.

In an article published in *Vpered*, Dan posed what could be considered a provocative question to the tribunal: "If libelous agitation in Soviet Russia is punishable by law, will the tribunal provide assur-

34. This order was published in Dan, "Pokhod protiv RSDRP," *Vpered*, 16 April 1918, p. 2. For further details, see also "V Rossii: RSDRP na zashchitu," *Bor'ba*, 29 May 1918, p. 3.

35. Dan, "Delo gazety *Vpered*: Kak velos' sledstvie po nashemu delu," *Vpered*, 21 April 1918, p. 3.

36. Dan, "Chto skazal sud," *Vpered*, 19 April 1918, p. 1.

37. Concerning a rally in Tula, see "Tula," *Vpered*, 21 April 1918, p. 3.

38. "Svideteli po delu *Vpered*," *Vpered*, 19 April 1918, p. 2.

ances that nonlibelous agitation is allowed?"[39] Dan informed the tribunal that he would furnish documentary evidence that reports of shootings of workers by the Bolshevik authorities were not libelous, but true. The editorial board requested that these documents be put on record.[40] Vpered published a list of witnesses from various cities who were ready to testify that such shootings had taken place on numerous occasions.[41] "As a part of our nonlibelous agitation," Dan posed a series of questions to the Bolsheviks: Why had they sworn allegiance to the Constituent Assembly in October 1917 and disbanded it in January 1918? Why had they denounced secret treaties in October and concluded some secret deals of their own in March 1918? Why, after Trotsky had shouted more loudly than anyone else about governmental accountability in October, had the Bolsheviks still not produced a financial accounting of their government's expenditures during their six months in office? Where was their famous accountability, where responsible government, and where the promised bread?[42]

The theme of "betrayal of principles," on which the Bolsheviks had harped in October, was prominent in these questions. The trial was turning into a bitter confrontation between the Menshevik opposition and the Bolshevik government, something the Bolsheviks had not anticipated.

On April 20, the tribunal held its public hearing on the charges against Vpered. N. V. Krylenko, acting as public prosecutor, announced that the investigative commission had rejected Dan's demand that the documents on the alleged shootings of workers be admitted into evidence. The Menshevik defense responded that, in that event, there were no legal grounds for prosecution. "Is it not the right of those accused of libel," insisted Dan, "to prove that the facts in question are not libel?" Dan strove to prove, moreover, that the charges against Vpered, like the charges against Martov, did not fall under the jurisdiction of this tribunal. The Menshevik "libel" against the Bolshevik party, according to Dan's argument, could not be equated with a call to overthrow the Soviet power, since the Bolsheviks were not the only party in the soviets, and in fact the Mensheviks had won majorities in many city soviets. Would the Revolutionary Tribunal recognize that there was a difference between the Bolshevik party, as merely a ruling party, and the Soviet power?[43]

39. Dan, "Agitatsiia ne klevetnicheskaia," Vpered, 20 April 1918, p. 2.
40. "Delo gazety Vpered," Vpered, 25 April 1918, p. 3.
41. "Svideteli po delu Vpered," Vpered, 19 April 1918, p. 2; see also "Vpered pered sudom," Vpered, 20 April 1918, p. 2.
42. Dan, "Agitatsiia ne klevetnicheskaia," p. 2.
43. "Publichnoe zasedanie sledstvennoi kommissii," Vpered, 21 April 1918, p. 3. For the Bolsheviks' view of the case, see "Revoliutsionnyi tribunal: Delo Martova," Izvestiia, 17 April 1918, p. 3.

After prolonged consultations, the tribunal acknowledged that such a difference did indeed exist. In that case, went on Dan, had some legal privilege been accorded to the Bolshevik party, that it alone could criticize other parties but it could not be criticized in turn? "We demand an official statement from the Revolutionary Tribunal! Are all parties equal before the law in Soviet Russia? This is a very important question. If there is an incorrect ruling, all political struggle in Russia, any criticism of the ruling party, will be stopped." The chairman insisted that *Vpered* was charged with libeling the ruling party, and hence a state authority. "If public criticism of political parties in power is prohibited in Soviet Russia," Dan retorted, "is it not fair to ask whether the Bolshevik party has a right to criticize the party of the Left SRs, which officially, at least, is a coalition partner of the Bolsheviks?" Krylenko tried to evade the issue: "There is no need to go into all these legalistic subtleties. A mere decision of the government is sufficient to bring you to trial as counterrevolutionaries." The Mensheviks could be tried for any article in their paper, he argued. "Just look at their headlines! Not a single vote to the Bolsheviks!" Krylenko's words infuriated the Mensheviks: "Admit that you are trying us for political views! Give us a straightforward answer!" demanded Dan. "Do we have the right to engage in political agitation against the Bolshevik party?" The chairman, Tsivkinadze, admitted that everyone had such a right, insofar as the Revolutionary Tribunal did not find such activity criminal. Vaguely alluding to the Martov-Stalin case, Tsivkinadze explained that "insofar as libel is directed against an individual member of the government, it still is only libel. But if it is directed against the government as such, it is tantamount to an uprising. One may prepare an uprising by stockpiling arms or by preparing minds." Dan, in an impassioned speech, responded that the Social Democrats had always been preparing the minds of the people to resist any autocracy and would continue to do so. The Bolshevik tyrants would not be able to shut the mouths of the opposition. The tribunal adjourned without a decision.[44]

It was relatively easy for the Bolshevik leaders to brush aside criticism that they were choking the press, as long as it was the bourgeois press. "Workers' rule" could easily justify the closing of newspapers of "class enemies." It was much more difficult to justify an attack on the press of the socialist parties, whose representatives often won elections to the workers' and peasants' soviets. Furthermore, some Bolsheviks still found it awkward to repudiate publicly the ideal of a free workers' press, which they themselves had extolled only six months earlier. Out of moral conviction, concern for their political reputation, or political expediency, some Bolsheviks had a hard time bringing themselves to

---

44. "Publichnoe zasedanie sledstvennoi kommissii," p. 3.

agree to an outright ban on the socialist opposition press; hence all the vacillation, temporary bans, and fines. The tribunal's official statement confirmed the opposition's right to criticize the government publicly, but the Commissariat of Justice nevertheless ordered an outright ban on Vpered. Evidently no decision had yet been made at the top.

The Press Besieged

The trial of Vpered was never completed. A full explanation of why the attacks on the Menshevik leaders and their newspaper stopped precisely at the moment when reprisals and arrests seemed inevitable is not easy to come by, partly because we do not know exactly what political moves individual Bolshevik leaders undertook. Some facts are clear enough, though. It is notable that neither Lenin nor Trotsky took part in the accusations against Martov. Only Krylenko, Sosnovskii, and Stuchka publicly defended Stalin. Many Bolshevik leaders had known Martov for years in emigration, and it seems likely that they preferred to distance themselves from Stalin's efforts at revenge. Lunacharskii maintained friendly relations with Martov, and Kamenev and Rykov preserved friendly personal contacts with several Menshevik leaders. Zinoviev, the Bolshevik boss of the Petrograd commune, was on good terms with A. N. Ioffe, a prominent Menshevik leader in Petrograd. Riazanov had on numerous occasions interfered on behalf of the editors of opposition papers, and his energetic efforts had secured the release of many arrested Mensheviks. Most important, Lenin, despite his irritation over the unabating Menshevik criticism, spoke respectfully of Martov. On the other hand, many Bolshevik leaders of both right and left factions, as we have seen, at that time held views critical of their party's foreign and domestic policies. They might have seen reprisals against the Mensheviks as a roundabout attack on their own position. Thus the ties of the past and the political commitments of the present probably accounted for a sort of tolerance among certain Bolshevik leaders. These Bolsheviks apparently prevailed and turned the outcome of the CEC session into merely a tacit warning to Martov: Be more restrained in your political criticism.

Even those Bolsheviks who wanted to eliminate the Mensheviks altogether may have had little enthusiasm for continuing the trials. Stalin must have feared that the issue of calling witnesses might again generate a political storm. Furthermore, it was all too obvious that the public trials, from the point of view of Bolshevik interests, had turned out to be counterproductive. The reports of the proceedings had been published in all the newspapers; everyone's attention had been riveted on the trials. The Mensheviks had asked all sorts of disconcerting questions and used the publicity to discredit the government and to earn political capital. All this was very embarrassing, especially the testimony about the shootings of workers. Now the Menshevik opposition had a written statement from the Revolutionary Tribunal to the effect that agitation against the Bolshevik party was legal in Soviet Russia. Who needed this sort of thing at the height of the election campaign to the city soviets?

It was presumably for such reasons that the cases of Martov vs. Stalin and of the newspaper *Vpered* remained unsettled. Officially, the charges were not withdrawn, yet the trials were never reopened. The whole affair ended in a draw. Martov had won twice in the courts, but the CEC had annulled one of the verdicts without debate. The editorial board of *Vpered* was charged with libel, yet neither Dan nor any other member of the board was arrested at that date, as the Commissariat of Justice had demanded. Nevertheless, as compensation to the Bolshevik hard-liners, *Vpered* was closed down "forever" at the beginning of May. On May 10, while the editorial board was working on the edition of a successor newspaper, *Vsegda Vpered*, a detachment of the Cheka surrounded the building. At first, the editors were not particularly worried. This had happened before, and closings for a month or so, perhaps accompanied by fines, were things the Menshevik editors had gotten used to. This time, however, the Cheka men announced that no paper of the Menshevik CC under any title could be published. The editors replied that the Cheka had no business interfering in the newspaper's affairs, since it had been duly registered with the Commissariat of the Press and the editors had a permit for publication. The Cheka representative responded with a surprising and ominous announcement: "From now on, registration with the Commissariat of the Press is no longer valid." All newspapers in Soviet Russia were to be registered henceforth with the Cheka and all materials submitted to its office for preliminary censorship.[45]

In the course of the press trials in the spring of 1918, the status and the function of the courts in Soviet Russia changed profoundly. The Revolutionary Tribunal for the Press was abolished after it had ruled in Martov's favor. The verdict of the Moscow Revolutionary Tribunal was peremptorily overruled by the CEC. Censorship was re-established. By June 1918, more than two hundred socialist publications had been

45. The incident is described in "Zaiavlenie fraktsii Moskovskogo soveta ispolkomu," *Nash golos*, 13 May 1918, p. 1. For a Soviet source on the background of the adoption of this practice, in Finn, "Antisovetskaia pechat'."

closed.[46] The Cheka had taken over the duties of the Commissariat of the Press, the Commissariat of Justice, and the Revolutionary Tribunal for the Press, while continuing to function as a political police organization as well. The Cheka was also running the anti-profiteering detachments, forming requisition squads, and disbanding opposition soviets.

This pattern of events in Moscow was essentially replicated in the provinces. There, too, Menshevik criticism of Bolshevik authorities was followed by court trials, Menshevik acquittals, and eventually Cheka retribution. The Martov-Stalin case was only one manifestation of a general trend. The Bolshevik government could no longer rely on the courts in its struggle with the Mensheviks and SRs. As a result, it turned to an extralegal, party-controlled strike force to crack down on the opposition. Only later would this method be ideologically justified and incorporated into the Soviet institutional structure.

The Martov-Stalin case demonstrates how crucial institutional changes were made by way of behind-the-scenes lobbying and how personal relationships were intertwined with political positions. The opposition could no longer criticize an individual if he happened to have a high position in the Bolshevik party. A crucial precedent had been established: the reputation of a single party leader was taken under the protection of the party. Key Bolshevik leaders did not or could not hinder Stalin's maneuvering to avoid having the witnesses in his case summoned. The establishment of the facts was less important to most of them than an unconditional defense of their party, even if it involved a cover-up and altered the very nature of political institutions. Those Bolsheviks who in the 1920s would expend so much effort in attempts to halt Stalin's rise to supreme power had lent themselves to his ends in 1918 by placing the protection of individual influential Bolsheviks above adherence to the law. Furthermore, by consenting to a ban on the opposition press, they seriously narrowed the range of political criticism permissible in Soviet Russia. Their control over "their" Cheka would prove to be a poor guarantee of their own political independence.

The Mensheviks' approach during all of these trials was meticulously

---

46. The number is given as 205 in A. A. Goncharov, "Bor'ba sovetskoi vlasti s kontrrevoliutsionnoi burzhuaznoi i melkoburzhuaznoi pechat'iu (25 oktiabria 1917–iiul' 1918)," *Vestnik MGU,* Journalism Series 11, no. 4 (1969):16. The periodicals closed between October 1917 and July 1918 are listed in "Spisok gazet zakrytykh organami sovetskoi vlasti v 1917–1918 godu," appendix to Okorokov, *Oktiabr' i krakh russkoi burzhuaznoi pressy,* pp. 357–76 (a Soviet source), and *Rabochii klass pod bol'shevistskoi diktaturoi,* p. 17 (a Menshevik source). For a recent discussion of this process by a Western historian, see Jeffrey Brooks, "The Breakdown in Production and Distribution of Printed Material," in Gleason, Kenez, and Stites, eds., *Bolshevik Culture,* p. 152.

legalistic. They attempted to justify and defend their every step by the existing laws. This kind of response adumbrated their decisions later in 1918, when, despite the intensification of Bolshevik repressions, Martov would attempt to make his party abide by Soviet laws and stay out of anti-Bolshevik uprisings. He continued to try to avoid giving the Bolsheviks an opportunity, as he saw it, to escalate political struggle into violent confrontation, which he feared would only strengthen the Bolshevik dictatorship and weaken his party.

The trials in the spring of 1918 were only one facet of the mounting Bolshevik pressure on the Menshevik-SR opposition. A related struggle was taking place in the provincial city soviets.

CHAPTER 5

The Elections to
the City Soviets

In the course of the spring of 1918, the Mensheviks and SRs attempted to regain their majorities in the city soviets and in this way to oust the Bolsheviks from national power. Menshevik policy with respect to the soviets has been somewhat obscure. One can find documented statements asserting that the Mensheviks had withdrawn voluntarily from the soviets, or that they had withdrawn only from the executive committees (ECs) while remaining in the soviet assemblies, or that they wanted to destroy the soviets from within, or that they supported the soviets. The problem is that at different times in different places, different Menshevik factions pursued different political goals.

The predominant view in the scholarly literature on this period is that the Bolsheviks rather quickly consolidated their hold on mass revolutionary organizations, notably the soviets, thus creating the institutional foundations for the Bolshevik dictatorship.[1] This view resembles the one that now prevails in the Soviet Union, that the Bolshevik seizure of power in Petrograd was followed by a "triumphal march" of soviet power across Russia. As John Keep has shown, the process was not quite so simple.[2] Nevertheless, even Keep asserts elsewhere that "by January 1918 the dictatorship had consolidated its grip upon the country to such a degree that it could only have been overthrown by

---

1. See, for example, Hough and Fainsod, *How the Soviet Union Is Governed*, pp. 81–83.

2. Keep, "October in the Provinces," pp. 180–219.

external force. This achievement was due in large measure to the astute use which Lenin and his followers made of the spurious legitimacy conferred upon their government by the Soviets." According to Keep, the Mensheviks inadvertently helped the Bolsheviks by creating in the soviets a "quasi-governmental authority with immense political prestige, a machine which in other hands could serve as the infrastructure of a dictatorship strong enough to sweep them from the political scene." The Bolsheviks turned the soviets into "sounding boards" as an element in their manipulation of the masses through the "command structure."[3]

In January 1918, the majority of city soviets in Russia were indeed controlled by the Bolsheviks. A closer look reveals, though, that their majorities were unstable and that the Bolshevik-controlled soviets, not to mention those controlled by the opposition, were often at odds with the Bolshevik central authorities.

There has been much discussion as to whether the "triumphal march" of soviet power can be attributed to a high degree of public support for the Bolsheviks at the end of 1917. Haimson analyzed in detail the returns of the elections to the Constituent Assembly and on the basis of that evidence concluded that "the Central Industrial Region had been turning into a Bolshevik stronghold even before the War." At the time of the elections, he asserted, "however 'blindly' or 'passively,' the vast majority of the Russian workers had supported and probably still supported the Bolsheviks, and this sense, more than any other, held the Menshevik party in a paralyzing grip."[4]

On closer examination, however, it appears that many of these supporters were, as one observer put it, "Bolsheviks by temperament only."[5] Haimson mistook the workers' revolutionary fervor for a pro-Bolshevik stand. The thesis that the Bolsheviks had mobilized, won over, mastered, or controlled the workers', soldiers', and peasants' movements at the end of 1917 becomes increasingly hard to defend when one considers not only the October euphoria but also the development of these movements in the months afterward. If the masses were successfully mobilized by the Bolsheviks by the end of 1917, and if the Soviet regime was consolidated by the spring of 1918, what accounts for the electoral victories of the Mensheviks and SRs in the soviets and for workers' strikes, protests, demonstrations, and uprisings? How can one explain the formation in July 1918 of an SR–Right Menshevik government in the Volga-Urals area?

3. Keep, *Russian Revolution*, pp. 337, 152, 471.
4. Haimson, "Mensheviks after the October Revolution," pt. 1, p. 469; pt. 2, p. 205.
5. Farbman, *Bolshevism in Retreat*, p. 162.

In fact, social upheavals did not end in October 1917. They were only one manifestation of discontent. The anti-Bolshevik mass movements in the spring and summer of 1918 were propelled by the same kind of sentiment that earlier had taken the form of pro-Bolshevik activity. These two radicalisms should be seen as a single emotional phenomenon. Spontaneous popular anti-Bolshevik movements, which the Mensheviks and SRs attempted to lead, continued their zigzags throughout the civil-war years.

Unfortunately, the elections to the soviets in the spring of 1918 have been subjected to little scholarly analysis. Keep cites cases in which the Mensheviks walked out of regional soviets, indignant at the Bolsheviks' seizure of power,[6] and such examples have been widely interpreted as an indication that the Mensheviks abandoned the soviets to the Bolsheviks. But other authors have shown that the Mensheviks remained in the soviets and that the soviets remained multiparty institutions until July 1918.[7] In the dozens of Soviet books on the strengthening of soviet power and on the "petty-bourgeois" parties, one looks in vain for data on election returns. Most such books either fail to discuss the period altogether or omit any reference to Menshevik-SR victories in the elections. L. M. Spirin, for example, provides figures for the period from March to August 1918 on the average number of opposition-party members in the soviets.[8] Such averages, however, make little sense, since in April, the Menshevik-SR bloc won elections in one city after another, yet by August, these parties had been expelled from the soviets. Some Soviet sources, however, do mention in passing the election victories of the "petty-bourgeois" parties. For example: "The Right SRs and the Mensheviks had a predominant position [*rukovodiashchee polozhenie*] in some soviets. In the province and city soviets of Arkhangelsk, Orel, Briansk, Tambov, Izhevsk, and some others, the majority belonged to the SR-Menshevik counterrevolutionary elements."[9] A few Western historians, notably Oskar Anweiler and George Denicke, have mentioned several cities where the Mensheviks won the elections to the soviets.[10] In his pioneering book on this subject, Leonard Schapiro goes so far as to say:

> By the middle of 1918 the Mensheviks could claim with some justification that large numbers of the industrial working class were now behind them,

6. Keep, "October in the Provinces," p. 213.
7. Helgesen, *Origins of the Party-State Monolith*, pp. 139–40.
8. Spirin, *Klassy i partii v grazhdanskoi voine*, p. 174.
9. Akademiia nauk SSSR, *Sovety v pervyi god proletarskoi diktatury*, p. 300 (hereafter cited as *Sovety v pervyi god*).
10. Anweiler, *Soviets*, p. 229; George Denicke, "From the Dissolution of the Constituent Assembly to the Outbreak of the Civil War," in Haimson, ed., *Mensheviks*, p. 123.

and that but for the systematic dispersal and packing of the soviets, and the mass arrests at workers' meetings and congresses, their party could eventually have won power by its policy of constitutional opposition.[11]

Local Menshevik party organizations faced such a diversity of circumstances in various parts of the country in the spring and summer of 1918 that only a few generalizations can be made. The structure of local government, economic conditions and the supply of food, and the tactics of local leaders varied from province to province. Labor relations, the Brest treaty, food shortages, and the arbitrariness of local Bolshevik authorities were at or near the top of the political agenda in all cities. Yet the prominence of such issues, the significance of the electoral victories that the Mensheviks scored, and the power settlements that they had to face were remarkably varied. Since these differences reflected the sociopolitical peculiarities of the diverse regions, it is helpful to investigate the Mensheviks' experiences in the Central Industrial Region, the Black Earth Zone, the Upper Volga–Urals area, and the Lower Volga–Don area.

The Central Industrial Region

The Central Industrial Region consisted of seven provinces clustered around Moscow. Some had large industrial centers employing thousands of workers in metal industries (Tula) or textiles (Vladimir); others had very small worker populations. Representation in the local soviets varied immensely from city to city. Since the soviets were supposed to represent the dictatorship of the proletariat, the propertied classes had no voting rights. Even among those who were eligible to vote—workers, soldiers, and peasants—the principle of one man, one vote was not always practiced. The Bolshevik-controlled ECs often packed the soviet assemblies with representatives of "revolutionary organizations," changed the norms of representation, and refused to hold new elections. That the Mensheviks and SRs managed to win elections even in such conditions is explained partly by the feuding among the Bolshevik centers of power. Particularly in the smaller provincial capitals, the city soviets disputed the authority of the province soviets, and the MRCs fought with the local CPCs.

The social milieu in such places as Kaluga, Riazan, and Tver was dominated by merchants, artisans, and peasants engaged in trade. Whereas the issues of industrial relations and foreign policy tended to

11. Schapiro, *Origin of the Communist Autocracy*, p. 191.

predominate in the larger cities, where tens of thousands of workers were concentrated in huge plants, the key issues in the smaller provincial capitals were the corruption of local officials, the arbitrary use of authority, the breakdown of local government, indemnities imposed on the bourgeoisie, and requisitions from the peasants.

The pattern of party politics in Kaluga was typical of that in the smaller provincial capitals of the Central Industrial Region. After the Bolsheviks seized power on November 28, the Mensheviks walked out of the city soviet in protest. On December 19, following the example of the Bolsheviks in the capitals, those in Kaluga disbanded the city duma and the victory of soviet power in Kaluga seemed to be secured.[12] In January 1918, however, the decrees of the Kaluga Bolsheviks were already referring to a "catastrophic economic situation and mass closure of factories and plants," and complaining that the Menshevik paper, *Kaluzhskii rabochii* (*Kaluga Worker*), was urging the workers to "overthrow the soviet power."[13] In fact, the reports of the Kaluga Mensheviks to their central committee suggest that they had demanded that the Bolshevik commissars account to the soviet for their monetary expenditures, citing the fact that three of the commissars had already been tried for embezzlement.[14] The entire Menshevik soviet faction was promptly arrested, though all were released the next day. On May 9, the Kaluga Mensheviks appealed to their CC for help because the editorial board of the *Kaluga Worker* had been brought to trial.[15] The local Menshevik organization, headed by I. A. Golubev, reported that "this whole policy of suppressing dissent led the workers (railway workers particularly) to turn completely away from the soviet. The sessions are attended less and less often. Their desire to have nothing to do with the authorities is obvious."[16] According to a report of the local Bolshevik organizers to their CC, by the end of May 1918 there were only 139 Bolsheviks in the entire city (competing with approximately 100 Mensheviks); the number of Bolsheviks was declining, "the Red Army was disintegrating . . . and some Bolsheviks were ready to accept the Menshevik-SR slogan of [reconvocation of] the Constituent Assembly."[17] When the soldiers' section of the soviet disappeared with demo-

12. Partiinyi arkhiv Kaluzhskogo obkoma KPSS, *Ustanovlenie sovetskoi vlasti v Kaluzhskoi gubernii*, document no. 164, p. 231 (hereafter cited as *Ustanovlenie v Kaluzhskoi gubernii*).

13. Ibid., document no. 180, p. 252.

14. "Kaluzhskie rabochie i sovet rabochikh deputatov: Pis'mo iz Kalugi," *Novaia zaria*, 1 May 1918, p. 40.

15. "Kaluga: Sudiat partiiu Men'shevikov," Nik. Col. no. 6, box 1, file 12.

16. "Kaluzhskie rabochie," *Novaia zaria*, 1 May 1918, p. 40. For the names of other provincial Menshevik leaders, see "Iz materialov partiinogo soveshchaniia," *Partiinye izvestiia*, no. 8 (June 1918), p. 13.

17. *Ustanovlenie v Kaluzhskoi gubernii*, pp. 339–41.

bilization, the balance shifted in favor of the opposition, since the 3,500 workers overwhelmingly supported the Mensheviks. In a report to the Second International, the Menshevik CC listed Kaluga as a city where the party won the soviet elections.[18] The Soviet volume on this period in Kaluga says only that on June 8 the Bolsheviks "found it necessary" to expel the Mensheviks and SRs from the soviet.[19]

In Orekhovo-Zuevo, Vladimir province, the workers did not go through a stage of pro-Bolshevik radicalism. To be sure, after October the Bolsheviks had a majority in the city soviet. The workers were reluctant to proceed with the nationalization of factories, however, and the old administration remained in charge at the Morozov and other textile mills. Nevertheless, numerous Bolshevik committees constantly interfered in production matters, and the workers grew increasingly displeased. An opposition correspondent quoted one worker as saying, "It's turned out to be pretty bad. We have so many masters now that the Devil himself couldn't count them all. Earlier they [the Bolsheviks] were shouting that the administrative expenses were too high, and now the expenses of all those damned committees have increased fivefold. So many masters you can't feed them all!"[20]

There was no sharp confrontation in Orekhovo-Zuevo between the Menshevik workers and the Bolsheviks, as there was in some larger industrial centers. The first post-October elections to the soviet were set for February 1918 but were delayed until March because of a workers' boycott. When they were held, the correspondent continued, "the mood in the broad working masses [was] anti-Bolshevik. This was revealed particularly clearly during the new elections to the soviet. . . . The results for the ruling party turned out to be pitiful: the majority of those elected were SRs, Mensheviks, and nonparty delegates." At first, the Bolsheviks wanted to void the returns; then, since they feared that new elections would bring even worse results, "the matter was somehow settled," as the correspondent put it.[21] Apparently the new soviet was tolerated by the Bolsheviks for some time.

The power struggle in Kostroma is of particular interest as an example of the Bolsheviks' bewilderment over the election results and the attempts by some of them to reach an accommodation with the Mensheviks and SRs. In early 1918, the Kostroma Bolsheviks were not perturbed by the Menshevik-SR opposition. They had a comfortable

---

18. M. Gurevich, "O polozhenii v Rossii i o RSDRP. Oktiabr' 12, 1918," a report of the Menshevik CC to the Second International, Nik. Col. no. 6, box 1, file 13.
19. *Ustanovlenie v Kaluzhskoi gubernii*, document no. 233, p. 334.
20. A. Orlov, "V rabochem kotle: Orekhovo-Zuevo: Ot nashego spetsial'nogo korrespondenta," *Zaria Rossii*, 11 May 1918, p. 1.
21. Ibid.

majority in the city soviet, and as late as March 1918, at the regional congress of soviets, the small Menshevik-SR faction did not represent a formidable force. The Bolshevik commissars reported proudly on the achievements of "socialist construction," particularly in the struggle with the bourgeoisie: 3 million rubles had been raised in tributes and indemnities.[22] On March 28, the city duma was disbanded and the supremacy of the soviet ensured.[23] However, drastic deterioration of the economic situation and a threat of famine in April and May sharpened the interparty struggle.

At a mass rally on May 23, election day, a Menshevik speaker, A. N. Diakonov, blamed the Bolshevik EC for a breakdown in the food supply.[24] Famine was no longer a threat but a reality. Bread riots had erupted in the neighboring towns. The Mensheviks called for the relaxation of state control over bread prices, in order to induce peasants to sell, and for the lifting of a ban on workers' travel out of town to purchase food. These measures would temporarily improve the situation, but the long-term solution, they insisted, lay in regaining the trust of the peasants and restoring the market, banking, credit, and duma procurement agencies: in a word, rebuilding what the Bolsheviks had destroyed in the previous seven months.[25] The food-supply crisis had become perhaps the major issue in the elections to the city soviet. On May 25, the city's Bolsheviks announced: "Comrades! The elections to the soviet of workers' deputies have just ended. Workers of all enterprises have expressed their will and elected the soviet to which they have given all power in the city. The elections gave the majority to the Mensheviks and Right SRs!"[26]

It was a peculiarity of the power struggle in Kostroma that the Bolshevik EC and the Menshevik-led soviet settled on a short-lived truce. Though the Menshevik faction in the soviet was now at twice its preelection strength,[27] the Bolsheviks did not disband the soviet. They did, however, refuse to relinquish their seats on the EC, which was supposed to be controlled by the soviet. In protest, the Mensheviks withdrew their delegates from the EC.[28] Thus the Bolsheviks controlled

22. Arkhivnyi otdel Upravleniia vnutrennikh del Kostromskogo oblastnogo ispolkoma, *Ustanovlenie sovetskoi vlasti v Kostrome,* document no. 195, pp. 260–63 (hereafter cited as *Ustanovlenie v Kostrome*).

23. Ibid., document no. 198, p. 266.

24. Soboleva, *Oktiabr'skaia revoliutsiia,* p. 290.

25. The Menshevik policy on the supply crisis was summarized in "Postanovlenie Moskovskogo biuro Moskovskoi oblasti RSDRP ot 29 maia 1918 goda, 'O golodnom dvizhenii,'" *Novaia zaria,* 10 June 1918, pp. 42–44.

26. *Ustanovlenie v Kostrome,* document no. 239, p. 305.

27. Nemov, "Pis'mo iz Kostromy," *Novaia zaria,* 10 June 1918, pp. 57–58.

28. *Ustanovlenie v Kostrome,* document no. 239, p. 301.

the EC, the Mensheviks the soviet assembly. Needless to say, the orders of the two bodies were in conflict.

In their announcement of the election results, the Bolsheviks admitted that "the Bolsheviks and the Left SRs have formed the city EC and have taken power without a majority in the soviet. . . . Since the events of May 23, we speak to the Mensheviks and Right SRs no longer as comrades but in the language of power."[29]

The Kostroma Bolsheviks seem to have been divided on how to react to the Menshevik-SR electoral victory. At a closed meeting of the Kostroma EC, some Bolsheviks said that since the majority had voted for the Mensheviks and SRs, the Bolsheviks should relinquish power without further struggle. Other speakers suggested a compromise: let the Bolsheviks keep half of the seats on the EC and offer the other half to the opposition parties.[30] These contradictory views were reflected in a resolution approved at the meeting. On the one hand, the resolution suggested that the Mensheviks should take over the EC if they considered that the working masses were behind them; on the other, the same resolution declared martial law in Kostroma and urged the Cheka to undertake measures against "counterrevolution": "all actions against the soviet power" were to be "suppressed by force of arms."[31] The Bolsheviks considered themselves to be the embodiment of soviet power, and they could not comprehend that the actions of a majority in the soviet against the Bolshevik EC could hardly be considered actions against the power of the soviets. Street processions were banned, and violators were threatened with execution on the spot.[32]

The Bolsheviks were obviously surprised that the election in Kostroma had brought them defeat. It was hard for the idealistic among them to come to terms with the need to preserve power by naked force. But in June the signs of hesitation were gone. As in other cities, the Cheka began to play the key role in local politics.

Naturally, the Menshevik and SR leaders attempted to organize resistance to the imposition of martial law. Following the examples of Petrograd and Tula, they called on the workers to elect delegates to a workers' assembly of *upolnomochennye*, or "fully empowered representatives," since the Bolsheviks refused to honor the results of the soviet elections. This appeal prompted a Cheka raid on the office of the local Menshevik paper and the arrest of its editor.[33] The Menshevik

---

29. Ibid., pp. 305–6.
30. "V Kostrome," *Nashe slovo*, 26 May 1918, p. 4.
31. *Ustanovlenie v Kostrome*, document no. 236, pp. 301–3; see also Soboleva, *Oktiabr'skaia revoliutsiia*, p. 290.
32. "V Kostrome," *Nashe slovo*, 26 May 1918, p. 4.
33. "Rabochii klass pod bol'shevistskoi diktaturoi," Nik. Col. no. 6, box 1, file 12.

newspaper in Moscow reported the arrests of members of the local SD committee and charged that "the authorities have declared a campaign against the Social Democrats."[34] Thus the peaceful competition between the Bolshevik authorities and the Menshevik-SR bloc in Kostroma had run its course by June 1918.

The political struggle in Riazan revolved around the imposition of indemnities on the local bourgeoisie. In contrast to Orekhovo-Zuyevo, where most of the workers were concentrated in fairly large factories, most of the 127 enterprises in Riazan were artisans' shops.[35] The indemnities therefore affected a fairly large stratum of the population and amounted in the eyes of many voters to plain robbery. Anti-Bolshevik sentiment was intensified by misuse of the "expropriated funds" and by a feud between the city soviet and the MRC, which, as Lenin said, "considers itself independent of the soviet and imposes its own taxes without accounting to the soviet."[36] The Mensheviks and SRs pointed out in the election campaign that the city duma had managed its finances much better than had the "vanguard of the proletariat."[37] The duma was disbanded on April 1, 1918, but the Bolsheviks' opponents won a majority in the elections to the soviet.[38]

In Tver, the corruption and high-handedness of the Bolshevik commissars were prominent issues. The commissar of city defense, A. Abramov, was notorious for his arbitrary killings. He even arrested the commissar of labor, Baklaev.[39] On March 26, A. Abramov was himself arrested. Such incidents certainly must have compromised the local administration in the eyes of the voters. No less important was the effect of the sharply deteriorating economic situation. Increasing numbers of workers were being laid off at Tver factories. A Petrograd newspaper published by the printers' union reported that the Mensheviks and SRs received a majority in elections to the city soviet, though data recently published in the Soviet Union indicate a Bolshevik majority.[40]

At the end of May, workers at Tver's three main factories went on strike, demanding a return to free trade, recall of the Constituent As-

34. "Aresty, obyski, i zakrytie SD gazety v Kostrome," Iskra (newspaper of Menshevik CC), 29 June 1918, p. 3.

35. Elufimova, "Pervye meropriiatiia bol'shevikov," pp. 108–24.

36. "Rech' po finansovomu voprosu na zasedanii TsIK, 18 aprelia 1918 goda," in Lenin, Polnoe sobranie sochinenii, 36:226–27.

37. "Riazan'," Vpered, 21 April 1918, p. 4.

38. Arkhivnyi otdel Riazanskogo oblispolkoma, Bor'ba za ustanovlenie i ukreplenie Sovetskoi vlasti v Riazanskoi gubernii, document no. 162, p. 186; Gurevich, "O polozhenii v Rossii."

39. "Abramovskaia epopeia," Novaia zaria, 1 May 1918, p. 36.

40. "Vybory v sovet," Utro Petrograda, 8 April 1918, p. 2; Novyi den', 9 April 1918, p. 2 (see also Gurevich, "O polozhenii v Rossii," p. 2); Perepiska Sekretariata, 3:168.

sembly, and the creation of a new government. Angry workers would not listen to the Bolsheviks.[41] These actions led to the imposition of martial law, as in Kostroma. The martial-law resolution of the extraordinary session of the Tver province EC, approved on June 1, 1918 (but omitted from later Soviet histories on the events in Tver), is a remarkable document. Its militant language reveals the intensity of the Bolsheviks' fear of losing their power. The resolution banned all meetings and processions, established an 11 P.M. curfew, annulled all identification cards issued before the introduction of martial law, and ordered all citizens to register with their local committees within twenty-four hours. Possessors of firearms were to be summarily executed. Perhaps the most extreme provision came in paragraph 6: "All robbers, bandits, instigators, suborners, and all those who foment the overthrow of soviet power will be executed on the spot."[42]

These political maneuverings in the smaller provincial capitals of the Central Industrial Region have certain similarities but also significant differences. The Bolsheviks' response to the opposition's victories varied from reluctant acceptance of the election results, at least initially, to abrupt imposition of martial law. Increasingly repressive measures posed acute problems for both local Menshevik leaders and the CC in Moscow. What should local party organizations strive to accomplish after a soviet in which they had won a majority had been disbanded? Right Mensheviks had always been reluctant to pin their hopes on a victory in the soviet elections.[43] Profoundly hostile to the Bolsheviks, they had warned that the Bolsheviks would not abide by the election returns. What was necessary, they argued, was independent workers' organizations strong enough to force the Bolsheviks to relinquish power. There was no unanimity among the Mensheviks as to exactly what role such workers' assemblies were to play. The center-left Mensheviks felt the task of these groups was to ensure fair elections to the soviets, a precondition for future reconvocation of the Constituent Assembly. In this connection, the Menshevik CC wrote to the local organizations:

> Agitation for elections to such assemblies should be recommended wherever the struggle for new elections to the soviets encounters insurmountable obstacles and wherever some local events set the masses in motion, giving us an opportunity to shape and organize the new tendencies that

41. "Trevozhnoe polozhenie v Tveri," *Novaia zhizn'*, 25 May 1918.
42. "Postanovlenie chrezvychainogo sobraniia Tverskogo gubernskogo ispolnitel'-nogo komiteta, 1 iiunia 1918 goda," *Izvestiia Tverskogo soveta*, 4 June 1918, p. 1.
43. See, for example, Liber's resolution at the May 1918 Menshevik party conference, "Sovety i nasha taktika," *Novaia zaria*, 10 June 1918, pp. 86–88.

demonstrate that the masses are beginning to pull away from the Bolshevik utopias.[44]

Such workers' assemblies played a crucial role in Tula. Tula's political life was centered in the two huge armament plants, which employed some 40,000 workers.[45] The city's Menshevik organization had a solid following among the local workers, even in the October days. The Bolsheviks seized power only in December 1917.[46] Even then they encountered a Menshevik-SR majority in the city soviet (143 vs. 117).[47] In the following months, when the Bolsheviks had secured control over the soviet, the Mensheviks concentrated their efforts on organizing a workers' assembly of upolnomochennye, which quickly became a rallying point for discontent and a counterweight to the Bolshevik soviet. The organizers in Tula were following the example of their comrades in Petrograd, where an assembly of upolnomochennye was to become a national center of workers' opposition to the Bolsheviks.

Initially the Tula assembly dealt with such problems as unemployment, wages, and strike funds.[48] In March, however, these issues were overshadowed by the turmoil over the Brest treaty, which, with its provisions for disarmament, was not popular with the workers of the armament plants: they feared that the Germans would demand that production at the plants be stopped. The Mensheviks responded to these fears by calling on the workers to arm themselves and to be ready to repel a German offensive.[49] The Bolsheviks, who had signed the "sellout at Brest," could not be relied on to organize the defense of the country. The workers would form a People's Army, to be armed with weapons manufactured in Tula. Everyone would be eligible to join; universal arming of the people had always been part of the program of Russian Social Democracy. The Bolsheviks had betrayed that principle by creating their elite units of Red Guards.

The Menshevik initiative threw the local Bolsheviks into panic. Hectic correspondence with Moscow ensued. The People's Army would be a Menshevik army, they feared. In addition, the workers' assembly was gaining authority and now demanded new elections to the soviet (which had not met for two months), to take place not later than April 13.

44. A. A. Troianovskii, "Sovety i rabochie konferentsii," *Partiinye izvestiia*, nos. 6–7 (May 1918), pp. 4–6.

45. Arkhivnyi otdel UVD Tul'skoi oblasti, *Uprochenie sovetskoi vlasti v Tul'skoi gubernii*, pp. 378–79.

46. Arkhivnyi otdel UVD Tul'skoi oblasti, *Oktiabr' v Tule*, p. 316.

47. "Po tsentral'noi oblasti: V polose terrora," *Novaia zaria*, 22 April 1918, p. 32.

48. "Stroptivye Men'sheviki, Tula," *Vpered*, 16 April 1918, p. 4.

49. G. Baturskii, "Sredi rabochikh," *Delo*, no. 2 (7 April 1918), pp. 16–17.

Focusing on the issues of the economy, Brest, and the structure of local authority, the Tula Mensheviks defined the tasks of a new soviet in the following platform:

> 1. Organization of the working class; 2. struggle for re-establishment of the democratic republic; 3. struggle for the reconvocation of the Constituent Assembly, and of all bodies of local self-government; 4. a number of planned measures against unemployment and supply breakdown; 5. organization for the defense of the country against the invasion of the imperialist hordes.[50]

I. I. Akhmatov, a local Menshevik leader and member of the CC, invited Dan to come to Tula to campaign for the party. The local Bolsheviks likewise requested help from their CC, bringing a comment from the secretariat that it was "necessary . . . to send an energetic comrade with a big name to Tula. . . . There is a serious Menshevik danger in Tula."[51]

Shortly after the Menshevik-SR victory, the soviet was disbanded, the local Menshevik newspaper was shut down, and several Menshevik leaders were arrested.[52] The workers' assembly remained, however. In mid-May, the premises of the Menshevik party committee were raided, the Menshevik-run workers' club was vandalized, and more arrests were made. There were casualties.[53] The Moscow Menshevik newspaper Vpered charged that the organizer of the assault was one V. L. Paniushkin, who in April had been wanted for murder in Petrograd and had disappeared with the help of the Cheka. He was said to have gone on a "business trip" (komandirovka) to Tula. The nature of his "business" now seemed clear.[54] Even before the assaults of mid-May, the popular mood had turned sharply against the Bolsheviks, the local Mensheviks reported: "The working class, except for a tiny minority, is leaning away from the Bolsheviks. These feelings sometimes reach such intensity, especially when they cannot be vented, that our comrades have to work very hard to contain them within the bounds of the organized struggle."[55]

---

50. "Tula," Novaia zaria, 22 April 1918, p. 46.
51. Perepiska Sekretariata, 3:168 (document no. 206).
52. Gawronsky, Bilanz des Russischen Bolschewismus, p. 45. The author was an SR representative at the Second International. The Menshevik-SR victory is reported in Gurevich, "O polozhenii v Rossii." See also Aksel'rod to the leaders of the European Socialist parties, 10 November 1918, Nik. Col. no. 16, box 1, file 13, and N. A. Roslavets, "Deiatel'nost' Tul'skogo gubispolkoma i ego otdelov," Vlast' sovetov, no. 1 (January 1919), p. 15.
53. "Razgrom Men'shevikov v Tule," Novaia zhizn', 18 May 1918, p. 3.
54. Martov, "Kto on?" Vpered, 21 April 1918, p. 2.
55. "Tula i Tul'skaia guberniia: Iz partiinogo otcheta," Novaia zaria, 1 May 1918, p. 52.

In Yaroslavl, as in Tula, the SD organization had solid support among the workers even during the October wave of radicalism. The repressive Bolshevik measures against the Menshevik leaders had started somewhat earlier there than in other cities.[56] As early as December 1917, the MRC had attempted to arrest B. V. Diushen and M. M. Ravich, respectively secretary of the local Menshevik organization and editor of its newspaper, *Trud i bor'ba*.[57] Both were Menshevik candidates for the Constituent Assembly and members of the city duma and of the city soviet. The key issue in Yaroslavl was undoubtedly the Bolsheviks' industrial policy.

Rising unemployment, rampant inflation, and approaching famine gave the Mensheviks the opportunity to reiterate that the Bolsheviks' hectic nationalizations and confiscations were at the root of the economic catastrophe.[58] The Mensheviks and the SRs argued that only through cooperation, labor-business partnership, and political democracy could the problems be resolved. The thrust of this campaign was directed against what they perceived as a Bolshevik-inspired *pugachevshchina* masquerading as "socialist construction." Diushen and I. I. Shleifer reported to the CC that the number of Menshevik-sponsored resolutions adopted by Yaroslavl workers had greatly increased. Inspired by this success, the Menshevik faction in the soviet three times introduced a motion to hold new elections. Each time, however, the Bolshevik majority blocked the proposal. Shleifer was arrested three times, but each time he had to be released. On March 29, the commander of the Red Guards, Rubtsov, published an announcement: "Those who are spreading Menshevik counterrevolutionary literature will be shot on the spot."[59] The Menshevik newspaper was closed. Rubtsov's severity, however, not only failed to silence the Mensheviks but added vigor to their campaign. A Central Bureau for New Elections to the soviet was set up. The Mensheviks emphasized that Rubtsov's Red Guards were not in practice accountable to the soviet, although in theory it was supposed to hold all power. The soviets were being turned into bureaucratic state agencies, argued the Mensheviks, whereas they should continue to be independent proletarian organiza-

56. "V provintsii: Pod bol'shevikami. Ot nashego korrespondenta," *Novyi luch'*, 22 December 1917, p. 4.
57. For short biographies of Diushen, Ravich, and other leaders of the Menshevik organization in Yaroslavl, see the brochure (with photos) *Nasha platforma i nashi kandidaty v Uchreditel'noe sobranie*, Nik. Col. no. 200, file 5. For data on the Yaroslavl Menshevik organization, see Ravich papers, Nik. Col. no. 200, file 5, "Iaroslavskii komitet RSDRP."
58. Solomon Shvarts, "Kapitalizm i sotsializm," *Delo*, no. 2 (7 April 1918), p. 4.
59. I. B. Rybal'skii, "Iaroslavskii proletariat na skam'e podsudimykh," pt. 1, *Vpered*, 24 April 1918, p. 2.

A campaign poster produced by the Yaroslavl Social Democratic party organization in preparation for the elections to the Constituent Assembly. Under the headline "Firm authority in the hands of the people," the poster introduces "our candidates." Boris I. Nikolaevsky Collection, Hoover Institution Archives, box 200, file 5.

tions defending workers' rights. The Mensheviks pledged to restore accountability, to put an end to requisitions and indemnities, and to hand over the management of municipal affairs to the city duma. The long-term solution to the country's problems could lie only in the reconvocation of the Constituent Assembly.

The harder the Bolsheviks tried to postpone the elections, the more the idea of holding new elections became an issue in itself. Finally the

Bolsheviks yielded, apparently realizing that delay was only playing into the hands of the Mensheviks. The elections were held on April 9, with the result that the Mensheviks won 47 of the 98 seats, the Bolsheviks 38, and the SRs 13.[60] The new soviet opened its first session in a tense atmosphere. The roll call for chairman produced 60 votes for Shleifer.[61] But then, after some fruitless bargaining over seats on the EC, the chairman of the province soviet, the Bolshevik Dobrokhotov, declared the elections void and the present soviet illegal.[62] The Mensheviks and SRs refused to leave the building. The Red Guards were called in. Holding hands, the Mensheviks and SRs tried to resist being dragged out one by one. In the end, the soviet was disbanded and the building locked up, and Shleifer was arrested again.[63] At first it looked as though the Bolsheviks had managed to disband the Menshevik-SR soviet, as they had the Constituent Assembly, without much trouble. But trouble was yet to come.

The Menshevik and SR soviet delegates aroused the whole town. The news that the soviet had been disbanded quickly reached the factories. Overnight, a conference of workers' upolnomochennye in defense of the soviet was formed, and several strikes were declared.[64] At this point the Bolsheviks made another mistake. Instead of trying to find some accommodation with the striking workers, the MRC published an order threatening to fire the strikers.[65] Three hundred printers were in fact fired. On April 15, Yaroslavl was paralyzed by a general strike.[66] Even workers who had voted Bolshevik protested the dismissals. The strike spread to the railway workers in Rybinsk.[67]

The Bolsheviks decided to back down. New elections were scheduled to take place between April 20 and April 30. Apparently in order to counter the impression that they were on the defensive, the Bolsheviks staged a trial of Shleifer and other Menshevik leaders on April 18.[68] The Mensheviks again turned the Bolshevik offensive to their own advantage. A large demonstration was held and workers marched through the city to the courthouse. The Bolsheviks could hardly make a

---

60. "Dans le royaume des commissaires; (1) Qu'est-ce passe a Iaroslavl'?" *Echos de Russie*, nos. 20–21 (1 September 1918), p. 18.

61. N. Rostov, "Poslednie razgromy, razgony, rasstrely," *Novaia zaria*, no. 1 (22 April 1918), p. 39.

62. "V Moskovskoi oblasti: Iaroslavl'," *Vpered*, 13 April 1918, p. 4.

63. "Iaroslavl'," *Partiinye izvestiia*, nos. 6–7 (1918), p. 29.

64. Rostov, "Poslednie razgromy," p. 39.

65. "Sovetskaia vlast' protiv rabochikh: Iaroslavl'," *Vpered*, 21 April 1918, p. 4.

66. G. D. Kuchin, "Zadachi i puti proletarskogo dvizheniia," *Novaia zaria*, no. 1 (22 April 1918), p. 24.

67. "Iaroslavl'," *Partiinye izvestiia*, nos. 6–7 (1918), pp. 29–30.

68. Rybal'skii, "Iaroslavskii proletariat," pt. 2, *Vpered*, 25 April 1918, p. 2.

case for a Menshevik counterrevolution to that audience. All those who had been arrested were released on the spot, to the cheers of the crowd.

As expected, the new elections ended in another victory for the Menshevik-SR bloc. The Mensheviks received 4,786 votes, the SRs 1,014, and the Bolsheviks 2,688.[69] Most of the nonparty delegates joined the Menshevik-SR faction, which controlled the assembly. This soviet was also disbanded, however. Martial law was declared and all protests were ruthlessly suppressed.[70] The cycle of strikes and lockouts continued, culminating in the famous Yaroslavl uprising in July (to be discussed in chapter 9).

The Black Earth Region

The political atmosphere of the southern provinces differed in several respects from that of the Central Industrial Region. First, in the aftermath of October, the Bolsheviks enjoyed a certain measure of social support in the industrial cities, but the southern provinces remained strongholds of the SRs and the Mensheviks. The Bolsheviks did not manage to seize power in Kursk until February 1918; in Voronezh, they had only 24 of the 120 seats in the soviet; and in Tambov, they had only 3 seats at the end of 1917.[71] Second, the southern provinces, unlike the northern and central ones, did not suffer from a grain shortage. On the contrary, the grain surplus in these provinces became a bone of contention between local Bolsheviks and the emissaries from Moscow. The local Bolshevik leaders did much to prevent or slow down shipments to the north. Thus the struggle of the Mensheviks with local Bolsheviks paralleled the region's friction with Moscow. Third, the proximity of the front lines of the war contributed to the instability in the region. The issue of the peace treaty certainly enhanced the Menshevik-SR appeal to the electorate, since these provinces were threatened by a continuing German offensive. Finally, the sociopolitical profile of the local Menshevik leaders differed significantly from that of their party comrades in the industrial region. In such cities as Tula the Mensheviks were closely attuned to the political life of huge factories and were accustomed to dealing with thousands of workers, but there were no large plants in such places as Orel. Here politics was

---

69. "Iaroslavl'," *Vpered*, 10 May 1918, p. 2. The Menshevik victory in the elections is also mentioned in *Sovety v pervyi god*, p. 308, but not in Partiinyi arkhiv pri Iarovslavskom oblastnom komitete KPSS, *Ustanovlenie sovetskoi vlasti v Iaroslavskoi gubernii*.

70. "Dans le royaume des commissaires," p. 18.

71. Keep, "October in the Provinces," pp. 200–201.

centered in the city duma and in a number of affiliated economic, cultural, and administrative organizations. Most of the local Mensheviks were not worker-organizers; they belonged to the provincial socialist intelligentsia. They were teachers, physicians, statisticians, and the like.

The reports of local Mensheviks to the CC in Moscow show that they were shocked to see the results of their efforts to improve education, medicine, and agriculture being ruined, as they believed, by the Bolsheviks. Their experience and lifelong commitments led them to believe that the radicalized Bolshevik soldiers would only mismanage and wreck the local economy. Thus the peace treaty, the local economy, the breakdown of administration, and later the issue of grain requisitioning stood at the center of local politics. A Menshevik reporter wrote in April 1918: "All over Orel province we see the same picture: financial breakdown, only the remnants of economic agencies; those in power have no credit, no authority with wide masses of the populace; a socioeconomic crisis is imminent."[72] The Bolsheviks had disbanded the duma in Orel, continued the report, but had soon run out of money. Shortly thereafter, the city went bankrupt. The soviet, controlled by the Bolsheviks, voted to raise funds by imposing a tribute on the bourgeoisie. Six million rubles were raised in this fashion, but that did not solve the economic problems. The local Menshevik organization—headed by E. Kogan, a physician and the editor of Delo Sotsial Demokrata, and V. Pereverzev, who had been chairman of the Orel soviet until November 25, 1917—started to campaign for new elections to the soviet. Whereas in Tula the Mensheviks had the support of a powerful workers' assembly, in Orel they had only the disbanded city duma. Economic normality could be achieved, argued the Mensheviks, if management of the city's affairs were returned to the duma. The new city soviet should work with the city duma, as it had done before October.

Elections to the Orel soviet took place in mid-May. The Menshevik-SR bloc won 162 seats, including the 100 nonparty delegates who joined it at the first session.[73] The Bolsheviks and their sympathizers won 62 seats and the Left SRs 20. A familiar denouement followed. The soviet was disbanded, the Menshevik leaders D. Glukhov and Volubaev

---

72. Novaia zaria, 22 April 1918, p. 62.

73. It is noteworthy that the official history of the establishment of Soviet power in Orel does not mention the Menshevik-SR victory; see Partiinyi arkhiv Orlovskogo obkoma KPSS, Bor'ba trudiashchikhsia Orlovskoi gubernii. Other Soviet sources, however, do mention it—e.g., Malashko, K voprosu ob oformlenii odnopartiinoi diktatury, pp. 144–45; Sovety v pervyi god, p. 300.

Рисунокъ Яка.

„Самоопредѣленіе" Самарской конки.

A cartoon in the Samara provincial satirical journal *Gorchichnik*, January 1918: "Self-determination of the Samara horsecar." Russian Serials Collection, Hoover Institution Archives.

were arrested, and, as in other cities, the cycle of violence continued.[74] On May 15 the SR newspaper *Delo naroda* informed its readers that "disorders took place in Orel. The soviet asked Trotsky to send in troops. In soviet circles here it is said that the movement in Orel is directed by the city duma, which was disbanded after October."

Meanwhile, disbandment of the duma, elections to the soviet, and social unrest were also roiling the political waters in neighboring Voronezh. The official Soviet history of the struggle for soviet power in that city contains only one brief mention of the soviet elections; it does not say which party won.[75] In Kursk, according to a Menshevik source, the soviet as well as the SR-led duma was disbanded in April by Bol-

74. "Die Bolschewiki und die Arbeiterbewegung," *Stimmen aus Russland*, 1918, nos. 4–5 (15 August 1918), citing *Iskra*, 13 June 1918, p. 15.

75. Partiinyi arkhiv Voronezhskogo obkoma KPSS, *Bor'ba za sovetskuiu vlast' v Voronezhskoi gubernii*, pp. 258, 451.

shevik marauders.[76] Also in April, an anti-Bolshevik rebellion broke out. Local Bolsheviks complained in a letter to Moscow that they had no forces of their own; there were only 100 Communists in the entire province of Kursk, and only 20 of them were workers.[77] In the judgment of a Soviet historian, "the position of the Mensheviks and SRs in Orel and Kursk provinces was strong."[78] Soviet power had to be propped up in Kursk by the troops of Commissar Nikolai Podvoiskii.[79] Yet the situation remained unpromising. Almost in despair, a local Bolshevik wrote that "the EC's position is such that you want to lock everything up and leave. . . . There are no factories, the trams are not running, trade is banned, and there are no funds."[80]

In Tambov, as in other cities of the Black Earth Region, the Bolsheviks could not seize power for several months. They were quite outspoken at that time about their problems (although their revelations did not find their way into Soviet histories). At a regional conference of Bolshevik commissars in Saratov, the Tambov delegates Zinger and Zatuzov enlightened their colleagues on the difficulties in Tambov:

> "Of course, we wanted to shake up the old soviet, but we had to reckon with the hostility of the Tambov population toward the Bolsheviks. . . . As a result, we decided to lie low. . . . In view of the great imbalance of forces, the struggle would have led nowhere. All this made us tolerate the old soviet of the Mensheviks and SRs. We had no forces; no help came from Moscow. Then we decided to try another way: to isolate the city soviet. . . . As Petrograd sent the Tambov soviet no funds, it was finally forced to recognize the power of the people's commissars by a vote of 73 to 72."[81]

This frank description is a rarity. It suggests that the Bolsheviks at the time were openly debating their scheming and plotting, not only against the dumas or the "bourgeoisie" but also against the soviet, even when, as in this case, they knew it had been supported by the electorate. The problems of the Tambov Bolsheviks did not end, however, with the seizure of power. A feud between the province soviet and the city soviet enabled the Mensheviks and SRs to press for new elections to the city soviet.

In February, according to a report by three special emissaries dis-

---

76. "Razgon trekh sovetov i gorodskoi dumy: Kursk," *Vpered*, 13 April 1918, p. 4.

77. "Doklad o sushchestvovanii i deiatel'nosti Kurskogo ispolnitel'nogo komiteta," *Vlast' sovetov*, no. 25 (7 November 1918), p. 33.

78. Malashko, *K voprosu ob oformlenii odnopartiinoi diktatury*, p. 144.

79. *Kurskaia guberniia*, p. 322.

80. "Doklad . . . Kurskogo ispolnitel'nogo komiteta," *Vlast' sovetov*, no. 25 (7 November 1918), p. 33.

81. "Zasedanie oblastnogo s''ezda kommissarov finansov," *Izvestiia Saratovskogo soveta*, 31 March 1918, p. 1 (cited hereafter as *Izv. Sar. sov.*).

patched by Deputy People's Commissar of Internal Affairs M. Latsis—later to hold a high post in the Cheka—the Mensheviks and SRs had a majority in the Tambov city soviet, but the province soviet was controlled by the Bolsheviks. The province soviet, the emissaries said, had "lots of enthusiasm, but not enough experienced personnel, a lack of intelligentsia. Untrustworthy . . . measures are being undertaken."[82] These measures were part of a struggle between the soviets of the province and the city. On March 1, the province soviet ordered that the city soviet be disbanded. The city soviet, however, not only did not submit to force but called on the Red Guards to defend it. On March 8 the province soviet shelled the city soviet. The Bolshevik minority in the city soviet, apparently resentful of the province soviet's grab for power, joined in the Menshevik-SR effort to repel the attack. Finally an agreement was reached whereby power in the city would be exercised by a newly elected city soviet.

The key issue in the election campaign was the Brest treaty. The Mensheviks reiterated the official position of the party that the treaty would not stop the German advance. The fact was that the Germans were continuing to move eastward in the supposedly independent Ukraine, conquering one province after another. "Where are the guarantees," Martov asked at the Fourth Congress of Soviets (being held in Moscow at the same time), "that the Germans will not march to the north?"[83] It was an embarrassing question for the Bolsheviks. Menshevik pamphlets pointed out, not without sarcasm, that the Bolsheviks were brave enough to fight against their domestic political opponents but not against the Germans.

Focusing on the issues of the peace treaty and the local economy, the election campaign brought an overwhelming victory to the Menshevik-SR bloc, which received three-fourths of the seats in the soviet assembly.[84] Soon it became apparent that the Bolshevik minority in the city soviet had made a secret deal with the province soviet at the expense of the Mensheviks and SRs. Changing sides, the local Bolsheviks agreed to expel the Mensheviks and SRs from the city soviet and take "all power."[85] At the first session of the newly elected soviet, the Bolshevik faction, now backed by the province soviet, demanded seven of the twelve seats on the EC. Naturally, the Menshevik-SR bloc refused, and

---

82. "Doklad emissarov Kommissariata Vnutrennikh Del," *Vestnik Kommissariata Vnutrennikh Del*, no. 9 (April 1918), pp. 12–13.

83. Martov, "Rech' na chetvertom s"ezde sovetov," *Vecherniaia zvezda*, 16 March 1918, p. 4.

84. I. Lazarev, "Razgon Tambovskogo soveta," *Vpered*, 13 April 1918, p. 2.

85. "Doklad emissarov," *Vestnik Kommissariata Vnutrennikh Del*, no. 9 (April 1918), p. 13.

the Bolsheviks walked out. The session continued, though, because the remaining delegates numbered more than the required quorom. An EC composed entirely of Mensheviks and SRs was elected, and a debate on the soviet's policy began. But the building was surrounded by the forces of the province soviet, and armed men burst inside. One of the Menshevik leaders later wrote to a Moscow Menshevik newspaper that at that point he asked the commander, "Where is your mandate? This must be a mistake! This is the session of the city soviet!" The commander of the detachment pulled out his gun and snarled, "This is my mandate!"[86] The agents of Latsis telegraphed, "The atmosphere in the city is tense. The rightist soviet is disbanded."[87] When the soviet attempted to meet again the next morning, it was confronted with a proclamation: "The soviet is disbanded forever! The time has come to establish not the power of the soviets but the dictatorship of the revolutionary parties."[88] The Menshevik and SR delegates to the soviet retreated to the railway station and convened there under the protection of armed workers.[89]

Thus the pattern of events in Orel, Voronezh, Kursk, and Tambov suggests that in the aftermath of October, the Bolsheviks' political priority was to oust the Mensheviks and SRs from the organs of local government. Lacking the manpower to run the local governments, the Bolsheviks turned to the radical soldier soviets, which took "all power," absorbing the smaller workers' soviets. By the spring of 1918, as the soldiers left for home, most of these soldier soviets disintegrated. A skeleton crew of Bolshevik zealots remained. The policy of "stifling the bourgeoisie" with indemnities set the majority of the population in these trade-oriented cities against the Bolsheviks, who found themselves embattled and isolated. The most prominent difference between the interparty struggles here and in the industrial centers was that in the Black Earth Region the dumas, in some cities intact until May, rather than the assemblies of upolnomochennye, played the crucial role of rallying centers for popular discontent. The reports of Latsis's agents reveal clearly what was at stake. If the Mensheviks and SRs continued to control the local soviets in addition to the dumas, how were the Moscow Bolsheviks to consolidate their power in the provinces? However, militant "local autocrats," such as the Tambov Bolsheviks, resisted pressure from the Moscow Bolsheviks. In May 1918, when the food-supply situation in the central provinces was critical,

86. Lazarev, "Razgon Tambovskogo soveta," p. 2. See also "Razgon Tambovskogo soveta," _Novaia zhizn'_, 11 May 1918, p. 4.

87. "Doklad emissarov," _Vestnik Kommissariata Vnutrennikh Del_, no. 9 (April 1918), p. 13.

88. "Po tsentral'noi oblasti," _Novaia zaria_, no. 1 (22 April 1918), p. 34.

89. Lazarev, "Razgon Tambovskogo soveta," p. 2.

the Tambov Bolsheviks proclaimed their province a consumer rather than a producer of food, though it was common knowledge that it had large stocks of provisions.[90] The Tambov Bolsheviks seem to have been more concerned with securing their own dictatorship than with "constructing socialism" or carrying out the orders of the Moscow Bolsheviks. The Menshevik and SR political strength, however, made the unruly Bolsheviks dependent on financial and military help from Moscow. As a result, the Moscow commissars were able little by little to assert control.

The Upper Volga–Urals Region

The Menshevik-SR bloc also did very well in the soviet elections in the cities of the Upper Volga and the Urals. The Volga basin had been a traditional stronghold of the SRs. In the grain-producing provinces of Samara, Saratov, Penza, and Simbirsk, the SRs were clearly the leading partner in the coalition; in the industrial centers—Nizhnii Novgorod, Viatka, and some cities in the Urals—the Mensheviks were dominant. In the course of the spring and early summer, the bloc won a majority in Nizhnii Novgorod, Tsaritsyn, Kazan, and presumably Saratov (as we shall see), and a parity with the Bolsheviks in Simbirsk.[91] In Kazan, the Menshevik-SR bloc held 180 seats, the Bolsheviks only 27.[92] In Penza, the Left SRs abandoned their Bolshevik partners and joined the Menshevik-SR bloc.[93]

Farther north, the Bolsheviks did not do any better. The Mensheviks and SRs won the city soviet elections in Vologda, and in Arkhangelsk they had majorities in both the city and the province soviets.[94] The Bolsheviks were much disturbed by these outcomes and what they portended. The Arkhangelsk Bolsheviks reported to their CC: "The new election of the local soviet has been fixed for June 15 owing to strong agitation by the Right SRs and the Mensheviks. All indications are that they would have a majority." To try to salvage the situation, the comrades from Arkhangelsk proposed more Bolshevik agitation and the dispatch of Red Army units of reliable Letts.[95]

90. "Kto sabotiruet?," *Delo naroda*, 17 May 1918, p. 4.

91. *Sovety v pervyi god*, p. 300.

92. On elections to the soviet in Kazan before the city was taken by the Komuch forces, see "Kazan'," *Rabochii internatsional*, no. 11 (14 August 1918). On the takeover of Kazan by the Komuch forces, see V. Arkhangel'skii, "Kazan' vo vremia bor'by s Bol'shevikami," *Volia Rossii* (Prague), nos. 8–9 (1928), pp. 267–85, and no. 10 (1928), pp. 135–55.

93. "Peints par eux-mêmes," *Echos de Russie*, nos. 20–21 (1 September 1918), p. 2.

94. Gurevich, "O polozhenii v Rossii"; *Sovety v pervyi god*, p. 300.

95. *Perepiska Sekretariata*, 3:274.

An almost complete run of the *Izvestiia* of the Saratov soviet for 1918 in Western libraries offers a unique opportunity to follow in detail the developments in post-October politics in a provincial capital in the Volga region. Bolshevik nationalizations and requisitions, the Menshevik critique, elections to the soviet, and an anti-Bolshevik uprising—all these familiar elements are encountered in Saratov; however, the case of Saratov illustrates, better than others, the process of interaction between the ruling and opposition parties during that brief period of multiparty competition in the soviets in the first half of 1918.

During the first three months of soviet power, the leaders of the Menshevik faction in Saratov—B. N. Guterman, V. Diakonov, and Abramovitch—faced few major obstacles in their criticism of Bolshevik socialism in the soviet. The Bolshevik leaders, V. A. Antonov, chairman of the soviet, and I. V. Mgeladze, seemed to be preoccupied with world revolution rather than with the Saratov Mensheviks. This was a time of heady declarations, denunciations of world imperialism, and speeches full of pathos. Several hundred workers' representatives, assembled in the soviet, enthusiastically applauded the Bolshevik speakers as they spoke of the victory of the socialist revolution in Russia; they applauded with equal enthusiasm as their Menshevik opponents called for unity among all socialists. Indeed, an observer might have noted elements of theatricality in the sessions of the soviet assembly. The atmosphere started to change in March 1918, when the serious issues of unemployment, financial breakdown, and the Brest treaty forced the soviet to come down from the clouds to the mundane business of governing Saratov.

As in other cities, the Menshevik-SR faction in the soviet focused its critique on Bolshevik economic policy. Dimant (SD), Belin (SR), and others pointed out that the nationalization of housing had turned out to be a financial burden for the city, and that the nationalization of the banks was destroying monetary circulation, since the merchants and peasants were keeping banknotes at home. The catastrophic economic situation in a basically grain-rich province, they asserted, was caused by the Bolsheviks' "quasi-socialist" experiments.[96] Many Bolshevik speakers described the problems in not dissimilar terms. At a regional conference of Bolshevik finance commissars, for example, the speaker from Saratov complained that nationalizations had resulted in an unbearable financial burden for the city: "Now we have to finance the railroad, city maintenance, and the detachments struggling with counterrevolution. . . . We have to provide loans for the army units and

96. This and all other proceedings of the Saratov soviet appeared under the title "Sovet rabochikh i krestianskikh deputatov," in *Izv. Sar. sov.*, 13 April 1918, p. 1.

factories. We had to pay a million rubles to the garrison in order to save [garrison] property from plunder and theft!"[97] In order to finance all these projects, the Bolsheviks seized thirty people from the business community as hostages and demanded that the Saratov bourgeoisie pay ten million rubles as an indemnity.[98]

Against this background, an election campaign opened in early April. *Izvestiia* explained in an editorial:

> Like any constitutional power, and particularly as a socialist power, the soviet must be re-elected from time to time so that it reflects the will of the toiling masses. For the first time since October, such elections are scheduled here in Saratov. At the factories and plants, two elements of our social life will be competing with each other: the Bolshevik and the Menshevik. By the will of the masses, the Bolsheviks have power. Recently, however, the Mensheviks have been trying to regain their strength, exploiting some failures of the soviet power. They want to challenge the Bolsheviks at the coming elections![99]

The Bolsheviks at this point did not dispute the right of the opposition party to challenge them at elections. This was still described as normal practice under soviet power. Only with the successes of the opposition would the Bolshevik reasoning change.

In addition to criticizing the requisitions, the Menshevik campaign focused on two specific issues. The first was the common workers' complaint that they could purchase food only from the Bolshevik-run agencies. The second revolved around the so-called obligation (*povinnost'*), as the Mensheviks sarcastically called the practice of conscription into the Red Guards.[100] The workers resented the conscriptions and the city Council of Trade Unions was not pleased to have its members turned into auxiliaries of the police agencies. Menshevik pressure did succeed in halting the conscriptions. Meanwhile, the Bolsheviks, fearing that they would lose the elections, changed the electoral rules.[101] The new procedures allowed either secret or open balloting; open balloting would obviously make it more difficult to cast a protest vote. Furthermore, in addition to the delegates elected directly at the factories, the trade unions—but only those that supported soviet power, that is, the Bolsheviks and Left SRs—were given separate representation, and the

97. "Zasedanie oblastnogo s"ezda kommissarov finansov," *Izv. Sar. sov.*, 31 March 1918, p. 1.

98. "Sovet ... deputatov," *Izv. Sar. sov.*, 13 April 1918, p. 1. See also *Khronika revoliutsionnykh sobytii v Saratovskom povolzh'e*, p. 249.

99. "K predstoiashchim vyboram v sovet," *Izv. Sar. sov.*, 16 April 1918, p. 1.

100. "Po Rossii: Saratov," *Vpered*, 25 April 1918, p. 4.

101. The rules were printed in *Izv. Sar. sov.*, 14 and 16 April 1918.

political parties that supported soviet power automatically received 25 seats in the soviet. Needless to say, these rules heavily favored the ruling parties. Nevertheless, the campaign proceeded without the scenes of violence that had shaken other cities. The Saratov Mensheviks invited Mark Liber, soon to be a member of the Menshevik CC, to come from Moscow and campaign for their candidates. At numerous workers' rallies, Liber, Epshtein, and other Mensheviks vied for the workers' support with Antonov, Mgeladze, and other prominent Bolsheviks.[102]

On April 30 the new soviet assembled. No data on its exact composition are available; however, the absence of jubilant articles in the Bolshevik press, its wrath at the voting of the nonparty faction, and the statements of the Mensheviks at the end of May suggest that the opposition, aided by the nonparty delegates, had a majority.[103] As we have seen, in many other cities the nonparty delegates joined the Mensheviks and SRs. In Saratov, their support was apparently crucial, as Izvestiia intimated on May 25:

> At the recent elections to the soviet, a large group of nonparty delegates was elected. Who are they? . . . In reality, in their voting behavior the nonparty delegates break down into certain party factions. . . . A rather considerable part of the nonparty delegates at the recent sessions of the soviet turned out to have a very partisan attitude toward the soviet parties [i.e., Bolsheviks and Left SRs]. Hiding under their nonparty status, these citizens wholeheartedly voted with the Right SRs and the Mensheviks and turned out to be "nonparty" Mensheviks and SRs.

The Bolsheviks undertook a number of reprisals against their opponents. On May 13, a wave of strikes broke out, and on May 17 there was an uprising of Red Army soldiers (as we shall see in chapter 9).

A Menshevik-led workers' movement that was more radical than that of Saratov battled the Bolsheviks in Nizhnii Novgorod. A huge complex of plants in the suburb of Sormovo, employing some 20,000 workers, dominated Nizhnii politics. Menshevik and present-day Soviet sources provide identical accounts of the general direction of politics there. According to a Soviet historian, there were 6,000 Bolsheviks in Nizhnii in March 1918; by summer, fewer than 3,000 remained. Conversely, the provincial congress of local Menshevik organizations reported in March "a noticeable increase in our influence."[104]

102. For a report on these rallies, see "V saratovskikh masterskikh," *Izv. Sar. sov.*, 8 April 1918, p. 4.
103. Victory for the anti-Bolshevik faction was reported in *Den' Vladivostoka*, 9 May 1918.
104. Spirin, *Klassy i partii v grazhdanskoi voine*, p. 124. See also "Po tsentral'noi oblasti," *Novaia zaria*, no. 1 (22 April 1918), p. 36.

Front-page headlines in *Izvestiia* of the Saratov soviet, 24 May 1918. The first line of this Bolshevik election appeal reads: "There is no longer any place for Mensheviks and SRs in the Soviet." In bold type: "Comrades, hurry to correct your mistake. Recall these bandits from the Soviet." Newspaper Collection, Hoover Institution Archives.

Some of the grievances of Sormovo workers were reminiscent of complaints in other cities—the heavy-handed ways of local commissars, food shortages, and the like. One issue, however, received particular attention. The Sormovo plants, producing steel and locomotives, were owned by a powerful group of financiers and industrialists, headed by Aleksei Meshcherskii.[105] In March 1918 the Bolshevik government held discussions with Meshcherskii's group concerning their proposals for the reconstruction of Russian industry. No agreement was reached, but the discussions did not pass unnoticed. The Menshevik press in the capitals seized upon the occasion to debate the Bolshevik change of heart in relation to the industrialists in the context of the New Course. The Menshevik leadership welcomed the Bolshevik call for an end to the "Red Guards' attack on the bourgeoisie" and asked when the attacks on the socialists would end as well.[106] Locally, the Mensheviks and SRs related workers' grievances to the broader context of the Bolshevik negotiations with the industrialists on the one hand and suppression of workers' organizations on the other. Their leaders, N. Bykhovskii and I. G. Upovalov, demanded new elections to the soviet. A. Troianovskii, soon to be a Menshevik CC member, came to Nizhnii to campaign for the party and spoke at a huge rally under a banner reading "All power to the Constituent Assembly!"[107]

The Bolsheviks tried to delay elections, but an outbreak of strikes forced them to give way. N. Bykhovskii reported that the election returns had brought 21 seats in the EC of the new soviet to the Mensheviks and SRs and 18 to the Bolsheviks and Left SRs—an exact reversal of the representation in the old EC, which had been elected in October 1917.[108] I. G. Upovalov later related that the new EC soon discovered that less than half of the 275,000 rubles levied on the bourgeoisie could be accounted for. The Bolsheviks not only declined to make an accounting but refused to hand over power to the new majority.[109]

The Bolsheviks' defeat in Nizhnii was so alarming that Moscow sent a special envoy to investigate. He reported that "the Bolsheviks lost

105. Aleksei Meshcherskii was at the time an important figure in the Moscow Council of People's Economy. For his contacts and negotiations with the Bolsheviks, see P. N. Kolokol'nikov, "Podpol'naia koalitsiia," *Delo*, no. 3 (14 April 1918), pp. 2–3. (Kolokol'nikov, a Right Menshevik, had been a high-ranking official of the Ministry of Labor in 1917.) See also Aleksandr Martynov, "Bol'shevistskaia natsionalizatsia promyshlennosti," *Vpered*, 14 April 1918, p. 1.

106. Dan, "Pokhod protiv RSDRP," *Vpered*, 16 April 1918, p. 2.

107. *Sovety v pervyi god*, p. 306.

108. N. Bykhovskii, "Perevybory soveta rabochikh deputatov," *Vpered*, 16 April 1918, p. 4.

109. I. G. Upovalov, "Kak my poteriali svobodu," *Zaria*, no. 2 (1922), cited in Bernshtam, ed., *Nezavisimoe rabochee dvizhenie*, document no. 75, p. 273.

part of their popularity in Sormovo because of the dwindling of supplies and the good organization of anti-Bolshevik propaganda by the workers' organizations of the Right SRs and Mensheviks." The envoy urged the eighteen Bolsheviks and Left SRs on the EC to retain "all power," promising aid from Moscow.[110] The Menshevik-SR majority was not prepared to concede power without a fight.

Local politics in Samara during the spring of 1918 followed a pattern more typical of small provincial capitals of central Russia. Constant feuding among the Bolshevik organizations was the chief source of troubles in the city. In May the Brotherhood of Sailors declared war on the MRC. After street fighting had gone on for several days, the sailors approached the Menshevik workers, and offered them an alliance against the MRC.[111] The Mensheviks refused, perplexed by the offer, since a few days earlier the Brotherhood had condemned the Mensheviks and SRs as counterrevolutionaries. At a rally at the tube works, the Mensheviks called on the plant's 5,000 workers to take prompt action, because the authorities had, "in the name of the working class, disbanded workers' rallies and opened fire on workers' assemblies, as has also happened in Tula, Kaluga, and Kovrov. In the name of the proletariat, all civil liberties were abolished."[112] The local Menshevik party organization, headed by Belov, introduced a resolution to recall the seventy-two workers' delegates from the soviet and fix a date for elections to an independent workers' assembly of upolnomochennye.[113] The resolution was passed, but on June 8, before elections could be held, Bolshevik authority in Samara was overthrown by the Czech legion and the SR underground, and the government of the Committee of the Constituent Assembly (the so-called Komuch government) was established.

A peculiarity of industrial geography in the Volga-Urals region was that a large plant was often located in a small town. Naturally, the political life of such towns was dominated by these large plants. Such industrial centers sometimes were more important politically than the provincial capitals. This was the case in the industrial towns of Izhevsk and Votkinsk, in Viatka province. In early 1918 the Izhevsk armaments plant employed more than 30,000 workers. The wave of Bolshevik radicalism did not affect the Izhevsk workers to the same extent as it did the Petrograd workers. Menshevik and especially SR influence re-

---

110. "Doklad v Kremle o sobytiiakh v Sormove," *Vecherniaia zvezda*, 21 May 1918, p. 3.
111. Zalivchii, "Likvidatsiia besporiadkov v Samare," *Vecherniaia zvezda*, 21 May 1918.
112. S. Mikhailov, "Sozyv rabochei konferentsii, Samara," *Vpered*, 23 April 1918, p. 4.
113. "Sozyv rabochei konferentsii v Samare," *Novaia zaria* no. 2 (1 May 1918), p. 62.

mained strong among these workers, most of whom were local people with their own houses and often a small plot of land.

The Bolsheviks came to power in Viatka province only in January 1918, just when the plants' production was drastically curtailed.[114] Many workers were laid off. The opposition parties naturally blamed the Bolsheviks. In elections to the Izhevsk soviet in February 1918, the Menshevik-SR bloc, together with the nonparty delegates, won a majority.[115] A Menshevik, A. I. Sosulin, was elected chairman of the EC. While returning home after a session of the EC, Sosulin and a colleague, Stepan Naslegin, were ambushed and shot. Sosulin was killed and Naslegin wounded.[116] On the following day, February 20, another newly elected member of the soviet, V. I. Buzanov, who had been an SR delegate at the Constituent Assembly, was attacked and wounded. The Bolsheviks refused to honor the election results and insisted on new elections in May, at which they were soundly defeated: only 22 Bolsheviks were elected out of 170 delegates.[117] The Menshevik-SR bloc had an overwhelming majority and elected Buzanov chairman of the new soviet. This soviet was disbanded as well.[118]

In the EC formed in Zlatous following elections there, the Bolsheviks held three seats, the Menshevik-SR bloc nine, and nonparty delegates nine. The chairman elected by the Menshevik, SR, and nonparty votes was arrested and the soviet disbanded. On March 17, Red Guards occupied the city and made numerous arrests.[119] A Menshevik-SR victory was reported at the Motovilikha steel mill, not far from Perm.[120] In Ufa, the Mensheviks and SRs also had success in the soviet elections; according to a Soviet historian, "railway workers, under the influence of antisoviet agitation, disarmed the Bolsheviks and came out to greet the Czechoslovaks."[121] In Syzran, the newly elected soviet, with a Menshevik-SR majority, was disbanded and its chairman arrested.[122]

The extent of Bolshevik repressions in the wake of lost elections seems to have been much higher in the Urals than in the Central Indus-

---

114. "Doklad delegata Piatogo Vserossiiskogo S"ezda Sovetov S. I. Kholmogorova Narodnomu Kommissariatu Vnutrennikh Del o politicheskom polozhenii na Izhevskom zavode," cited in Bernshtam, ed., *Ural i Prikam'e*, p. 279.

115. Ibid., p. 280. For a non-Bolshevik source, see "Iz-za ugla," *Delo naroda*, 28 March 1918, p. 1.

116. "Iz-za ugla," *Delo naroda*, 28 March 1918, p. 1.

117. "Doklad delegata," in Bernshtam, ed., *Ural i Prikam'e*, p. 280.

118. Spirin, *Klassy i partii v grazhdanskoi voine*, p. 263. See also *Sovety v pervyi god*, p. 308.

119. Dioneo, *Russia under the Bolsheviks*, p. 11.

120. "Kurze Nachrichten aus dem Alltagsleben im 'Kommunistischen' Russland," *Stimmen aus Russland*, nos. 4–5 (15 August 1918), p. 31.

121. Malashko, *K voprosu ob oformlenii odnopartiinoi diktatury*, p. 145.

122. "Razgon Syzranskogo soveta," *Vpered*, 28 April 1918, p. 2.

trial Region. Arbitrary arrests, executions of political opponents without trial, and beatings and even public whipping of arrested workers were reported as early as March. A correspondent of a Menshevik newspaper reported shootings of workers by the Bolsheviks in Nizhnii Tagil, Beloretsk, Kizel, Zlatous, and other industrial towns.[123] Particularly brutal were the actions of the Bolsheviks at the Berezovskii plant, near Ekaterinburg. On May 9, at a workers' protest rally, speakers condemned the Bolshevik commissars for appropriating the best houses in town for themselves and for spending funds (150,000 rubles levied on the bourgeoisie) without an accounting. They called on the commissars to come to the rally and answer these charges. Instead, the commissars sent the Red Guards, who opened fire on the workers. Fifteen people died. The next day the Bolsheviks declared martial law and warned that "persons who agitate against soviet power and those detained after seven in the evening will be shot without mercy."[124] On May 10, five people were executed; on May 11 and 12, six more; and on May 13, another two.

By June, clashes between Bolsheviks and workers in many cities were turning into uprisings and armed struggle. Led by the SRs and Right Mensheviks, these uprisings were successful in numerous places, especially when they were backed by the Czech-SR military formations of the Committee of the Constituent Assembly.

The Lower Volga, Kuban, and Don Region

In the vast nonindustrial area of the lower Volga, Kuban, and Don, the Menshevik-SR bloc was a significant but not a decisive factor in local politics. Here, too, the Mensheviks scored victories in soviet elections, where they were held; but the political weight of the soviet and the outcome of the power struggle varied from city to city. The region as a whole, however, was distinguished by three characteristics. First, in contrast to the industrial, Black Earth, and Volga-Urals provinces, a broad spectrum of political and military forces competed for power. Besides the Mensheviks, the SRs, and the local Bolsheviks, the forces vying for power included Cossacks, White volunteers, Germans, itinerant anarchist bands, and armed detachments of Bolsheviks from Moscow. Second, the local feuds among the Bolsheviks and between the Bolsheviks and their Left SR and Communist-anarchist allies at-

123. "Vesti s Urala (ot sobstvennogo korrespondenta)," *Novaia zhizn'*, 8 May 1918, p. 4.
124. "Po Rossii: Berezovskii zavod na Urale (ot sobstvennogo korrespondenta)," *Novaia zhizn'*, 1 June 1918, p. 4.

tained here the proportions of open warfare. Third, the shaky Bolshevik regime in some cities of this region was a military one, established in the wake of a military conquest.

The case of Rostov-on-Don is the prototype of the political trajectory that many Russian cities were to follow later in the civil war. After October 1917, the Bolsheviks briefly seized power in Rostov. Even Martov admitted that they enjoyed popular support at first. Soon afterward, however, Martov wrote, "The Bolshevik methods generated a strong reaction, and the workers have abandoned the Bolsheviks." A government under General Kaledin of the Cossack forces was established in the Don region, but Martov, citing reports from B. S. Vasil'ev, the leader of the Rostov Mensheviks (and in 1917 chairman of the city duma), asserted: "The workers who used to be Bolsheviks declared that 'we will comply neither with the orders of the Don government nor with those of the people's commissars. We recognize only the authority of the Constituent Assembly and, until its convocation, that of the city duma.' "[125] The Menshevik chairman of the Rostov soviet, M. B. Smirnov, assured Martov that the workers overwhelmingly supported the Mensheviks.

In February 1918, Bolshevik troops entered Rostov. A unique document, the minutes of the proceedings of a session of the city soviet held on February 15, 1918, reveals the complexity of the political struggle in the city.[126] The issue that triggered stormy debate in the assembly was the assumption of two commissars sent from Moscow that they had the right to carry out searches, requisitions, and executions. The secretary of the local MRC, M. I. Ravikovich, complained that there was a "dual power" in the city. Moscow's commissars, V. A. Antonov (Ovseenko) and Voitsekhovskii, had declared themselves to be the supreme power in Rostov, but the MRC recognized that power only insofar as it did not violate the MRC's policy. Ravikovich claimed that Voitsekhovskii had threatened to arrest the members of the MRC and had begun to censor its newspaper. Vasil'ev suggested that the conflict between the MRC and the Moscow commissars should be seen against the background of the executions, raids, and arrests then being carried out. "Who has the right to do that?" he asked. All power in the city was supposed to belong to the soviet. Ravikovich retorted that Antonov had told him, "Truly, power belongs to the soviet, but your soviet is no good and we will disband it!" Another local Menshevik leader, Aleksandr Loker-

125. Martov, "Rol' partii proletariata," *Novyi luch'*, 22 December 1917, in Nik. Col. no. 6, box 2.
126. All of the following quotations from speeches at this session are taken from "Istoricheskoe zasedanie Rostovo-Nakhichevanskogo na Donu soveta rabochikh deputatov," Nik. Col. no. 6, box 2.

man, declared that in the interests of the workers, a concerted effort to repulse the Moscow commissars should be made. Ravikovich agreed that Rostov did not need "governor generals" from Moscow. The Mensheviks declared that they were ready to support the MRC in its struggle with the commissars.

Passions flared after a speech by a commander of the workers' detachment from Petrograd, E. A. Trifonov, who had arrived under Voitsekhovskii's command. Trifonov said he had witnessed numerous killings of innocent people on the way from Petrograd to Rostov, and he added that he was afraid that he might be killed himself "by a hired assassin" for having reported what he had seen to the soviet. There were shouts from the floor—"Bolshevik murderers! Scoundrels! There is blood on your hands!" The session adjourned in a highly tense and emotional atmosphere.

The rivalry among the Bolshevik organizations did not abate in the following weeks. Administrative authority simply ceased to exist, while control of the streets constantly changed hands. One band of "revolutionary" soldiers from the MRC would declare another band of "revolutionary" soldiers to be counterrevolutionary and would then seize "power." These rotating "powers" were virtually indistinguishable from one another. They all imposed indemnities, raided the bourgeoisie, assaulted the Menshevik-SR clubs and newspapers, and fought each other. Indemnities, requisitions, confiscations, "socializations," and raids often amounted to plain robbery. Whole railway trains were stopped, passengers searched, and possessions "socialized." The bands were often referred to as Red Hundreds (*Krasnosotentsy*).[127] The Mensheviks' sharpest attacks were directed against the Brotherhood of Revolutionary Cossacks and Sailors, a band notorious for its raids on the bourgeoisie. One of its chief political slogans was "Kill all the bourgeoisie and the Jews!" and it warned that it was preparing for a "St. Barthelomew's night" (*Varfalomeevskaia noch'*) in Rostov against the bourgeoisie.[128]

The local Mensheviks complained that all these "ruling" bands called themselves Bolsheviks, Communists, Anarcho-Communists, Left Revolutionary Socialists, and the like, thus discrediting socialists of all persuasions. The Mensheviks believed that anarchism was the outcome of the degeneration of Bolshevism, and indeed, most anarchists were former Bolsheviks. The Mensheviks accused the Bolsheviks of having perverted the whole idea of socialism by appealing to the lowest instincts of the masses.[129] "Seize! Loot! Overthrow!"—these

127. Spiridonova, *Otkrytoe pis'mo.*
128. Lokerman, *74 dnia*, pp. 60–61, 71.
129. Editorial, "V roli partii poriadka," *Vpered*, 14 April 1918, p. 1.

were the Bolsheviks' slogans. When they requisitioned luxury goods, perfume, and women's clothing from a Rostov store, the Mensheviks sarcastically asked, "Is this necessary for the suppression of the bourgeoisie or for the strengthening of socialism?"[130] New elections to the soviet, they claimed, would end the artificial Bolshevik majority. They appealed to the trade unions, the departments of the city duma, and the soviet itself. As in other cities, the Menshevik platform called for a decisive struggle with the anarchists and the restoration of a popularly elected city government. Elections were held, and the returns brought the Mensheviks a majority in the city soviet.[131]

The Mensheviks' victory could have ended tragically for them. It turned out that the Bolsheviks were planning to install machine guns in the soviet building and shoot the "Menshevik counterrevolutionaries" during the session.[132] Cooler heads prevailed, however, and the soviet was simply disbanded, the Menshevik paper was shut down, and the Menshevik and SR parties were declared to be counterrevolutionary.[133] By mid-May the population was so tired of Bolshevik rule that outbursts could no longer be contained. When the Germans entered the city, they were greeted, to their surprise, as liberators.

The Mensheviks also won the soviet elections in Tsaritsyn in the spring of 1918.[134] A Menshevik newspaper in Petrograd reported a War Ministry announcement that "in Novorossiisk, power had been seized by the railway workers, who were hostile to the Bolsheviks. The Bolshevik soviet and sailors' organizations were disbanded."[135]

Bolshevik rule in the Don and Kuban areas had ended by June 1918. General Krasnov, in the Don area, and General Alekseev, in the Kuban area, declared all the laws both of the Bolsheviks and of the Provisional Government of 1917 to be void and the laws of the Russian Empire restored. The threat of a tsarist restoration haunted the local Mensheviks and their leaders in Moscow. Local Menshevik organizations requested guidance from the CC. What should the party policy be under the Whites? Was any cooperation with the Bolsheviks possible? The CC had to define the party's policy for those cities where the overthrow of

---

130. Lockerman, *Bolcheviks à l'oeuvre*, pp. 74–76.
131. Lokerman, *74 dnia*, p. 43. The Menshevik victory was also reported in "Pobeda Men'shevikov," *Utro Petrograda*, 1 April 1918, p. 2, citing *Izvestiia Rostovskogo na Donu soveta*, 26 March 1918.
132. Lockerman, *Bolcheviks à l'oeuvre*, p. 54. It is noteworthy that this French edition of Lokerman's *74 dnia* dropped the description of White atrocities and emphasized Bolshevik atrocities.
133. For a detailed description of these events, see "Otkrytoe pis'mo Donskogo komiteta RSDRP," *Bor'ba*, 23 May 1918, p. 3.
134. Gurevich, "O polozhenii v Rossii."
135. "Novorossiisk," *Vecherniaia zvezda*, 21 May 1918, p. 3.

the Bolsheviks might lead to a tsarist restoration. This was the problem the Mensheviks had to tackle throughout 1919 and 1920.

The Bolshevik Crisis of 1918

Three factors in the political process in Russia in 1918 emerge from the evidence we have examined. The first is the impressive success of the Menshevik-SR bloc in the soviet elections in all regions of the country. The second is the Bolshevik practice of disbanding the soviets that came under Menshevik-SR control. The third is the subsequent wave of anti-Bolshevik uprisings. These factors reveal fundamental changes in political developments during the first half of 1918. The election returns impel a reconsideration of the Bolsheviks' popular support in the country. The disbanding of the soviets necessitates a re-examination of the institutionalization of the Bolshevik regime. The anti-Bolshevik uprisings call for an explanation of the subsequent Menshevik policy.

Taken together, the evidence suggests that by the summer of 1918, Bolshevism as a mass movement was in deep crisis. It is therefore necessary to take a second look at the allegiance of the Bolsheviks' supporters at the end of 1917. It seems that as soon as the interests of the workers collided with the interests of the Bolshevik state, workers' "Bolshevism" tended to wane. The Menshevik-SR bloc won the city soviet elections in nineteen of the thirty provincial capitals or large industrial cities of European Russia where soviet power actually existed. One of these cities, Pskov, was occupied by the Germans; in two provinces, no elections were held; and for six provinces we have no data. Therefore, in all provincial capitals of European Russia where elections were held and on which data have survived, the Mensheviks and SRs won majorities in the city soviets in the spring of 1918.

The case studies of local politics presented here show that workers' concerns focused on such problems as famine, unemployment, police brutality, and the threat of foreign intervention. The fruits of Bolshevik socialism had proved to be much less desirable than the October slogans had led them to believe. Euphoria over "immediate socialism" had given way to more sober thoughts. The elections held six months after the Bolsheviks came to power reflected the electorate's attitudes toward Bolshevik rule rather than toward Bolshevik promises. The opposition parties showed flexibility, resourcefulness, and responsiveness to the needs of their constituencies. The Mensheviks regained the workers' support and, together with the SRs, staged a remarkable political comeback in the spring of 1918.

In short, the "triumphal march of soviet power" existed only in Lenin's imagination, though it has become the standard portrayal in official histories. The cases of Tambov, Rostov, and Yaroslavl demonstrate not only that the Mensheviks and SRs were much stronger than has generally been believed, but also that the local Bolsheviks who seized military control of the cities were not, for the most part, the instruments of Moscow. They seized power for themselves, and they often resisted interference by the Moscow commissars. Not a consolidation of power but rather regionalism in local politics and fragmentation of central authority prevailed in the first half of 1918. In early 1918, the soviet assemblies were not yet "sounding boards" in the Bolshevik command structure; rather, they were still popular revolutionary centers, albeit without much power, and they continued to reflect the changing moods of the electorate. Neither the Moscow nor the local Bolsheviks had the manpower with which to govern the country. The personnel with the expertise to maintain the structure of taxation, food supply, and administration were to be found predominantly among the moderate, democratic, socialist intelligentsia. The radicalized soldiers who were the backbone of Bolshevik local "government" mismanaged the local economy and quickly lost popular support, and with it their capacity to maintain their hold on the cities.

In addition to winning the elections to the soviets, the Mensheviks and SRs retained control of the local trade unions and dumas. They thus presented a serious threat to the Bolsheviks. In order to stay in power, the Bolsheviks disbanded the soviet assemblies in most cities and villages and turned for institutional support to the ECs, the Cheka, the military, and special emissaries with "unlimited dictatorial power." This chain of events culminated in the crisis of June and July 1918, when the Bolsheviks expelled the socialist opposition parties from the CEC, ending the period of election politics. Armed clashes escalated into a full-scale civil war, which was to alter the soviet political system profoundly.

By the summer of 1918, the country was sliding into chaos. The Menshevik leadership had to reexamine their party's policies in the aftermath of the disbandings of the soviets, the general strikes, the overthrow of the Bolsheviks by Czech-SR forces in the east and by the Whites in the south, and violent anti-Bolshevik rebellions. As we shall see, this reexamination led to a new division among the Mensheviks during the first phase of the civil war.

CHAPTER 6

Shifting
Political Allegiances

The politics of elections to the soviets in the spring of 1918 were intrinsically connected with the activities of the workers' assemblies of upolnomochennye. In the provincial capitals of Tula, Nizhnii Novgorod, Samara, and Voronezh, these assemblies became rallying centers of protest and played an important part in exerting pressure on the Bolshevik authorities to hold new elections to the soviets. In Petrograd, where the upolnomochennye movement started, the Workers' Assembly of Upolnomochennye from the Factories and Plants acted as a powerful political force confronting the Bolshevik-controlled soviet, in the face of the continuing Bolshevik refusal, until June 1918, to hold new elections.[1] The Bolsheviks and the Socialist opposition parties competed for workers' support in scores of other working-class organizations, such as the factory committees, the soviets, and the trade unions.[2] After the Bolsheviks' seizure of power, however, these organi-

1. Some attempts to describe the movement of upolnomochennye and the role of the Menshevik party in it were made in the 1950s and 1960s by emigre Mensheviks. These otherwise valuable accounts gloss over the disunity and weakness in the movement, which, in the end, must have contributed to its failure. See Abramovitch, "Bolshevistskaia vlast' i rabochie vesnoi 1918 goda," *Sotsialisticheskii vestnik* (New York), nos. 8–9 (1960), pp. 170–76; G. Aronson, *Rossiia v epokhu revoliutsii*, especially the chapter "Rabochie protiv diktatury," which is a variant of the manuscript "Dvizhenie u-polnomochennykh ot rabochikh fabrik i zavodov v 1918 godu," and the many documents on the movement of upolnomochennye in the Aksel'rod papers, Nik. Col. no. 16, file 119. file 119.

2. On other workers' organizations in 1918, see, for example, Solomon Shvarts, "Fabzavkomy v pervye gody revoliutsii," Nik. Col. no. 86, file 3. Of interest among other emigre Menshevik studies on this subject is Aronson, *K istorii pravogo techeniia*.

zations were gradually turned into state economic agencies, in accordance with the Bolshevik ideas about government, and soon lost the political significance they had had in 1917. On the other hand, the unique conditions during the New Course in the spring of 1918 permitted the opposition parties to work all but unimpeded to organize new workers' groups, independent of the state, which would become political forums parallel to the state-controlled soviets.

As a result of their political experience during 1917, many workers embraced the classic social-democratic assumptions that the workers had to organize themselves, that they could exert pressure on the government for or against certain policies, and that they must have unions, disability funds, self-help boards, and so on. To understand the pattern of struggle between the Menshevik-SR opposition and the Bolshevik authorities in Petrograd, which was the center of Bolshevik support in October 1917, it is necessary to examine the nature of workers' grievances, their political demands, the character of their strikes, and the organization, composition, development, and effects of the upolnomochennye movement.

The Workers' Assembly of Upolnomochennye in Petrograd

The question as to when the Workers' Assembly of Upolnomochennye was founded and by whom has generated considerable controversy.[3] Perhaps the major impetus to the creation of the organization was the chaos during the evacuation of Petrograd industries at the time of the brief German offensive in February 1918.[4] The Red Army units had fled in panic. Zinoviev, the chairman of the Petrograd soviet, admitted that the German troops were within two days' march of the city. Urgent orders to evacuate large plants were given and then withdrawn. At the plants, no one seemed to know who had given what orders. The orders of the soviet contradicted those of the factory committees, and sometimes both contradicted the orders of the Commissariat of Labor. At the Izhorskii plant in Kolpino, a Petrograd suburb, the first order following news of the German offensive was to remain calm and continue to manufacture armor; then came an order to blow up the plant, then yet another to begin evacuation as soon as possible.[5] Some machinery was packed and loaded, but remained at the train station; other

3. Iurii Denike, "Bogdanov v nachale 1918 goda," *Sotsialisticheskii vestnik* (New York), nos. 2–3 (February–March 1960), p. 48.

4. On the beginning of the movement, see "Rabochie Petrograda o Bol'shevikakh," *Sotsialist revoliutsioner* (journal of SR Central Committee), no. 2 (April 1918), pp. 15–16.

5. "Nastroenie rabochikh," *Delo naroda* (newspaper of SR CC), 28 March 1918, p. 4.

machinery was dispatched, but no one seemed to know where. Production came to a halt; some workers had to be laid off, and the factory committee could not find funds to pay their wages. Such cases were described by angry workers at their first spontaneous protest meetings at the end of February.

At the Tube Works in Petrograd, an order came to evacuate to Penza. Three trains with equipment were hastily sent out. Eighty more trains would have been needed to complete the evacuation, but that many trains were simply unavailable. At a general meeting, the plant's workers asked the Bolsheviks why the three trains had been dispatched when it was evident that the evacuation could not be carried out. Production had been disrupted and the plant had to be closed temporarily. A Menshevik correspondent reported: "The workers are embittered and blame the Bolsheviks, who promised golden mountains to them, for what is going on. At the rally, the workers would not let the Bolsheviks speak and shouted at them: 'Down with them! Out! You liars!' The Bolsheviks brought in the Red Guards and threatened to shoot."[6]

In short, fragmentation of authority, exacerbated by poor management and the commissars' high-handedness, had brought Petrograd industry to a standstill.[7] The confusion over the evacuation made it evident that the Bolsheviks were doing no better at governing Petrograd than the Provisional Government had done. The food supply had dwindled sharply, the ranks of the unemployed were increasing, and inflation was getting out of hand. The euphoria over socialism, the hopes for great improvement under the dictatorship of the proletariat, were shattered.

On February 23, representatives of various Petrograd Menshevik organizations—trade unions, local district soviets, party committees, and so on—met with the Menshevik CC to discuss the feasibility of organizing an independent workers' assembly. The idea found support, and a series of district meetings took place the following week. The initiative was taken by the Mensheviks and SRs from the Nevsky district, who on March 3 elected a district bureau of upolnomochennye. The Right Mensheviks, in particular were looking for alternative organizational forms with which to oppose the Bolshevik regime. In Petrograd they acted somewhat independently of the CC. They published their own newspaper, *Den'* (edited by A. N. Potresov) and their own journal, *Delo* (whose chief editor was Vladimir Levitskii). Among the editors and

---

6. "Rabochaia zhizn': Trubochnyi zavod," *Den'*, 30 March 1918, p. 7.

7. For data on the number of workers in Petrograd and the disintegration of Petrograd industry, see A. Gel'fgot, "Tragediia rabochego klassa," *Narodovlastie* (Ekaterinodar), no. 1 (1919), p. 28; A. B. Eliashevich, "Razrushenie promyshlennosti i rabochii klass," *Narodovlastie* (Moscow), no. 2 (1918), pp. 35–41.

frequent contributors were B. O. Bogdanov, G. Baturskii, A. N. Smirnov, and other leading Mensheviks, all of whom played an important role in founding the Workers' Assembly of Upolnomochennye. On March 5, a citywide Menshevik conference discussed the progress that had been made toward organizing the assembly. Dan, Zaretskaia, Bogdanov, and others reported on the political situation. The proceedings of this meeting leave no doubt that the Menshevik party leaders welcomed the creation of a new workers' forum.[8]

As in January, after the disbanding of the Constituent Assembly, the workers sent delegations to other factories to coordinate their protests. This response to the Mensheviks' and SRs' call for elections reflects the workers' heightened dissatisfaction with the Bolsheviks' performance during the crisis.[9] Menshevik and SR workers who had been known as outspoken critics of the Bolshevik policies were elected as upolnomochennye to the new assembly, but they were not the only ones. According to data compiled by the assembly's leaders on the basis of questionnaires filled out by the 110 elected representatives, 35 were Social Democrats, 33 were SRs, 1 was a People's Socialist, and 41 had no party affiliation.[10] Despite the Menshevik-SR majority, it was decided to call the new organization a "nonparty" (*bespartiinaia*) institution.[11] Its status vis-à-vis the Menshevik and SR parties was conceived to be the same as that of the trade unions: it was to be an organization involving large numbers of workers who did not necessarily have a party affiliation, although, like the trade unions, it had party groupings within it. It was to have its own voice and remain independent of the central committees of the socialist parties. Commenting on the political composition of the assembly, G. Baturskii (who before December 1917 had been a member of the Menshevik CC) wrote: "At the present workers' conferences, we have representation of wide factory masses, which only recently were following the Communist flag of the Bolsheviks and which are still infected by the maximalist fury [*stikhiia*] and are still in the process of disillusionment with the socialist experiments."[12]

In the proceedings of the early meetings of the assembly, one detects not so much a fighting spirit as feelings of bitterness, fear, and almost

8. "K chrezvychainomu sobraniiu upolnomochennykh fabrik i zavodov," *Partiinye izvestiia* (Petrograd), no. 3 (11 March 1918), p. 7.

9. Aronson, *Rossiia v epokhu revoliutsii*, p. 185.

10. "Sobranie upolnomochennykh fabrik i zavodov," *Novyi den'*, 2 April 1918, p. 6.

11. Soviet historians have interpreted the assembly's claim to nonparty character as a ploy designed to disguise the Mensheviks' dominance of the gathering. See Vladimirova, *God sluzhby sotsialistam kapitalistam*, pp. 196–99.

12. G. Baturskii, "Sredi rabochikh: Sobranie upolnomochennykh fabrik i zavodov Petrograda," *Delo*, no. 3 (April 1918), pp. 14–16.

despair over the workers' grievances, as in this passage from a declaration adopted at the first session on March 13:

> The war is over, but our misfortunes are only beginning. There are few jobs. Senseless and hectic evacuation is destroying industry completely. Tens of thousands of workers are thrown out into the streets. There is nowhere to go, and in any case it is forbidden. Everywhere, not enough jobs. The last money is being used up. A hungry summer is coming. There is no one we can expect help from. How much are the trade unions doing for the unemployed? They are busy not with the unemployed but with those who are working. The unions are organizing, all right, but the administration and not the workers. Factory committees have become commissions for firing the workers; they have become bureaucratic state institutions that do not need our trust and have long since lost it. And they will not help us. And from the soviets we can hope for nothing, because they are now only trying, punishing, levying taxes, organizing the Red Guards, and sometimes shooting.[13]

The plain, despairing language of these lines, with their repetition of concern over jobs, strongly suggests that they were written by workers themselves, who probably drew on the mandates of several workers' groups. Most striking in these words is the sense of helplessness. The workers seem to be disoriented and frustrated, having lost the confidence and assurance they had had in October 1917:

> We are faced with the horrors of long-lasting unemployment. We are deprived of the means to cope with it. The trade unions are destroyed. The factory committees will not defend us. The city duma is disbanded. The work of cooperatives is hindered. Fleeing Petrograd, the CPC abandoned us to the will of fate, closing the factories and plants, throwing us out into the streets without money, without bread, without jobs, without means of self-defense, without any hope for the future.[14]

Such words reveal a change from rebelliousness to passivity. The workers expected that the "workers' government" would tend to their needs; when it did not, they felt deceived and powerless. One of the themes that runs through the resolutions of the assembly is the unfulfilled promises of the Bolsheviks: "We were promised the soviet workers' and peasants' republic. We were promised immediate democratic peace, bread, and freedom. But we were deceived. The most

13. The text of the declaration is here cited from "Slushai, rabochii," *Severnaia zaria* (Vologda), no. 13 (25 March 1918); the text is included in Bernshtam, ed., *Nezavisimoe rabochee dvizhenie*, pp. 87–90. For the entire text, see "Dokumente der Russischen Arbeiterbewegung Unter dem Regime des Bolschewistischen Kommunismus," *Stimmen aus Russland*, nos. 6–7 (15 October 1918), pp. 37–41.

14. "Slushai, rabochii."

important questions of national life are decided without the soviets. We were given the obscene Brest peace, famine, and shootings without trial."[15]

At first glance, it may appear incongruous that the same workers who had been so brave and self-assured in their fight against the industrialists, and so articulate in their demands to the Provisional and Bolshevik governments in the fall of 1917, felt so helpless in March 1918. The underlying reason for this change was that in October the workers had been propelled by heightened expectations and hopes for a bright future following the victory of socialism. Everything had seemed easy and within reach in October. All one had to do was overthrow the bourgeoisie. Subsequently, however, the workers discovered that the "stifling of the bourgeoisie" or the "looting of the looters" did not bring about the promised socialism. The wave of radicalist destruction had ended in painful disappointment.

The political apathy of the workers presented a problem for the Mensheviks. Iurii Denike wrote at the time that the workers, "having suffered from a worthless policy, now believe in none. Having deceived themselves about their own strength, they now feel completely powerless."[16] Similarly, a representative of the Nevskii shipyard said at the first session of the Assembly of Upolnomochennye: "In many shops of our plant, the elections to the Workers' Assembly have been completed. The attitude toward the Bolsheviks is hostile. However, it is necessary to point out another phenomenon, that is, the psychological reaction among the working masses—the feeling of being at a dead end, and apathy as a result."[17] In a letter to Aksel'rod, Levitskii paraphrased workers as saying, "A curse on you all—Bolsheviks [and] Mensheviks—with all your politics."[18] Workers' disillusionment manifested itself in other ways as well. Some workers supported the anarchists, who accused the Bolsheviks of betraying communism for the sake of state power.[19]

Nevertheless, resolutions adopted at many factories and the speeches at the Workers' Assembly make it evident that the Menshevik and SR parties were eliciting new interest. At a general meeting of the Putilov plant on March 6, the workers not only elected representatives to the Workers' Assembly but also adopted resolutions demanding that the

15. Baturskii, "Sredi rabochikh," p. 14.
16. Iurii Denike, "Odin iz urokov," *Novaia zaria*, no. 2 (1 May 1918), p. 20.
17. "Protokoly chrezvychainogo sobraniia upolnomochennykh fabrik i zavodov 13 marta," document no. 14, in Bernshtam, ed., *Nezavisimoe rabochee dvizhenie*, p. 70.
18. *Martov i ego blizkie*, p. 63.
19. See the interesting discussion of the relationships between Bolsheviks and anarchists in "Poslednie 'soglashateli'," *Novyi den'*, 13 April 1918, p. 1.

ban on Menshevik and SR newspapers be lifted immediately and expressing a lack of confidence in the CPC. Similar resolutions were adopted at the Old Lessner, Erikson, Rechkin, Obukhov, and other plants.[20] At the first session of the Workers' Assembly, a representative of the Rechkin plant summarized the situation there in these words: "There is a turnabout in workers' attitudes. But it was not possible to carry out elections to the Workers' Assembly because of the workers' apathy. . . . The [Bolshevik] members of the soviet from our plant declared that if the plant adopted the Menshevik resolution, they would resign. But they nevertheless did not resign."[21]

At other plants, one could observe a strong sentiment against the Bolshevik dictatorship and for unity among all socialist parties. At the assembly's first session, a representative of the Baltic plant said, "Recently we have circulated a questionnaire: Who is for the Council of People's Commissars, and who is for a united and common revolutionary front? For the CPC, there were 113 [votes] and for a united democracy, 1,899."[22] It should be recalled that after October 1917, the Mensheviks had advocated the formation of a united coalition government of all socialist parties. As we saw earlier, after the Bolsheviks disbanded the Constituent Assembly, the Mensheviks' position changed: now they demanded the resignation of the CPC and the reconvocation of the Constituent Assembly.[23] At the first session of the Workers' Assembly, this demand was voted upon, accepted by the majority, and included in a declaration that was sent to the Fourth Congress of Soviets. N. N. Glebov, a representative of the Putilov plant who was an ardent proponent of unity among socialist workers and a sharp critic of factionalism, attempted to promote his ideas by organizing a United Workers' Party. Attacking the Bolshevik and Menshevik party bureaucrats alike, Glebov asserted that the workers had only been used by the functionaries for their own ends. "We will never forget the burning words of the Communist Manifesto, that the liberation of the working class is the task of the working class itself!"[24]

There was no unanimity either among the workers or among the

---

20. "Mitingi i sobraniia," *Partiinye izvestiia*, 11 March 1918, p. 7.

21. "Protokoly chrezvychainogo sobraniia," in Bernshtam, ed., *Nezavisimoe rabochee dvizhenie*, p. 70.

22. "Nastroenie rabochikh Petrograda," *Sotsialist revoliutsioner* (April 1918), p. 16.

23. This position was reiterated continually by the Menshevik leadership. See, for example, "Rezoliutsii partiinogo soveshchaniia," *Partiinye izvestiia*, no. 8 (10 June 1918), p. 4.

24. Bernshtam has suggested that this current of political thought reflected the workers' break with all socialist parties. See Bernshtam, ed., *Nezavisimoe rabochee dvizhenie*, p. 92. Glebov's efforts are discussed in P. Golikov, "Vserossiiskaia edinaia rabochaia partiia," *Delo*, no. 3 (14 April 1918), pp. 8–9.

assembly leaders. Just as in October, some demanded a united socialist government, others the convocation of the Constituent Assembly. A new element in this disunity was that the workers were beginning to get tired of arguments over the great issues, such as universal suffrage and the dictatorship of the proletariat, and were becoming more interested in doing something about the problems that affected their daily lives—unemployment, food supply, wages. Thus when the Menshevik and SR leaders proposed a political declaration, the representative of the Tube Works said, "I was elected to discuss the issues of evacuation and unemployment, and I was not authorized to vote for the declaration, because these questions were not discussed at the plant's meeting." Some Mensheviks were disappointed with this concentration on mundane issues. The Menshevik leaders pointed out that in the long run, the small problems could not be resolved until the fundamental institutional and constitutional issues had been settled. "All the problems that we deal with," said Bogdanov, "are connected with problems of general politics. In our every effort we will encounter 'big' questions. Our every step will mean a struggle with the government." The Petrograd workers could do little themselves about supplies that were transported to the city from other parts of the country. Only when the Bolshevik "socializations" were halted could normal economic life be restored. Anatolii Diubua objected that it was ridiculous to tell the workers that as long as the Bolsheviks' power existed, nothing could be done. "We should do what we can, here and now!"[25] Finally, it was decided to put aside the big questions for a while and to direct attention to the day-to-day workers' grievances.

The two most pressing problems were evacuation and unemployment. Special commissions to deal with these problems were set up by the assembly. Representatives of the Petrograd duma, the union of engineers, the city soviet, and the unemployed were invited to take part in the deliberations. The Bolsheviks ignored the invitation, an action that did nothing to enhance their standing in the eyes of the unemployed. At the fourth session of the assembly, it was decided to begin general registration of the unemployed.[26] Furthermore, whenever a factory closed, the commission on unemployment was to investigate the causes, report them in the press, and undertake measures to reopen the plant. The commission's report on unemployment stated that the difficulties with supply and marketing were compounded by the incompetence of the Bolshevik factory committees. It was necessary to return to a joint system of management, with the participation of experienced

25. Baturskii, "Sredi rabochikh," pp. 14–16.
26. "Evakuatsiia i bezrabotitsa," *Vecherniaia zvezda*, 25 March 1918, p. 3.

technical personnel and the industrialists. To alleviate hardship among the unemployed, the commission recommended the creation of a special fund, supported by contributions from the state, the trade unions, and employed workers.[27] The commission on evacuation came to the conclusion that most of the factory stoppages were caused by disorderly evacuation attempts by various Bolshevik agencies. In the existing administrative and managerial disarray, plants could not be evacuated, and efforts to evacuate them only paralyzed industry. These seemed like reasonable observations, but attempts to act on them soon brought the Workers' Assembly into conflict with the Bolshevik authorities. Most of the conflicts revolved around the issues of bread rations, the right to enter and leave the city, and the elections to factory committees and to the Petrograd soviet.

With the worsening of the food situation in Petrograd until supplies never exceeded one week's needs, by Zinoviev's own admission, the Petrograd soviet had to determine bread rations for each group of the population.[28] The workers' ration was not the smallest, but they were antagonized by the fact that rations for the Red Guards and the commissars were larger. Trying somehow to regulate the number of mouths in Petrograd, the city soviet imposed restrictions on travel in and out of the city.[29] Armed patrols at the railway stations, searches of passengers, and raids on the bagmen became a daily routine. Many workers were trying to go to the countryside, individually and in groups, sometimes to buy provisions from relatives. At the railway stations they were often searched and arrested by the Cheka. Their demand that travel restrictions be abolished became one of the most intensely disputed issues. The workers at the Putilov dockyard, declaring that the only "way out of the current crisis" was through "the combined efforts of the socialist parties," not through "a war of all against all," demanded "freedom to import provisions into Petrograd; an increase in the bread ration to two pounds a day, equal with the Red Guards; and the transfer of funds appropriated for the May Day celebration to the fund for the unemployed."[30]

What angered the workers most was that the local district soviets, the factory committees, and even the Petrograd soviet refused to hold new elections, even though officially their mandates had expired. At almost

27. Iu. D., "Vokrug rabochich konferentsii," *Novaia zaria*, 1 May 1918, pp. 56–60.

28. See "Rech' na chrezvychainom sobranii Petrogradskogo soveta 18 maia 1918 goda," in Zinoviev, *Dve rechi*, pp. 25–30. For a later Soviet account of the food-supply situation in Petrograd, see "Prodovol'stvennoe polozhenie Petrograda v 1918 godu," in Potekhin, *Pervyi sovet*, pp. 285–301.

29. For a debate among the workers on these restrictions, see "Rabochaia konferentsiia," *Den'*, 30 March 1918, p. 7.

30. "Rabochaia zhizn'," *Novyi den'*, 30 April 1918, p. 4.

every session of the Workers' Assembly, the upolnomochennye gave detailed accounts of the election bans at their factories. Thus the Tube workers had been unable to hold elections to the factory committee for two months, though the general meeting had voted four times for elections.[31] The workers expressed surprise at hearing of so many Bolshevik refusals to abide by the electoral rules, for some of them still perceived the Bolsheviks as a workers' revolutionary party. At the assembly's second session, a representative of the Obukhov plant said: "Our factory committee has always been SR, but the Bolsheviks rigged the elections and now they have a majority on the committee. We already passed a resolution of no confidence in the factory committee four months ago, but this doesn't help. They only laugh when 'no confidence' is passed against them."[32] Workers from Siemens-Schuckert reported in early March that the Bolsheviks had disbanded their factory committee and shut down the plant.[33] At the assembly session of April 10, the representative of the Lessner plant also reported that the factory committee had shut down the plant and refused to hold elections.[34]

In the spring of 1918, the workers still took it for granted that there were to be elections and re-elections. These reports provoked indignation, but the upolnomochennye did not quite know what could be done. Indeed, for some time the Workers' Assembly appears to have been merely a forum for discussing grievances. At its second session, however, the assembly resolved to make the struggle for election of public officials one of its main political objectives. The representative of the First State Printing Shop said, "It is imperative to start a campaign for new elections to the trade-union boards, the factory committees, and the soviets."[35] But this was easier said than done. The Menshevik faction in the Petrograd soviet had several times called for new elections to that body. At the soviet's session on April 5, S. Iu. Semkovskii, leader of the Menshevik faction, brought up this issue again. A newspaper described the scene:

> The majority of those assembled try to prevent the speaker from saying anything after his first words, when he begins to say that the Petrograd soviet as it is constituted today does not represent the views of Petrograd's proletariat. "You," he says, "have turned yourselves into the agents of the

31. "Nastroenie rabochikh Petrograda," *Sotsialist revoliutsioner*, no. 2 (April 1918), p. 16.

32. "Protokoly chrezvychainogo sobraniia," in Bernshtam, ed., *Nezavisimoe rabochee dvizhenie*, p. 82.

33. "Mitingi i sobraniia," *Partiinye izvestiia*, 11 March 1918, p. 8.

34. "Chrezvychainoe sobranie fabrik i zavodov," *Novyi den'*, 11 April 1918, p. 3.

35. "Protokoly chrezvychainogo sobraniia," in Bernshtam, ed., *Nezavisimoe rabochee dvizhenie*, p. 84.

Bolshevik power! Remove the stigma of bureaucracy from yourselves! Stage elections!" Unbearable noise and shouts ring out in the hall. "You do not have the courage to do it!" Semkovskii tries to shout louder: "This is the debt of honor which the Moscow soviet has already paid." Because of the incredible clamor and shouts, the speaker cannot finish his speech.[36]

The Menshevik proposal was finally put to a vote and was defeated by the Bolshevik majority.

A general meeting at the Sestroretsk plant on February 27 adopted a resolution demanding new elections to the Petrograd soviet. After the meeting, the Bolsheviks arrested the Menshevik who had introduced it.[37]

The issue of the elections to the Petrograd soviet became highly explosive by June 1918. A. N. Ioffe, coleader of the Menshevik faction in the Petrograd soviet, reported to the assembly of upolnomochennye on April 24 on the problems the opposition had encountered in the soviet.[38] The reason the Bolshevik delegates so strongly resisted elections, he said, was that in effect they represented "dead souls." Many of the factories where they had been elected in September 1917 had closed. Thus, even if the remaining workers continued to support the Bolsheviks, many of the present soviet delegates could not be re-elected. In fact, it was common knowledge that the majority of the workers by now supported the Mensheviks and SRs. "If the majority of seats [in the soviet] belonged to non-Bolshevik delegates," Ioffe said, "the workers would find ways to remove the Bolsheviks from power painlessly."[39]

The economic and political demands of the workers—equalization of bread rations, freedom to leave and enter the city, and elections—remained unfulfilled. The Petrograd Bolshevik leaders did not want to reduce the bread ration for the Red Guards and risk protests from them at a time when the Bolsheviks needed an armed presence in the city to secure their shaky power. Indeed, urgent measures were being undertaken to recruit Red Guards, and one of the incentives was a good bread ration. Free movement into and out of the city could not be easily allowed, either, for that would have amounted to abandoning the Bolshevik food-supply policy and dismantling the Cheka anti-profiteering detachments. To hold new elections, at least at the factory-committee

36. "Delovaia chast', o perevyborakh soveta," *Vecherniaia zvezda*, 6 April 1918, p. 3.
37. "Mitingi i sobraniia," *Partiinye izvestiia*, 11 March 1918, p. 8.
38. "Fabrichnye upolnomochennye," *Strana*, 25 April 1918, p. 4. For another report on this session of the Workers' Assembly, see "Chrezvychainoe sobranie upolnomochennykh fabrik i zavodov Petrograda," *Novyi den'*, 25 April 1918, p. 4.
39. "Fabrichnye upolnomochennye," *Strana*, 25 April 1918, p. 4.

level, was admissible in theory, but it hardly seemed a wise policy from the Bolsheviks' point of view, because of the likelihood that they would lose control of the committees. Thus the Bolsheviks had little to offer the workers at that point, and the image they tried to project bore little resemblance to the reality. Their newspapers repeatedly proclaimed that power belonged to the workers, that the soviets were the most democratic of institutions, representing the will of the masses, and that the Bolsheviks were the vanguard of the proletariat. But if power belonged to the workers, asked numerous resolutions of the time, why did the Petrograd soviet refuse to hold new elections?[40]

The workers continued to press for changes in the soviet and to support the opposition parties. When the Bolsheviks at one plant proposed that the workers end their support for the Workers' Assembly, the workers responded that one allegiance did not contradict the other. The Workers' Assembly was their own organization, and they would not let anyone attack it. Workers at some factories returned a vote of confidence in both the CPC and the assembly of upolnomochennye.[41] It is hard to judge what such a vote actually meant. Perhaps the workers expressed confidence in the CPC because they were afraid of reprisals, or perhaps their disappointment at Bolshevik policies did not yet extend to the Bolsheviks themselves. It may be said with a fair degree of certainty, though, that the workers' support for the Mensheviks did not yet signify outright hostility to the Bolsheviks.

Since general elections to the Petrograd soviet were not possible, the Menshevik leaders concentrated their efforts on building centers of opposition at the local level: workers' cooperatives, self-help loan associations, trade-union branches, workers' clubs, and district assemblies of upolnomochennye. Most of these organizations were occupied with routine matters: lack of provisions or of raw materials, a conflict with a factory committee or with the Red Guards.[42] The task of the district assemblies, in particular, was to counter the actions of the factory committees when they ran contrary to the wishes of the workers. Workers were urged to report to their upolnomochennye any conflicts with the Bolshevik authorities. In a matter of weeks, it became customary to hold large workers' meetings at the plants, at which the upolnomochennye in turn reported to the workers on their activity in the assembly. Throughout March and April, the Workers' Assembly and the Pet-

40. See, for example, "Rabochaia zhizn': Nastroenie rabochikh: Putilovskii zavod," *Delo naroda*, 26 March 1918, p. 4.

41. Such incidents are discussed in "Vokrug rabochikh konferentsii," *Novaia zaria*, 1 May 1918, p. 59.

42. For a discussion of the local Menshevik organizations and their factional disputes, see Aronson, *K istorii pravogo techeniia*.

rograd soviet peacefully coexisted. The assembly's activity was legal and open and so far not banned. Its own paper, *Billiuten' chrez-vychainogo sobraniia upolnomochennykh*, appeared regularly. The upolnomochennye movement was spreading across the country. At the beginning of April, the Petrograd assembly sent a delegation to Moscow to coordinate efforts to establish a workers' conference there.[43] As we saw in chapter 5, workers' assemblies played an important role in campaigns for new elections to soviets in Tula, Yaroslavl, Nizhnii Novgorod, Voronezh, and other cities in April 1918.[44] A proposal was also made to start preparations for a convocation of an All-Russian Congress of Workers' Assemblies of Upolnomochennye.[45]

The upolnomochennye movement was strongest in Petrograd. The number of factories sending representatives to the assembly steadily increased. It was decided that every chairman of a district assembly would automatically be a member of the city bureau of the Workers' Assembly, the executive organ that conducted affairs between plenary sessions. The chairman of the assembly elected at the first session was a worker from the Obukhov plant, Efrem Berg, an SR; the chairman of the bureau was A. N. Smirnov, a Menshevik from the Cartridge plant. The other members of the bureau were N. N. Glebov and Rozenshtein of the Putilov plant, supporters of the wished-for United Workers' party; M. S. Kefali of the Union of Printers, a Menshevik; S. I. Kononov of the Arsenal plant, an SR and a member of the Menshevik-SR bloc in the Petrograd soviet; Ragozin, a Menshevik representing the First State Printing Shop; N. K. Borisenko of the Tube plant, a Menshevik; and two men, Zimin and Iakovlev, whose party affiliations are unknown.[46]

Many of the assembly's leaders were simultaneously engaged in other Menshevik or SR activities. Kononov and Orlov were members of the opposition faction in the Petrograd soviet. Kefali combined his responsibilities in the assembly's bureau with work in the Union of Printers, which was led by the Mensheviks. Smirnov, the bureau chairman, and G. Baturskii had been Menshevik CC members until December 1917 and editors of *Delo*. O. A. Ermanskii was a member both of the Menshevik CC and of the Menshevik faction in the Petrograd soviet. A.

---

43. For the details of this initiative, see "K sozyvu v Moskve bespartiinoi rabochei konferentsii," *Edinstvo*, 1 May 1918, pp. 6–7.

44. For a summary of the upolnomochennye movement in various cities, see Gel'fgot, "Tragediia rabochego klassa."

45. On this and other initiatives of the Workers' Assembly, see the letter of Pavel Aksel'rod to the leaders of the European Socialist parties, Nik. Col. no. 16, box 1, file 13, and Aronson, *K istorii pravogo techeniia*, p. 186.

46. "Chrezvychainoe sobranie upolnomochennykh fabrik i zavodov," *Novyi den'*, 11 April 1918, p. 3. See also "Protokoly chrezvychainogo sobraniia," in Bernshtam, ed., *Nezavisimoe rabochee dvizhenie*, p. 87.

P. Krasnianskaia, the secretary of the assembly, was a candidate member of the Menshevik CC and a frequent contributor of articles on the assembly's proceedings to various Petrograd Menshevik newspapers, particularly *Utro Petrograda*, a publication of the printers' union.[47] Ioffe, coleader of the Menshevik faction in the Petrograd soviet, often reported on the faction's activities to the Workers' Assembly. Several of the assembly's plenary sessions were held at the club of the Right Mensheviks, at 9 Baskova Street. There is thus no question that the upolnomochennye movement was led by the Mensheviks and SRs.

Local Menshevik party committee coordinated the activities of the various Menshevik-led organizations, gathered information for the party dailies and weeklies, and kept in touch with the Menshevik faction in the soviet and with the party's central committee. Workers were encouraged to discuss their problems at the committee's headquarters. One notice, typical of those appearing in the Menshevik newspapers, read: "For matters concerning the business of local organizations, my office hours are from 12 to 6. For matters concerning unlawful searches and arrests, I receive comrades with no waiting in line."[48] Such notices suggest that it was still possible to go to the office of an opposition party and complain about unlawful searches and arrests. But what could the Mensheviks do in such cases? They usually organized an investigation and contacted a sympathetic lawyer, who might file a complaint with the court against the offending agency. The Menshevik newspapers published details of these cases in an effort to arouse public concern and apply pressure on the Bolshevik authorities.

Many other initiatives were launched. Local Menshevik party headquarters set up canteens for the unemployed. Menshevik clubs organized discussion groups and workers' libraries. The printers' union began publication of morning and evening dailies in both capitals, and all the revenues, according to a notice on the front page, were donated to the fund for unemployed printers. Other Menshevik trade-union activists, in conjunction with the trade-union commission of the Workers' Assembly, campaigned for elections to the union boards and for the unions' independence of the state.

The Mensheviks' initiatives and their organizational drive in the spring of 1918 to a certain extent recaptured the infrastructure of the socialist labor movement, which had been lost to the Bolsheviks in

47. Krasnianskaia had been nominated as a candidate CC member before the December 1917 Menshevik party congress. For a list of the CC members at that time, see "Iz zhizni RSDRP," *Luch'*, 19 November 1917, p. 4. For the list of the CC members in June 1918, see *Partiinye izvestiia*, no. 8 (10 June 1918), p. 13. See also the appendix to this book.

48. *Novyi luch'*, 19 December 1917, p. 2.

October 1917. By the end of April, the Petrograd Mensheviks could be satisfied with the results of their efforts. Their comeback as a factor in the workers' movement was indisputable.[49]

Rising unemployment, inflation, and imminent famine no doubt provoked dissatisfaction with the government's performance, but it would be a mistake to regard these factors as the only cause for this turn in the Mensheviks' fortunes. Equally important was the fact that the Mensheviks' organizational drive responded to the workers' need to have an outlet for their grievances. As the Bolsheviks turned the unions and soviets into state institutions, the channels for communicating disagreement, criticism, and complaints were profoundly altered. These organizations began to represent the interests of the state, as the Bolsheviks defined them. Encountering in their daily experience an impenetrable wall of bureaucratic insensibility in dozens of Bolshevik-run agencies and organizations, the workers felt isolated and frustrated. The creation and protection of workers' organizations independent of the state was a cornerstone of Menshevik policy, and that was a major reason for the Mensheviks' new popularity among the workers. The workers as a social group and the Mensheviks as an organized political party shared an interest in opposing the Bolsheviks' claim to speak on behalf of the workers—a claim made at the same time that the Bolsheviks were consolidating their party dictatorship.

The workers applauded Menshevik speakers who said that the dictatorship of the proletariat had been replaced by the dictatorship of the Communist party. The workers condemned the new bosses, the "leather jackets" of the Cheka, and demanded free elections to the soviets, independent workers' organizations, a free press, and the freedom to strike. In their positive programs, however, the workers showed far less unity. At some plants they supported the Menshevik-SR demands for reconvening of the Constituent Assembly and restoration of universal suffrage. At other plants, while they might approve the idea of exercising power through elected soviets, they perceived the restoration of universal suffrage as a return to the old order.[50] G. D. Kuchin, a prominent Menshevik leader and one of the founders of the Workers' Assembly, quoted some workers as saying, "All we need to do is send other [non-Bolshevik] honest people to the soviets and they would govern very well."[51]

On the basis of available evidence, it is impossible to judge accurately

49. Anweiler, *Soviets*, p. 229.

50. "Itogi vyborov," *Vpered*, 3 May 1918, p. 1.

51. G. D. Kuchin, "Zadachi i puti proletarskogo dvizheniia," *Novaia zaria*, 22 April 1918, pp. 24–25.

which idea—support for the Constituent Assembly or for newly elected soviets—enjoyed more popularity. In any event, the Menshevik-SR alliance was heading a movement without a coherent positive program. At the end of April, however, the differences in the movement had not yet hurt it. Its potentially divergent currents had coexisted so far, held together by a common opposition to Bolshevism. It was easier to paper over fundamental differences with ambiguous resolutions than to coordinate political action in a moment of crisis. But in May 1918, when the struggle with the Bolshevik authorities escalated into an open confrontation, the lack of unity was to play a crucial role in the fortunes of the Mensheviks and SRs.

The Shootings at Kolpino

By early April, the Bolsheviks were beginning to feel somewhat nervous about the assembly of upolnomochennye. Its reports on the causes of unemployment undermined the prestige of the Bolshevik commissars. Its calls for new elections embarrassed the leaders of the soviet. The Bolshevik newspapers started to label the upolnomochennye counterrevolutionaries, capitalist agents, and the like.[52] To disband the assembly, in view of its popularity, was politically hazardous, yet to let the Mensheviks continue building their campaign against the government was unacceptable. Apparently to feel out what the workers' reaction would be, the Bolsheviks launched attacks on individual upolnomochennye. At a meeting in the Cartridge plant, the Bolshevik leaders V. Volodarskii and D. Evdokimov demanded cancellation of the scheduled reports of the upolnomochennye. The workers' shouts and protests drowned out the Bolshevik speakers. The incident ended with a fist fight between the workers and the Red Guards.[53]

At the end of April, the Cheka raided the Workers' Assembly headquarters and confiscated "counterrevolutionary" literature. Information about similar Bolshevik plans was leaked to the opposition press, and the right Menshevik newspaper reported:

> Zinoviev declared in his last speech that the Bolsheviks were going to be "extremely decisive" in dealing with the Mensheviks and SRs, even though these Mensheviks and SRs were the working masses. It is reported by informed SR circles that the soviet authority of the Petrograd commune

52. See, for example, "Men'shevistskii obman," Izvestiia, 6 April 1918, p. 1. For an SR commentary on the Bolshevik press campaign against the Mensheviks, see "Men'sheviki—palachi," Strana, 3 April 1918, p. 1.
53. "Chrezvychainoe sobranie fabrik i zavodov," Novyi den', 11 April 1918, p. 3.

gave a number of directives to the district Red Army headquarters along those lines.[54]

The exact content of these directives is not known, but it is not unlikely that the Bolshevik leaders indeed ordered the Red Guards to respond "decisively" to the Menshevik-SR "provocations."[55] Whether there is any connection between these orders and the shooting in Kolpino just ten days later is uncertain. In any case, at the beginning of May, the language of workers' resolutions was becoming increasingly impatient. They no longer stopped at expressing disapproval of Bolshevik policies, but more and more often called for the Bolsheviks' ouster and the reconvocation of the Constituent Assembly. At a rally in the Obukhov plant, which by then had become a Menshevik-SR stronghold, the workers whistled in derision at the Bolshevik speakers and chased them away. It was decided to stage a May Day demonstration under the slogans of the Workers' Assembly. The resolution they adopted read in part:

> After hearing the report about the search at the headquarters of the Extraordinary Workers' Assembly, carried out on orders from Uritskii [the Petrograd Cheka chief], we, the workers of the Obukhov plant, having assembled at a general meeting on April 29, protest the actions of the Bolshevik government, which, on the eve of May Day, is acting like the Tsarist Autocracy. And we declare that we will struggle for our upolnomochennye against the ravishers and traitors of Russia.[56]

Some workers' protests were colored by panic, fear of famine, and despair. This general anxiety, although it had found an outlet in the Workers' Assembly, still led to outbursts of popular anger. One protest demonstration, unplanned and unorganized, led to a violent confrontation in Kolpino, an industrial suburb of Petrograd. Throughout April, workers' demands there, as in the rest of Petrograd, had focused on new elections, equalization of bread rations, and the right to make independent food purchases in the countryside. These demands, as usual, had been turned down. On May 9 a crowd of demonstrators, many women among them, marched to the Kolpino soviet to reiterate these demands. The Red Guards opened fire and the crowd scattered. Three workers were killed and several were wounded.

When news of the event reached the Izhorskii plant nearby, work came to a halt. A spontaneous workers' rally condemned the shootings

54. "1-oe maia," *Novyi den'*, 28 April 1918, p. 3.
55. For a Menshevik discussion of the Bolshevik measures against them, see "Bor'ba s men'shevizmom," *Novyi den'*, 26 April 1918, p. 3.
56. "Proval Bol'shevikov na Obukhovskom zavode," *Novyi den'*, 4 May 1918, p. 4.

and demanded an immediate investigation and strict punishment for those who had fired at the crowd, immediate new elections to the soviet, and disarming of the Red Guards. If these demands were not met, they would strike. A delegation of the plant's workers was sent to the Workers' Assembly and to other factories. The Kolpino Bolsheviks, instead of attempting reconciliation or even admitting that an unfortunate incident had occurred, ordered the Izhorskii workers to be fired upon as they left the plant after the protest rally; many were wounded. All those who had spoken at the rally were arrested, and mass searches were conducted.[57] Martial law was declared in Kolpino. This incident added fuel to the fire, and protest rallies erupted all over Petrograd.

Although at first glance the resolutions adopted at these rallies appear very similar, subtle differences can be noted. Most of them repeated demands for new elections to the Petrograd soviet, reconvocation of the Constituent Assembly, and the right to elect officials answerable to the people. The resolution at the Arsenal plant also called for "complete freedom of speech, press, assembly, and strikes" and for the release of several recently arrested comrades. Perhaps most important, it added: "With regret we note such a quick transformation of Socialist-Communists into oppressors of the workers." Of the 1,500 workers present at the rally, only 36 voted against the resolution and 24 abstained.[58]

At the Putilov works, protest demonstrations went on for four days. Zinoviev himself was sent to address the workers. He admitted that the food-supply situation was critical but insisted that the Bolshevik party, the vanguard of the proletariat, was doing everything in its power to improve it. The bourgeoisie, the bagmen, and the Menshevik instigators were undermining the government's efforts, exploiting the temporary difficulties, and inciting the workers.[59] The Bolsheviks at the rally demanded tougher measures against the Menshevik saboteurs, provocateurs, and instigators, and called for the removal of the chairman of the meeting, N. N. Glebov. The majority voted against this last demand. In his own speech, Glebov said that the commissars, instead of responding to the workers' demands, were "only arguing with the socialist parties, blaming the saboteurs and justifying themselves. . . . But we want to ask only one question. Can the people's commissars feed the hungry and guarantee peace on the domestic and foreign fronts?" At Glebov's suggestion, the meeting adopted a mandate to the Petrograd soviet demanding equal bread rations for workers and Red Guards, abolition of the restrictions on bringing food into the city, and convocation of a con-

57. "Besporiadki v Kolpino," Novyi den', 11 May 1918, p. 3; "Voennoe polozhenie v Kolpino," Novaia zhizn', 11 May 1918, p. 3.

58. "Posle Kolpinskikh rasstrelov, rezoliutsii," Delo naroda, 14 May 1918, p. 3.

59. "Rabochaia zhizn'," Novyi den', 11 May 1918, p. 4; "Miting po gudku," Novaia zhizn', 10 May 1918, p. 3.

ference on the food supply, with participation of all socialist and democratic organizations, for a speedy resolution of the food-supply crisis.[60] In practical terms, they were calling for the Bolshevik-led soviet, the opposition Workers' Assembly, the state food-supply agencies, and the Menshevik-led workers' cooperatives to sit down together and work out measures to combat the looming famine. Whatever the merits of this proposal, some opposition leaders thought it was highly unlikely that the Bolsheviks would agree to hold such a conference.[61] Yet the Putilov workers, while opposing Bolshevik policies, still pinned their hopes on making the authorities cooperate with opposition organizations. Nevertheless, the mandate also demanded "new elections to the Workers' and Soldiers' Soviet based on the principle of a general, direct, equal, secret, and free ballot."[62]

At the Sestroretsk armament plant, the local Bolsheviks, fearing food riots, had earlier made a few arrests. When the workers learned of the shootings in Kolpino, they called a strike. Several Bolsheviks were beaten up. The workers drew up a petition and dispatched a delegation to the Petrograd soviet and to the Workers' Assembly to demand immediate release of those arrested and new elections.[63] A chain reaction had been set off: workers' protests were followed by increasingly harsh actions by the Bolsheviks, which in turn intensified the workers' protests.

Workers at the Nevsky shipyard protested the Kolpino shootings, and after hearing a report from a representative of the Obukhov plant, they unanimously voted for a resolution that repeated the now familiar demands. An additional factor in the situation here was that the workers had held elections to the soviet in April, but the Bolsheviks on the soviet's credentials commission had refused to admit the new delegates. Apparently because the meeting was voting for one anti-Bolshevik resolution after another, a Bolshevik, Lisovskii, burst out, "This is a nest of counterrevolutionaries!" The chairman tried to calm him, but he went on: "We'll shoot people like you without mercy!" Whistles, clamor, shouts and threats against him and the commissars followed, and he finally had to leave the meeting. The opposition speaker who then took the floor urged the workers to avoid violence. The objective was not to fight the Bolsheviks but to vote them out and force them to recognize the election results.[64]

The protest resolution passed by workers at the Vulkan plant de-

---

60. "Na Putilovskom zavode," *Novaia zhizn'*, 11 May 1918, p. 3.
61. D. Kol'tsov, "Starye illiuzii na novyi lad," *Delo*, 3 June 1918, pp. 6–7.
62. "Miting po gudku," *Novaia zhizn'*, 10 May 1918, p. 3.
63. "Vie politique et sociale," *Echos de Russie*, nos. 18–19 (1 August 1918), p. 20.
64. "Obshchee sobranie: Nevskii sudostroitel'nyi i mekhanicheskii zavod," *Delo naroda*, 14 May 1918, p. 4.

manded "freedom of speech, a ban on arrests for political views, freedom of assembly, freedom for workers' and peasants' organizations."
The resolution of the Russian-Baltic plant declared, "Only the Constituent Assembly can lead the country to the path of salvation."[65] Protest
resolutions expressing similar political demands were adopted at all
major Petrograd factories and plants.

Perhaps the most radical anti-Bolshevik protest was made at the
Obukhov plant. A delegation of workers from the Izhorskii plant reported on the Kolpino shootings, and then, one after another, Menshevik and SR speakers condemned the "so-called workers' government" that was shooting the workers. In an emotional speech, one
worker said: "Let the soviet power know that even if we are dying of
hunger, the Constituent Assembly will save our motherland!" In addition to the demands made elsewhere, the Obukhov workers proclaimed
that they were ready "to support any workers' action in defense of
violated rights and justice."[66]

The openly hostile tone of this resolution provoked the Petrograd
Bolshevik leaders. On the night of May 12, the chairman of the meeting
and several others were arrested at their homes, by order of the district
soviet. The arrests sparked a strike, another stormy rally, and a proposal that the EC itself be seized and held hostage until those arrested
were released. The workers were persuaded to drop that idea and instead to send a delegation to the Smolny Institute, where the Petrograd
soviet had established its headquarters, to demand the immediate release of those arrested.[67] Their actions left no doubt, however, that they
had lost hope that the Bolsheviks would negotiate or cooperate with the
opposition parties. They seemed willing to try to drive the Bolsheviks
out of power.

The protests in the wake of the Kolpino shootings reveal conflicting
attitudes among the workers. All of the resolutions called for new elections to the Petrograd soviet and reconvocation of the Constituent Assembly, but the workers' actions varied widely. The Putilov workers'
call for a joint effort by all socialist organizations to resolve the food-
supply crisis implied that they still perceived the Bolsheviks as a
workers' party. The Arsenal workers, on the other hand, expressed
shock that the Bolsheviks had turned into oppressors. The Nevsky
shipyard workers booed the Bolsheviks, the Sestroretsk workers beat
them up, and the Obukhov workers referred to them as traitors and
executioners.

65. "Golod i rabochie," *Novaia zhizn'*, 12 May 1918, p. 3.
66. "Na Obukhovskom zavode," *Novaia zhizn'*, 11 May 1918, p. 3; "Rabochaia
zhizn'," *Novyi den'*, 12 May 1918, p. 4.
67. "Vie politique et sociale," *Echos de Russie*, nos. 18–19 (1 August 1918), p. 19.

The workers' understanding of the Menshevik-SR platform also varied immensely. For some, new elections to the soviets and reconvocation of the Constituent Assembly meant first and foremost the continuation of workers' power through the soviets, in which legitimately elected Bolsheviks would work together with Mensheviks and SRs in a united socialist front. For others, new elections meant "soviets without Bolsheviks" (as the rebellious Kronstadt sailors were to demand in 1921), which would cooperate with the bodies elected by universal suffrage, that is, the dumas and the Constituent Assembly. Still others lost faith in the soviets altogether and saw a solution exclusively in the reconvocation of the Constituent Assembly. The Menshevik and SR leaders may have deliberately avoided accentuating these differences. They realized that the workers' movement could be successful only if it was unified. The task of the moment was to force the Bolsheviks to hold new elections: the relationship of newly elected soviets to the Constituent Assembly could be defined later.

The wave of protest rallies at the Petrograd plants in mid-May was handled badly by the Bolsheviks. Sometimes, as at Kolpino and the Nevsky shipyard, they panicked and overreacted. The Cheka's heavy-handed shootings and arrests, intended to subdue the workers, produced the opposite effect. Zinoviev and other leaders of the Petrograd soviet refused to negotiate and compromise, apparently because, in the volatile atmosphere of those days, they were unable to control or coordinate the actions of the local Bolshevik militants. It is not clear whether Zinoviev himself ordered the Kolpino Red Guards to open fire, but once they had done so, he felt he had to stand by them. At the root of these Bolshevik actions was a tendency to regard workers' protests and demands as Menshevik provocations. Indeed, from this time on, the Bolsheviks became increasingly firm in their conviction that things would return to normal once the Menshevik and SR instigators were removed.

The workers' resolutions and the actions of the Workers' Assembly represented no immediate threat to the Bolsheviks' power. The workers were not armed; their protests were of political but not military significance. Much more dangerous for the Petrograd Bolsheviks was the rising discontent among the Baltic sailors and the Red Army soldiers, which jeopardized the Bolsheviks' ability to use armed force in the event of riots. In the spring of 1918, many of the Baltic ship crews openly supported the Workers' Assembly and its political stand. In Kronstadt, which had been a stronghold of Bolshevism, the Bolsheviks' share of seats in the newly elected soviet shrank from 131 to 53.[68] The chief cause of the sailors' discontent was the Brest treaty and the ever-

68. "Rabochaia zhizn': V Kronshtadte," *Strana*, 12 April 1918, p. 4.

mounting German demands, which threatened the existence of the Baltic fleet. The dictatorial actions of the Bolshevik commissars and the possibility that the ships would be disarmed also angered the sailors. In April 1918, at a Congress of Sailors in Moscow, speeches critical of the CPC were heard. The sailors complained that the Bolsheviks were ready to sacrifice the Baltic fleet for the sake of their own political and military survival.[69] In April and May their discontent crystallized into specific political declarations. Some of them sounded like the criticism voiced by the Left Communists and the Left SRs: that the government was capitulating to German imperialism and abandoning the ideals of the October Revolution. Others called for unity among all socialist parties; still others, echoing the Mensheviks and SRs, demanded resignation of the CPC and reconvocation of the Constituent Assembly. Politically, the sailors' movement was rather fragmented; the seamen were united only by dissatisfaction with Lenin's government. At a conference of Baltic sailors in Petrograd in the middle of April, speakers accused the CPC of having "broken away from the masses and barricaded itself from the people behind many tiers of guards in the Kremlin" and of having "turned the CEC into a voting machine." They complained that the Bolsheviks had deceived the sailors, no longer heeded their opinions, and were only using them for their own purposes. "To whom are Lenin and Trotsky indebted? To us, the sailors! We brought about the October uprising! We shed our blood all over Russia, and now those we raised to power want to disarm us! They call us a gang of brigands and have decided to get rid of us!"[70]

The worst development from the Bolshevik point of view would have been a convergence of the workers' and sailors' protest movements. It was such a convergence that had swept aside the Provisional Government in October. The Baltic fleet's mining unit, which was stationed not far from the Obukhov plant, had already developed close contacts with the protesting workers. It appears, however, that the Mensheviks paid much less attention to contacts with the sailors (and with the soldiers) than did the SRs. In addition to open and public organizations, the SRs had armed underground cells (*druzhiny*).[71] Though little is known about these cells, it is reasonably certain that the SRs planned

69. "Rezoliutsiia moriakov," *Novyi den'*, 18 April 1918.
70. B. Rossov, "Sredi nedovol'nykh moriakov," *Utro Petrograda*, 22 April 1918, p. 2.
71. For a general description of the SR underground, see V. M. Zenzinov, "Bor'ba rossiiskoi demokratii s bol'shevikami v 1918 godu," Nik. Col. no. 7, box 1, file 24. Zenzinov was a member of the SR CC. His positive appraisal contrasts with the memoirs of Grigorii Semenov, who was an SR functionary engaged in underground work; see Semenov, *Voennaia i boevaia rabota*. On aspects of legal SR activity, see the Shreider papers, "Iz deiatel'nosti SR posle 1917 goda," Nik. Col. no. 104. (G. I. Shreider was mayor of Petrograd in 1917.)

to use armed force in the event of an uprising or a drastic Bolshevik police action against them.

On May 9, the Baltic mining unit made public a resolution demanding the abolition of the Petrograd soviet, the resignation of the CPC, and the reconvocation of the Constituent Assembly.[72] By taking this step, the unit may have been trying to attract other crews of the Baltic fleet to their side. The resolution was the main item on the agenda of the Baltic fleet conference in Petrograd on May 11.[73] It is important to note that the sailors invited representatives of the Workers' Assembly of Upolnomochennye to take part in the conference. Bolshevik speakers were interrupted by shouts: "We want freedom! Where are the elections? What kind of socialism is this?" Said one of the sailors: "What kind of workers' power is this, when the workers of the Tube Works and many others recall their representatives from the soviet? They no longer reflect the will of the workers but rely on soldiers' bayonets." The Bolshevik speakers talked about the world revolution that would save the socialist revolution in Russia, and they appealed for patience and calm. But the sailors' patience was at an end. They shouted such biting personal insults at some of the Bolshevik commissars that the Bolshevik faction walked out in protest. A representative of the Kolpino workers then told the sailors that the Petrograd soviet had refused to listen to a report on the Kolpino shootings. "From January on," he said, "we have been struggling for new elections to our soviet, but the old representatives are holding on to power with bayonets and refuse to go."[74]

The atmosphere at this conference seems to have been reminiscent of the September-October days in 1917. At that time, too, government representatives had tried to calm the sailors, and they had refused to listen. The opposition party, at that time the Bolsheviks, had been gaining strength and popularity. Now, in May 1918, the roles had changed: the Bolsheviks, representing the government, were trying to calm the sailors, and the opposition parties were gaining popularity. The sailors' attitude toward the socialist parties of the Provisional Government must have changed since October. Under the Provisional Government, workers had not been shot at, elections had taken place, and defeated deputies had turned over their seats in the soviets and dumas to their elected successors. The comparison could not have been favorable to the Bolsheviks. It is extremely difficult to pinpoint the party leanings of the sailors. In general, they were socialist, idealistic, uncompromising, and antigovernment. The fact that the Menshevik-SR

---

72. Bernshtam, ed., *Nezavisimoe rabochee dvizhenie*, document no. 44, pp. 176–79.
73. "Sobranie matrosov," *Delo naroda*, 14 May 1918, p. 3.
74. Pestovskii, "Konferentsiia moriakov," *Utro Petrograda*, 13 May 1918, p. 3.

leaders of the Workers' Assembly were invited to the sailors' conference suggests a certain degree of political cooperation between them. But more important for the political struggle in May than the sailors' party orientations was their marked independence, their readiness to intervene in politics, express demands, and take sides, and their firm conviction that they were a force that could not be ignored.

At the same time that the sailors were convening, the Red Army soldiers were also meeting in Petrograd. The conference of the Red Army—the last resort of the Bolshevik authorities if workers' unrest got out of control—opened with two defeats for the Bolsheviks. First, a Left SR, Berezin, was elected as chairman. The Bolshevik delegates demanded his ouster; the majority threatened to remove the Bolsheviks instead. Second, the conference voted to consider all of its decisions binding on the soviet authorities. Again the Bolsheviks objected, but they were in a weak position, for their newspapers had been constantly saying that the decisions of the masses were "law" for the soviet government. A Bolshevik commissar, Boris Pozern, accused the soldiers of reluctance to sacrifice: "Indignation reigns at all the factories because the Red Army soldiers get a ration of a whole pound of bread." The soldiers responded with counteraccusations: "Why is there so much hubbub against the reconvocation of the Constituent Assembly? It's not the Constituent Assembly one should be afraid of, but a new Skoropadskii!" They were referring, of course, to the general who was leading counterrevolutionary forces in the Ukraine (see chapter 3).

Turning to the problems facing the Bolshevik government, Pozern said:

> "At the present time, the soviet power is living through the most critical moments in the whole of its existence. Even we ourselves doubt that our rule can survive. We're surrounded by enemies on all sides. Skoropadskiis and Kornilovs and their ilk are standing at our doorstep. We have no support. Everywhere, all over, on the streets and in the restaurants, in the squares, even at the factories and plants, the masses have turned away from us and are already talking openly about the need to abolish soviet power and convene the Constituent Assembly."[75]

Pozern was not the only Bolshevik to hold such views, as we shall see, but few were expressing them so openly. Meanwhile, the soldiers' discontent was manifesting itself in other ways as well. In Saratov it escalated to armed struggle with the Bolsheviks; soldiers in Petrograd were reported to have sided with striking workers numerous times at the end of May.[76] Obviously the reliability of these units for antiworker actions was doubtful.

75. "Konferentsiia krasnoarmeitsev," *Delo naroda*, 14 May 1918, p. 3.
76. Bernshtam, ed., *Nezavisimoe rabochee dvizhenie*, document no. 41, p. 168.

Toward the end of May, in a letter to local party organizations, the Bolshevik CC itself described the situation in terms strikingly similar to those Pozern had used: "Never have we lived through such a difficult moment." A week later, in another letter, it admitted that "this crisis is very, very acute. . . . Every active party comrade has had to take note of the decline in party membership; in larger centers, a decline in quantity goes hand in hand with a decline in quality. . . . General decline in party work, disintegration in the party organizations are beyond doubt."[77]

The October coalition among the workers, the soldiers, the sailors, and the Bolsheviks was breaking down. The very social classes that had supported the Bolsheviks in October were turning against them in May. Bolshevism as a social movement was in deep crisis. The numbers of Bolshevik party members in Petrograd had dropped from 35,000 in October 1917 to 15,000 in May 1918.[78] If these trends continued, the Bolsheviks' hold on power could be loosened. Something had to be done, particularly about the most pressing problem of the day, food supply.

The Food-Supply Crisis

The debates on the food-supply crisis in the Petrograd soviet and in the Workers' Assembly shed light on the Bolsheviks' and Mensheviks' thinking about the options open to them. The Bolsheviks regarded free movement in and out of the city, free trade, and free elections as steps too risky for them to allow. At the soviet session on May 9, M. M. Lashevich, a Bolshevik, and S. Iu. Semkovskii, leader of the Menshevik faction, clashed over food-supply policy. Semkovskii reiterated the Menshevik view that the arbitrariness and incompetence of the Bolshevik dictators was at the root of the crisis and that the Constituent Assembly had to be reconvened. Lashevich's answer is most interesting:

"If those sitting on the right could give assurances that with the reconvocation of the Constituent Assembly, the peasantry would deliver bread, then we could strike a bargain [*stolkovat'sia*] with them. But the peasants would not give bread. They wouldn't take 30 rubles for a pud of grain

77. "Tsirkuliarnoe pis'mo TsK RKP(b)," *Pravda*, 22 May 1918, p. 2, and "Ko vsem komitetam, gruppam, chlenam RKP(b)," *Pravda*, 29 May 1918, p. 1. For Menshevik and SR discussions of the crisis of Bolshevism, see K., "Na zakate," *Delo*, 12 June 1918, pp. 4–5, and "Krizis sovetskoi vlasti," *Sotsialist revoliutsioner*, no. 2 (April 1918), pp. 7–9.

78. *Perepiska Sekretariata*, document no. 174, 3:136. See also Astrakhan, *Bol'sheviki i ikh politicheskie protivniki*, p. 235.

when they have to pay outrageous sums for iron and cloth. Even Germany
is ruled not by the Reichstag but by food-supply dictators."[79]

As we saw earlier (chapter 3), Lashevich's opinion that the only way to
resolve the crisis was to give dictatorial powers to the managers of the
food supply was not shared by all Bolshevik leaders. Like him, however, many of them saw no need to come to an understanding with the
opposition parties. In their view, the abolition of trade restrictions, the
reconvocation of the Constituent Assembly, and a compromise with the
Mensheviks and SRs would not have eased the food-supply problem,
anyway. To accept the opposition's demands amounted in their minds
to capitulation. In a reconvened Constituent Assembly, the Bolshevik
party would not have been able to claim anything approaching the one-
quarter of the national vote it had once had. Even the limited-franchise
elections to the city soviets had demonstrated their weakness. The
Bolsheviks had either to hold on to all power or to face the prospect of
having close to none. That realization was the basis of Lashevich's
intransigence and his advocacy of dictatorship.

The first part of the soviet's session on May 11 was devoted to a
commemoration of the hundredth anniversary of Karl Marx's birth. The
Bolsheviks had been preparing for this event for some time; it was
unfortunate that the Kolpino shootings marred the celebration, but they
decided to go ahead with it anyway. The Mensheviks, however, would
not permit the shootings to pass unnoticed. Semkovskii mounted the
podium and demanded that the soviet hear a report by the Kolpino
workers. His words were greeted with catcalls, shouts, and clamor.
Semkovskii shouted over the commotion, "Marx would turn over in his
grave if he knew that the regime that's celebrating his birth has been
shooting hungry workers!"[80] This was too much for the Bolsheviks.
"Arrest Semkovskii!" "Down with him!" "Hang him!" came the cries
from the Bolshevik benches. The Red Guards rushed to the podium and
dragged Semkovskii away. The representative of the Kolpino workers
was arrested and the Menshevik faction walked out in protest. The
session then proceeded without further interruption.

At the very end of the session, Zinoviev abruptly and hurriedly announced that the Bolsheviks had decided to relax some of the restrictions to which objections had been raised. Individuals would now be
permitted to bring into the city 1.5 puds (about 54 pounds) of potatoes,
and some private initiative would be tolerated in food supply.[81] He did

79. "Zasedanie Petrogradskogo soveta," *Novyi den'*, 10 May 1918, p. 2.
80. "Zasedanie Petrogradskogo soveta," *Novyi den'*, 12 May 1918, p. 2.
81. Ibid.

not explain what form that initiative would take or why potatoes were being singled out as permissible for private importation, and the Menshevik faction was not there to ask him. These ambiguities notwithstanding, the purpose of Zinoviev's move was clear enough: he wanted to appease the workers without going so far that the militants in his own party would accuse him of capitulating to the Menshevik demands.

This episode gives us an instructive glimpse at the interaction between the Bolsheviks and the Mensheviks in the soviet. The Petrograd soviet was a much rougher place than the CEC, where some parliamentary norms were still observed. In the soviet, threats, insults, and outright force were frequent occurrences. The soviet was neither a decision-making nor a policy-deliberating institution. Decisions were made in advance and deliberations were all but impossible in its theatrical atmosphere. The Bolshevik leaders and the representatives of the "revolutionary masses" applauded each other, and the Bolshevik activists were told that they were the embodiment of the dictatorship of the proletariat, the workers' vangard. The Mensheviks did what they could to put an end to this spectacle. Not only did they point to the Bolsheviks' mistakes and incompetence, and accuse them of usurping workers' rights by refusing to hold new elections; using their frequently superior knowledge of Marxism, they also argued that the Bolshevik dictatorship had nothing to do with Marxism, that its socialism was no more than a caricature. Interestingly, the newer members of the Bolshevik party seemed to find reconciliation with the Mensheviks more difficult than Zinoviev and the old-guard Bolsheviks: the Mensheviks' criticism undermined their confidence in themselves.

The Menshevik workers hailed the partial lifting of restrictions on food brought into the city as a victory. It strengthened the position of those who had maintained that it was possible to force changes in Bolshevik policies by public pressure. According to a contemporary Soviet historian, permission to bring 1.5 puds of potatoes into Petrograd loosed a flood of people on the countryside to purchase provisions, and a new term—*polutoropudnichestvo*, the "one-and-a-half-pud movement"—was coined to describe the phenomenon.[82]

These events brought the realization that the Workers' Assembly was potentially a major political force. In the two months of its existence its membership had doubled to 200 upolnomochennye representing 100,000 Petrograd workers, or about two-thirds of all employed workers in the city.[83] The underlying springs of the assembly's political

82. Sokolov, *Revoliutsiia i khleb*, p. 79.
83. "Sostav sobraniia upolnomochennykh," *Novaia zhizn'*, 19 May 1918, p. 3; "Vie

strength lay not only in numbers but also in its translation of workers' grievances into a concrete program of action. At the assembly's sessions on May 11–13 and 15, the Bolsheviks' opponents, encouraged by the concessions, discussed further steps that could be undertaken to alleviate the food shortage.

The Menshevik economist S. Zagorskii, an editor of *Delo* and a frequent contributor of articles to the socialist press, pointed out that in the long run the problem of the food supply in Petrograd could not be resolved without political changes in the country. So long as the Bolshevik authorities in the provinces were disbanding the opposition-led soviets and confiscating goods in transit, normal economic life could not be restored. Only the removal of the Bolshevik dictatorship and the reconvocation of a Constituent Assembly that would enjoy popular support could ensure eventual economic recovery.[84]

No one objected in principle to this assessment of the situation, but sharp differences emerged over how the Bolshevik government could be forced to resign. In a speech at the May 15 session, Smirnov brought out the Mensheviks' by-now familiar frustrations. He agreed that the problem of the food supply was intrinsically connected with the problem of who held power. And the Petrograd proletariat could not resolve the problem of power by itself, without organized and concerted action in other cities. Moreover, there was a danger that popular wrath against the Bolsheviks might lead to pogroms and mob rule. The prospect of food riots was repugnant to the Mensheviks, who feared that the extreme right would be the beneficiary. In terms of practical policy, all that Smirnov could suggest was that confrontation and violence be avoided and that the workers exert peaceful pressure on the government.[85]

Some speakers, especially at the session on May 12, were more inclined to go ahead with direct action against the government. The details of this crucial debate, which largely determined the assembly's policy at the time, are not known. Few names are given in the newspaper reports, obviously out of caution. It is clear, though, that the proponents of direct action were arguing that the question was not

---

politique et sociale," *Echos de Russie*, nos. 18–19 (1 August 1918), pp. 18–20. For a summary of the excellent statistical data on the numbers of employed workers in Petrograd, by industry, see M. Kapitsa, "Petrogradskaia tiazhelaia promyshlennost'," *Delo naroda*, 15 May 1918, p. 2. For official Soviet data, see Khesin, *Stanovlenie proletarskoi diktatury*, p. 276. See also "Rabochie Petrograda," in Drobizhev, ed., *Rabochii klass Sovetskoi Rossii*, pp. 83–103.

84. "Ekstrennoe zasedanie tsentral'nogo i raionnykh biuro Chrezvychainogo sobraniia upolnomochennykh fabrik i zavodov," *Delo naroda*, 14 May 1918, p. 4; "Sobranie upolnomochennykh fabrik i zavodov," *Delo naroda*, 18 May 1918, p. 1.

85. Bernshtam, ed., *Nezavisimoe rabochee dvizhenie*, document no. 32, p. 143.

whether the workers should seek open confrontation with the Bolsheviks, but when. The opponents of immediate action evidently prevailed, for "not a single speaker considered it necessary or possible to call on the workers to rise." Such a call would have amounted, in the opinion of the moderates, to "promising the masses bread immediately, when in fact no power was capable of delivering it." In any case, "food riots occur spontaneously; they do not lend themselves to organization and may have unforeseen consequences."[86] Thus there was no support for a rush to the barricades. But the debate barely concealed the dilemma facing the leaders of the Workers' Assembly: What were they to do if the workers' protest movement escalated into strikes and riots? Should they yield to the workers' impulses or try to contain them?

A compromise resolution was worked out. The assembly, it said, "found it necessary to stage a one-day general protest strike against the violence and overall policy of the Bolshevik regime and entrusted the bureau to introduce this question for deliberation at the plenary session of the assembly of upolnomochennye." As far as practical measures to deal with food shortages were concerned, the assembly leaders recommended increases in the fixed prices of bread in order to encourage private trade; abolition of all restrictions on entering and leaving the city; abolition of the antiprofiteering detachments; encouragement of workers' self-help boards and individual as well as collective purchases of food in the countryside; insistence on full accounting by the Bolshevik food-supply agencies; and genuine workers' control over the actions of the Bolshevik authorities.[87] Such a resolution amounted to an open challenge to the Petrograd Bolsheviks. If implemented, this program would have ended their control over the food supply.

The Bolshevik newspapers reacted angrily. *Izvestiia* accused the assembly leaders of "irresponsible demagoguery in deftly using the understandable discontent among some strata of the workers, those suffering from the collapse of the economy and food supply and frantically rushing about in search of a way out," and lashed out at "the main contingent of their followers"—"the old guard of acquiescers [*soglashateli*] and social traitors, of unrepentant bourgeois lackeys, Mensheviks, and SRs, and also of a mixed bag of nonparty types, at best benighted and indifferent, at worst counterrevolutionaries and Black Hundreds."[88]

Still, some action had to be taken to deal with the food-supply situation. A session of the Petrograd soviet was convened on May 18, and

86. "Ekstrennoe zasedanie," *Delo naroda*, 14 May 1918, p. 4.
87. Ibid.
88. "Kommivoiazhery sotsial predatel'stva," *Izvestiia*, 21 May 1918, p. 1.

factory committees were invited to participate in an attempt to coun-
teract the popularity of the Workers' Assembly. When Zinoviev addressed the session, he acknowledged that "in very large segments of
the population the view is spreading that at this time perhaps free
trade, even though it would be a violation of our principles, would
nevertheless give us a breathing spell, and would truly save us, at least
for a short time, from the horrors [of famine] we face at present. Let us
think it over: maybe the Mensheviks and SRs are right that free trade
would save us."[89] He then proceeded to demolish the argument. Free
trade, he said, would only strengthen the bourgeoisie, a solution that
the vanguard of the proletariat could not accept. Apparently alluding to
the Menshevik-sponsored workers' demand for new elections, Zinoviev said, "The workers are now going against their representatives [in
the soviet], but the representatives must have the courage to go against
the current."[90] Despite what he had said a week ago about "concessions
to private initiative," Zinoviev now affirmed the party's line of intensified struggle against the bagmen. The Bolshevik solution to the food-
supply crisis was to send armed detachments to the countryside to
requisition grain from the "peasant bourgeoisie" by force. Those who
joined the detachments would receive 150 rubles a month and a food
allotment.[91] This tactic was, in effect, an effort to divert the workers'
anger from the government to the "class enemy." As in October, the
Bolsheviks wanted to unleash the aggressive instincts of the masses in a
campaign to "loot the looters," except that now it was the peasants that
were to be looted.

At a session of the Workers' Assembly on May 22 the speakers unanimously condemned the Bolsheviks' war on the peasantry. "Why is it
necessary to send armed detachments and confiscate grain by force
when the antiprofiteering detachments didn't let the traders who
wanted to sell bread enter the city?" asked one representative. A
worker from the Obukhov plant suggested a workers' boycott of those
who joined the requisition detachments. The upolnomochennye of the
Baltic, Arsenal, Obukhov, and other plants urged the assembly to proceed immediately with a political strike against the detachments. By
unanimous vote, the assembly approved a proposal to launch a general
strike at all factories represented at the assembly if the Bolsheviks took
action against it.

One of the most important decisions of the session was to send a

---

89. Grigorii Zinov'ev, "Rech na chrezvychainom sobranii Petrogradskogo soveta 18
maia 1918 goda," in *Dve rechi*, p. 35.
90. "V Petrogradskom sovete," *Vecherniaia zvezda*, 20 May 1918, p. 4.
91. "Prizyv Zinov'eva vstupat' v otriady," *Znamia bor'by*, 25 May 1918.

delegation to Moscow to coordinate workers' actions in the two capitals.[92] The mandate that the delegation was to bring to the Moscow
workers was a remarkable document, full of despair and indignation,
intertwining old workers' complaints with new ones:

> We, the Petrograd workers, entrust our delegates with the following mes-
> sage: Our life has become unbearable. The plants are idle. Our children are
> dying of hunger. Tens of thousands of proletarians are in need of public
> canteens. To the starving they give bullets, and all who dare to talk about it
> they call enemies of the people. Freedom of speech is stifled. We can no
> longer speak and write freely. Our organizations are persecuted. Strikes
> are banned. There are no courts. We are ruled by uncontrollable people in
> whom we have long since lost trust, whom we have not elected, who taunt
> us, who do not respect law, rights, and honor, who love only power and
> have betrayed us for it. . . . The regime hid behind our name, a regime
> inimical to us, a regime that has brought us only suffering and dishonor.
> We want it to go! . . . It has promised us socialism and has destroyed the
> economy with its meaningless experiments. . . . Instead of socialism,
> empty plants, cold furnaces, thousands of unemployed, misery. . . . Our
> organizations are destroyed. Since [the soviets] have become the organs of
> power in a "socialist motherland," they no longer defend us. We are
> dispersed, disarmed, defeated, without unions, without the right to strike,
> without freedom of the press; we are defenseless against our own and
> German capitalists, against state capitalism, which is defended by ma-
> chine guns, more defenseless than under tsarism.[93]

Perhaps the most striking element of this appeal is its rendering of the
Menshevik critique of Bolshevik socialism. Like the first declaration of
the Workers' Assembly, this one is full of complaints against the Bolshevik rule, but now the workers no longer express surprise that the
"workers' government" does not defend them. Now the Bolsheviks are
perceived as "uncontrollable people" who hide behind the workers'
name. Furthermore, the workers now have a clearer idea of what they
want: freedom of speech and of the press, independent unions free to
strike and to elect their own leaders, the rule of law. In short, they want
the Bolshevik regime to disappear.

In a starving city with 100,000 unemployed, no doubt many were
willing to join the requisition detachments with a guaranteed bread
ration. On the whole, though, the workers' reaction to the Bolsheviks'
new food-supply policy was one of astonishment and indignation. At a
general meeting at the Putilov plant on May 28, shouts of "Down with
autocracy!" interrupted speeches by the Bolsheviks, whose attempts to

---

92. Bernshtam, ed., *Nezavisimoe rabochee dvizhenie*, document no. 35, pp. 149–50.
93. "Nakaz delegatsii k Moskovskim rabochim: Sredi rabochikh: Na perevale," *Delo*,
12 June 1918, pp. 15–16.

blame the bourgeoisie for troubles with the food supply fell on unsym-
pathetic ears. An opposition speaker, on the other hand, received enthusiastic applause when he said that the task of food supply should be
entrusted to the workers themselves. Unrestricted collective purchases
by workers in the countryside, rather than grain requisitioning, were
the answer. A Red Army soldier said in an emotional speech that the
Red Army had nothing to do with requisition detachments, that they
were the business of the Cheka. The Red Army soldiers would never go
against the people. His words, too, were greeted with loud applause.[94]
A strongly worded protest resolution was adopted: "We, the workers of
the Putilov plant, protest against sending the Red Army to war against
the peasants, and we declare that we are not guilty of the blood that is
being shed in our name, and we ourselves will take no part in this."[95]
The resolution reiterated the long-standing demands for freedom to
import food into the city without limit; abolition of restrictions on
entering and leaving the city; equalization of bread rations for workers
and Red Guards; freedom of press, assembly, and unions; abolition of
the death penalty; and an end to the civil war.

On the same day, to the surprise of the leaders of both the Workers'
Assembly and the city soviet, a strike movement broke out in Petrograd.
Over the next three days, strikes were called at many factories. The
Bolsheviks sent speakers to the factories to urge the workers to stay
calm; in some plants, the workers refused to listen. The assembly of
upolnomochennye debated the question of a general strike. The representatives of some plants, particularly those of the Nevskii district,
where most of the plants had already been struck, urged the assembly
to convert the separate strikes into a general strike and to demand the
resignation of the Bolshevik government. At an assembly session on
May 29, an Obukhov plant representative declared that his colleagues
were ready to carry out the decisions of the Workers' Assembly. The
Putilov representative said that the workers at his plant, too, were
prepared to strike. The speeches of the upolnomochennye clearly indicated that what the workers needed most was political leadership. A
railway worker called on the assembly "to take the movement into its
own hands and explain to the workers what to do."[96] Present at this
session were specially delegated representatives of some Red Army
units and of the railroad workers. Their presence was significant, for
the soldiers' support of the strikers and the railroad workers' readiness
to block the arrival of any troops sent from Moscow would be essential
if a general strike was to succeed.

94. "Brozhenie sredi rabochikh," Novaia zhizn', 29 May 1918, p. 3.
95. "Na Putilovskom zavode," Petrogradskoe ekho, 29 May 1918.
96. Bernshtam, ed., Nezavisimoe rabochee dvizhenie, document no. 40, p. 164.

The leaders of the assembly were suddenly faced with decisions about matters they were not prepared to deal with. The Workers' Assembly had started out as a forum on evacuation and unemployment. Now it had to answer such questions as: Would the call for a general strike to force the Bolsheviks to resign be supported by all Petrograd plants? How many Red Army units would support the strikers or at least stay neutral? How strong were the Cheka forces in Petrograd? Would the Moscow workers support the movement? Fearing to risk action before these questions could be answered, the assembly's bureau deferred a decision until the issues could be discussed by the district assemblies of upolnomochennye.

On May 29, as strikes were breaking out, the Petrograd soviet adopted a new system of bread rations. The population was divided into several categories: members of the bourgeoisie were allotted 25 grams of bread a day, employees 50 grams, workers 100 grams, and those engaged in heavy labor 200 grams. Zinoviev declared that the bourgeoisie were getting just enough bread to keep them from forgetting how it smelled, while the workers' rations demonstrated their privileged position—a position they could have achieved nowhere but under the dictatorship of the proletariat.[97] The Bolsheviks were well aware that during the earlier campaigns, the mobilization of the bourgeoisie to dig trenches and their eviction from their apartments had been hailed by the Petrograd workers.

The Bolsheviks' new rationing system was not altogether successful. Resolutions adopted at various plants spoke of the "paltry dole" [*podachka*] for workers.[98] At the same time, some workers refused to accept higher rations at the expense of the rest of the population. The upolnomochennye reported that the workers felt embarrassed to receive a higher ration while the clerks at their own plants were starving. On the day the new system was announced, the assembly appealed to the Petrograd workers with the following declaration:

> The soviet authority has come up with a new means of struggling against famine—to feed the hungry workers at the expense of the rest of the population. People are dying of hunger on the streets; little children are dying; but for us they increase the bread ration. . . . The soviet authority is offering a bribe to the working class which will cause hostility toward it among other groups of the population. We . . . reject with indignation the authorities' attempts to bribe the workers with an additional portion of bread, and we call on the Petrograd proletariat to protest with all its might against this attempt.[99]

97. "La Famine et les ouvriers," *Echos de Russie*, nos. 18–19 (1 August 1918), pp. 21–22.

98. Bernshtam, ed., *Nezavisimoe rabochee dvizhenie*, document no. 40, p. 169.

99. The entire text is in *Echos de Russie*, nos. 18–19 (1 August 1918), pp. 18–20.

It appeared possible that the new rations would bring elements of disunity into the workers' ranks.

Debate continued the next day, May 30, over whether to expand the strike movement to a general strike. Some speakers proposed a large demonstration to converge on the Smolny from various parts of the city. This demonstration, unlike the one on January 5 in support of the Constituent Assembly when it was disbanded, would be protected by the sailors of the mining unit, then docked along the Neva River. It was not clear, however, what the attitude of other navy and army units would be. Furthermore, the reports of the upolnomochennye from some plants suggested that some workers, even though they condemned the Bolsheviks, were still willing to accept the higher bread ration. Most important, some speakers voiced the fear that if a decisive confrontation between the Bolsheviks and the proletariat should bleed both sides white, "some third force"—presumably the monarchists—"might be the beneficiary."[100] Semkovskii, the Menshevik leader in the Petrograd soviet, though speaking hopefully of "a spontaneous movement . . . that can sweep away the Bolshevik regime," urged the workers not to rush blindly into action but to prepare themselves for a well-coordinated effort.[101] In the end, the assembly decided to put off a general strike, and the next day work was resumed at some factories in the Nevskii district.

The proponents of a general strike did not give up, however. At the Workers' Assembly session on June 1, an Obukhov plant representative declared that his plant was ready to stop work as soon as the call came from the assembly. Another speaker argued that a general strike would fail because the workers were not ready for a showdown with the Bolsheviks. A general strike and a march to the center of the city, if not well prepared, could lead to violence and bloodshed. Izmailov, representing the workers of the Putilov plant, presented their proposal that the assembly "discuss the question of the revolutionary elections of the soviet."[102] On May 29 the Putilov workers had resolved to "recall our representatives from the soviet because the comrades who represent our plant at present do not reflect our interests. We consider only the newly elected delegates to be our genuine representatives."[103] The Putilov representative urged this course of action upon the assembly, and it proved to be an acceptable compromise. The assembly passed a

100. Bernshtam, ed., *Nezavisimoe rabochee dvizhenie*, document no. 41, p. 169.

101. S. Semkovskii, "Stikhiinoe dvizhenie i soznatel'naia bor'ba," *Rabochii internatsional* (journal of Menshevik CC, Petrograd), nos. 3–4 (June 1918), pp. 3–4.

102. "Chrezvychainoe sobranie upolnomochennykh," *Utro Petrograda*, 3 June 1918, p. 1.

103. "Na Putilovskom zavode," *Petrogradskoe ekho*, 29 May 1918.

resolution calling on "the workers of Petrograd energetically to prepare the workers' masses for a political strike against the current regime." The strike's objectives were to be "the transfer of power to the Constituent Assembly, restoration of the organs of local self-government, and a struggle for the unity and independence of the Russian republic" (this last objective reflected opposition to the Brest treaty).[104] This resolution echoed the position taken at the All-Russian Menshevik Party conference that had taken place shortly before (see chapter 7). Meanwhile, after lengthy and heated debate, a general strike was again postponed, though preparation for it was declared to be the assembly's most important task.[105]

Bolshevik newspapers throughout the country covered the assembly's proceedings fairly accurately, though they embellished their stories with a few insults. Here, for example, is the report on the session of June 1 published by the Saratov *Izvestiia*:

> The parties of the social traitors have decided to use the food-supply crisis for their own ends. By demagogical agitation, the Mensheviks and SRs have managed to arouse backward elements of the Petrograd proletariat and to create a provocateur organization parallel to the soviet, the so-called Assembly of Upolnomochennye of the Factories and Plants, which was not in fact elected by anyone. Here open propaganda is going on for a political strike directed at the overthrow of soviet power. At the meeting on June 1, the right SRs were for an immediate strike and the Mensheviks against it, because it was clear that an immediate strike would not be successful. Both groups of social traitors decided to postpone the strike in order to prepare energetically for a political strike.[106]

The Turning Tide

Important changes occurred in the spring of 1918 in the triangular relationship among the workers, the Bolsheviks, and the Mensheviks. The high pitch of worker radicalism orchestrated by the Bolsheviks in October had been followed by a brief period of euphoria, a celebration of the victory of the proletariat, which in turn had gradually given way to disillusionment with Bolshevism. Unrealized expectations, unemployment, and famine generated a sense of disorientation and helplessness among Russian workers. When the mounting number of griev-

104. *Utro Petrograda*, 3 June 1918, p. 1.
105. V. Mirov, "Politicheskoe obozrenie," *Delo*, no. 9 (3 June 1918), pp. 12–13.
106. "Sotsial predateli gotoviat politicheskuiu stachku," *Izv. Sar. sov.* 5 June 1918, p. 1.

ances and demands were met with repressive measures, the pace of the protest movement quickened. The Workers' Assembly started with a moderate critique of Bolshevik policies and recommended changes. When their recommendations were ignored, the workers became increasingly impatient and the first confrontations occurred. The Red Guards' firing at protesting demonstrators generated more protests, followed by arrests, lockouts, and more shootings. At the end of May, for the first time since October, some workers staged political strikes against the Bolshevik government in Petrograd. Instead of merely recommending or pleading, they now *demanded* political changes. The workers had shifted their support from the Bolsheviks to the Mensheviks—a shift that has gone largely unacknowledged. The strength of the Mensheviks' appeal to the workers lay in their commitment to independent workers' organizations, in response to workers' fears of defenselessness and helplessness vis-à-vis the new "workers'" state. Therein lay the significance of the Workers' Assembly of Upolnomochennye.

The Mensheviks' preoccupation with "conscious" as opposed to "spontaneous" struggle, however, created difficulties and misunderstanding between the leaders and the workers. During the crucial days at the end of May, the Menshevik leaders tried to contain the workers' anti-Bolshevik radicalism. They sought to force the Bolshevik government to resign by public pressure rather than by a violent uprising. Out of fear that a rebellion might help the rightists, out of scruples about promising too much, and out of a desire to preserve the precarious unity of the movement, the Mensheviks cancelled the ongoing strikes without exacting tangible concessions from the Bolsheviks. Thus, on the eve of the coming showdown with the government, the Menshevik leaders were faced with a series of problems. How were they to unite potentially divergent currents into an effective movement? How could they keep a "conscious" struggle from degenerating into a "spontaneous" rebellion? And how could they exert pressure on the Bolshevik government without lending strength to the rightists or provoking an all-out onslaught by the Cheka?

PART III

THE SHOWDOWN

May–October 1918

CHAPTER 7

Discord among the Socialists

By June 1918 the withdrawal of political support by the majority of the social groups that had supported the Bolsheviks in October—workers, soldiers, and peasants—was plunging the regime into crisis. The problems included rising unemployment, galloping inflation, and the onset of famine; popular unrest, both peaceful and violent; and the possibility that the opposition parties might replace the Bolshevik–Left SR coalition by winning majorities in the soviets. On more than one occasion Lenin wondered whether his government would survive until the next day.

The showdown in the summer of 1918 may be considered to have begun on June 8, with the fall of Samara to the Czech-SR forces and the formation of the SR-led Komuch government. The army of the Komuch government represented the most serious military threat to the Kremlin at that point. Other anti-Bolshevik forces were gathering strength, but they did not yet pose a danger to the regime. Meanwhile, the measures taken against the internal opponents—the Menshevik workers among them—had great influence on the shape of the Bolshevik regime as it emerged from the summer crisis. In the chaos of military battles, strikes, demonstrations, assassinations, lockouts, arrests, and shootings, no single factor was decisive. Only by analyzing the interaction of opposing forces and between adopted policies and institutional change can we understand what led to the banning of non-Bolshevik workers' organizations, the prohibition of strikes, the suppression of the non-Bolshevik press, the expulsion of opposition parties from the soviets, and the imposition of the Red Terror.

The Menshevik Party Conference of May 1918

A number of difficult questions confronted the Menshevik party in the spring of 1918: Should it continue its efforts to win majorities in the local soviets, or should it abandon the soviets as institutions too closely associated with the Bolshevik dictatorship? Should local party organizations take part in anti-Bolshevik uprisings when and if they broke out? And finally, if the allied armies undertook military intervention in Russia's internal affairs, what should the Menshevik policy be? To consider these and other problems, the Menshevik CC summoned an All-Russian Party Conference, to begin in Moscow on May 20.

Accounts of the proceedings tend to accept the Mensheviks' claim that the conference secured party unity.[1] The party's right wing, formerly known as the Defensist faction, is thought to have overcome its differences with Martov and Dan's center-left majority, formerly known as the Internationalists and Revolutionary Defensists. Soviet histories point to an alleged shift by Martov to the right, which made the rapprochement with the right wing possible.[2] Western studies tend to regard the newly established Menshevik unity as the result of a carefully worked-out compromise.[3] While neither interpretation is incorrect, both are inadequate. Behind the facade of party unity the Menshevik factions were still dangerously divided.

The Menshevik CC would have preferred to summon a full congress of the party, but since the delegates from many provinces would probably be unable to reach Moscow, the gathering was called a party conference. When the conference opened, however, the CC found that a surprising number of delegates had managed to come, despite the chaotic conditions of transportation and communication. "It turned out," stated the official report, "that the conference was much more fully representative than might have been expected."[4] The CC did not know the exact membership figures for local organizations, but that was hardly surprising. The SRs' eighth party congress, held that same month, produced many "discoveries" for its CC as well, and the Bolshevik CC, too, was uncertain about the numerical strength of its local organizations.[5]

1. Sivokhina, *Krakh melkoburzhuaznoi oppozitsii*, p. 193; Malashko, *K voprosu ob oformlenii odnopartiinoi diktatury*, p. 140.

2. Spirin, *Klassy i partii v grazhdanskoi voine*, p. 159; Ruban, *Oktiabr'skaia revoliutsiia i krakh men'shevizma*, p. 385.

3. See, for example, George Denicke, "From the Dissolution of the Constituent Assembly to the Civil War," in Haimson, ed., *Mensheviks*, pp. 144–45.

4. B. I. Gorev, "Vserossiiskoe soveshchanie pri TsK RSDRP," *Partiinye izvestiia* (Moscow), no. 8 (10 June 1918), p. 2.

5. V. M. Zenzinov, "Obshchenarodnyi front i voennaia pomoshch' soiuznikov (Vos'moi sovet partii SR)," *Narodovlastie* (SR journal, Moscow), May 1918, p. 5; *Perepiska Sekretariata*, 3:168.

The documents of the Menshevik party conference state that 60 delegates arrived from 50 local organizations, representing 60,000 party members.[6] This last figure is usually quoted as the best estimate of party membership in May 1918.[7] Compared with the 150,000 represented at the December 1917 party congress, it seems to indicate a loss of 90,000 party members.[8] Citing these figures, Soviet historians write of the collapse of the Menshevik party, the Bolshevization of the masses, and so on. They overlook the fact that the figure of 60,000 represents not the total Menshevik party membership but only the members represented at the party conference. It was explicitly stated that since not all delegations had been able to come, the gathering lacked the required quorum and thus did not qualify as a party congress.[9] Of the 50 delegations present, 9 came from district (uezd) main towns and 6 from Siberia and the Far East; 9 were sent by the Bund (the General Union of Jewish Workers) and other Menshevik organizations; 4 by non-Russian borderlands, and 22 were from province party organizations (see table 2). Of the major provincial capitals of European Russia, ten (Riazan, Orel, Simbirsk, Nizhnii Novgorod, Perm, Rostov, Novorossiisk, Vologda, Petrozavodsk, and Pskov) sent no delegates. The fact that the Mensheviks had earlier won majorities in the elections to the soviets of five of these cities suggests that it was not a lack of Mensheviks that accounted for their lack of representation at the party conference. Representation from the outlying areas was sparser still. In the Ukraine, only the Kharkov organization was able to send a representative; only the Gomel delegation came from German-occupied Belorussia, and only the Baku representative from the Caucasus. It is unclear whether the delegations from the Urals, eastern Siberia, and the Far East represented the entire Menshevik membership in those areas or only the main party organizations. In any event, it seems reasonable to estimate that at least a third of the Menshevik party members were unrepresented at the conference. That estimate yields a total party membership of about 90,000. An official Menshevik document published shortly after the conference claimed 100,000 dues-paying members.[10]

Also unrepresented at the May party conference were several right-wing groups that had ended their affiliation with the Menshevik party

6. Gorev, "Vserossiiskoe soveshchanie," p. 2. Table 2 contains 65 names of delegates, but only 60 of them represented local organizations. Table 2 lists 49 organizations rather than 50 because I counted Izhevsk and Votkinsk delegates as one delegation from Viatka province.

7. Spirin, *Klassy i partii v grazhdanskoi voine*, p. 158; Ruban, *Oktiabr'skaia revoliutsiia i krakh men'shevizma*, p. 385.

8. "Polozhenie finansov partii," *Partiinye izvestiia* (Petrograd), no. 8 (20 January 1918), p. 22.

9. Gorev, "Vserossiiskoe soveshchanie," p. 2.

10. "Protest RSDRP," *Novaia zhizn'*, 8 June 1918.

TABLE 2

Delegates of the Menshevik organizations at May 1918 party conference, by area and province

Area and province	Delegate(s)
Central Industrial Region	
Moscow	Romanov, Novikov
Tver	Zabelin
Yaroslavl	Shleifer, Gol'dman
Kostroma	Denin
Vladimir	Abzianidze, Kaufman
Kaluga	Golubev
Riazan	(Not represented)
Tula	Akhmatov, Kogan
Black Earth Region	
Kursk	Pavlov
Tambov	Podobedov
Orel	(Not represented)
Voronezh	Tatarchukov
Upper Volga–Urals Region	
Saratov	Epshtein
Simbirsk	(Not represented)
Penza	Pligala
Kazan	Bruk, Nelidov
Nizhnii Novgorod	(Not represented)
Ufa	Shik
Viatka (Izhevsk, Votkinsk)	Mikhailov, Zalomov
Perm	(Not represented)
Samara	Belov
Lower Volga–Don Region	
Astrakhan	Abdusheli
Rostov	(Not represented)
Novorossiisk	(Not represented)
Northern Region	
Arkhangelsk	Rozin
Vologda	(Not represented)
Petrozavodsk	(Not represented)
Petrograd	Kliachko
Pskov	(Not represented)
Novgorod	Abramovitch
Western Region	
Smolensk	Davidovich
Vitebsk	Kvasman
Siberia and Far East	
Tomsk	Iukhnevich
Cheliabinsk	Voitov
Blagoveshchensk	Efimov
Eastern Siberian committee	Cherkunov, Konstantinov
Far Eastern committee	Kolko
Urals party committee	Shneerov, Fedoseev
Non-Russian borderlands	
Gomel (Belorussia)	Braun
Kharkov (Ukraine)	Liubimov

TABLE 2 (*Continued*)

Area and province	Delegate(s)
Baku (Caucasus)	Ozidziguri
Tashkent (Central Asia)	Demidov
Uezd towns	
Briansk (Orel)	Tovbin
Eletsk (Orel)	Miamlin
Belevsk (Tula)	Elshin
Viazniki (Vladimir)	Klinkov, Shtein
Velikii Ustiug (Vologda)	Zapalov
Rybinsk (Yaroslavl)	Vitolin
Tsaritsyn (Saratov)	Poluian
Velikie Luki	Lobanov
Syzran (Simbirsk)	Kalugin
Other party organizations	
Petrograd city committee	Klimov, Prushitskii, Bogdanov
Moscow city committee	Kipen, Kopralov
Moscow region bureau	Kuchin
CC of RSDWP	Gorev, Martynov, Ezhov
Moscow bureau of Bund	Abramovitch
Northern bureau of Bund	Erlikh
Western bureau of Bund	Goldshtein, Melamed
Occupied-lands bureau of Bund	Aizenshtadt
CC of Latvian RSDWP	Vetskalkha

Source: "Iz materialov partiinogo soveshchaniia," *Partiinye izvestiia*, no. 8 (10 June 1918), p. 13.

in protest against Martov's policies but still considered themselves Mensheviks. It should be recalled that during the Vikzhel negotiations, eleven members of the Menshevik CC resigned because of their objections to negotiations with the Bolsheviks (see chapter 1). Though they were persuaded to return to the CC on the eve of the December 1917 congress, many of them nevertheless decided to boycott the new CC, now headed by Martov and Dan. Grouped around Potresov's newspaper *Den'* and Plekhanov's *Edinstvo*, these Social Democrats were known as the "unaffiliated opposition." There is no accurate estimate of the membership of these local organizations. Some Right Mensheviks remained in the party but pursued a policy that was partly independent of the CC's. They were known as the "internal opposition."

As I have suggested, the usual picture of reconciliation between party factions that is supposed to have occurred at the conference must be qualified.[11] It is true that the Right Mensheviks Mark Liber and G. D.

11. A Soviet depiction of this reconciliation may be found in Solov'ev, *Velikii oktiabr'*, p. 193; a Menshevik depiction is in Aronson, *K istorii pravogo techeniia*, pp. 54–55.

Kuchin were elected to the CC. If, however, the number of Right Mensheviks elected to the CC in May 1918 is compared with the numbers elected at the December 1917 and August 1917 party congresses, it becomes strikingly clear that the return of the Right Mensheviks to the party leadership was merely symbolic.[12] The proportion of seats held by Right Mensheviks was lower in December 1917 than it had been in August 1917 and was lower still in May 1918. Many of the then Defensist Mensheviks had been supporters of the Provisional Government during 1917 (some had even held public office in its agencies), whereas the Internationalists, or Left Mensheviks, had then been in opposition. The changes in the Menshevik party leadership point to a shift of power away from the prominent figures who had supported the Provisional Government and toward the left-of-center Mensheviks. The latter were more likely to be found working in the soviets and more willing to seek a compromise with the Bolsheviks. Despite the rhetoric of unity, such differences of opinion came out into the open during the debates at the May 1918 conference. Although the voting records available are far from complete, it is nevertheless possible to identify the basic attitudes of the center-left majority and of their opponents.

On the eve of the conference, Iurii Denike outlined the problems facing the Menshevik leaders. "We can hide neither from ourselves nor from those we call to follow us," he wrote, "that our victories [in elections] are leading to the destruction of the soviets." As a result, the Menshevik majority in a soviet disbanded by the Bolsheviks found its position worse than it had been before the elections. Local leaders were baffled by this problem, and Denike quoted some of them as admitting that they were "afraid to win elections." If they won an election, either the soviet was disbanded or they capitulated to the Bolsheviks and carried out their orders. In either case, Denike pointed out, an election victory was hollow.

> Our victory in the elections unfortunately does not end the so-called soviet, in fact Bolshevik, power. The power is "soviet" as long as the soviets are Bolshevik; the change in the composition of the soviets reveals the true nature of power, for the Bolsheviks disband disobedient soviets and realize "soviet power" without the soviets.

Somehow, Denike was saying, the soviets had to be defended against the Bolsheviks; the struggle for new elections to the soviets had to go on

12. The names of the Menshevik CC members elected at the August 1917 party congress are listed in L'vov-Rogachevskii, *Sotsialisty o tekushchem momente*, p. 263; at the December 1917 party congress, in *Vpered*, 26 April 1918; and at the May 1918 conference, in *Partiinye izvestiia*, no. 8 (10 June 1918), p. 13. These lists are reproduced in the appendix to this book.

despite Bolshevik threats. "Not only can we dare to win at elections, but we must at all costs strive for victory," he concluded.[13]

Denike's article reflected the views of the Mensheviks who were committed to working within the soviets and who valued their newly acquired majorities there. It remained unclear, though, by what means the soviets were to be defended, and whether the Mensheviks had a duty to defend them even when the Bolsheviks won the elections.

The Left Mensheviks had to deal with an internal contradiction in their political philosophy. As democrats, they believed in universal suffrage. Hence, if they (or they together with the SRs) won a majority in a soviet, their duty was to vote to pass power to the city duma, since that body was elected by universal suffrage. Yet as socialists they were bound by the wishes of their worker constituents, among whom the idea that power should belong to the soviets was still quite popular. The workers wanted "honestly elected" or "good" soviets; they did not necessarily want to see power transferred to the dumas. Thus the Menshevik defense of universal suffrage gave the Bolsheviks the opportunity to portray the Mensheviks as "agents of the bourgeoisie in the ranks of the proletariat." To ward off these politically damaging accusations, the Mensheviks in the soviets increasingly emphasized their role of protecting the soviets against the Bolshevik-appointed commissars. As we shall see, the wishes of these Mensheviks had a great deal to do with the changes in the party's program in the fall of 1918.

The Right Mensheviks stressed the negative consequences of the Menshevik presence in the soviets. First of all, there were examples, asserted Kuchin, of Menshevik efforts to reach a compromise with the Bolsheviks in the soviets.[14] The danger, he said, was that the newly elected soviets with Menshevik majorities still remained prisoners of the Bolshevik state agencies. Menshevik-led soviets thus found themselves saddled with responsibility for policies they opposed. Second, the very fact that the elections were being held tended to support the Bolsheviks' contention that "soviet democracy" existed. One Right Menshevik wrote, "To go into the soviets in order to struggle with this power is the same as if someone suggested entering the tsar's Supreme Council to struggle with tsarism!"[15] To the Right Mensheviks, the soviets were sham institutions, their only purpose to conceal the Bolshevik dictatorship: "More and more the soviets are arousing general hatred. The working class is turning away from them. They have been turned into bureaucratic, parasitic institutions that oppress not only

13. Iurii Denike, "Perevybory sovetov i nasha taktika," *Novaia zaria*, nos. 3–4 (20 May 1918), p. 21.
14. G. D. Kuchin, "Iz prochitannogo doklada," ibid., p. 28.
15. D. Kol'tsov, "Starye illiuzii na novyi lad," *Delo*, no. 9 (3 June 1918), pp. 6–7.

the bourgeoisie and the propertied classes but also the laboring masses and above all the proletariat.''[16] Consequently, the Right Mensheviks at the party conference favored a boycott of the soviets.

Despite such differences of opinion, Menshevik CC publications later went out of their way to emphasize that a spirit of party unity had prevailed at the conference. One report said that, for the first time in the history of the Social Democratic party, separate factional meetings had not been held before the plenary session of the conference, and votes had not been registered by faction.[17] Nevertheless, it is the case that key decisions at the conference were usually compromises. Factionalism was seemingly inevitable in the Menshevik party, as elsewhere.

Some revealing details of the divisions within the party appeared in publications issued by Menshevik bodies other than the CC, by the unaffiliated opposition, and especially by the Bolsheviks. Generally speaking, the leaders of Russia's political parties in 1918 were very well informed about what was going on in their opponents' CCs. The Mensheviks and SRs, for example, seemed to know a great deal about the Bolsheviks' dealings with the German ambassador, just as the Bolsheviks seemed to be aware of the SRs' contacts with the Allied missions. The statements of major figures, no matter how firmly closed the doors behind which they were made, were almost always leaked to the opposition party and were often published in the press. News about the Mensheviks probably reached the Bolsheviks through former Mensheviks who had joined the Bolshevik party. News about the Bolsheviks reached the opposition through the Left SRs and those Bolsheviks who opposed Lenin's policy on such issues as the peace treaty and grain requisitioning. The network of informal communications among the parties was an essential part of the political process in the spring and early summer of 1918.

At the end of May, *Izvestiia* carried detailed accounts of events at the Menshevik conference. One featured a clash between Liber and Martov. As the editors must certainly have known, Martov favored continued Menshevik participation in the soviets and Liber opposed this policy. *Izvestiia* reported this exchange:

> Liber: "The population, and not only the bourgeoisie, has every right to be bitter about all these 'leather jackets.' The soviets are Bonapartist clubs that gather together all these déclassé dregs." Martov could not contain himself and asked the epileptic of social treason, "And what were the soviets when their policies were made by you, Mr. Liber?"[18]

16. M. Amginskii, "Vserossiiskoe soveshchanie rossiiskoi Sotsial Demokratii," ibid., p. 10.
17. Gorev, "Vserossiiskoe soveshchanie," p. 2.
18. "Salon otvergnutykh," *Izvestiia*, 26 May 1918, p. 1.

Repeating the major Right Menshevik arguments, Liber asserted that the soviets could no longer play the role of rallying centers for workers' opposition against the Bolshevik dictatorship. The time had come to abandon the soviets and concentrate instead on consolidating the Workers' Assemblies of Upolnomochennye. Liber offered a resolution to recall all the Mensheviks from the soviets and urge the masses to boycott the "discredited institutions."[19] He proposed the slogan "Bypass the soviets," arguing that the Mensheviks' final goal was not a "soviet democracy" but a parliamentary democracy based on universal suffrage. His resolution was soundly defeated by a vote of 29 to 9.[20] A boycott of the soviets was not likely to be popular with the provincial leaders who had won seats in so many city soviets.

Abramovitch argued that since the Mensheviks recognized the soviets as having originally been mass revolutionary organizations and since they themselves were a party of the working class, they had to remain in the soviets to organize the workers' struggle for free elections and protect the soviets against disbandment.[21]

The final resolution on the soviets adopted by the conference was a political compromise in the Menshevik tradition. It consisted of three parts: the first defined the nature of the soviets, the second explained the Menshevik policy objectives, and the third provided guidelines for Menshevik conduct in the local soviets. The first part described the Bolshevik-controlled soviets as "bureaucratic institutions in the hands of party cliques and adventurist bands that tyrannically, irresponsibly, and uncontrollably rule the country." The Bolshevik commissars had developed the habit of using a gun to ensure the supremacy of the so-called soviet power. When the opposition parties won or seemed likely to win elections, said the resolution, the Bolsheviks arbitrarily changed the election rules, canceled elections, falsified results, refused to step down after defeat, and finally disbanded the soviets. "Therefore, during the half year since the October overturn, the soviets have had time to become, in the eyes of the broad popular masses, the incarnation of unbearable tyranny, hotbeds of corruption, stiflers of personal freedom and of citizens' political rights. . . . "[22] This part of the resolution was unanimously approved. Its description of the Bolshevik-controlled soviets demonstrates a remarkable change since October in the center-Left Mensheviks' perceptions of soviet power. No longer were the soviets criticized only for going too far in their attempts to take over the

---

19. "Uchastie Sotsial Demokratov v sovetakh i ikh uchrezhdeniiakh, proekt rezoliutsii Libera," *Partiinye izvestiia*, no. 8 (10 June 1918), pp. 18–19.

20. "Soveshchanie Men'shevikov," *Nashe slovo*, 26 May 1918.

21. "Vserossiiskoe soveshchanie RSDRP v Moskve, 20–28 maia," *Rabochii internatsional*, nos. 5–6 (June 1918); typewritten copy in T. S. Russia Collection.

22. "Sovety i taktika Sotsial Demokratii," *Novaia zaria*, nos. 5–6 (1918), pp. 82–83.

governing of the country. Now the party condemned them in much the same terms that the Right Mensheviks had used before.

Nevertheless, in the second part of the resolution, the local Menshevik organizations were urged to remain in the soviets in the role of an "irreconcilable opposition to the Bolshevik regime."[23] Their task was to struggle to restore the democratic nature of the soviets. In places where the soviets had been disbanded, the Mensheviks should organize workers' assemblies to support free elections to the soviets. Actually, these policies were already in effect, and in this respect the resolution introduced nothing new. Liber's faction abstained from voting on this part of the resolution.

The third part of the resolution allowed the Mensheviks in the soviets to assume positions of authority in food-supply and other agencies if those positions entailed no political responsibility for Bolshevik actions. The Right Mensheviks voted against this provision. In their view, it amounted to de facto recognition of soviet power and contradicted the party's commitment to the Constituent Assembly. The party leaders, the Right Mensheviks declared, were refusing to draw the conclusions implicit in their own analysis. If the soviets were what the conference said they were, how was it possible to call on the party to remain in them? The political consequences, warned the Right Mensheviks, would be devastating for the party. In the eyes of the masses, the Mensheviks would share the guilt for the Bolsheviks' crimes. Not only should the Mensheviks have nothing to do with the Bolshevik regime; they must actively oppose it.[24]

Mainstream Menshevik opinion, though, favored peaceful accommodation with the Bolsheviks, as this resolution makes clear. It may seem strange that the party majority was in favor not only of remaining in the soviets but also of taking responsible positions within a political structure ultimately controlled by the Bolsheviks. One possible explanation is that after the Constituent Assembly and the dumas were disbanded early in 1918, the soviets remained the only institutions whose members could be elected, at least in theory, by the masses, albeit on the basis of a limited franchise. Furthermore, during the spring of 1918, local Menshevik organizations had put so much effort into the election campaigns that they had acquired a stake in them. Local leaders valued their dearly won electoral victories and favored compromise with the Bolsheviks in order to avoid losing what they had won, and the party's recognition of their right to hold responsible positions in the soviets was a concession to them. Some of them were willing to go even further

---

23. Ibid., p. 83.
24. Amginskii, "Vserossiiskoe soveshchanie," pp. 6–7.

and accept the principle of soviet power rather than uphold the current party position that power had to be vested in the dumas and the Constituent Assembly. They may well have sincerely wished for reconvocation of the Constituent Assembly, but they probably did not want the party's commitment to reconvocation to jeopardize their position in the soviets. What mattered most to these local leaders, it seems, was their ability to take part in the political process—something they could do only in the soviets.

What was most important to the Right Mensheviks, though, was that the party maintain its commitment to the principle of universal suffrage and to reconvocation of the Constituent Assembly.[25] They accepted a compromise on the question of the soviets apparently because they were convinced that the expulsions and disbandments would continue and the necessity of active struggle against the Bolshevik dictatorship would then become evident to everyone. Thus the resolution satisfied both factions. As long as reconvocation of the Constituent Assembly remained at least a theoretical possibility, unity seemed to be possible.

The differences between the factions over another issue were harder to reconcile: Could the Constitutional Democrats (Kadets) be considered allies of Social Democracy in its struggle with Bolshevism? This was a thorny problem, dating back to debates before October over the possibility of a coalition with the Kadets. At the May conference, all the speakers agreed that the Kadets' efforts to eradicate Bolshevism by supporting the German occupation forces in the Ukraine had completely discredited them. Both Dan's and Liber's resolutions condemned the "treason" of the Kadets and spoke of the necessity of consolidating Russia's democratic forces.[26] Liber's resolution, however, stated that the fact that a part of the Kadet party had adopted a "German orientation" and had concluded an alliance with the monarchists did not mean that the entire Russian bourgeoisie was guilty of such a turnabout. Liber advocated "detaching the objectively progressive part of the bourgeoisie" from the reactionary camp, since it was "driven into the circle of monarchist aspirations only by Bolshevik maximalism and anarchy."[27] Dan's resolution was unclear as to whether the entire Kadet party was to be excluded from the ranks of "democratic forces."

Public endorsement of a possible alliance with the Kadets would, in practical terms, have given the Bolsheviks an excuse to harass the Mensheviks as "agents of the bourgeoisie." The final conference resolution

25. "Sovety i taktika Sotsial Demokratii," p. 83.

26. "Tezisy i proekty rezoliutsii o voine i mire (tezisy F. Dana priniatye soveshchaniem)," *Partiinye izvestiia*, no. 8 (10 June 1918), p. 14; Mark Liber, "O voine i mire," ibid., p. 17.

27. G. D. Kuchin, "Itogi," *Novaia zaria*, nos. 5–6 (1918), pp. 20–24.

on this subject therefore stated simply that the "elimination of the Bolshevik dictatorship must be carried out by the forces of Democracy alone."[28] The phrase "the forces of Democracy" could be interpreted by each faction as it wished, and explicit reference to the Kadets was avoided.

The attitude toward a possible Allied intervention was potentially an even more divisive issue. Right Mensheviks wondered whether the term "forces of Democracy" could be extended to include the armed forces of the Allied countries. Martov's and Dan's resolutions, however, unequivocally opposed any cooperation with foreign powers in the struggle with Bolshevism. Dan's said: "The RSDWP decisively rejects the inclination apparent in some democratic circles toward an Anglo-French orientation in terms of counting on help from foreign armed forces in the overthrow of Bolshevik power and the constitution of democratic statehood."[29] Liber's proposed resolution, in contrast, stated:

Social Democracy recognizes the possibility of some agreement between Russia and the Allies in the struggle against imperialist Germany. However, if such an agreement is not to prove harmful to Russia's internal development, a necessary precondition is the rapid growth of a democratic movement inside Russia.[30]

According to Martov and Dan, in other words, the Bolshevik dictatorship had to be overcome by the socialist parties alone, without cooperation with either the Kadets or the Allies; according to Liber, cooperation with some of the Kadets was necessary and cooperation with the Allies was possible. Dan's and Martov's resolutions were adopted at the conference.

The difference in phrasing between Dan's and Liber's resolutions perhaps seemed trivial at the time. After all, what difference did it make whether the socialist parties first eliminated the Bolshevik dictatorship and then joined the Allies against Germany or cooperated with the Allies in the process of fighting both Bolshevism and German imperialism? Ten days after the conference ended, the difference assumed unexpected importance. The Czech legion, closely linked to the French high command, joined hands with the SRs and seized power in Samara.[31] Armed struggle against the Bolsheviks under the banner of

28. "Tezisy i proekty rezoliutsii," p. 14.
29. F. Dan, "O voine i mire," and L. Martov, "Gosudarstvennyi raspad Rossii," both in *Partiinye izvestiia*, no. 8 (10 June 1918), pp. 14–15.
30. Liber, "O voine i mire," p. 18.
31. For a recent Soviet treatment of this event, see Gusev and Eritian, *Ot soglashatel'stva k kontrrevoliutsii*, pp. 318–21.

the Constituent Assembly with the assistance of Allied troops became a reality.

The compromise resolutions adopted at the May 1918 Menshevik party conference preserved party unity by leaving room for divergent interpretations by local organizations. For the Right Mensheviks, the party was not decisive enough in active struggle with the Bolshevik regime, and for the center-Left Mensheviks, such decisiveness would threaten the party's very existence. In May and June 1918, the cracks in Menshevik unity were evident, and in July and August, at the height of the anti-Bolshevik uprisings, the Menshevik party split over the issue of armed struggle against the Bolshevik dictatorship (see chapter 9).

The Rift between the Mensheviks and the SRs

The differences between Menshevik and SR party leaders on such issues as policy toward the soviets, relations with the Kadets and the Allies, and the admissibility of armed struggle against the Bolshevik dictatorship closely resembled the divergence between the center-left and the right within the Menshevik party. On some issues, however, such as the use of terrorism, all Mensheviks vehemently disagreed with the SRs. While no exhaustive discussion of SR history can be attempted here, a few comparisons with the Mensheviks may be fruitful.

The Menshevik and SR parties had long been very close allies. In fact, contemporary Soviet historians, unlike the Bolsheviks in 1918, seldom distinguish between the policies of the two, treating them both as "petty-bourgeois" parties.[32] Indeed, for the period between March 1917 and June 1918, the Mensheviks and SRs remained, though sometimes not without difficulties, each other's most important allies, and they frequently stressed their unity. During the election campaigns in the spring of 1918, the platforms of the two parties were virtually identical on all major political issues, such as the Brest treaty, grain requisitioning, reconvocation of the Constituent Assembly, and the role of the soviets. The Mensheviks and SRs cooperated so closely that they presented joint lists of candidates, as has already been pointed out. The two parties often formed a single opposition bloc in the soviets. Several local Menshevik and SR organizations published periodicals together. The CCs of the two parties jointly published in Stockholm *Les Echos de*

32. See, for example, Soboleva, *Oktiabr'skaia revoliutsiia*, p. 6. On the "petty-bourgeois" character of the Mensheviks, see L. M. Spirin, "Nekotorye teoreticheskie i metodologicheskie problemy izucheniia neproletarskikh partii v Rossii," in *Bankrotstvo melkoburzhuaznykh partii*, p. 14, and Malashko, *K voprosu ob oformlenii odnopartiinoi diktatury*, p. 142.

Russie, a journal edited by Pavel Aksel'rod (Menshevik) and Nikolai Roussanoff (SR). Furthermore, as Martov later acknowledged, the top Menshevik and SR party leaders often shared information and discussed policy matters together.[33] Menshevik and SR publications even discussed the feasibility of a formal merger of the two parties.[34]

Nevertheless, even at the height of Menshevik-SR harmony, serious differences separated the allies. Unlike the SRs, the Mensheviks did not think of themselves as necessarily a ruling party. The trauma of 1917, the unsuccessful coalition with the Kadets, and the disaster of October convinced the Mensheviks that power ought not to be the ultimate goal of the party. They believed that the best way for them to promote workers' interests was to create powerful, independent working-class organizations that could exert pressure on any government.

The self-image of the SRs was altogether different. Their historical identification was with the peasants, but they did not want to be a one-class party; they aspired to be the party of all the people. To that end, they sought members among all social groups. The SR membership—at 1 million the largest of any Russian party in 1917—included intellectuals and peasants, industrialists and workers, generals and soldiers.[35] The SRs were much more confident of their strength than the Mensheviks ever were, and their confidence was solidified when they obtained a majority in the elections to the Constituent Assembly.[36] The SRs believed that they had received a mandate from the Russian people.[37] They felt that the power that rightfully belonged to them had been usurped by the Bolsheviks. Hence their hostility toward the Bolsheviks was compounded by bitterness.

The SRs were less dependent than the Mensheviks on capturing votes that had once been cast for the Bolsheviks. In Tambov, Orel, Voronezh, and elsewhere, as we have seen, they preserved a strong popular following of their own. Although it is hard to generalize, as the Mensheviks and SRs presented joint slates in many elections, it is reasonable to surmise that the SRs generally did better in the grain-producing provinces and the Mensheviks in the industrial regions. The

33. "Martov o partii v 1918, 1919 godu," *Sotsialisticheskii vestnik* (Berlin), 4 April 1927, pp. 3–10.

34. See Zaslavskii, "Partiia i liga," *Den'*, 30 March 1918, p. 2; Boris Nikolaevsky, "Iu. O. Martov i Esery (istoricheskaia spravka)," *Sotsialisticheskii vestnik* (New York), 15 May 1944, p. 114.

35. On the number of members in the SR party, see "Polozhenie partii SR v Rossii (1 aprelia 1923; sekretno)," Nik. Col. no. 7, box 2, file 45. For an interesting discussion of the SRs' identity, see Radkey, *Sickle under the Hammer*, pp. 2–3.

36. Radkey, *Elections*.

37. This belief is clearly indicated in the letters of the SR CC to local organizations: "Tezisy dokladov dlia partiinykh agitatorov i propagandistov" (January–February 1918), Nik. Col. no. 7, PSR archive, box 3, file 52.

Volga area became the bastion of SR support, whereas the industrial centers, such as Tula and Yaroslavl, were Menshevik. Thus the tactics of the two parties were determined to some extent by the fact that they appealed to different social groups.

The heterogeneity of the SRs turned out to be a source of weakness. There was little in common between Mariia Spiridonova, the leader of the Left SRs, who hailed the peasants' rebellion against the landlords, and Boris Savinkov, a commissar of the Provisional Government, who was involved in the Kornilov putsch. The left and right wings of the party not only ignored CC policy on numerous occasions but were each other's bitter political enemies. The friction between Right and center-Left Mensheviks appears to have been a minor problem in comparison with the warfare among the SR factions. Constant infighting virtually paralyzed the SR leadership in the October days.[38] In the party's right wing, Kerensky vied with the Preparliament chairman, N. D. Avksent'ev; the left wing, led by Spiridonova, openly rebelled against the Provisional Government; and the party center under Chernov bogged down in helpless inaction. The outright secession of the Left SRs in November 1917 brought no peace to the party, but rather produced chaos in its local organizations.[39] The party center, deprived of support from the left, was in danger of becoming a prisoner of the right wing. Unlike Martov and Dan in the Menshevik party, Chernov, the ill-fated chairman of the Constituent Assembly, never managed to consolidate his authority in the SR party. Hated by the right wing, repudiated by the left, he was isolated in his own CC. To be sure, he was accorded formal respect; when he arrived in the late summer of 1918 in Samara, capital of the SR-led Komuch government, he was provided with honorary guards at his office in the best hotel.[40] Yet the chairman of the Constituent Assembly had very little influence on the policies of the Komuch government; indeed, according to his memoirs, he vehemently opposed them.[41] The key decisions in the SR party and in the Komuch government were made by those who had engineered the Samara uprising and by the military leaders. Thus in the months after October, when the Menshevik party leadership was becoming increasingly dominated by its center-left wing, the SR leadership was dominated by its right wing. These developments did not augur well for the durability of the coalition.

38. For a detailed account of the factional infighting in October 1917, see Viktor Chernov, "Kommentarii k protokolam TsK," ibid., file 54.

39. Radkey, *Sickle under the Hammer*, p. 163.

40. I. M. Maiskii, a Menshevik minister in the Komuch government and later a Bolshevik functionary, describes Chernov's arrival in Samara in *Demokraticheskaia kontrrevoliutsiia*, p. 66.

41. Viktor Chernov, "SRy v 1918 godu," Nik. Col. no. 7, PSR archive, box 3, file 53.

Perhaps the most serious problem in Menshevik-SR relations was the dispute over the form that the struggle against the government was to take. This problem had a long history, going back at least a decade to the division between the Social Democrats and the Socialist Revolutionaries over the forms of underground activity under tsarism. The Mensheviks held that their success as a political party depended on organization of the workers for action. The more numerous their political, economic, and cultural organizations, the greater their ability to exert pressure on the government, be it Bolshevik or Tsarist. This tenet was shared by all Mensheviks, right and left. The SRs, on the other hand, regarded the organization of workers as only one of the possible methods of building opposition to the Bolshevik regime. Equally important in their view were underground armed strike groups. According to Vladimir Zenzinov, a member of the SR CC, the SR leadership periodically mobilized such groups in the churches of Moscow and other cities, readying them for deployment in case of an uprising against the Bolsheviks.[42]

The SRs were proud of their "heroic past" and often reminisced about the days when SR terrorists had "liquidated" tsarist officials and "expropriated" bank funds. This aspect of the SRs' political culture was much closer to the Bolshevik than to the Menshevik tradition. Conspiratorial organizations of professional revolutionaries were alien to the Menshevik philosophy. The Mensheviks' very identity was rooted in the 1903 split with the Bolsheviks over this issue. The Mensheviks believed in Marx's "objective laws of historical development," and they operated with such notions as class interest, mass movement, and social revolution. The only way to achieve social and political change, in their view, was through the organization of the laboring classes for the defense of their interests. A party could be successful only if it voiced class interests. In Menshevik eyes, underground professional revolutionaries were nothing but laughable adventurers.

The Mensheviks thus condemned the SRs' espousal of terrorist activities. Both under the tsars and under the Bolsheviks, such tactics tended to provoke government repression without producing any positive results. During the election campaigns of 1917 and 1918, many Mensheviks assumed that the SRs' terrorist activity was a thing of the past. With the end of election politics, however, the old tradition was revived. When, in May 1918, the Bolsheviks threatened to expel the SRs from the Moscow soviet, the SR leaders retorted that the party would go underground. This would be nothing new for them, they

42. V. M. Zenzinov, "Bor'ba rossiiskoi demokratii s Bol'shevikami v 1918 godu, Moskva, Samara, Ufa, Omsk," Nik. Col. no. 7, PSR archive, box 1, file 24, p. 18.

pointed out. They had functioned underground for fifty years and had shot a great many tsarist officials; now they would shoot the Bolshevik commissars.[43]

The differences between the Mensheviks' and SRs' self-perceptions, political traditions, and ideology led inevitably to differences in policy toward the Bolsheviks. In the spring of 1918 the SRs had no interest in seeking an accommodation with the Bolsheviks—the party that had disbanded the Constituent Assembly. For the Mensheviks, victories over the Bolsheviks in the soviets were indispensable to their morale, as proof that the Bolsheviks could be beaten in their own bailiwick, among the workers. Victories in the elections to the soviets were less important for the SRs, who were much more concerned about the reconvocation of the Constituent Assembly. For the Mensheviks, the democratically elected soviets were of great value in themselves, with or without the Constituent Assembly. This difference was not immediately apparent during the election campaigns, because both parties were committed to the reconvocation of the Constituent Assembly. When the Bolsheviks disbanded soviets controlled by the Mensheviks and SRs, however, and anti-Bolshevik uprisings broke out, the divergent attitudes of the two parties became increasingly evident.

At an SR party congress that met two weeks before the Menshevik conference began in May 1918, the question arose as to whether cooperation with the Allies against the Bolsheviks was admissible. Even more unequivocally than the Right Mensheviks, the SRs welcomed the prospect of Allied intervention. A resolution of the congress stated, "It is hardly possible for Russia to extricate herself from her sad and critical position without aid from outside. For Russia, the transfer by the Allies of sufficient armed forces to Russian territory is not only acceptable but actually desirable."[44] To be sure, the resolution added that the Allied forces were not to interfere in Russian internal affairs unless requested to do so by the Russian government, but even this phrasing—in May 1918, almost a month before the creation of a "Russian government" friendly to the Allies—suggests that the SRs deemed the creation of such a government feasible and likely.[45] The memoirs of SR leaders describing their contacts with the French mission confirm the impression that the SRs considered undertaking a number of anti-Bolshevik

43. This incident was reported in "Presledovaniia Men'shevikov i SRov," *Petrogradskoe ekho*, 29 May 1918.

44. "8-oi sovet partii SR," *Delo naroda*, 18 May 1918, p. 2. Other reports of the proceedings of the congress appeared in ibid., 12–17 May 1918, and in "8-oi sovet partii SR," *ESER*, 19 June 1918.

45. This is also clear from such documents as I. Brushvit, "Kak podgotovlialos' Volzhskoe vystuplenie," *Volia Rossii* (Prague), nos. 11–12 (1928), pp. 89–95, esp. p. 93.

operations.[46] Thus, on this issue as well, the SRs and Mensheviks were moving in very different directions.[47]

A survey of the Menshevik and SR press in the late spring and early summer of 1918 clearly indicates that the two parties were engaged in an intense debate. Often without naming the targets of their criticism, editorials would scoff at "the fear of a restoration in certain socialist circles" or at "prisoners of illusions." The SRs criticized the Mensheviks for their refusal to recognize that the Bolsheviks were no longer a party of Russian democracy. One SR writer told of the psychological difficulty "some socialists" experienced when they thought of armed resistance to the Bolshevik dictatorship. Such guilt feelings, according to the writer, were rooted in the Russian intelligentsia's long tradition of serving the people. As the masses supported the Bolsheviks in October, "some socialists" reasoned, true socialists could not fight them now. Thus, the author went on, some socialists remained prisoners of the old dogmas. What they failed to realize was that

> the correspondence of the Bolshevik slogans with the elemental [sti-khiinye] moods and aspirations of the masses is to a considerable degree of an external and superficial sort; furthermore, Bolshevism is gradually losing credit with the masses, is pulling away from them, and is coming into sharp contradiction with their interests and aspirations.

Finally, popular support of the Bolsheviks in no way guaranteed the revolutionary or socialist nature of Bolshevism. Many social movements that the masses had supported were reactionary—attacks against Jews and other religious minorities, for example. From this perspective, the Bolshevik bands that were plundering the countryside and exterminating the "bourgeoisie" had to be seen as counterrevolutionary.[48]

This message was obviously directed against the widely known Menshevik position that Bolshevism was a temporary "zigzag," a leftist deviation of socialism which could best be dealt with by patient efforts to win over the masses from "maximalist" influences. Since the Bolsheviks recruited their supporters from the laboring classes, an armed struggle against them would mean a civil war in the ranks of the proletariat. This was exactly what the Menshevik party wanted to avoid.

Some articles make it clear that the SRs were losing patience with the Mensheviks. A front-page editorial in the SR CC's journal warned that

46. Zenzinov, "Bor'ba rossiiskoi demokratii," p. 33. See also Robien, *Russisches Tagebuch*, p. 327.
47. G. Aleksinskii, "Moskovskie SRy o vnutrennei i vneshnei politike," *Edinstvo*, 1 May 1918, pp. 5–6.
48. V. Vadimov, "Sotsializm, Bol'shevizm, i massy," *Za rodinu* (Moscow), 20 April 1918, pp. 10–11.

"the one who eliminates Bolshevism will establish the new regime. If Democracy is unable to do this, it will have to give way to those forces that will carry out some restorationist work"[49]—a thinly veiled allusion to the possible return of tsarism, which was a concern of both the Mensheviks and the SRs. The difference between them was that the Mensheviks were inclined to see the lesser evil as the Bolsheviks while the SRs saw it as the bourgeoisie and the officers. The SRs wanted the socialist parties to lead a movement to overthrow the Bolshevik regime.[50]

Echoing the arguments of the Right Mensheviks, the SRs defended cooperation with the industrialists and the officers' corps, most of whom they expected to incorporate in a democratic anti-Bolshevik movement. Thus the monarchist minority would be isolated. According to the SRs, the fear of inadvertently helping the Whites was paralyzing the Mensheviks. Their irritation with the Mensheviks was aggravated in mid-June, when it became clear that the longtime ally was in no hurry to join the Komuch government on the Volga in its battle with the Bolsheviks. The SRs accused the Mensheviks of procrastination and indecision when the new government desperately needed their support.

The Menshevik leaders tried to postpone an open break with the SRs as long as possible, because they feared, with justification, that it would provoke a split with the Right Mensheviks as well. Furthermore, the Mensheviks and SRs were still acting as a united bloc in the elections to the Petrograd soviet in mid-June (as we shall see in chapter 8). The Menshevik CC held several joint sessions with the SR CC, trying in vain to convince them that the path they had chosen was risky at best and catastrophic at worst.[51] The proceedings of these sessions are not available, but the public pronouncements of Martov and Dan are revealing enough.

In June 1918, Dan published a response to the SR criticism of the Menshevik policy. If a "democratic liquidation" of the Bolshevik regime had been possible, if indeed the regime could have been replaced by a government formed at the Constituent Assembly, he wrote, the Mensheviks would have supported such an effort. The Menshevik leadership had severe reservations, however, about the Komuch government's right to act on behalf of the future Constituent Assembly. Its reliance on Czech troops and Allied support, as well as its dependence

49. "Zashchita strany i zashchita revoliutsii," *Sotsialist revoliutsioner*, coll. no. 1 (Moscow: TsK PSR, March 1918), p. 3.

50. Zenzinov, "Bor'ba rossiiskoi demokratii," p. 33.

51. "Martov o partii v 1918, 1919 godu," *Sotsialisticheskii vestnik* (Berlin), no. 7 (1927), pp. 3–10.

on the officer corps, gave the Bolsheviks an opportunity to discredit the idea of the Constituent Assembly.[52]

Dan admitted that his understanding of the constellation of social forces in Russia led to a pessimistic evaluation of the prospects for a "democratic outcome." The bourgeoisie had at one time been willing to come to an understanding with the socialist parties. Now they were terrorized by the Bolsheviks in the name of socialism. Bolshevik violence, terror, and the unremitting "Red Guards' attack on the bourgeoisie" (a phrase endlessly repeated in the Bolshevik press) generated a strong reaction among the bourgeoisie, who had always been suspicious of the socialists and now could hardly bear to hear the word "socialist" at all. Terror had driven the propertied classes to embrace any monarchist general, any dictator who would restore "law and order," as witness the flirtation by Pavel Miliukov, the Kadet party leader, with the German occupation forces in Kiev and with General Krasnov's dictatorship on the Don. "Broad strata of the intelligentsia and the officer corps are driven to despair and are ready to seek salvation in any form of statehood in order to escape from the iron grip of hunger, insults, and direct physical violence."[53] This characterization suggests that the Mensheviks did not regard the officer corps as an inherently monarchist group. Only the Bolshevik terror, they believed, was driving the officers into the camp of reaction.

The anti-Bolshevik rebellions in the countryside, Dan argued, showed that "the peasants are ready to give up all achievements of democracy and accept any regime as long as they can retain land."[54] This statement must have especially offended the SRs, since it implied that the peasants were far from espousing socialist and revolutionary (i.e., SR) views.[55] In the Mensheviks' eyes, peasant excesses committed against the Bolsheviks represented the same phenomenon as their excesses against the landlords in 1917. The peasants' wrath was an unreliable ally.

Dan was no more optimistic in evaluating the leadership potential of the working class. Always a tiny minority in Russia, the working class had by this time been completely dispersed. The great decrease in the numbers of employed workers, the ruthless Bolshevik repressions, the shootings and arrests had generated a feeling of hopelessness among the workers. At least for the time being, they could hardly be the vanguard of a democratic movement in Russia. Dan's conclusion was that what the Mensheviks had been predicting since October had become a

---

52. F. Dan, "Nado poniat'," *Iskra*, 29 June 1918, p. 1.
53. Ibid.
54. Ibid.
55. Dan had addressed this question even earlier as well, in "Zadachi partiinoi raboty," *Partiinye izvestiia* (Petrograd), nos. 1–2 (5 March 1918) p. 2.

reality: the Bolshevik regime was arousing in all classes a strong reaction that was paving the way for a monarchist restoration. The SRs had let themselves be deceived, he said, by their new allies on the right, who paid lip service to the principle of universal suffrage: "It is easy for counterrevolutionary elements to accept the [SR] program in word when they know they can count on social forces that will carry them far from the democratic SR shore indeed."[56]

Martov's main fear was that the SRs would not manage to integrate the bourgeoisie and the officers in a democratic movement; that the rightist forces would use the Komuch government as a shield to provide legitimacy and then would turn against the SRs when they no longer needed them. In the fall, Martov wrote to a colleague abroad that "an ever-greater role in the anti-Bolshevik struggle is being played by all sorts of officers' and cadets' units whose sympathies are Kornilovite at best and monarchist at worst, and they are becoming a more decisive factor in the 'national' coalition than Komuch and similar elements." Displaying remarkable foresight, Martov added that an Allied victory over Germany would swing all of Russia's right-wing parties behind the Entente. The Allies would then drop their flirtation with the SRs, and the SR cause would be lost.[57] This perception of the SRs' prospects was vindicated in November 1918, when Admiral Kolchak staged his coup d'état.[58] Martov later commented that, "just as we had foreseen, the movement encouraged by the uprising of the Czechoslovaks and by the landing of British forces in Arkhangelsk, after a brief interlude of a powerless democratic republic, ended with the military dictatorship of Kolchak and Denikin."[59]

For all these reasons, the Menshevik leaders found it impossible to support the SRs' armed struggle against the Bolsheviks, though they could not side with the Bolsheviks either. In the struggle between the Bolsheviks and the SRs, the Mensheviks were determined to remain neutral. On such crucial issues as the role of the soviets, Allied intervention, cooperation with the Kadets, the forms of underground activity, and, most important, armed struggle against the Bolsheviks, the Mensheviks and the SRs chose very different courses of action. The two allies had in fact come to a parting of the ways by mid-June 1918.

56. Dan, "Nado poniat'."
57. Iu. O. Martov to A. Stein, 25 October 1918, Nik. Col. no. 17, Martov archive, box 1, file 3.
58. For documents on the background of Kolchak's coup, see Zenzinov, ed., *Gosudarstvennyi perevorot.*
59. "Martov o partii v 1918–1919 godu," pp. 3–10.

CHAPTER 8

The Mensheviks
under Attack

In the maelstrom of strikes, demonstrations, arrests, and shootings during the summer of 1918, so many things were going on at the same time that the causal relationships among them tend to blur. Yet when one focuses on each problem individually, one risks oversimplifying what in reality was a chaotic situation. Still, by focusing on the three great blows dealt to the Mensheviks that summer—their expulsion from the CEC and the soviets, the rigging of the elections to the Petrograd soviet, and the suppression of the upolnomochennye movement—we may identify the links in the chain of events that altered Russia's politics so profoundly.

The Expulsion from the Central Executive Committee

On June 14, 1918, the CEC expelled the Mensheviks and SRs from its ranks and recommended that all soviets do the same.[1] A compromise formula legitimated the expulsion in those cities where it had already occurred and yet did not require it everywhere. Bolsheviks in the provinces were much more impatient to crush the opposition than were those in Moscow; by June 1918 the Mensheviks and SRs had already

---

1. "Postanovlenie VTsIK ob iskliuchenii iz sostava VTsIK sovetov i mestnykh sovetov predstavitelei kontrrevoliutsionnykh partii Sotsialistov Revoliutsionerov (pravykh i tsentra) i Rossiiskoi Sotsial Demokraticheskoi Partii (men'shevikov)," *Sobranie uzakonenii i rasporiazhenii rabochego i krestianskogo pravitel'stva* (Moscow), no. 44 (20 June 1918), document no. 536, p. 538.

been expelled from many provincial soviets, well before any major anti-Bolshevik uprisings had taken place.[2] In addition to pressure from the provinces, two other factors must have influenced the decision to go ahead with the expulsion from the CEC, which Martov called a "small coup d'état."[3] One was the threatening proportions that the upolnomochennye movement was assuming, and the other was the Bolsheviks' fear that their opponents might overcome their differences and form a united bloc against them both within the CEC and at the forthcoming Fifth Congress of Soviets.

The Spread of the Upolnomochennye Movement

By the end of May 1918, workers' assemblies of upolnomochennye were spreading across the country with astonishing speed. This form of organization was particularly popular in cities where the disbandment of the soviets left no other medium for workers' interaction. In the last week of May, the Petrograd bureau of upolnomochennye sent a delegation to the Moscow workers.[4] Its arrival evidently gave impetus to the upolnomochennye movement in Moscow.[5] The Petrograd delegation reported to the assembly leaders that a bureau, or executive body, had been established there, and elections of upolnomochennye were under way at numerous factories.[6] A rally of four thousand workers was held on June 5 at the Aleksandrovskii railworks, at which the proposal of the Petrograd workers was accepted with but a single dissenting vote. The railworkers' clubhouse was turned over to the bureau of upolnomochennye and a volunteer detachment was formed to guard it. The visit of the Petrograd delegation also sparked steps toward the formation of workers' assemblies in Briansk, Kolomna, and Sormovo, where the Menshevik-SR bloc held or soon won majorities in the soviets, as well as in other cities.[7] On June 3, the Petrograd Workers' Assembly voted to convene an All-Russian Congress of Upolnomochennye.[8]

---

2. A number of crucial documents on the expulsions have never been made public. For Soviet accounts, altogether inadequate, see T. A. Sivokhina, "Rukovodiashchaia rol' rabochego klassa v gosudarstvennom stroitel'stve, oktiabr' 1917–iiul' 1918," *Vestnik Moskovskogo universiteta*, ser. 9 (History), no. 2 (1972), p. 16; and E. G. Gimpel'son, "Iz istorii obrazovaniia odnopartiinoi sistemy v SSSR," *Voprosy istorii* (Moscow), no. 1 (1965), p. 18.

3. Iu. Martov to A. Stein, 16 June 1918, in *Sotsialisticheskii vestnik* (Berlin), nos. 7–8 (25 April 1926), pp. 16–18.

4. "Petrogradskaia delegatsiia," *Novaia zaria* (Moscow), nos. 5–6 (10 June 1918), pp. 4–5. See also "Nakaz delegatsii Moskovskim rabochim," ibid.

5. Aronson, *Rossiia v epokhu revoliutsii*, p. 195.

6. "Organizatsiia sobraniia upolnomochennykh v Moskve," *Novaia zhizn'*, 7 June 1918, p. 3.

7. "K Petrogradskim rabochim," *Delo naroda*, 19 June 1918, p. 4.

8. "O sozyve Vserossiiskogo rabochego s"ezda," *Novaia zhizn'*, 4 June 1918, p. 3.

The Bolsheviks were of course alarmed by these developments. The Cheka intensified surveillance of the Petrograd upolnomochennye, and whistles and shouts drowned the words of Mensheviks when they tried to speak at workers' rallies.[9] At Kolomna, a town not far from Moscow, the arrival of the Petrograd upolnomochennye at the machine-building plant was greeted enthusiastically by the local workers, but Bolshevik gunfire broke up the rally. At Ozery, not far from Kolomna, the Petrograd delegation was arrested upon its arrival and locked up in a room of the soviet building. Local workers tried to storm the soviet four times to free them. The delegates could hear machine-gun fire and explosions. Finally the workers managed to free the prisoners and helped them flee to Moscow; then, fearing retribution by the authorities, they dismantled the railroad tracks.[10]

At the CEC session on May 27, Dan introduced a motion protesting the arrests of opposition leaders. People were being arrested, he pointed out, not for any offense that the government recognized as grounds for prosecution, but for no identifiable misconduct at all; "one by one, the members of our organizations are simply arrested. I have in my hands a whole string of such telegrams." The motion was politely put to a vote and defeated by the Bolshevik majority. At the next session, on May 29, Martov tried to bring up the issue of arrests again: "We have the example of the Kolomna workers, when the entire plant rose to struggle with the Soviet power after attempts were made to arrest members of our party." Bolsheviks expressed indignation at the Mensheviks' temerity in introducing such questions. Sosnovskii exclaimed, "Comrades! Here we are mobilizing forces, while behind our backs Martovs are organizing strikes."[11]

Sosnovskii was succinctly expressing the Bolsheviks' perception of the situation: in their eyes, the cause of the strikes was not the arrests by their own forces but agitation by the Mensheviks. If only the "troublemakers" could be removed, nothing would disturb the unity of the masses and their Communist vanguard. According to a report in a Left SR newspaper, Sosnovskii demanded "a decisive and merciless struggle with the Mensheviks and SRs, who are capitalizing on the difficulties the country is going through."[12]

At that point the Bolsheviks in the Moscow soviet were even blunter than their colleagues in the CEC about the way to deal with the Men-

9. At one rally, the hecklers evidently became confused about the party membership of the speaker and set up a clamor against a Bolshevik speaker until they were silenced by their leader (Makhno, *Pod udarami kontrrevoliutsii*, p. 108).

10. "Rabochie i sovetskaia vlast'," *Novaia zhizn'*, 13 June 1918, p. 3.

11. *Protokoly TsIK*, pp. 314, 341–42.

12. "TsIK," *Znamia truda* (Moscow), 30 May 1918.

sheviks. On May 25, the EC of the Moscow soviet expelled one Menshevik delegate, Egorov.[13] When the Mensheviks and SRs condemned the expulsion as illegal, P. G. Smidovich, the chairman of the soviet, threatened to expel all of them. The menacing remarks by Sosnovskii and Smidovich were the first indications that the Bolsheviks were considering drastic measures against the opposition parties.

A few days later, two members of the Petrograd upolnomochennye delegation, Krakovskii from the Sestroretsk plant and Kuz'min from the Obukhov plant, as well as their host, Rashkovskii, a Menshevik member of a district soviet in Moscow, were seized by the Cheka and imprisoned in the Butyrki jail.[14] Kuz'min was arrested following a rally at the Savelovskii plant, where he had given a well-received speech. When the Bolsheviks proposed that the workers vote either to support soviet power or to reconvene the Constituent Assembly, the overwhelming majority voted for the reconvocation of the Constituent Assembly.[15] It was reported that Kuz'min and Krakovskii were interrogated personally by Feliks Dzerzhinskii, the head of the Cheka, who then briefed the Council of People's Commissars.[16] Apparently the Bolsheviks were trying to test their limits, to learn how strong the workers' protests would be if more drastic operations were launched.

News of these arrests was immediately published by the opposition press. The Obukhov and Sestroretsk plants threatened to strike unless their upolnomochennye were released. New delegates were elected to replace the arrested ones and dispatched to Moscow. Delegations were also sent to the Moscow soviet to demand the release of those arrested. The Moscow bureau of upolnomochennye urged the city's workers to protest.[17] In the Moscow soviet, the leader of the Menshevik faction, I. A. Isuv, demanded that the authorities demonstrate the legality of the arrests.[18] P. G. Smidovich flatly refused to give an explanation but declared that the upolnomochennye were "sowing counterrevolution" and that the Cheka was authorized to deal with such "social traitors."[19]

The next day the SR faction introduced an interpellation concerning the arrests. An SR delegate, Rozanov, said that he had been sent to the soviet by 1,050 workers who wanted to know why the soviet power was

13. "Konflikt v Mossovete rabochikh deputatov," *Nashe slovo*, 26 May 1918, p. 3.
14. "K arestu delegatsii Petrogradskikh rabochikh v Moskve," *Novaia zhizn'*, 12 June 1918, p. 3.
15. "Arest chlenov Petrogradskoi delegatsii," *Novaia zhizn'*, 11 June 1918, p. 1.
16. "Aresty delegatov," *Novaia zhizn'*, 9 June 1918, p. 3. Krakovskii was killed later in the summer by the Cheka.
17. "Chrezvychainoe sobranie upolnomochennykh," *Delo naroda*, 15 June 1918, p. 3; "Protest Petrogradskogo biuro," *Nashe slovo*, 12 June 1918.
18. "Obvinitel'nyi akt protiv Men'shevikov," *Utro Petrograda*, 10 June 1918, p. 1.
19. "Men'sheviki i SRy—kontrrevoliutsionery," *Molva*, 10 June 1918, p. 1.

"acting like the old gendarmes." Smidovich now adopted a conciliatory tone: "The presidium will have to look into the matter of whether there was any abuse. We must prove to the workers that these measures were necessary in the interests of the revolution. . . . Let the presidium gather information to shed light on the matter."[20] If the arrests were not necessary, he continued, they would have to be stopped. Mistakes would be corrected; only "instigators"—"agents of the bourgeoisie"— would be arrested.

The Bolsheviks were trying to discredit the Mensheviks and SRs and to isolate them from the workers. But Smidovich's statement was damaging, for it amounted to an admission that the leadership of the Moscow soviet, which in theory held all power in the city, was not informed about the arrests being made. Nevertheless, on June 25, the Moscow soviet voted to expel the SRs and to bar Mensheviks from positions of authority in the EC.[21]

In the meantime, the "merciless struggle" that Sosnovskii had called for had apparently begun in Sormovo, an industrial suburb of Nizhnii Novgorod. On June 10, news reached Moscow that a regional congress of upolnomochennye being held there had been fired upon.[22] At the CEC session on the next day, Dan protested the attack and proposed that the CEC conduct an official inquiry into the incident.

> "One hundred eighty delegates representing forty thousand workers assembled in Sormovo. But even before the meeting could open, the building was occupied by Red Guards and machine guns were placed on street corners. . . . We must demand that our government answer the question: Is it not possible in Soviet Russia to have the kind of workers' conferences that were possible even under Nicholas II?"[23]

At this point the Bolshevik and Menshevik accounts of the session diverge.[24] According to the Bolshevik account, the chairman replied that Dan's charge was not based on fact, and he then put Dan's proposal to a vote (meaning certain defeat by the Bolshevik majority). According to the Mensheviks, however, Dan's accusation was met by laughter from the Bolshevik benches, followed by this exchange:

20. "Aresty rabochikh: Zasedanie Mossoveta," Nashe slovo, 12 June 1918.
21. "Zasedanie Moskovskogo Soveta," Novyi vechernii chas, 26 June 1918, p. 1.
22. "Po Rossii: V Sormovo," Novyi vechernii chas, 17 June 1918, p. 4.
23. Protokoly TsIK, p. 398.
24. The Menshevik account was published in a newspaper and journal of the party in 1918: "TsIK: Zapros o Sormovskikh sobytiiakh," Nashe slovo, 12 June 1918, p. 2; "Sprengung einer Arbeiterkonferenz," Stimmen aus Russland, nos. 4–5 (15 August 1918), p. 18. The Bolshevik version, in Protokoly TsIK, was published two years later and omits several statements by Bolshevik leaders as well as the interruptions from the floor.

Sosnovskii: "If we are to discuss this question, we must have facts. Where and when did all this happen?" "In Sormovo!" they shout at him from the Menshevik benches. "The PTA [Petrograd Telegraph Agency, which was under Bolshevik control] reports it!" shouts Sukhanov. "Take the newspapers and read!" Sosnovskii: "Sukhanov customarily distorts the CEC's activities. There is not a single word of truth in anything he writes in his articles about the CEC. And in what Dan has said, too, there is probably very little truth. These accusations are all unsubstantiated." Clamor. Protests. "What do you mean, unsubstantiated?" "This is reported by your own agency!"[25]

The Bolsheviks were of course reluctant to admit on the floor of the CEC that the Red Guards had opened fire on a workers' demonstration. From their point of view, the Mensheviks were using the forum of the CEC to discredit the government. To make matters worse, they would have a difficult time closing down opposition newspapers for reporting the proceedings of the "Soviet parliament." Such embarrassments must have fired the Bolsheviks' determination to get the Mensheviks and SRs out of the CEC.

Convergences within the Opposition

A second factor in the Bolsheviks' decision to expel the Mensheviks and SRs from the CEC was a desire to prevent the formation of a united opposition against them. Their fears were justified: after the Left SRs broke with the Bolsheviks later that month, they and the Mensheviks adopted very similar positions on the Brest treaty, grain requisitioning, and the disbandment of soviets.[26] They also vehemently protested the establishment of the so-called committees of the poor in the villages, which were supposed to replace the unruly soviets. For the SRs and Left SRs, the fate of the peasant soviets they led was at stake.

At the CEC session on June 11, Dan condemned the establishment of the committees of the poor. The Bolsheviks' plan to incite the poor peasants to confiscate grain from the more affluent ones, he warned, would trigger a bloodbath in the countryside. Dan specifically referred to his agreement "to a certain degree" with a similar criticism made by V. A. Karelin, a Left SR leader and also a member of the CEC, and until March 1918, people's commissar of state properties. Establishment of

25. "TsIK: Zapros," *Nashe slovo*, 12 June 1918, p. 2.
26. A Left SR account of the break with the Bolsheviks is given in Spiridonova's open letter to the Bolshevik CC, "Otkrytoe pis'mo TsK Bol'shevikov," January 1919 (copy in Hoover Institution Library); for the Soviet account of the Left SRs' "drift to the right" and rapprochement with the Mensheviks and SRs, see Gusev, *Krakh partii Levykh SRov*, pp. 185–88.

the committees, said Dan, would bring no bread to the cities but only aggravate hostilities between the cities and the countryside and between different groups of peasants. The real reason for the committees, he asserted, was that the Bolsheviks had lost their hold on the peasant soviets.

So the village Red Army [i.e., the peasants' grain-requisitioning detachments] is going to be organized like the Red Guards in the cities, and to be sure, this army will take bread that the peasants need for their own nourishment. There will be general famine, but there will also be what you [Bolsheviks] now need to hold on to power—there will be a general melee and a free-for-all. There will be civil war. Just like every government that resorts to war after it loses social support, you too, since you can't wage a foreign war on a foreign front, subserviently kowtow to Mirbach [the German ambassador]—you want to hold on by means of civil war! . . . You know that every new set of elections leaves you in the minority in the soviets![27]

At the same CEC session S. A. Lozovskii, of the United Social Democrats, also condemned the Bolsheviks' intentions:

"As for the committees of the poor which you are creating, I will say that these committees give you a pretext to abolish the peasant soviets; and if the majority is against you at the next congress of soviets, then you'll say that these representatives are counterrevolutionary and you'll invite a few dozen committees of the poor to replace the congress."[28]

This prediction turned out to be quite accurate. Three weeks later, several hundred Left SR delegates to the Fifth Congress of Soviets—supposedly the highest legislative body—were declared counterrevolutionary after an open confrontation with the Bolsheviks.

By establishing the committees of the poor to replace the soviets, then, the Bolsheviks were trying to create some institutional leverage of their own in the countryside for use against the SRs. In this light, the Bolsheviks' measures against the Menshevik-led city soviets and assemblies of upolnomochennye and against the SR–led village soviets may be seen as a two-pronged attempt to stem the tide that threatened to leave them in the minority at the Fifth Congress of Soviets.[29]

27. *Protokoly TsIK*, p. 405.
28. Ibid., p. 422.
29. For the Left SRs' data on their standing in the soviets, as well as their protest against the "unfair norms of representation" at the Fifth Congress of Soviets, see "K s"ezdu sovetov," *Znamia bor'by*, 6 July 1918, p. 1. According to both Left SR and Soviet sources, the Left SRs were doing extremely well against the Bolsheviks in the elections to the village soviets in the spring of 1918. The Soviet data are in "Tablitsa izmeneniia v partiinom sostave delegatov s"ezdov uezdnykh sovetov v 1918 godu," in Spirin, *Klassy i partii v grazhdanskoi voine*, p. 175.

A comparison of the CEC minutes with reports in the non-Bolshevik papers suggests that intensive bargaining was going on between the Left SRs and the Bolsheviks over the norms of representation at the Fifth Congress of Soviets. The official minutes state only that at the June 10 session of the CEC, which lasted only fifteen minutes, it had been announced that the Fifth Congress would convene on June 27. The session was so brief because the Left SRs wanted to postpone deliberation on issues related to the convocation of the congress until they had had time to devise a way to change the norms of representation, which favored the cities over the countryside. M. L. Kogan-Bernshtein, an SR, spoke openly of the political struggle that was taking place when he addressed the June 14 session of the CEC—the last the SRs and Mensheviks were to attend: "It is clear that hectic preparation . . . for the Fifth Congress of Soviets is now going on; and it is no coincidence that on the same day [June 10] that the issue of convocation of the congress arose, at the same session, this question [of expulsion] came up. . . . They tried to . . . pass this proposal with your help, but somehow it dragged on until today."[30] Apparently the proponents of expulsion had encountered opposition not only from the Left SRs but among some Bolsheviks as well. To tip the balance, they needed some way to compromise the opposition, and on June 13 they believed they had found it in a series of resolutions passed by an intercity conference of upolnomochennye then being held in Moscow—resolutions condemning the Bolshevik dictatorship and calling for the reconvocation of the Constituent Assembly. By declaring the resolutions "counterrevolutionary" and arresting the delegates attending the conference, the Bolsheviks hoped to silence those in their ranks who were concerned about the legality of expulsions from the CEC.[31]

The Bolsheviks on the CEC met for several hours before the June 14 session, which did not begin until 10 P.M., an unusually late hour.[32] Evidently some Bolsheviks (their identity is unknown) were still reluctant to agree to the expulsions. Their reluctance stemmed not from sympathy for the SRs or Mensheviks but from concern over violations of the "principles of October." The government had no legal or moral right to expel representatives elected by the workers and peasants. *Novaia zhizn'*, a Menshevik newspaper reputed to be well informed on Bolshevik party affairs, reported that heated debates were going on behind closed doors among high-ranking Bolsheviks on the propriety

30. *Protokoly TsIK*, p. 424.
31. "Bol'shevistskaia vlast' i rabochie," *Nash golos*, no. 9 (18 June 1918). The documents confiscated at the time of the arrest of the delegates are described in "Kompromentiruiushchie dokumenty," *Molva*, 15 June 1918, p. 1.
32. "Zasedanie VTsIK," *Novyi vechernii chas*, 15 June 1918, p. 1. See also "Iskliuchenie iz VTsIK oppozitsii," *Novaia zhizn'*, 16 June 1918, p. 3.

of expulsions.[33] The clash was primarily between "idealists" and "pragmatists," who believed the time had come to put an end to the Menshevik "counterrevolution."

The June 14 Session of the CEC

As soon as the June 14 session opened, Martov took the floor and demanded that the CEC include on the agenda a Menshevik interpellation about the arrest of the conference of upolnomochennye the day before. He went on:

> "I must bring to your attention that the attempts of workers from various plants to send their delegations here to the CEC to take part in today's session ran up against a special order not to let anyone but the Bolsheviks and the Left SRs through. These comrades, workers—those elected by hundreds and thousands of workers—are standing now in the street waiting in vain . . . to be allowed to sit at this session, where our faction is trying to bring up the question of this new act of tyranny and violence against the proletariat."[34]

Martov's request was put to a vote and of course rejected.

The session then moved toward expulsion of the non-Bolshevik members. The CEC chairman, Ia. M. Sverdlov, called for "the most merciless struggle against the adventure [avantiura] of the Mensheviks and the Right SRs, which has manifested itself in the creation of the so-called councils of upolnomochennye." No inquiry into the arrests was needed; it was common knowledge that they were justified. Latsis sought to demonstrate the "counterrevolutionary nature" of the council of upolnomochennye and thus to rationalize the expulsion of the "counterrevolutionary parties" from the CEC: "Out of fifty-nine people arrested at the upolnomochennye conference, it turned out that only fifteen had no party cards and called themselves nonparty delegates. As for the others, they all turned out to be members of the Menshevik and SR parties."[35] Evidently, then, mere membership in the Menshevik or SR parties was, to Latsis's way of thinking, sufficient proof of counterrevolutionary activity.

Sosnovskii summarized the Bolshevik accusations against the Mensheviks and SRs and said that the word "socialist" should not blind the Bolsheviks; it was high time to recognize that the so-called socialist parties had become the parties of counterrevolution. How could they

33. "Fraktsiia Bol'shevikov protiv iskliucheniia oppozitsii iz sovetov," Novaia zhizn', 19 June 1918, p. 3.
34. Protokoly TsIK, p. 419.
35. Ibid., p. 434.

still be sitting in the CEC and have the same rights as the Bolsheviks? Menshevik and SR counterrevolutionary activity was shown by their preparation of all kinds of secret plots and uprisings to overthrow the soviet power.[36] "The Mensheviks and SRs are trying to overthrow soviet power in the same way that we once overthrew the power of the bourgeoisie."[37] The validity of Sosnovskii's charges was not to be investigated: the decision had already been made.

"You are disbanding the soviets!" someone shouted to Sosnovskii from the opposition benches. "And you," he retorted, "disbanded the soviets in the Don [area] and in other places!" Voices from the right: "In Yaroslavl, for instance, who disbanded them?" Sosnovskii: "In Yaroslavl the soviet has not been disbanded—the Mensheviks left of their own accord."[38] When Bolshevik speakers could no longer deny the disbandings and arrests, they offered justifications. Iurii Steklov, the editor of *Izvestiia*, said, "If measures are taken against some soviets, and I don't deny that sometimes mistakes can be made in this respect, that's only the self-defense of the working class against those renegades."[39]

The Bolshevik speakers must surely have known that it was the Whites, not the Mensheviks, who were disbanding the soviets in the Don area; that the Mensheviks had not voluntarily abandoned the Yaroslavl soviet, and that it had been twice disbanded by the Bolsheviks; and that the upolnomochennye at the intercity conference had been elected by the workers. The facts were no longer important, only the elimination of the political opponents. Clearly the Bolsheviks' attitudes had undergone a sharp change since October. By June 1918 they were no longer willing to grant the possibility of workers' parties other than their own. The Mensheviks' real fault was that they were competitors, rivals of the Bolsheviks among the workers.

It may appear that the Bolsheviks had valid reasons for expelling the SRs, a party that had staged an antigovernment uprising in a provincial capital, openly defied the very principle of soviet power, and demanded a new constitutional order through reconvocation of the Constituent Assembly. The SRs' position in June 1918, however, was not dissimilar to that of the Bolsheviks in September 1917. At that time the Bolsheviks, an opposition party, likewise defied the government, then partly led by the SRs; demanded a transfer of power to alternative institutions, the soviets; and were preparing an uprising to achieve that goal. Yet the Bolsheviks were not expelled from the dumas. From the SRs' point of

---

36. Ibid., p. 421.
37. "Zasedanie VTsIK," *Novyi vechernii chas*, 15 June 1918, p. 1.
38. Ibid.
39. *Protokoly TsIK*, p. 436.

view, then, the Bolsheviks had no right to expel them from the CEC or the soviets for refusing to recognize the legitimacy of the existing power structure or for working to alter it. As Kogan-Bernshtein pointed out at the June 14 session, when the Bolsheviks disbanded the Constituent Assembly in January 1918, they claimed that the soviets represented a superior form of democracy; now that they were losing elections, they could find no better way to secure "democracy" than to expel the opposition parties from the soviets. There was nothing "counterrevolutionary" in demanding the reconvocation of the Constituent Assembly, he went on; and as for participation in anti-Bolshevik uprisings, he declared: "Our party will agree to that only if the laboring masses in one place or another are no longer able to bear your rule. And if there is an open insurrection, then of course our organization will be marching with the masses."[40] Such a bold statement was hardly likely to allay the Bolsheviks' fears.

In contrast to Kogan-Bernshtein, Martov stressed that the Mensheviks had no plans to take part in any anti-Bolshevik insurrections. Responding one by one to Sosnovskii's charges, Martov accused the Bolsheviks of malicious insinuation and slander: They knew very well that they had arrested workers' delegates, not officers and lawyers, the Bolshevik papers said. The Bolsheviks were trying to create the impression that there were Menshevik plots and conspiracies against them; since they were losing social support, they needed a villain to blame. The Mensheviks, declared Martov, had quite different aspirations:

> "We are not preparing an armed uprising. We are taking no part in either the Siberian or any other government brought into being at the point of foreign bayonets. We are taking one path, the path of organizing the working masses. . . . And we are happy to state that there is not a single place around Moscow or across the entire expanse of Russia where a Bolshevik demagogue could freely speak at a free workers' rally and not be brought to account for the evil and humiliation your government has brought to the working class."[41]

Dan continued this theme by emphasizing the Mensheviks' efforts in the election campaigns. The atmosphere was now tense; anti-Bolshevik speakers were frequently interrupted by shouts, insults, and threats, and according to some eyewitness accounts, their voices sometimes could not be heard. Still Dan spoke on, apparently determined to use the full ten minutes the rules allotted him: "You have the arrogance to write that if the workers don't like the government of Lenin and Trot-

40. Ibid., p. 427.
41. Ibid., p. 426.

sky, they can always vote to change it. This is a lie! . . . The workers can't vote freely in the elections to the soviets, which are supposed to be the most democratic institutions, reflecting the latest will of the masses."[42] The Bolsheviks were rigging the elections, he went on, disbanding the soviets, arresting objectionable workers' leaders, and even firing on the workers' demonstrations. Catcalls, shouts, and curses filled the hall. "Down with him!" "Out! Get him out!" "Arrest him!" "Shoot them!" Such shouts were omitted from the official minutes, which summarized them as "clamor." Waving his fist, Dan yelled back: "You are not going to intimidate us with any shootings and *okhranka* [a derogatory term for the tsarist secret police, here obviously a reference to the Cheka]!"[43]

V. A. Karelin, speaking for the Left SRs, branded the proposed expulsion bill illegal, since the Mensheviks and SRs had been sent to the CEC by the Congress of Soviets, and only the next congress had the right to withdraw their representation. Furthermore, the Bolsheviks had no right to pose as defenders of the soviets against the alleged SR counterrevolution when they themselves had been disbanding the peasants' soviets and creating committees of the poor to replace them.[44]

When the move for expulsion came to a vote, only the Bolsheviks supported it, but their votes were sufficient to pass it. The Menshevik and SR members rose from their seats and walked out, to the accompaniment of whistles, insults, and threats. As they were leaving, a member of the SR faction, Disler, was arrested by the Cheka. In a private letter abroad, Martov wrote two days later that the Bolsheviks' action had destroyed the very principle of free worker representation in the soviets, which had been the basis of soviet power. Prophesying what was to come, he wrote that "we expect an intensification of terror." Indeed, he said, some Bolsheviks had proposed that he himself be seized as a hostage.[45]

The expulsion of the opposition parties from the CEC marked a turning point in the establishment of one-party dictatorship in Russia. Until now, expulsions of opposition members from various soviets had been ad hoc affairs and their legality had been subject to debate. The speeches and interpellations in the CEC between October 1917 and June 1918 indicate clearly that many Bolsheviks had difficulty accepting the emerging principle that soviet power was equivalent to Bolshevik power. After the expulsion from the CEC, the opposition parties, though

42. Ibid., p. 433.
43. "Zasedanie TsIK: Po telefonu, ot spetsial'nogo korrespondenta," *Molva*, 15 June 1918, p. 1.
44. *Protokoly TsIK*, p. 428.
45. Martov to Stein, 16 June 1918, Nik. Col. no. 17, box 1, file 3.

still tolerated in some soviets, could no longer count on coming to power within the system of soviets by winning elections. What had been a de facto practice had become a de jure reality. The expulsion is thus as significant for the development of the new regime as the disbandment of the Constituent Assembly. On the other hand, it would be a mistake to believe, as some opposition leaders did at the time, that their cause was lost beyond recovery on June 14, 1918.

The Mensheviks felt that their party had been the hardest hit. The expulsion could not have come at a worse time for them. Just when the Menshevik center-left was beginning to move toward a basic accep-tance of the soviets, the expulsion undercut their position vis-à-vis the Right Mensheviks, who were now to gain great strength in the party. The fragile unity between the Menshevik factions, achieved with such difficulty only two weeks before at the party conference, was now a shambles.

The expulsion made considerably less difference to the SRs; it only served to redouble their efforts to overthrow the regime, now that no legal opportunities existed for them in Bolshevik Russia. The Left SRs viewed the expulsion of the right socialists as a dangerous precedent and a bad omen. If the Bolsheviks could do this sort of thing with impunity, what could stop them from turning one day against the Left SRs? In the event, nothing did: in July they too were expelled.

With the opposition gone, the CEC had little purpose left, and it scarcely met for the remainder of the year. Now that no one was left to debate bills, key decisions were made in the Council of People's Com-missars, and new decrees were not even submitted for the CEC's ap-proval, as the law required. Ironically, the Bolsheviks on the CEC also suffered from the expulsion of their opponents. As part of the Commu-nist party, they could not demand accountability from the CPC. As a result, the Bolshevik commissars became less open to public criticism, less accountable to other state institutions, and less bound by any legal or other constraints. When we seek to understand the reasons for the CEC's downfall and the ascendancy of Lenin's Council of Commissars, we find that the CEC engineered its own atrophy when its Bolshevik members closed ranks against their opponents.

The Elections to the Petrograd Soviet

The CEC's recommendation that the Petrograd soviet follow its exam-ple created special difficulties for the soviet's Bolsheviks because the workers at the Putilov and Obukhov plants threatened to strike unless new elections were held. Expulsion of the opposition now would make a mockery of the elections and could provoke the very strike they were designed to avert. Yet going ahead with new elections was equally risky, in view of the opposition's popularity. Signs of hesitation and conflict between moderate and militant Bolsheviks appeared as early as the June 15 session of the Petrograd soviet.

Zinoviev harshly condemned the opposition, especially the "treason" of the SRs on the Volga and in Siberia, where they had overthrown the Bolsheviks. Electing Mensheviks and SRs to the soviets was equivalent to handing power to the bourgeoisie. By the same token, voluntarily or involuntarily, such people as N. N. Glebov, one of the Putilov plant upolnomochennye and an advocate of a united socialist party, played into the hands of the bourgeoisie. Nevertheless, Zinoviev's speech showed some moderation: he made it clear that the CEC expulsion resolution was only a recommendation to other soviets and he admitted that "when famine was particularly acute, the SR and Menshevik gentlemen had some success among a narrow circle of workers in Petrograd." He even recognized the opposition parties' right to seek political power within the Soviet system: "In the framework of democracy, the framework of Soviet Russia, [if] any party wants to attain power—this is a lawful right of every party."[46]

As far as the Mensheviks and SRs were concerned, Zinoviev's moderation was no more than an exercise in hypocrisy. They wanted deeds, not words: an investigation into the shooting of the workers in Sormovo, an immediate release of their arrested comrades in Moscow (two of whom, Kuchin and Troianovskii, were members of the Menshevik CC), guarantees of fair elections, and the appointment of a multiparty credentials commission.[47] All of these demands were, as usual, voted down.

M. M. Lashevich and others among the more militant Bolsheviks were growing impatient with Menshevik demands. In contrast to Zinoviev's more or less parliamentary approach, Lashevich burst out in abuse: "What do they want, those milksops who are putting up a fuss here! They don't want power, because they don't know how to use it— they'd only pass it over to Miliukov [of the Kadet party]. They've become so barefaced because they're treated too gently!" When clamor and protests broke out, Lashevich pulled out a gun, waved it in the air, and went on: "There's been too much ceremony with you scoundrels among scoundrels! You can kill us, but we won't give up without a fight, and if it comes to a fight, then fourteen bullets for you and the last one for us!"[48] Someone from the opposition benches commented sar-

46. Zinov'ev, *Kontrrevoliutsiia*, p. 5.
47. "V Petrogradskom sovete," *Utrenniaia molva*, 16 June 1918.
48. "Pod zanaves," *Novyi vechernii chas*, 17 June 1918, p. 3.

castically, "What an unfair distribution of metal!" Volodarskii, the commissar for press, propaganda, and agitation, said: "War has been declared, and it will be a merciless war! Either us or them!"[49]

In these outbursts we can see the Bolsheviks' increasing boldness, intolerance, and mercilessness toward the "enemies of the proletariat." Yet the bravado may well have been a reflection of an underlying insecurity: the Bolsheviks were unwilling to face the decline in their support among the workers. When their power, status, and jobs were at stake, they forgot the principles of soviet democracy and the "will of the masses" in favor of the "iron dictatorship of the proletariat"—their own dictatorship. In the end, however, the Bolsheviks agreed to go along with new elections—but with new norms of representation that would ensure a Bolshevik victory no matter what the popular vote might be.[50] (These norms will be discussed below.) Thus the appearance of democratic elections would be maintained and the workers' demands fulfilled with no risk to Bolshevik power. Evdokimov's comments on the decision—he was then an important Bolshevik functionary in the Petrograd soviet and in the Cheka—are revealing. Asked by a newspaper correspondent why the soviet had finally agreed to new elections, he replied, "We have to knock the last weapon out of the Mensheviks' and SRs' hands and make clear to them that the satisfaction of their insistent demands [for new elections] will show their lack of support among the workers." When the correspondent asked why this lack of support could not have been demonstrated earlier and why the elections had been postponed so many times, Evdokimov replied:

> "Even now it's been difficult for us to decide on elections because they distract a number of specialists working in such areas as food supply, transport, and the court from their duties at a difficult moment. They'll all have to interrupt their work in order to take part in the [election] meetings. Besides, the new elections mean the breakup of the old executive committee, as well as of other organizations that have already been set up."[51]

The Election Campaign

On June 16 the Menshevik party city conference assembled to discuss the new norms of electoral representation. Two courses of action were proposed. One, advocated by the Right Mensheviks, was to boy-

---

49. "V Petrogradskom sovete," *Utrenniaia molva*, 16 June 1918.

50. Concerning the Bolshevik decision to go ahead with the elections, see "K perevyboram Petrogradskogo soveta," *Molva*, 14 June 1918, p. 3.

51. "Perevybory v Petrograde," *Molva*, 17 June 1918, p. 3.

cott the elections and call a general strike, since campaigning was a waste of time and participation in the elections would enable the Bolsheviks to boast of their victory at the polls. Furthermore, participation would create the illusion among the workers that some kind of electoral competition was still going on, whereas a Bolshevik "victory" was in fact assured. The other course of action was to take part in the elections in order to "expose the Bolshevik machinations." The center-Left Mensheviks wanted to remain in the soviet as the elected representatives of the workers, even if they could not win a majority.

The text of the resolution that was adopted reflected the ideas of both factions. The influence of the Right Mensheviks can be seen in this passage: "By the disbandments, arrests, and shootings . . . and by the expulsions . . . from the CEC and the soviets, the Bolsheviks have exposed the regime of soviet power as the dictatorship of a Bonapartist, autocratic clique that is waging civil war against the people, the working class, and its independent organizations." The resolution called the norms of representation "fraudulent" (*moshennicheskie*), but then declared: "In order to expose the fraud of this Bolshevik "victory" made possible by . . . falsifications of all kinds, and to reveal the true will of the working masses . . . against the Bonapartists and autocrats who cloak their crimes in the name of the proletariat, the city conference of the RSDWP resolves to take part in the elections." Finally, as another concession to the Right Mensheviks, the last paragraph stipulated that the Mensheviks would boycott the new soviet after the elections.[52] Though the radicals and moderates had clearly worked out a compromise, some newspapers wrote of an open split between them,[53] and indeed the Menshevik faction in the Petrograd soviet, who had been urging continued participation in its work, now split over the election issue.

On June 17 the Mensheviks and SRs were reported to be negotiating specific forms of cooperation during the election campaign.[54] The details of these negotiations are unknown, but their outcome was a decision that the two parties would continue as a bloc and, "in the majority of cases," would present joint slates of candidates. Outwardly, the longtime Menshevik-SR alliance seemed undisturbed. In reality, however, it was encountering strong opposition within the Menshevik ranks. Too close an association with the SRs, and especially joint slates, would hinder the Mensheviks' freedom of action. At some plants,

52. "Perevybory Petrogradskogo soveta," *Utro Petrograda*, 17 June 1918, p. 2.
53. E.g., "Perevybory Petrogradskogo soveta," *Novyi vechernii chas*, 20 June 1918, p. 2.
54. "Perevybory v sovet," *Novyi vechernii chas*, 17 June 1918, p. 2.

workers were reported to have "categorically refused to abide by that decision."[55]

Relations between the Bolsheviks and the Left SRs had also been deteriorating. At separate sessions of the soviet, both the Bolsheviks and the Left SRs rejected the idea of acting as a coalition in the new elections. Grain requisitioning, the establishment of the committees of the poor, the disbandments of the soviets, and the Brest treaty were the major issues of disagreement. At last the Petrograd Left SRs announced that in the new soviet their faction would be in the ranks of the opposition to the Bolsheviks.[56] Thus the election campaign put a strain on the established party alliances and on the individual parties. A sense of increasing friction colored this election campaign.

The Workers' Assembly decided to back the opposition candidates, and so informed the Bolshevik authorities. The assembly set up a campaign headquarters in conjunction with the Menshevik party city committee, and together they staged thirty-six rallies on June 18 alone. One campaign leaflet read: "1. Down with representation by "dead souls" and by Bolshevik bureaucrats! 2. Down with the counterrevolutionary regime of the antiworkers' power! 3. Down with the armed crusade against the peasants! 4. Down with the policy of Brest treason and of subservience to Mirbach! 5. Long live the Constituent Assembly."[57]

A rotating schedule was drawn up to permit speakers to appear at as many rallies as possible. Candidate lists and a description of the party platform were widely circulated. This campaign was among the last in Soviet Russia during which opposition parties could present their platform to the workers relatively unobstructed and openly call on them to vote against "Soviet" power. At plant meetings, both Bolshevik and Menshevik-SR leaders usually addressed the workers and then put their platform up for a vote. At many factories, however, the credentials commissions that controlled the election procedure reversed their earlier practice and refused to admit the opposition to membership. Secret ballots were seldom used. At the Cartridge plant, when Volodarskii counted the hands that were raised and announced that the majority had voted for the Bolshevik slate, the opposition demanded another vote, this time by secret ballot. The new count produced 369 votes for the Menshevik-SR slate and 241 for the Bolshevik slate.[58] The election

---

55. "Sredi oppozitsii: Perevybory v Petrogradskii sovet," *Novyi vechernii chas*, 19 June 1918, p. 2.

56. "Levye SRy: Perevybory," ibid.

57. "Perevybory Petrogradskogo soveta," *Utro Petrograda*, 17 June 1918, p. 2.

58. "Perevybory v Petrogradskii sovet," *Molva*, 18 June 1918, p. 1. For a Bolshevik story on the Menshevik election campaign, see "Burzhuaznaia lovushka," *Pravda*, 21 June 1918, p. 1.

meeting at the Arsenal plant produced 74 votes for the Bolsheviks, 21 for the Left SRs, 11 abstentions, and 1,894 for the Menshevik-SRs.[59] Workers at the Sestroretsk plant agreed to listen to a campaigning Bolshevik only after persistent urging by the Menshevik-SR campaigners.[60] Workers at the Putilov plant shouted Lashevich out of the room when he tried to speak, and adopted a resolution that protested against "disbandment and persecution of workers' organizations, shootings and lynchings, arrests, and all other repressions directed by the existing government against the working class, which used to support it." Workers at the Siemens-Schuckert plant supported the Menshevik-SR platform by an overwhelming majority; at the Porokhovye plant, 350 voted for the opposition and 3 for the Bolsheviks. Election campaigning at the Obukhov plant was particularly rowdy. Catcalls and clamor forced Zinoviev to cut his speech short, while boisterous applause greeted Ioffe's reference to "a bunch of Bolshevik committees directed against the workers and peasants." The opposition platform received 3,900 votes, the Bolsheviks' 100.[61] In a resolution adopted two days earlier, the plant's workers had declared:

> Yielding to pressure from the workers, the soviet power has fixed new elections to the Petrograd soviet. We, the workers of the Obukhov plant, will take part in these elections under the slogan "Regeneration and cleansing of the soviets." . . . The soviets must not be a weapon for establishing an antidemocratic dictatorship; [they must not be] bureaucratic agencies or police headquarters, or executors of demands by the German reaction that triumphed in Brest. The newly elected soviets must raise their voice for the restoration of universal suffrage, of democratic institutions, for the reconvocation of the Constituent Assembly.[62]

During the last days of the campaign, the Bolsheviks engaged in drastic repressive measures. A Menshevik worker, I. V. Vasil'ev, was arrested after making an anti-Bolshevik speech at an election rally; later in the day, his dead body was found in a ditch.[63] On June 22, a worker from the Putilov plant, Grigor'ev, who had already been elected to the soviet, disappeared. Many people were arrested, among them one of the upolnomochennye from the Obukhov plant and a member of the soviet, Korokhov.[64] Apparently to prevent disturbances among the anti-Bol-

59. "V Arsenale," *Novaia zhizn'*, 20 June 1918, p. 3.

60. "Perevybory Petrogradskogo soveta," *Novaia zhizn'*, 19 June 1918, p. 2.

61. "Perevybory Petrogradskogo soveta," *Novaia zhizn'*, 21 June 1918, p. 3.

62. "Perevybory Petrogradskogo soveta," *Novaia zhizn'*, 19 June 1918, p. 2.

63. "K ubiistvu Vasil'eva," *Izvestiia*, 2 July 1918, p. 2. An independent source is Chessin, *L'Apocalypse russe*, p. 77. See also Ivan Kubikov, "Dve smerti," *Delo*, 1 August 1918, pp. 11–12.

64. "Sobytiia v Petrograde 22–25 iiunia 1918 goda," in Bernshtam, ed., *Nezavisimoe rabochee dvizhenie*, document no. 85, pp. 265–70.

shevik workers at the Obukhov plant, it was shut down on June 25 and the work force dismissed.[65] When the workers tried to approach the gates of the plant, Bolshevik troops fired into the air and charged the crowds, which dispersed in panic. Troops occupied the entire Obukhov and Nevskii districts; a 6 P.M. curfew was imposed, searches and arrests were widespread, and all meetings were banned.[66] The Obukhov workers expected support from the sailors of the mining unit, but six hundred reliable Kronstadt sailors disarmed the unit; the troublemakers were arrested and the ships were ordered to move from their positions near the Obukhov plant.[67] Zinoviev later said that many Bolsheviks in the EC of the Petrograd soviet favored a similar move against the Putilov works.[68]

Thus it was a hectic election campaign. A document published abroad that year said that "the soviets arrested the opposition leaders at bayonet point, stopped meetings, suspended newspapers, and closed factories and workmen's clubs."[69] Nor did the Bolsheviks themselves escape unscathed. Commissar Volodarskii was assassinated during the campaign, apparently by an underground SR group.[70]

The Election Results

Analysis of the Petrograd election returns presents difficulties. Both the Bolsheviks and the opposition parties claimed victory. The Bolsheviks tried to substantiate their claim by pointing out that hundreds of Bolshevik deputies had been elected and only a few dozen Mensheviks and SRs. The opposition charged that the Bolsheviks had created an artificial majority by manipulating the norms of representation.[71] A

65. Chessin, *L'Apocalypse russe*, p. 78.

66. "Repressii," *Novaia zhizn'*, 26 June 1918, p. 3. Contemporary Soviet historians seem to be more embarrassed by the Bolsheviks' actions against the workers than the Bolsheviks themselves were in 1918. In 1968 Soboleva wrote that the plant was closed at the request of the workers themselves (*Oktiabr'skaia revoliutsiia*, p. 285).

67. An eyewitness described the disarmament of the mining unit at the session of the Petrograd soviet on June 27; see "Novyi sovdep," *Vechernie ogni*, 28 June 1918, p. 3. According to the commissar of the Baltic Fleet, "armed force" was used against the mining unit; see I. Flerovskii, "Miatezh mobilizovannykh matrosov v Petrograde 14 oktiabria 1918 goda," *Proletarskaia revoliutsiia*, no. 8 (1926), p. 237.

68. "K Putilovskim rabochim," *Severnaia kommuna*, 18 August 1918, p. 3.

69. Slobodin, *Questions on the Bolsheviks*, p. 12.

70. "Ubiistvo Volodarskogo," *Izvestiia*, 22 June 1918, p. 3. For a vivid description of the preparation for the assassination, see the confessions of a former SR terrorist published in 1922, probably to discredit the SRs at the time of the trial: Semenov, *Voennaia i boevaia rabota*, p. 31. For the SRs' response to Semenov's charges, see *Golos Rossii*, 23 July 1922, p. 1.

71. Vassili Soukhomline, "Le Bluff bolcheviste des élections de Petrograd," *Echos de Russie*, nos. 18–19 (1 August 1918), p. 13.

Menshevik report to the Second International stated, "The large factories voted for the representatives of the opposition by an overwhelming
majority."[72] If this knot of assertions and denials is to be untangled, the
election returns and the new Petrograd soviet's composition and norms
of representation must be compared with those of the preceding soviet.

The preceding soviet had been elected largely in September and October 1917, at a time of increasing worker radicalization, which resulted in a Bolshevik majority. The most complete list of names of its
members has been published by the Soviet historian M. N. Potekhin.
This list does not show party affiliations, but it does show the organizations that the delegates represented. More than half of them (440 of the
791) came from military units. The second largest group, 259, were
workers. In addition to these delegates, elected by direct vote, 60 members represented trade unions; 17, the railways; 12, political parties;
and 3, district soviets.[73] Even if these figures are incomplete, there is no
doubt that the overwhelming majority of delegates in the soviet were
elected by popular vote rather than by organizations. It is significant,
however, that this kind of "corporate" representation already existed at
that time. Still, the soviet elected in the fall of 1917 was a fairly democratic institution: any delegate could be recalled by his constituency or
could switch to another party faction; the credentials commission was
a multiparty organ; and when a party lost its majority, it handed leadership over to the new majority.

In the following months, the soviet underwent significant changes.
With the demobilization of the army, the soldiers' section dwindled
and was finally abolished. It was replaced by the Red Army section, but
these delegates were appointed by the Bolsheviks rather than popularly
elected, and there were only fifty-eight of them. The workers' right to
recall delegates was revoked early in 1918, when it no longer served the
Bolsheviks' interests. New elections were postponed several times,
though the soviet's term had expired in the early spring. The opposition parties no longer held seats on the credentials commission. Most
important, the norms of representation established on June 15 dramat-
ically changed the composition of the soviet.

Although the number of workers in Petrograd was smaller than it had
been eight months earlier, the number of workers' deputies remained
almost the same (260, compared with 259). On the other hand, the
numbers of representatives of agencies and organizations substantially
increased. According to the new norms of representation, two seats
went to each trade union that had more than 2,000 members; the Cen-

72. Gurevich, "O polozhenii v Rossii," Nik. Col. no. 6, box 1, p. 3.
73. Potekhin, *Pervyi sovet*, pp. 318–29.

tral Council of Trade Unions had one delegate for every 5,000 organized workers; and three seats were allotted to each district soviet.
Political parties were no longer directly represented. The Bolsheviks
had created new "revolutionary organizations" to counterbalance the
Workers' Assemblies of Upolnomochennye, and these Bolshevik-domi-
nated workers' conferences were allocated eighty-eight seats. In theory,
any workers' organization had a right to be represented in the soviet; in
practice, opposition-led workers' organizations were denied seats. Finally, the new electoral rules specified that the unemployed were to be
represented by the trade unions to which they had once belonged. The
Union of the Unemployed was denied seats in the soviet, probably
because it openly supported the opposition parties.[74]

These new norms made it possible for one worker to be represented
in the soviet five times—by the district soviet, by the trade union, by
the Central Council of Trade Unions, by the workers' conferences, and
by the factory committee—without voting once. Furthermore, contrary
to the electoral rules, most union boards, factory committees, and district soviets held no elections before the general elections; indeed, they
had held no elections since October 1917, and their claim to represent
the popular will was thus questionable.[75] Many enterprises had been
closed in the months after October; the Bolshevik delegates from such
firms were the "dead souls" of whom the opposition frequently complained. The Petrograd soviet was no longer a popularly elected assembly: it had been turned into an assembly of Bolshevik functionaries.
The trade unions now had 144 delegates instead of 60; the railways, 72
instead of 17; the district soviets, 46 instead of 3. Added to the 88
delegates of the workers' conferences, the 58 of the Red Army, and the
10 of the navy, corporate representatives now made up 418 of the 677
members of the city soviet.[76]

Table 3 presents data from Menshevik, Bolshevik, and contemporary
Soviet sources on the party composition of the Petrograd soviet elected
in June 1918. There are numerous and substantial differences among
the figures. Even the total number of delegates varies, ranging from 582
to 682. The number of delegates reported to be Bolsheviks or Bolshevik
sympathizers ranges from 405 to 477. There is less variation in the
number of Left SR delegates, from 75 to 87. Perhaps the most important

74. "Kak budut proiskhodit' perevybory," Molva, 17 June 1918, p. 1, and "Perevybory
Petrogradskogo soveta," Utro Petrograda, 17 June 1918, p. 2. For the new norms of
representation, see "Polozhenie o vyborakh v Petrogradskii sovet," Severnaia kommuna,
18 June 1918, p. 1.

75. Semkovskii, "Perevybory Petrogradskogo soveta," Utro Petrograda, 17 June 1918,
p. 2.

76. Potekhin, Pervyi sovet, pp. 318–29.

TABLE 3

Party affiliation of delegates elected to Petrograd soviet in June 1918, according to six sources

Party affiliation	Menshevik-SR sources		Bolshevik sources		Contemporary Soviet sources	
	(1)	(2)	(3)	(4)	(5)	(6)
Bolsheviks and sympathizers	—	—	405	432	474	477[a]
Left SRs	—	—	75	—	87	84
Mensheviks	40	40	—	—	—	35
Mensheviks and SRs	—	—	59	—	81	—
SRs and sympathizers	77	87	—	—	—	44
Other and no party affiliation	30	—	43	—	35	37
All affiliations	—	—	582	682	677	677

Sources: (1) "Na obshchegorodskoi konferentsii Men'shevikov," Utro Petrograda, 1 July 1918, p. 2; (2) Vassili Soukhomline, "Le Bluff bolcheviste des élections de Petrograd," Echos de Russie, 1918, no. 18–19:13; (3) Pravda, 29 June 1918, p. 3; Lenin, Polnoe sobranie, 36:626; Chugaev, ed., Rabochii klass, p. 308; (4) Severnaia kommuna, 6 July 1918, p. 3; (5) Krasnikova, Na zare sovetskoi vlasti, p. 196; (6) Potekhin, Pervyi sovet, p. 69.
[a]424 Bolsheviks, 53 sympathizers.

discrepancy is that between Bolshevik and Menshevik sources on the number of Menshevik and SR delegates. Pravda's figure, 59, was less than half the figure of 127 (40 Mensheviks and 87 SRs) given in the Menshevik-SR journal Echos de Russie and barely more than half of the 117 (40 Mensheviks and 77 SRs) printed in a Menshevik newspaper in Petrograd. (Interestingly, the numbers in the contemporary Soviet sources fall between these extremes.)

The number of delegates in a given party faction is not an accurate indication of the party's strength in the elections, because that number combines delegates chosen by popular vote with those sent by organizations. Table 4 shows the party affiliations of the delegates who represented the workers and of those sent by the various organizations. It may be seen that of 477 Bolsheviks and sympathizers, 327, or 69 percent, were representatives of the Bolshevik-controlled organizations, and only 150, less than one-third, belonged to the workers' section (only part of which had been elected by direct vote of the workers). Similarly, of the 84 Left SR delegates, only 32 belonged to the workers' section. On the other hand, the workers' section contained the majority of the Menshevik and SR delegates (as well as of the unaffiliated).[77]

77. Similar figures on the party affiliation of delegates in the workers' section are given in Mandel, Petrograd Workers, p. 406. According to A. L. Mil'shtein, "Rabochie Petrograda v bor'be za ukreplenie sovetov," in Rabochie Leningrada, p. 104, the workers' section had only 217 delegates. However, since the norms of representation provided for one delegate per 500 workers, and there were 133,000 employed workers in Petrograd at the time of the elections, 260 is the more likely figure.

TABLE 4

Party affiliation of delegates elected to Petrograd soviet in June 1918, by group represented

Party affiliation	Workers	Railways	Organizations Trade unions	District soviets	Workers' conferences	Red Army	Navy	All organizations	All delegates[a]
Bolsheviks and sympathizers	150	44	118	32	72	55	6	327	477
Left SRs and sympathizers	32	7	10	14	16	3	2	52	84
Mensheviks and sympathizers	20	1	14	0	0	0	0	15	35
SRs and sympathizers	31	13	0	0	0	0	0	13	44
Other and no party affiliation	27	6	2	0	0	0	2	10	37
All affiliations	260	71	144	46	88	58	10	417	677

Sources: Workers and all delegates: Potekhin, Pervyi sovet, p. 69; organizational representatives: Novaia zhizn', 26, 27, and 30 June 1918.
[a]Utro Petrograda, 1 July 1918, p. 2, gives totals of 40 Mensheviks and sympathizers, 77 SRs and sympathizers, and 30 with other or no affiliation.

Among plants in the metal industry, the Bolsheviks could claim a victory only at the Nobel toolmaking factory. All told, the delegates from sixteen plants in the metal industry included 48 Mensheviks and SRs, 34 Bolsheviks, 10 Left SRs, and 5 without party affiliation.[78] In the plants of the electrical, chemical, and porcelain industries, the Bolsheviks again won at only one, the Treugol'nik rubber factory. In all others, the opposition won. Among the printers, too, the opposition bloc received 9 delegates, whereas the Bolsheviks had only 4 and the Left SRs 1. In tobacco factories the opposition parties won as well: 8 Mensheviks and SRs, 3 nonparty, and 5 Bolsheviks were elected. The textile and food enterprises elected 13 Mensheviks and SRs, 2 nonparty delegates, 1 Left SR, and 27 Bolsheviks. The municipal enterprises (the port, city canteen employees, etc.) returned 4 opposition delegates and 1 Bolshevik. Five more opposition delegates were elected by the various groups of unemployed. And finally, 5 Mensheviks and SRs and 2 sympathizers, 1 Left SR, and 3 Bolsheviks were returned from railway stations and depots. The total number of delegates elected by workers came to 123 Mensheviks and SRs, 82 Bolsheviks, 15 Left SRs, and 10 unaffiliated.[79]

The Aftermath

Immediately after the elections, Bolshevik policy toward the opposition parties hardened. Having secured their "victory," the Bolsheviks felt confident enough to ban the Workers' Assembly of Upolnomochennye. At the first session of the new Petrograd soviet, on June 27, one speaker after another denounced "the traitors in the ranks of the proletariat," "the capitalist agents," "the provocateurs paid by world imperialism," "the upolnomochennye of tsarist generals." One of the Bolshevik speakers said, "The Assembly of upolnomochennye is trash and we will take it where it belongs!" Hecklers prevented the assembly's representative, Filipov, from speaking. Shouts came from the floor: "Remove him! Out! Arrest him!" As an independent paper described the scene:

Some members of the soviet charge, fists raised, toward the podium. Someone tries to pull Filipov down by his feet. But Commissar Zalutskii, who stands next to the speaker, prevents this. Filipov leaves. The repre-

---

78. *Novaia zhizn'*, 26, 27, 28, and 30 June 1918; Mandel, *Petrograd Workers and the Soviet Seizure of Power*, p. 408.

79. *Novaia zhizn'*, 26–28 June 1918. C. F. Gogolevskii says that more than 200 delegates of the "petty bourgeois parties" were elected to the Petrograd soviet. See his *Petrogradskii sovet*, p. 29.

sentative of the Rechkin plant tries to speak in defense of the Assembly of Upolnomochennye. Shouts: "Lies! Out! Down with him!"[80]

The Bolsheviks' hostility was in part a reaction to their opponents' accusations that the new soviet represented not the Petrograd workers but the Bolshevik agencies. The more the opposition speakers denounced the electoral tinkering, the more furious the Bolshevik delegates became. At the end of the session, the soviet declared the Workers' Assembly a counterrevolutionary organization and banned its further existence.[81] After June 27, 1918, the only legal workers' organizations were to be those controlled by the Bolsheviks.

The rigged elections, the lockout of the Obukhov workers, and the banning of the Workers' Assembly created a new crisis in the camp of the opposition over the appropriate response. At a Menshevik party city conference that opened in Petrograd on June 30, moderates and radicals clashed over a proposal that the party refuse to take part in the new soviet. The radicals said it would be a disgrace to remain in a soviet created by fraudulent rules. "Wherever the elections went fairly, the overwhelming majority voted against the Bolsheviks and for the opposition."[82] The moderates joined in the condemnation of the electoral machinations but insisted that a walkout would accomplish exactly what the Bolsheviks wanted: to drive the opposition out of the soviet. The Mensheviks must remain in order to struggle against the representation of "dead souls."[83] Finally a compromise resolution was adopted, to the effect that the Menshevik faction would walk out if attempts to change the electoral law failed. In addition, at the insistence of the radicals, the conference endorsed a call by the Petrograd Workers' Assembly for a one-day general protest strike on July 2, with the proviso that food-supply workers should stay on the job.[84]

Meanwhile, the Petrograd Workers' Assembly was preparing for a meeting of the All-Russian Congress of Upolnomochennye, which had been scheduled before the ban on the workers' assemblies. An organizing committee had been set up to establish norms of representation (which were set at one delegate for every 5,000 workers), draw up an agenda, and tend to other practical matters.[85] The call for the congress

80. "Novyi sovdep," *Vechernie ogni*, 28 June 1918, p. 3.

81. "Peterburg: Sovet protiv rabochikh," *Iskra*, 29 June 1918, p. 3.

82. "Men'shevistskaia konferentsiia," *Novyi vechernii chas*, 1 July 1918, p. 2.

83. "Na obshchegorodskoi konferentsii Men'shevikov," *Utro Petrograda*, 1 July 1918, p. 2.

84. "Na konferentsii Men'shevikov," *Novyi vechernii chas*, 1 July 1918, p. 2. For the resolution calling for a one-day strike, see "Sobranie upolnomochennykh fabrik i zavodov," *Iskra*, 27 June 1918.

85. "K rabochemu s"ezdu," *Utro Petrograda*, 17 July 1918.

combined a cry of desperation with the tacit hope that the Bolsheviks would not dare disband it or arrest those who attended it:

> Life has become harsh and difficult. More and more factories are being closed. The army of the unemployed is getting bigger and bigger. Hunger and arbitrary rule are getting stronger and stronger and there is no way out. . . . In these dire and troubled hours we can expect no help from anywhere. We must help ourselves; we must save ourselves. . . . Workers of all Russia, we, the upolnomochennye of the Petrograd factories and plants, call you to the All-Russian Congress. Freely elected representatives of the working class will come from all cities, and together they will look for and find a path to salvation for themselves and for the whole country: food supply, unemployment, general ruin, the people's lack of rights, and the rebirth of our organizations—all must be discussed and decided upon.[86]

An atmosphere of fear and fearlessness, panic and determination, hung over these last days of the assembly's existence. The representatives of the Obukhov plant told of the workers' bitterness and anger toward the Bolsheviks.[87] The lockout at their plant showed that the Bolsheviks were now ready to undertake repressive measures not only against individuals but also against whole plants. Instead of leading to caution in dealings with the Bolsheviks, though, the workers' plight provoked outrage:

> We are strangled by hunger. We are mangled by unemployment. Our children are dropping from lack of food. Our press has been crushed. Our organizations have been destroyed. The freedom to strike has been abolished. And when we raise our voices in protest, they shoot us or throw us out, as they did with the Obukhov comrades. Russia has again been turned into a tsarist dungeon. We can't go on living like this.[88]

Preparations were also going forward for the one-day general strike. Smirnov, a Menshevik who was chairman of the city bureau of the Petrograd Workers' Assembly and a member of the strike committee, reported to the assembly about the preparations being made there and in Yaroslavl, Tula, Nizhnii Novgorod, Vladimir, Rybinsk, and other cities.[89] The railway workers in Bologoe (between Petrograd and Mos-

86. "V sobranii upolnomochennykh fabrik i zavodov Petrograda 15 iiunia 1918 goda," *Novaia zhizn'*, 16 June 1918, p. 3.

87. "Zakrytie Obukhovskogo zavoda," *Novaia zhizn'*, 26 June 1918. See also Aronson, *Rossiia v epokhu revoliutsii*, p. 192.

88. Aronson, *Rossiia v epokhu revoliutsii*, p. 193. The wording of the last sentence in the quotation—*Tak dol'she zhit' nevmogotu*—indicates that this resolution, unlike many others, was written by workers rather than by intellectuals.

89. "Sobranie upolnomochennykh fabrik i zavodov," *Iskra*, 27 June 1918.

cow) were already striking, to protest the arrest of their leaders by the Cheka. They threatened to block passage of all trains between the two capitals. From other stations along the line, workers sent messages of solidarity, expressing their readiness to join the general strike. The Bolshevik-controlled Moscow soviet described the activity of the railroad strike committee thus:

> Here and there on the railroads, strikes broke out in response to counter-revolutionary agitation by the Mensheviks and right SRs, who are playing on the famine among the laboring classes. Strike committees have been set up which are sending [telegraph] messages along the railroad lines without paying, calling for a general strike, and using locomotives for their own purposes.[90]

Other actions were being taken as well. A recent study has found evidence of eighteen strikes "with an explicitly anti-Bolshevik character" and some seventy other incidents in Petrograd alone—demonstrations, protest rallies, and anti-Bolshevik factory meetings—between the shootings at Kolpino and July 2, the date set for the general strike.[91]

The scheduled strike date was to coincide with the opening of the Fifth Congress of Soviets, which was to ratify a new constitution. Speeches about the triumph of Soviet democracy would be inappropriate against the background of a general strike. Moreover, relations between the Bolsheviks and the Left SRs were at their worst. (A Left SR uprising broke out on July 6, while the Congress of Soviets was in session.) The Bolsheviks were in panic. Indeed, Lenin, according to some accounts, wondered whether they would still be in power the next day.[92] Harsh measures against the planned general strike were initiated. The Cheka ordered all its local branches to strengthen the struggle against the "counterrevolution." A special railroad section was created at the Cheka to deal with what was referred to as "sabotage on the railroads," and a state of emergency was declared on major lines.[93] Members of the railway workers' strike committees were arrested. An "Extraordinary Commission to Struggle with the White Guards' Strike" was set up in Petrograd. ("White Guards" was here being used as a derogatory term for Mensheviks and SRs. Other epithets employed were "traitors," "agents of imperialism," "upolnomochennye of the

---

90. "Postanovlenie zheleznodorozhnogo raiona soveta Moskvy ot 28 iiunia 1918 goda," in *Uprochenie sovetskoi vlasti v Moskve*, pp. 130–31.

91. Rosenberg, "Russian Labor and Bolshevik Power," *Slavic Review* 44 (Summer 1985): 233.

92. I. I. Vatsetis, "Grazhdanskaia voina: 1918 god," *Pamiat'*, p. 27. These are the memoirs of a Red Army commander, never published in the Soviet Union.

93. Soboleva, *Bor'ba Bol'shevikov protiv SRov*, p. 68.

Entente," and "lackeys of the bourgeoisie.") All "counterrevolutionary" newspapers were shut down and some editors were arrested. A
special detachment of 1,000 Communists was mobilized to be sent to
critical areas.[94] Machine guns were installed on housetops in strategic
locations. Reinforced Red Guard units patrolled the streets. These steps
seemed excessive even to *Izvestiia*, which called for a more orderly
struggle with the "Menshevik-SR counterrevolution." Nevertheless,
the Bolshevik newspaper also said that "it is sometimes necessary to
call to order individual workers or even whole groups of workers who
by their actions willingly or unwillingly play into the hands of the
bourgeois counterrevolution . . . this is inevitable although rather
sad."[95]

The organizers of the Congress of Upolnomochennye feared that the
Bolsheviks would move against them, too. One of them, the Right Menshevik Levitskii, said that the meeting was called "realistically, without unnecessary illusions and utopias. After all, the legacy of the past
year has been a great deal of realism. We'll be working on its preparation, unless . . . we are crushed by those in power. It seems that a
crusade against us is being prepared on their side, and in their last
throes perhaps they will try to hit even harder."[96] These fears were of
course not unjustified. Such terms as "counterrevolutionary" and "social traitors" were being applied to the congress and its organizers.[97] A
new element was that the Bolsheviks may have begun to see the opposition's political initiatives as part of a conspiracy (*zagovor*), with the
Mensheviks in charge of propaganda and the SRs in charge of military
operations. They may well have believed that a secret plot was being
hatched in which the Congress of Upolnomochennye would assemble
and, backed by strikes and demonstrations, demand the resignation of
the government, while SR underground armed detachments attacked
government forces and seized power in the name of the Constituent
Assembly.[98] The Bolshevik newspapers in July 1918 conveyed an ob-
session with conspiracies—and several conspiracies were indeed
afoot. Their fear prompted them to brand any strike or demonstration,
the formation of a strike committee, a demand for new elections, or any
other opposition activity as a new anti-Soviet conspiracy.

According to official Bolshevik sources, the "yellow strike" on July 2

94. Krasnikova, *Na zare sovetskoi vlasti*, p. 197.
95. "Sovetskaia vlast' i rabochie," *Izvestiia*, 27 June 1918, p. 1.
96. Levitskii to Aksel'rod, 16 June 1918, in *Martov i ego blizkie*, p. 66 (ellipses are
Levitskii's).
97. "Azhitatsiia i agitatsiia: K slukham o sotsial predatel'skom rabochem s"ezde,"
Pravda, 13 June 1918, p. 1.
98. Sosnovskii described this scenario in a speech to the CEC on June 14, 1918; see
Protokoly TsIK, p. 422.

failed: only a "bunch of counterrevolutionaries" participated.[99] The non-Bolshevik papers—the few that still remained—also spoke of the strike's failure.[100] The latter, however, were not necessarily referring to a failure by the workers to heed the strike call. One provincial newspaper reported that 80,000 Petrograd workers had participated;[101] that would amount to 80 percent of the workers represented in the city's assembly of upolnomochennye. Other reports, however, did speak of hesitation, procrastination, and fear on the part of some workers.[102] In any case, the strike was a failure in the sense that it won no concessions. On the contrary, the repressions intensified. Many strikers were blacklisted; some were fired, arrested, or ordered to leave Petrograd. The sense of failure was heightened by the realization that what had previously been thought of as the workers' ultimate weapon, the general strike, had proved ineffective against the Bolshevik dictatorship. The lessons of July 2 for the opposition were that firmly entrenched ideas about forms and methods of workers' struggle no longer fitted with Russia's reality. The protesting workers had to cope not only with the Bolsheviks' readiness to inflict the entire gamut of repressive actions but also with the baffling realization that the Bolsheviks were doing all this in the name of the proletariat. The striking workers were facing not gendarmes in uniform but other workers like themselves, who had been recruited into the Red Guards. Another cause for confusion and hesitation was the infighting between moderates and radicals, which had always been a disruptive factor in the assembly of upolnomochennye. Despair alternated with self-assurance, bold initiative with inaction.

The failure of the strike also reflected the extraordinary, not to say catastrophic, conditions in Petrograd. The newspapers were filled with stories about cholera, famine, and the flight of workers from the city. For lack of raw materials, many factories, particularly in the metal and textile industries, had to cease operations.[103] In such conditions, a strike was more threatening to the workers than to the government. When the call for a general strike was first being heard, a Left SR newspaper characterized it as "thoughtless" and asked plaintively: "Where will a strike lead? To what concrete results, now that production has almost completely stopped, when there are so few workers left

99. Vladimirova, *God sluzhby sotsialistov kapitalistam*, p. 197. See also "Proval zabastovki," *Izvestiia*, 3 July 1918, p. 5.

100. "Nesostoiavshaiasia zabastovka," *Novyi vechernii chas*, 2 July 1918, p. 1.

101. "Petrograd: K zabastovke protesta," *Golos iuga*, 5 July 1918.

102. "Zabastovka 2 iiulia v Petrograde," *Novaia zhizn'*, 3 July 1918, p. 3.

103. See, for example, "Evakuatsiia Petrogradskikh bezrabotnykh," *Izvestiia*, 6 June 1918, p. 4; "Peterburg: Grazhdanskaia voina i bezrabotitsa," *Iskra*, 29 June 1918; *Utro Petrograda*, 17 July 1918.

in Petrograd. . . ? A general strike can only add to the numbers of the hungry and to the destruction of industry, nothing else."[104]

Thus the workers' protest movement, called to life by ever-worsening conditions, could achieve little precisely because conditions were so appalling.

Repression in the Provinces

In the two weeks following the expulsion of the opposition from the CEC, general strikes took place in Tula, Nizhnii Novgorod, Yaroslavl, Kaluga, Tver, and other cities, despite repressive measures by the Bolsheviks.[105] The events in Tula were typical of those elsewhere. On June 10 the Bolshevik EC declared martial law in Tula, supposedly to prevent a strike at two large plants. The factory committees, led by Mensheviks and SRs, refused to recognize the legitimacy of the declaration and said they would not abide by it. Adding to the Bolsheviks' anxiety was a large quantity of arms stored at the plants. To make things worse, expressions of discontent had been heard among the Red Army soldiers. The Bolsheviks were unsure of their next move. As one of them said at an EC session, "We will accomplish nothing by repressive measures alone, but will only kindle the wrath of the masses."[106] In a public appeal, they admitted that "the masses had begun to turn away" from their party.[107]

In the Tula Metalworkers' Union Bolsheviks were outnumbered by Mensheviks 3 to 1,[108] and the Tula council of upolnomochennye commanded the workers' overwhelming support. When the news reached Tula that the Menshevik chairman of the council, Aleksandrov, was among those who had been arrested in Moscow on June 13, the workers demanded his immediate release and threatened a general strike. The Bolsheviks responded with more arrests, and on June 17, workers at the two plants struck.[109] A Menshevik-led strike committee appealed to other plants to join the strikers. The Bolsheviks arrested the twenty members of the strike committee—including its chairman, N. I. Kise-

104. *Znamia bor'by*, 26 May 1918, p. 1.

105. For a vivid description of these strikes, see Serge, *Year One*, pp. 241–42.

106. "Protokol zasedaniia Prezidiuma . . . , " document no. 64 in Arkhivnyi otdel UVD Tul'skoi oblasti, *Uprochenie sovetskoi vlasti v Tul'skoi gubernii*, pp. 119–21 (cited hereafter as *Uprochenie v Tul'skoi gubernii*).

107. "Obrashchenie Tul'skogo komiteta RKP(b) k Kommunistam ob usilenii raboty . . . ," document no. 66, in ibid., p. 124.

108. Helgesen, *Origins of the Party-State Monolith*, p. 213.

109. "17 iiunia v Tule ob"iavlena vseobshchaia zabastovka zavodov," *Delo naroda*, 19 June 1918, p. 4.

lev, and the secretary of the Tula Menshevik organization, V. A. Kogan—and warned that participation in the strike would be considered
tantamount to treason.[110] In response, the metalworkers formed a new
strike committee. The Bolsheviks—in a resolution published as if it
were a decision of a general meeting of the workers—demanded an end
to the strike and said that anyone who did not return to work immediately "will be tried by us as a person who is consciously acting
against the working class and playing into the hands of the bourgeoisie.
Furthermore, the general meeting is to hand over all members of the so-
called strike committee to the Revolutionary Tribunal for trial for their
policy of deceiving the workers."[111] No trials actually took place, and
the arrested strike leaders went on a hunger strike in prison, demanding that they be either put on trial or freed.[112] In defiance of the martial-
law declaration, the workers held marches and rallies and demanded
the immediate release of their arrested comrades, not only those in Tula
but those in Moscow as well. They also demanded that martial law be
rescinded and that the Constituent Assembly and a congress of upolnomochennye be convened.[113]

On June 21, the new strike committee set up a picket line in front of
the main gate of the armaments plant. At a rally of striking workers,
speakers demanded that their comrades be freed immediately. According to a Bolshevik source, the commander of the military detachment,
Tsutskov, "shot into the air with a revolver."[114] Somehow, one worker
was killed. Naturally, the workers' protests intensified. Since the Tula
Bolsheviks realized they could not force the workers to return to work,
they decided to shut down the armaments plant indefinitely and dis-
miss all the strikers.[115]

In new elections held by the Tula Metalworkers' Union in July, the
Mensheviks again won a clear majority.[116] The Bolsheviks then evicted
their political opponents from public office by force. In June the Tula
committee of the party had already declared that "the Mensheviks and
Right SRs must be kicked out [vybity] of the factory committees, the
trade union boards, the [workers'] insurance boards, out of all organiza-

110. "Sredi politicheskikh zakliuchennykh," Novaia zhizn', 30 June 1918, p. 2.
111. Soboleva, Oktiabr'skaia revoliutsiia, p. 286.
112. "V Tule," Iskra, 29 June 1918.
113. "Zabastovka v Tule," Vozrozhdenie, 20 June 1918, p. 3; Soboleva, Oktiabr'skaia
revoliutsiia, p. 286.
114. "Protokol ob"edinennogo zasedaniia Prezidiuma. . . ," in Uprochenie v Tul'skoi
gubernii, p. 138. The shooting was later discussed at a session of the assembly of u-
polnomochennye in Petrograd on June 26; see Bernshtam, ed., Nezavisimoe rabochee
dvizhenie, document no. 86, pp. 269–71.
115. "Protokol ob"edinennogo zasedaniia Prezidiuma. . . ," in Uprochenie v Tul'skoi
gubernii, p. 139.
116. Ibid., p. 18.

tions!"[117] Strikes must be banned, troublemakers arrested, and Mensheviks driven out. In describing developments in Tula, *Izvestiia* wrote: "Tula has always been a bastion of Menshevism. . . . The factory committees, which until now consisted to the last man of Mensheviks and SRs, are being dismissed and replaced by supporters of soviet power."[118]

Events followed a similar course in Nizhnii Novgorod. On June 10, delegates representing 40,000 workers assembled in Sormovo for a regional conference of upolnomochennye.[119] The Bolsheviks declared martial law in both Nizhnii Novgorod and Sormovo, and all public meetings were banned. The Red Guards occupied all buildings in the city that could have been used for assembly and installed machine guns in strategic locations. The conference nevertheless opened, in a Menshevik club. Workers demonstrated in the streets; according to an official Bolshevik report, after "provocateur shots" were fired at the Red Guards from the crowd, "the soviet troops shot into the air and five people turned out to be wounded."[120] According to a Menshevik report, one worker was killed and many were wounded and beaten up by the Red Guards.[121]

The next day, the conference assembled at the plant and voted to stage a general strike. The secretary of the local Menshevik party committee, Ridnek (who was killed by the Cheka later that year), reported that the mood of the workers was combative. A description of the shooting was widely circulated.[122] The Bolsheviks threatened to "take merciless measures against counterrevolution."[123] On June 17, the Sormovo workers went on strike, supported by workers in the smaller enterprises and commercial establishments of Nizhnii Novgorod.[124] The authorities responded with searches, arrests, and shootings. An SR newspaper in Moscow reported that the enterprises that had been struck had been shut down and that the Cheka was "threatening" those

117. "Obrashchenie Tul'skogo komiteta RKP(b) k chlenam partii ob usilenii raboty i ukreplenii partiinoi distsipliny," *Revoliutsionnyi vestnik*, 16 June 1918, p. 2, reprinted in Chugaev, ed., *Rabochii klass Sovetskoi Rossii*, document no. 77, pp. 74–75.

118. "Perelom," *Izvestiia*, 23 June 1918, p. 1.

119. For a Soviet source on the conference of upolnomochennye in Nizhnii Novgorod, see Arkhivnyi otdel UVD Gor'kovskogo oblispolkoma, *Pobeda oktiabr'skoi sotsialisticheskoi revoliutsii v Nizhegorodskoi gubernii*, document no. 495, p. 513 (cited hereafter as *Pobeda v Nizhegorodskoi gubernii*). See also "Sprengung einer Arbeiterkonferenz," *Stimmen aus Russland*, nos. 4–5 (15 August 1918), pp. 18–19.

120. Quoted in "Bol'sheviki v provintsii: Nizhnii Novgorod," *Nashe slovo*, 12 June 1918, p. 4.

121. "Po Rossii: V Sormove," *Novyi vechernii chas*, 17 June 1918, p. 4.

122. "Spisok arestovannykh rabochikh upolnomochennykh soderzhashchikhsia v Taganskoi tiur'me," *Novoe delo naroda*, 18 June 1918, pp. 3–4.

123. *Pobeda v Nizhegorodskoi gubernii*, document no. 495, p. 513.

124. "Po Rossii: V Sormovo," *Novyi vechernii chas*, 17 June 1918, p. 4.

who had joined the strike.[125] On June 26, two workers were killed and ten wounded in Sormovo during the dispersal of a demonstration protesting the arrest of I. G. Upovalov, a Menshevik member of the local soviet.[126] Delegations of upolnomochennye were dispatched to Moscow, Tula, Yaroslavl, Viatka, Vologda, Arkhangelsk, and other cities.[127]

News items from other cities at this time illustrate the magnitude of the protest movement and the determined Bolshevik effort to suppress it:

Kostroma: About 1,000 workers of the Sotov factory protest against arrests and terror directed against the representatives of workers and the Petrograd delegation.

Tver: As a consequence of worker unrest, martial law has been declared.

Voronezh: The sale of non-Bolshevik publications is forbidden.

Kaluga: The Bolsheviks have expelled the Social Democrats and the Socialist Revolutionaries from the soviet.

Zlatous: The workers are on strike. Commissar Podvoiskii has asked Moscow to dispatch 300 unemployed to replace those on strike.[128]

Also in Tver, where the Menshevik and SR party organizations were reported to be strongly influential, railway and textile workers went on strike. The Cheka arrested the members of the strike committee and fired some of the strikers.[129]

New elections to the soviet were held at a toolmaking plant in Kolomna, near Moscow, at the end of June. The Bolsheviks received only one seat; the rest went to Mensheviks, SRs, and nonparty delegates. In what had by then become standard practice, the Bolsheviks disbanded the soviet. Many Menshevik and SR workers and trade-union leaders were arrested. The local Menshevik organization was essentially destroyed.[130]

In Vitebsk, a province-wide conference of 300 workers' upolnomochennye assembled and was immediately repressed. A few Mensheviks were arrested and charged with organizing a "counterrevolutionary

125. "Posledstviia Nizhegorodskoi zabastovki," Vozrozhdenie, 20 June 1918, p. 3. "V Petrogradskom sovete," Golos Kieva, 21 June 1918.
126. "Sormovskii rasstrel," Iskra, 29 June 1918.
127. "Vserossiiskii rabochii s"ezd: Beseda so Smirnovym," Novyi vechernii chas, 26 June 1918, p. 4.
128. "Kurze Nachrichten aus dem Alltagsleben im 'Kommunistischen' Russland," Stimmen aus Russland, nos. 4–5 (15 August 1918), pp. 27–30.
129. "Soobshchenie gazety Izvestiia o deiatel'nosti mestnykh chrezvychainykh kommissii," document no. 160 in Belov, Iz istorii Vserossiiskoi chrezvychainoi kommissii, p. 191.
130. "Kolomenskii mashinostroitel'nyi zavod," Vsegda vpered, 16 February 1919, p. 2.

A cartoon in the satirical journal *Novyi Satirikon*, no. 18 (1918). Under the heading "Radiant future" is this dialogue: Chairman of the tribunal: "So, defendant, you are sentenced to confinement, food will be water and bread only. . . . But I don't understand why you have such a happy face?" Defendant (joyfully): "For God's sake! I'm going to get bread!" Russian Serials Collection, Hoover Institution Archives.

conspiracy." The socialist party organizations in the province were declared illegal and all socialists were ordered to leave the province immediately. One worker, a Menshevik, was killed by the Cheka for posting Menshevik protest declarations.[131]

In the spring of 1918, after losing elections, the Bolsheviks had disbanded the soviets; now in the summer of 1918, after the general strikes, they demanded the "liquidation of Menshevism."[132] Especially in smaller towns, the local Cheka units raided Menshevik party premises, confiscated printing presses, and seized hostages.[133] Plots, con-

131. Aronson, *Na zare krasnogo terrora*, p. 38.
132. For a Soviet description of the purge of the Mensheviks from the trade unions, see Krasnikova, *Na zare sovetskoi vlasti*, p. 182.
133. Martov, *Le Parti ouvrier Socialiste Democrate*, Nik. Col. no. 6, box 1, file 16 (2), p. 11.

spiracies, and attempts at rebellion were discovered in increasing numbers. Popular unrest was attributed to Menshevik agitation. A few opposition papers continued to appear sporadically despite the bans; one published in Moscow said that the actions of the Bolsheviks were proof that the government had lost touch with reality:

> Let the "workers' and peasants'" government scream about bands of kulaks, landlords, and White Guards raising the banner of rebellion against the soviet power. But after the events in Sormovo, Nizhnii Novgorod, Kolpino, Petrograd, Sestroretsk, Orekhovo-Zuevo, and Moscow, after the June 18 political protest strike, only the blind and power-hungry can fail to see that it is a matter not of the intrigues of the socialists but of a genuine, spontaneous workers' movement.[134]

According to data collected by the Menshevik CC on the strikes in central Russia in June and July 1918, thousands of protesters were arrested and hundreds fled; in some places, resistance took the form of armed insurrection.[135]

On July 23, forty upolnomochennye from Petrograd, Moscow, Tula, Sormovo, Kolomna, Tver, Vologda, and Votkinsk assembled in Moscow for a conference. The gathering was a mix of Menshevik and SR workers active in the upolnomochennye movement, Menshevik party functionaries and intellectuals and old-guard Social Democrats. On the second day the Cheka burst in, guns in hand. The conference was disbanded and those in attendance were arrested. The Bolshevik press claimed that the conference had been part of a conspiracy planned in conjunction with Kadets and Western imperialists and that gold, diamonds, and thousands of rubles had been found. The arrested delegates were held in prison but no charges were brought against them.[136]

At a session of the Petrograd soviet on July 30, the Bolsheviks hurled

---

134. "Natsional'nyi front," Vozrozhdenie, 20 June 1918, p. 1.

135. Gurevich, O polozhenii v Rossii, p. 6.

136. A discussion of the background of the conference and an account of its disbandment are contained in a report to the Second International by Aksel'rod on behalf of the Menshevik CC, dated 10 November 1918, in Nik. Col. no. 16, box 1, file 13. Among the documents about this incident that have been published in the West are a telegram of the Menshevik CC to the Western socialist parties, in The Case of Russian Labor, p. 7, and an appeal of the arrested delegates from prison, in Slobodin, Questions on the Bolsheviks, pp. 38–39. The names of those arrested may be found in Vladimirova, God sluzhby sotsialistov kapitalistam, p. 199, and Case of Russian Labor, p. 7. The Bolsheviks' charges of conspiracy appeared in Izvestiia, 25 July 1918, p. 3. Abramovitch's account of the incident is in "Ein offener Brief aus dem Moskauer Gefaengnis," Stimmen aus Russland, nos. 6–7 (1918), pp. 43–48, and in his memoirs, Soviet Revolution, p. 165. In the latter, Abramovitch relates that in the fall of 1918, Riazanov, a high-ranking Bolshevik to whom he was related, visited him in prison and intimated that Abramovitch was to be executed but later returned and said that the execution had been called off.

imprecations at Menshevik speakers. Lashevich, as he had done before, advocated the toughest possible measures against the "traitors of the working class": "The Right SRs and Mensheviks are more dangerous enemies of soviet power than the bourgeoisie. Yet these enemies still have not been shot and are enjoying freedom. The proletariat must finally get down to business. The Mensheviks and SRs must be finished off once and for all!"[137] No longer were the Bolsheviks debating the admissibility of Menshevik participation in the soviet elections; at issue now was whether they were to live or die. It was becoming dangerous for Menshevik representatives to remain in the soviet.

Although the workers' protest movement had begun as a response to deteriorating economic conditions in the spring of 1918, political concerns overshadowed economic ones by the summer. The movement embraced Russia's major cities and industrial centers, and it was especially strong in the large factories of the metal industry in such cities as Petrograd, Tula, Sormovo, Briansk, Kolomna, and Izhevsk. It was difficult for the Bolsheviks to claim that they represented the proletariat when Russia's largest industrial centers remained hotbeds of Menshevik-SR opposition. In these circumstances, the Bolsheviks' uncompromising and brutal repression is understandable. At stake was not only their power but their very identity. It is important to realize that the repressive measures taken by the Bolshevik regime were responses to the regime's internal crisis and not to the external pressures of the civil war, which was only just beginning.

137. "V Petrogradskom sovete," *Sovremennoe slovo*, 31 July 1918, p. 3.

CHAPTER 9

The Civil War and
the Party Split

The term *civil war* is used in the scholarly literature to denote two different patterns of armed struggle. It may be defined as simply an armed struggle between different social groups and classes within a society, and in that case we could say that the civil war in Russia started soon after October 1917, or even earlier. It may also be defined, however, as a struggle of groups within a society involving organized armies, territorial bases, and front lines, and then we could say that the civil war in Russia began with the Czech-SR uprising in the summer of 1918. The advance of the Czech-SR troops, the Bolsheviks' panic, Trotsky's energetic efforts to create the Red Army, the execution of Tsar Nicholas II, and the onset of the Red Terror—all these dramatic events of that summer have been extensively covered in the historical literature.[1] What part did the Mensheviks play in the early stage of the civil war? The debate among the Mensheviks, which at the end of May had focused on whether to stay in the soviets or to boycott them, centered by mid-July on whether armed struggle against the Bolsheviks was admissible.

Anti-Bolshevik Uprisings

In the summer of 1918, the Bolsheviks' power was at its lowest ebb since October. The Menshevik CC described the situation in these terms:

1. Bradley, *Allied Intervention*, chap 4, esp. p. 101; Deutscher, *Prophet Armed*, pp. 405–48; Gerson, *Secret Police*, pp. 130–31.

Nourished by general indignation, attempts at uprisings have been going on almost uninterruptedly in recent times. Some of them are prepared by conspiratorial means, others burst out spontaneously, and still others represent conscious and organized action by the laboring masses (workers' political strikes, attempts at seizure of power in Moscow, Yaroslavl, and other cities, destruction of local soviets, peasant disturbances, active support by the population for the Czechoslovak advance).[2]

Contemporary Soviet historians likewise admit that scores of anti-Bolshevik uprisings were taking place. According to a recent study, the Cheka registered 245 large-scale counterrevolutionary insurgencies in the twenty central provinces in 1918.[3] It is difficult to classify these insurgencies in a meaningful way, because so many diverse social forces were at play, but in general terms, there were four categories, distinguished by the composition of the groups that took part or provided leadership.

No doubt the largest number of uprisings were those of peasants and small traders. These were primarily expressions of protest against grain requisitioning and restrictions on trade. Usually local, involving a small town or several villages, these rebellions were short and violent.

Red Army soldiers and sailors were the main fighting force in the second category. Linked by social origin and economic interest to the countryside, the soldiers and sailors expressed peasants' grievances. What made these uprisings particularly dangerous for the Bolsheviks was that the insurgents were well armed and organized. In addition, these revolts, unlike those in the first category, had undertones of political orientation, echoing the demands of political parties, most often of the SRs or the Left SRs.

The third category consists of uprisings organized and led by White officers' underground organizations. These uprisings were especially well planned and well timed, and they had specific political and strategic objectives. In some southern cities they coincided with the advance of the White army, and in some cities of central Russia, workers took a prominent part in them.

In the fourth category are uprisings led by SRs and Right Mensheviks. In some cases, the main fighting force consisted of workers; in others, peasants; and in still others, a combination of various social groups and the Komuch military formations. The only uprisings that had any success against the Bolsheviks were those in the last two categories.

The extent of Menshevik participation in these uprisings is still a matter of controversy. On the one hand, Soviet historians cite evidence

2. "Rezoliutsiia TsK" (27 July 1918), Nik. Col. no. 6, box 1, file 2 (published in *Rabochii Internatsional* [Petrograd], no. 10 [7 August 1918], pp. 2–3).
3. Sofinov, *Ocherki istorii Vecheka*, p. 88.

from archival sources to show that the Mensheviks wholeheartedly took part in the uprisings and supported the Komuch government.[4] On the other hand, a more objective student of the period has written that "the charge against the Mensheviks, as a party, of supporting armed anti-communist activity was manifestly false, although constantly reiterated."[5] A third view is that, although the Mensheviks were not involved in any uprisings against the Bolsheviks before their expulsion from the CEC, they did participate in some in the summer and fall of 1918.[6]

A judgment on this matter requires a careful definition of what can be considered "involvement" of a political party in an antigovernment uprising. If the Menshevik CC formally forbade party members to take part in uprisings, can one say that the party rejected insurrection, even though some members of the CC explicitly favored such a course? Furthermore, how does one evaluate the policy of the provincial party organizations in cases where it deviated from that of the CC? Moreover, involvement has to be seen in the context of the political conditions in each region. The question is not merely whether the Mensheviks participated in anti-Bolshevik uprisings, or in how many, but what kinds of uprisings these were. With which social and political groups were the Mensheviks collaborating when they did participate?

Most of the bloodiest clashes were in the first category. In small towns and villages, crises rapidly got out of control, and the authority of party leaders was quickly overrun by the furor of the mob. The cycle of events leading to spontaneous outbursts of violence was remarkably similar in these cases. Menshevik and SR activists denounced the Bolshevik requisitions and blamed them for the starvation of the local populace. The Bolsheviks overreacted and fired at the crowd, as in Kolpino, Kovrov, Rybinsk, and other towns.[7] "Troublemakers" were arrested and martial law was declared. Burials of the victims, processions, singing of revolutionary songs, speeches, and condemnation of the Bolsheviks followed. Telegrams from local Bolshevik leaders provide a vivid portrayal of the situation:

> Situation . . . most critical—reports of rebellions; work at factories coming to a standstill. Province on verge of anarchy. Save and help us with resources from Moscow! [Vladimir]

4. See, for example, Mints, *Men'sheviki v interventsii*, pp. 76–102.
5. Schapiro, *Origin of the Communist Autocracy*, p. 195.
6. Nikolaevsky, "RSDRP (men'shevikov)," Nik. Col., p. 36.
7. "Kovrov," *Novaia zaria*, 1918, no. 1:41; "Krasnogvardeiskii pogrom," *Vpered*, 3 May 1918, p. 2; "Vos'moi sovet partii Eserov," *ESER*, 3 May 1918; "Po bol'shakam i proselkam: Kartina revoliutsionnoi provintsii," *Vecherniaia zvezda*, 27 March 1918, p. 3. On the events in Kolpino, see chap. 6.

Send bread for the sake of the salvation of soviet power! [Bogorodsk]

Situation serious. Rebellion ripening! [Serpukhov]

Commissariat embattled by crowds of workers, peasants, and soldiers. Any day now, excesses are possible. [Briansk][8]

In Poreche, the mob stormed the soviet, shouting, "Beat them! Kill all the commissars!" In Belyi, all members of the soviet were killed. In Soligalich and other towns, the building housing the soviet was locked and burned with the members inside.[9] An SR newspaper described the dramatic events in Pavlovskii Posad:

> Angered by grain requisitions, the peasants of nearby villages came to the town. Assembled in front of the soviet, they demanded a change of government. When the commissar appeared, they would not let him speak. Shouts: "Down with the soviets!" Commissar: "Clear the square!" He threatened to open fire. Shouts: "Go away yourselves!" "We have nowhere to go! In any case, we'll starve!" The crowd became infuriated. People began to pick up paving stones. A shot was fired—according to one version, from the crowd; according to another, from the soviet. The fact is that after that, shots were fired at the crowd, which responded with a hail of stones. More and more people were converging on the square. By then a few people had been killed. The mob went completely wild. Someone shouted: "Let's burn them!" and this was enough: they brought a fire engine and sprayed gasoline on the soviet and set it on fire. Some of those inside tried to surrender but were immediately killed by the crowd. The others were burned together with the building. Twenty-three were killed among those in the crowd and eight or twelve burned in the soviet.[10]

A Menshevik journal noted that "sometimes these spontaneous movements acquired a certain religious character. In Klin the masses marched to the soviet in a semihysterical mood, singing, 'Christ is risen!' "[11] In Kostroma the mob cried, "Down with the commissars! It was better under the tsar!"[12] Rebellions of this kind were also reported in Orekhovo-Zuevo, Ivanovo-Voznesensk, Vologda, Cherepovets, Orel, and dozens of other towns.[13] Mensheviks were unable to play any organiza-

8. Sokolov, *Revoliutsiia i khleb*, p. 25.

9. G. D. Kuchin, "Za nedeliu," *Novaia zaria*, no. 2 (1 May 1918), p. 25; "Po tsentral'noi oblasti: V polose terrora," ibid., no. 1 (22 April 1918), p. 35; *Echos de Russie*, nos. 20–21 (1 September 1918), p. 22.

10. "Pogrom soveta v Pavlovskom Posade," *Delo naroda*, 15 May 1918, p. 2; "Besporiadki v Pavlovskom Posade," ibid., (17 May 1918), p. 4.

11. "Po tsentral'noi oblasti," *Novaia zaria*, no. 1 (22 April 1918), p. 35.

12. G. D. Kuchin, "Pod znakom goloda i narodnykh vosstanii," *Novaia zaria*, nos. 5–6 (10 June 1918), p. 37.

13. "Po tsentral'noi oblasti," ibid., no. 1 (22 April 1918), p. 35; "Golodnye bunty," *Novaia zhizn'*, 28 April 1918, p. 4; "Otchet kommissii TsK i Soveta Oborony tovarishchu

tional role in most of these struggles. They were swept aside by the tide of violence and sometimes they panicked in the face of the mob's hostility toward socialists in general. The members of the CC were just as shocked and perplexed by the course of events as were the local leaders. These outbursts of popular rage, reminiscent of October, were repugnant to the Mensheviks, even if some took consolation in the fact that they were now directed against the Bolsheviks. The Mensheviks had warned from the beginning that the Bolshevik methods would discredit socialism in the eyes of the masses and lead to the worst type of counterrevolution, but their prescience made it no easier to tolerate the upheavals, which simply did not fit into their notions of class struggle. The predominant mood in the party was one of alarm.

Rebellions of soldiers and sailors, the second category, were usually ignited by the Bolsheviks' failure to satisfy economic demands. In Tver, for example, at the end of May, soldiers had surrounded the local soviet, pointed machine guns at the soviet building, and demanded higher pay. The Bolsheviks yielded to the soldiers' demands.[14] A similar kind of disturbance had taken place in Yaroslavl, but this one erupted in an exchange of fire between the soldiers and the Red Guards.[15] In Syzran, 800 soldiers had rebelled against Soviet power on April 30.[16] In August, the First Proletarian Regiment refused to go to the front. Trotsky was shouted down when he attempted to plead with the soldiers.[17] In October, an abortive rebellion of the newly mobilized Baltic Fleet broke out in Petrograd. Judging by their slogans, the rebels were Left SRs, and they condemned "commissarocracy" and grain requisitioning.[18]

Perhaps the best-known rebellion of Red Army soldiers occurred in Saratov. To the Bolsheviks, this was another Menshevik-SR conspiracy; to the Mensheviks, it was a rebellion of anarchists.[19] The uprising had begun over the soldiers' refusal to obey orders to suppress anti-Bolshevik disturbances. Many soldiers had already been angered by the Bolshevik disbandment of the Union of War Veterans (Soiuz Frontovikov),

Leninu o prichinakh padeniia Permi v dekabre 1918 goda," in I. V. Stalin, Sochineniia, vol. 4, as quoted in Bernshtam, Ural i Prikam'e, p. 112.

14. "Armiia krasnykh naemnikov," Novaia zhizn', 24 May 1918, p. 1.

15. "Krasnoarmeiskie besporiadki v Iaroslavle," ibid., p. 3.

16. "Vystuplenie protiv sovetskoi vlasti," ibid., 3 May 1918, p. 3.

17. "Bunt pervogo proletarskogo polka," Bor'ba, 8 September 1918, p. 3.

18. I. Flerovskii, "Miatezh mobilizovannykh matrosov v Petrograde 14 oktiabria 1918 goda," Proletarskaia revoliutsiia, no. 8 (1926), pp. 218–38. (The author of this article had been commissar of the Baltic Fleet in 1918.) Some of those who took part in this rebellion were executed; A Collection of Reports on Bolshevism in Russia, p. 104 (cited hereafter as Bolshevism in Russia).

19. Nikolaevsky, "RSDRP (men'shevikov)," p. 35, discusses the Bolshevik allegations about this uprising. See also "Beschestnye i prezrennye," Partiinye izvestiia, 29 May 1918, pp. 8–10.

an SR-led organization. Litnov, an SR and the union's chairman, played an important role in the uprising. After shelling the Saratov soviet with artillery on the evening of May 17, a group of insurgents published an appeal to the citizenry, accusing the Bolsheviks of tampering with the elections, wasting huge sums of money without giving an account to the soviet, disbanding the Union of War veterans, and other misconduct. They defined their goals as follows:

> We want to destroy the predatory power of the Bolsheviks, which is based on violence and hated by all of you. We are not leading our struggle against them to seize power for ourselves. Instead of Bolshevik violence, we want to restore rights and freedom for all! Enough of violence and seizures! In a free country, political authority must derive from a direct, equal, and secret ballot! There can be no other authority.[20]

The SR party committee openly took the side of the insurgents and resumed publication of its newspaper, *Golos trudovogo naroda* (Voice of the Working People), which had earlier been banned by the Bolsheviks.[21] The Mensheviks published their own declaration, supporting the political aims of the insurgents but criticizing their use of violence. The Mensheviks offered to mediate a peaceful resolution of the conflict. Their caution might be explained partly by the fact that the insurgents had been joined by anarchists and other distasteful elements, and some cases of drunken looting were reported. It seems that neither the Menshevik nor the SR party committee knew about the uprising in advance. The local Bolsheviks appealed for help, and 600 Red Army soldiers arrived in Saratov. The Bolshevik newspaper said their tactic was to pretend to be the insurgents' friends; in that way, they "gained control of their weapons unnoticed, and then suggested that [the insurgents] surrender."[22] An armed struggle followed, with casualties said to be "very high"; at least 600 soldiers were arrested.[23]

In the first few days after the uprising, the wrath of the Saratov Bolsheviks was directed chiefly at the SRs. A member of the soviet said that the Mensheviks "could not decide themselves to take part in the events, though their sympathies were all on the side of the SRs."[24] However, another Bolshevik speaker objected: "How do you explain the fact that the counterrevolutionary insurgents . . . proclaimed purely

20. "Listovka krasnoarmeitsev i frontovikov," *Izv. Sar. sov.*, 20 May 1918, p. 2.
21. "Sobytiia 18 maia," ibid.
22. "Pomoshch' iz vne," ibid.
23. "Zasedanie Soveta," ibid., 26 May 1918, p. 1; "Soedinennoe zasedanie soveta," ibid., 2 June 1918, p. 1. See also "Likvidatsiia vosstaniia v Saratove," *Petrogradskoe ekho*, 29 May 1918, p. 1.
24. "Sovet Rabochikh Deputatov," *Izv. Sar. sov.*, 26 May 1918, p. 1.

Menshevik political slogans? . . . That proves the Mensheviks' participation."[25] The latter view eventually prevailed. The Bolsheviks passed a resolution urging the workers to recall the "social traitors" from the soviet within the week.[26] During the following days, the local Bolshevik newspaper referred to the Mensheviks and SRs as "bandits," "conspirators," and "traitors."[27] On June 12, fifteen members of the Menshevik party committee were put on trial. Peculiarly, no SRs were among the defendants. The explanation may be that on June 8 the SRs had seized power in neighboring Samara. The Saratov Bolsheviks may have feared that a trial of SRs in Saratov would trigger an attack from Samara. Whatever the reason, the Bolsheviks' wrath was now directed against the Mensheviks.

The Bolshevik prosecutors at the trial, still inexperienced at their task, had a hard time proving the guilt of the accused. The charge was counterrevolutionary agitation, as manifested in an appeal for the resignation of the CPC and the reconvocation of the Constituent Assembly. The commissar of the press, Venatovskii, testified that as he walked by the room where the Menshevik party committee was meeting, he had seen in the window a declaration of the Petrograd assembly of upolnomochennye which seemed to him to be counterrevolutionary. The defense attorney asked, "But what is the substance of the crime?" Venatovskii responded, "That the present power is referred to in the declaration as the power of the usurpers, which has done nothing for the people." The defense attorney suggested that in that case, it was the Petrograd proletariat that should be on trial; the Saratov Mensheviks could not be held responsible for a declaration made by the Petrograd proletariat.[28]

The prosecutor did not argue that the Mensheviks had participated in the uprising, apparently fearing that the charge would be difficult to prove. He focused instead on the Mensheviks' political position: "They point out the absence of freedom. . . . They want to ruin Bolshevism!" No longer, apparently, were the soviets conceived of as multiparty institutions. The prosecutor urged the workers and peasants "to drive out [of the soviet] those who sold them out to the bourgeoisie, just as Jesus Christ drove the money changers out of the temple."[29]

In the typical pattern of uprisings in the third category, those led by White officers, the local Mensheviks' initial enthusiasm at the Bolsheviks' overthrow quickly gave way to hostility toward the officers. The

25. "Nekotorye itogi," ibid.
26. "Sovet Rabochikh Deputatov," ibid.
27. See, for example, "Besposhchadnaia mest' predateliam," ibid., 9 June 1918, p. 1.
28. "V Revoliutsionnom Tribunale," ibid., 12 June 1918, p. 1.
29. "V Revoliutsionnom Tribunale," ibid., 13 June 1918, p. 3.

events in Tambov are a case in point. In mid-June the Mensheviks in Tambov found themselves in a frustrating situation. On the one hand, they had won, in alliance with the SRs, overwhelming majorities in the spring election to the soviet and to the provincial Congress of Trade Unions in June.[30] On the other hand, it was becoming obvious that they would be unable to translate this popular support into effective political power. On June 14 the Bolsheviks declared martial law in Tambov. On June 17 an uprising broke out in response to a decree on obligatory enlistment in the Red Army. The disbanded city duma convened, and some socialists began to celebrate their victory.[31] Real power in the city, however, belonged not to the duma but to the White general Bogdanov and his officers. The enthusiasm of many socialists subsided. Fear of the Whites and of a monarchist restoration turned some Menshevik workers against the officers.[32]

During the summer of 1918 popular uprisings broke out in Perm, Ufa, and Viatka provinces. To a certain extent they represented frustration over declining production, rising unemployment, and—still—grain requisitions. Since the social differences between workers and peasants in small industrial towns with large plants were often indistinct, workers' uprisings were often backed by the peasants of the surrounding villages, and peasants' uprisings were backed by workers. It would be misleading, though, to see only economic factors in this social upheaval. No less important is the fact that many such uprisings took place after a newly elected soviet was disbanded by the Bolsheviks and the workers saw no other way to oppose their self-proclaimed avantgarde.

The picture of upheaval that emerges from Bolshevik sources differs little from that delineated in Menshevik and SR sources. Local Bolsheviks in Perm province wrote of peasants storming soviets, killing grain-requisition officials, seizing arms, destroying railway lines, and ambushing Red detachments.[33] A high-ranking Bolshevik official in Ekaterinburg, R. I. Berzin, telegraphed to Commissar N. I. Podvoiskii on June 18,

30. "Razgon konferentsii professional'nykh soiuzov," *Iskra*, 29 June 1918, p. 3.
31. "Po Rossii: Tambovskii perevorot," *Novyi vechernii chas*, 29 June 1918, p. 4. See also an almost identical account in a Bolshevik source: "Podrobnosti Tambovskikh sobytii," *Izvestiia*, 20 June 1918, p. 3. It is noteworthy that no documents on this uprising were published in the official Soviet account of events in Tambov province during the Bolshevik Revolution (Partiinyi arkhiv obkoma KPSS i arkhivnyi otdel UVD Tambovskoi oblasti, *Bor'ba . . . za ustanovlenie i uprochenie sovetskoi vlasti v Tambovskoi gubernii*), except for Lenin's speech on the subject (p. 168).
32. "Po Rossii: Tambovskii perevorot," *Novyi vechernii chas*, 29 June 1918, p. 4.
33. "Beseda s voennym kommissarom tov. Postnikovym," *Golos kungurskogo sovdepa*, 25 July 1918, p. 4, reprinted in Bernshtam, *Ural i Prikam'e*, pp. 120–21. An SR source for the same events is *Novoe delo naroda*, 19 June 1918, p. 4, reprinted in ibid., p. 119.

"The workers are very hostile to the soviets."[34] Another Bolshevik participant in these events wrote, "We knew from our experience in Ufa that the majority of workers there did not support us."[35] When an uprising broke out in Nev'iansk, a small town not far from Ekaterinburg where an artillery plant employed 7,000 workers, "the insurgents' program was expressed by typically Menshevik-SR slogans: 'Down with the commissarocracy of the Bolsheviks! Long live the Constituent Assembly!'" The insurgents stormed the soviet, seized power, and formed a 5,000-man armed detachment. Peasants from nearby areas, organized by the SRs, supported the insurgents. After five days of fighting, the insurgents were defeated by a superior Bolshevik force.[36]

As a result of such experiences, many Mensheviks came to favor active struggle against the Bolsheviks. A Menshevik CC resolution of July 27, declared that "the task of the party is to organize the workers into an independent third force."[37] In the complex conditions of civil war, however, this was easier said than done. The Mensheviks' role in the Yaroslavl uprising reveals the difficulties.

After the disbandment of the newly elected Menshevik-led Yaroslavl soviet in April, the patience of many Menshevik workers was running out.[38] The activists in the party felt that the Bolshevik dictatorship could and should be resisted, with arms if necessary. When an uprising did break out, even though it was led by the former SR terrorist Boris Savinkov—who had played a major role in the Kornilov putsch and was allied with White officers[39]—I. T. Savinov, a Menshevik member of the Yaroslavl duma and soviet, joined it at the head of a large detachment of workers. B. V. Diushen had already established contact with Savinkov's underground forces. I. I. Shleifer, however, urged the workers to remain neutral in what he perceived to be a fight between the Reds and the Whites. The Menshevik CC agreed with Shleifer. It issued a resolution stating that the insurgents' leaders were only using the workers' protest movement for their own political ends:

> Whatever the outcome of this confrontation, it provides no guarantee to the proletariat or to democracy that the regime of the shameful Bolshevik

34. "Doklady po priamomu provodu . . . mezhdu R. I. Berezinym . . . i N. I. Podvoiskim," in G. Kh. Eikhe, Oprokinutyi tyl (Moscow: Voenizdat, 1966), pp. 46–47, reprinted in Bernshtam, Ural i Prikam'e, p. 91.

35. A. Kuchkin, "Pobitymi sobakami ostavliali my Izhevsk," Proletarskaia revoliutsiia, no. 6 (1929), pp. 156–61, reprinted in Bernshtam, Ural i Prikam'e, p. 323.

36. N. M. Matveev, "Nev'ianskoe vosstanie," in Za vlast' sovetov (Sverdlovsk, 1957), pp. 137–42, reprinted in Bernshtam, Ural i Prikam'e, p. 83.

37. "Rezoliutsiia TsK" (27 July 1918), Nik. Col. no. 6, box 1, file 2.

38. Boris Nikolaevsky, "Mikhail Markovich Ravich (1881–1962)," Sotsialisticheskii vestnik, nos. 5–6 (1962), pp. 86–88.

39. For more on Savinkov, see Golinkov, Krushenie antisovetskogo podpol'ia, p. 175.

dictatorship will not be replaced by a regime of counterrevolution, more or less concealed at first. Therefore . . . the CC once again points out that the party comrades must in no way take part in such uprisings or be used by groups organizing uprisings.[40]

Earlier uprisings of this kind had persuaded the Menshevik party leadership that if and when the Bolsheviks fell, the workers' organizations and the local socialists were not capable of holding power in their stead. Either the Mensheviks and their supporters would be overwhelmed by raging anti-Bolshevik mobs, with the consequent danger of bloodbaths and pogroms, or they would be pushed aside by conspiratorial organizations of White officers using popular protest movements to seize power, who would abolish all the political and economic changes brought about by the 1917 revolution. The resolution of July 27 explained the CC's view to local party organizations:

> The circumstances and progression of these events have confirmed that the correlation of social forces at present is such that the military, technical, and material means for the overthrow of Bolshevik power are concentrated primarily in the hands of either antidemocratic and even counterrevolutionary elements or of international imperialists. . . . Therefore, until these objective conditions change, Social-Democracy does not consider it possible at the present time to propose the organization of uprisings for the overthrow of Bolshevik power as an immediate task for the working class.[41]

Party members were forbidden to take part in anti-Bolshevik uprisings, and to demonstrate the CC's seriousness, Diushen and Savinov were expelled from the party.

Barely ten days after the adoption of this resolution, an anti-Bolshevik uprising broke out in Izhevsk. This time the workers were the main fighting force.[42] To the Right Mensheviks, they represented the third force for which the party resolution had called. To the center-Left Mensheviks, they posed a dilemma: to back the insurgent workers was to challenge the Bolshevik government; not to back them was to face a party split.

The Bolsheviks had been badly beaten in the elections to the Izhevsk

40. "Rezoliutsiia TsK RSDRP o Iaroslavskikh sobytiiakh" (16 July 1918), Nik. Col. no. 6, box 1, file 2 (published in *Rabochii internatsional*, 7 August 1918, p. 1). For more on the events in Yaroslavl, see Vasil'ev-Iuzhin, "Uchastie Men'shevikov v iaroslavskom vosstanii," *Pravda*, 26 July 1918, p. 1, and "Rasstrel aktivnykh uchastnikov iaroslavskogo miatezha," *Izvestiia*, 26 July 1918, p. 3. A collection of documents is Polgunov and Rozanova, *Shestnadtsat' dnei*.

41. Nik. Col. no. 6, box 1, file 1; also in English, as "The So-Called Dictatorship of the Proletariat," in *Case of Russian Labor*, p. 14.

42. Berk, " 'Class Tragedy.' "

soviet in June.[43] From the Bolshevik point of view, the loss of their local administration was intolerable. There was a large armament plant in Izhevsk, and with the Tula plant closed by a general strike, it was the only one then producing weapons. Determined to retain power, the Bolsheviks disbanded the newly elected soviet and intensified their repressions against the Mensheviks and SRs.[44] The Bolsheviks realized that most workers were supporting their opponents.[45] Furthermore, they were particularly concerned that the Union of War Veterans would play an active role against them.

When a call for voluntary enlistments in the Red Army failed to get more than a handful of recruits, a compulsory draft was ordered on August 5, and that announcement set in motion the chain of events that led to the uprising. On August 7 the Union of War Veterans organized a protest rally.[46] They refused to comply with the conscription order unless the men conscripted were armed on the spot. The Bolsheviks rejected this demand and arrested some of the union's leaders. The veterans, many of whom worked at the plant, seized some of the weapons they had just manufactured and demanded that their comrades be released immediately. On August 8 the Bolsheviks abandoned the city.[47] The prisoners were freed. The disbanded soviet was reconvened and proclaimed its loyalty to the Constituent Assembly and to the Committee of the Constituent Assembly—that is, the SR-led Komuch government in Samara. The 20,000 Izhevsk workers became a part of the Komuch People's Army.[48] The Menshevik party committee of the Urals region voted its support for the Izhevsk workers. Now a confrontation with the Menshevik CC was imminent.

The Rift between Right and Center-Left Mensheviks

Liber and other Right Mensheviks were angered by the CC resolution forbidding Menshevik participation in anti-Bolshevik uprisings. The

43. "Doklad delegata Piatogo vserossiiskogo s"ezda sovetov S. I. Kholmogorova Narodnomu kommissariatu vnutrennikh del o politicheskom polozhenii na izhevskom zavode," in Udmurdiia v period inostrannoi interventsii i grazhdanskoi voiny: Sbornik dokumentov (Izhevsk, 1960), pt. 1, pp. 66–69; reprinted in Bernshtam, ed., Ural i Prikam'e, p. 280.
44. D. I. Fedichkin, "Izhevskoe vosstanie v period s 8 avgusta po 20 oktiabria 1918 goda," in Bernshtam, ed., Ural i Prikam'e, p. 337.
45. "Doklad delegata," in ibid., p. 282; Kuchkin, "Pobitymi sobakami," in ibid., pp. 323, 325.
46. N. Sapozhnikov, "Izhevsko-Votkinskoe vosstanie," Proletarskaia revoliutsiia, nos. 8–9 (1924), pp. 5–11, reprinted in Bernshtam, ed., Ural i Prikam'e, p. 366.
47. D. Tomashkin, "Nachalo i pervyi den' Izhevskogo vosstaniia," in Bernshtam, ed., Ural i Prikam'e, pp. 370–71.
48. For the appraisal of sources on the numbers in the Izhevsk workers' army as well as in other insurgent armies in this area, see Bernshtam ed., Ural i Prikam'e, pp. 368–69.

CC had no right, they argued, to issue such a prohibition without a vote by the entire party. Furthermore, the resolution had dealt only with uprisings led by counterrevolutionary elements. The uprisings on the Volga and in the Urals were led by the SRs, the Mensheviks' allies. What was the Menshevik position to be in such cases? The resolution had been a forced combination of right and center-left views. On the one hand, it recognized that the Bolshevik dictatorship was arousing popular hatred and that there was evidence that the population was giving direct help to the advancing Czech-SR troops; on the other hand, it refrained from support of anti-Bolshevik uprisings because they would split the working class and give monarchist elements an opportunity to seize power. Nevertheless, it still called for the "elimination of the Bolshevik regime, in alliance with the forces of democracy." At one CC meeting, I. M. Maiskii, a Right Menshevik, called on the party to clarify its position: would it stand by its commitment to reconvocation of the Constituent Assembly, and if so, would it support the Committee of the Constituent Assembly (Komuch) in Samara? He urged the CC not only to do so but also to send a delegation to encourage the anti-Bolshevik struggle there.

Dan vehemently objected, brushing aside the SRs' action as a mere "adventure." From the Right Mensheviks' point of view, the CC's procrastination violated the decisions of the May party conference, as well as other party pronouncements in defense of the Constituent Assembly. As Maiskii recalled it, he had addressed Dan in the following way:

> Explain to me, please, why you're so quick to criticize and make fun of any attempts to revive the Constituent Assembly. Our party's platform is that of the Constituent Assembly. It's leading a tireless campaign in favor of the Constituent Assembly. It's trying to prove that there is no way out of the country's current situation except through the Constituent Assembly. It's calling on the workers to strike for the sake of the reconvocation of the Constituent Assembly. In a word, the party seems to be showing a maximum of interest and activity in struggle for the Constituent Assembly. And then? When people come along who try to put the reconvocation of the Constituent Assembly on a practical footing, you can find nothing better to do than shrug your shoulders in contempt and superciliously toss off: "Absurd *avantiura*." Where is your logic?[49]

In October, Maiskii wrote an open letter to the CC, arguing that to remain neutral during a civil war was "contrary to human nature and logic."[50]

Some Right Mensheviks, echoing the SRs, charged that the fear of

49. Maiskii, *Demokraticheskaia kontrrevoliutsiia*, p. 12.
50. Ibid., p. 14.

counterrevolution had paralyzed the CC's will to act. G. Erlikh, also a member of the CC, had written to Aksel'rod that "by its policies and its destruction of the democratic conquests of the revolution, Bolshevism has been preparing the ground for the victory of the counterrevolution. No—rather, in the guise of Lenin's government, we already have a most genuine counterrevolution."[51] All the achievements of the February 1917 revolution had already been lost: freedom of the press, assembly, speech, elections. In the name of socialism, ruthless Cheka gangs were running the country. The Brest sellout, the class war against the bourgeoisie and the peasantry, the disbandment of the dumas and soviets, and now even the shooting of workers—"What regime could be worse?" asked one Right Menshevik.[52] The arguments of Martov and Dan, said another, stemmed from an undispelled illusion about the nature of Bolshevism: they were still reluctant to admit that Bolshevism was no longer a part of Russian democracy.[53]

The fact that the material position of the working class was even worse in the summer than it had been in the spring was obvious, wrote the Right Mensheviks, but a still more serious problem was that the Bolsheviks were mercilessly suppressing any opposition activity. As a result, "the workers are many times more helpless and powerless . . . than in the era of capitalism."[54] The Bolshevik regime had not freed the working class but enslaved it. "Having proclaimed the dictatorship of the proletariat and the poorest peasantry, the Bolshevik regime has in fact turned into a dictatorship over the proletariat."[55] According to the Right Menshevik critics, the Bolshevik regime no longer reflected the interests of any social class in Russia. It was a new kind of regime, one that forced its will by armed Cheka detachments and an ever-growing civilian bureaucracy. One critic wrote, with remarkable foresight:

> The Bolshevik regime expresses and defends the interests of the new bureaucracy that was brought to life by this regime itself to take the place of the old self-perpetuating tsarist officialdom. But perhaps the worst is . . . the demoralization of the spirit. Communism has killed the idea of democracy for a long time. It has undermined belief in socialism for decades to come, making the very word socialism odious for several generations. By elevating class hatred and mob rule to a principle, by its system of feeding hundreds of thousands at state expense, it has sown so much

51. G. Erlikh to P. Aksel'rod, 14 June 1918, Nik. Col. no. 16, box 5.

52. V. M., "Politicheskoe obozrenie," *Delo*, no. 14 (1 August 1918), pp. 12–14.

53. M. Amginskii, "Vserossiiskoe soveshchanie Rossiiskoi Sotsial Demokratii," *Delo*, no. 9 (3 June 1918), p. 10.

54. V. Mirov, "Politicheskoe obozrenie," *Delo*, no. 10 (12 June 1918), pp. 13–14.

55. B. I. Gorev, "Sotsializm ili bonapartizm," *Novaia zaria*, nos. 5–6 (10 June 1918), pp. 14–20.

poison in people's souls that the possibility of normal labor is killed for many years in Russia.[56]

Clearly the perceptions of the Right Mensheviks had undergone significant changes since October 1917. They no longer spoke of Bolshevism as an anarchic rebellion by hungry soldiers or a peasant *pugachev-shchina*; now they saw it as a monopolistic, bureaucratic regime, a brutal dictatorship of irresponsible cliques that reduced the population to parasitic dependence on state support and enslaved the working class.

The Right Mensheviks regarded the wave of anti-Bolshevik uprisings as indisputable evidence that all social groups and classes of the population were rising against the Bolshevik dictatorship.[57] Expropriations and confiscations had angered the bourgeoisie, grain requisitioning had sown the seeds of peasant rebellion, and suppression of workers' organizations had provoked strikes. According to the Right Mensheviks and the SRs, the duty of any honest socialist was to take part in the genuinely popular anti-Bolshevik movement.[58] The Right Menshevik editor V. O. Levitskii hailed this movement, insisting that "it is not a White Guards' conspiracy, but a constantly growing people's uprising . . . a many-headed hydra that not all the commissars put together can cope with, despite all the military and technical means at their disposal." Without naming the Menshevik CC, Levitskii attacked its policy: "such supposed 'Marxists' see elements of counterrevolution and adventurism in the very turning to armed struggle against the soviet power."[59] Describing the situation to a friend and colleague abroad, Martov wrote that the party would probably have split formally had a party congress taken place in the summer of 1918. "The Bolshevik terror put such pressure on all of us that any public debate in the party became impossible."[60]

A conference of the party organizations of the Central Industrial Region was held at the end of July. This region had been an area of impressive Menshevik electoral victories in the spring elections (see chapter 5). The party leaders there, though angered by the Bolshevik repressions, were probably reluctant to abandon the possibility of legal existence in Soviet Russia. Instead, they were likely to support Martov's position and distance themselves from the anti-Bolshevik uprisings and the foreign intervention forces. The proceedings of this con-

---

56. V. M., "Politicheskoe obozrenie," *Delo*, no. 14 (1 August 1918), p. 13.
57. V. O. Levitskii, "Zagovor ili vosstanie," ibid., p. 1.
58. A. Korneev, "Sila shtyka," ibid., pp. 14–15.
59. Levitskii, "Zagovor ili vosstanie," ibid., p. 1.
60. L. Martov to A. Stein, 25 October 1918, Nik. Col. no. 17, box 1, file 3.

ference are not available, and no opposition press was left to cover it, so we know what happened at it only from the correspondence and memoirs of the participants. The Bolshevik press tried to minimize the differences between the two main factions, led by Martov and Liber.[61] In fact, however, the differences of opinion so carefully camouflaged at the May 1918 party conference had become irreconcilable. Martov managed to secure majority support, and the CC resolutions reflected his positions: neutrality in the struggle between the Moscow and Samara governments; no cooperation with the bourgeois parties; and vigorous opposition to the Allied intervention.[62] This last point acquired particular significance when, in the first days of August, British and American troops landed in Arkhangelsk. The CC resolution declared:

> Despite the horrors of the Bolshevik regime now reigning in Russia, which is founded on the suppression of all freedoms and on irresponsible tyranny; despite all the mass arrests and all kinds of repressions and executions perpetrated daily by a bunch of Bolshevik usurpers against Russia's socialist working class, it rejects any interference of the capitalist governments for its liberation from the bloody Bolshevik dictatorship and relies only on its own forces, the forces of the democratic masses, and on the help of the international proletariat for the liquidation of this regime.[63]

Martov feared that the Allies were only momentarily interested in supporting the socialists and that they would switch to supporting the conservative forces as soon as the opportunity presented itself.

The Right Mensheviks, unable to accept these policy statements, now formed a group that called itself the Committee for an Active Struggle for the Regeneration of Russia.[64] In their initial declaration, the Activists, as they came to be known, explained their decision: "No considerations of party discipline and of the authority of the central party institutions can keep us . . . from trying by ourselves to fulfill the task that is incumbent on Social Democracy and that the leading official party circles refuse to fulfill."[65] On specific issues, the Activists' declaration defended cooperation with the Allies and with all "economically progressive forces" for the overthrow of the Bolshevik regime, and it reiterated the call for the formation of a national anti-Bolshevik front.[66] No

---

61. "Stydlivye i besstyzhie," *Izvestiia*, 30 August 1918, p. 1.

62. Nikolaevsky, "RSDRP (men'shevikov)" (Nik. Col.), p. 24.

63. "Protiv inostrannogo vmeshatel'stva," Nik. Col. no. 6, box 1, file 2. The resolution was published in *Rabochii internatsional*, no. 10 (7 August 1918), despite the ban on the journal. For important material on the rule of the White forces in Arkhangelsk, see *Materialy k istorii grazhdanskoi voiny v Rossii*, Nik. Col. no. 95, box 1, file 13.

64. Martov to Stein, 25 October 1918, Nik. Col. no. 17, box 1, file 3.

65. Nikolaevsky, "RSDRP (men'shevikov)," p. 29. See also "Zhalkie uvertki," *Izvestiia*, 10 September 1918, p. 1.

66. Nikolaevsky, "RSDRP (men'shevikov)," p. 29.

list of names of the committee's members has ever been published, but from various sources it is clear that Liber, Kolokol'nikov, Kipen, and Levitskii were among them.[67]

It is important to note that the Activists did not actually secede from the Menshevik party. The committee, was intended to be a faction within the party, with the goal of marshaling support in as many local Menshevik organizations as possible against the "neutral" policy of the CC. The Right Menshevik leaders stressed their intention to act as an "all-Russian organizational center" for all democratic organizations that favored "active domestic and foreign policies."[68] They were openly challenging the right of the CC to speak for the party.

This action was very much in the Menshevik tradition. In fact, it resembled Martov's own tactics in 1917. At that time the International-ists—the Left Mensheviks—had been a minority in the party. They, too, had openly defied the CC, then dominated by the center-Right, and had publicly criticized its policy, set up independent newspapers, and built up grass-roots support that eventually brought them into the party leadership at the December 1917 party congress. Now the Right Men-sheviks were attempting to follow the same course.

The Beginning of the Red Terror

The summer of 1918 was a period of significant military victories for the Czech-SR forces. One city after another along the Volga and in the Urals was taken by the People's Army, aided by anti-Bolshevik upris-ings in the cities and peasant rebellions in the countryside. The history of the fighting and of the Komuch government is a separate topic that cannot be treated here.[69] Suffice it to say that the Komuch government's offensive, in conjunction with the Allied landing, presented a serious threat to the survival of the Bolshevik regime. As one historian has said, "even the most optimistic Bolsheviks saw the end of their regime in sight."[70] Lenin's communications with his lieutenants, dispatches of Red Army commanders to Moscow, and diplomatic reports testify that the Bolsheviks recognized the possibility of defeat.[71] In a dispatch to

67. See, for example, David Dallin, "The Outbreak of the Civil War" in Haimson, ed., *Mensheviks*, p. 181.

68. "Men'sheviki o deklaratsii aktivistov," *Utro Moskvy*, 30 September 1918, p. 2.

69. A summary of the events is in Stewart, *White Armies*, pp. 111–26. For SR sources on the preparation of the uprising in the Volga area, see I. D. Klimushkin, "Pered vol-zhskim vystupleniem," *Volia Rossii* (Prague), nos. 8–9 (1928), and I. Brushvit, "Kak podgotovlialos' volzhskoe vystuplenie," ibid., no. 10. Klimushkin and Brushvit were among the Komuch leaders.

70. Ullman, *Anglo-Soviet Relations*, p. 286.

71. See, for example, Lenin to Zinoviev, Lashevich, and Stasova, 20 July 1918, in *Iz*

Berlin on June 21, the German ambassador, Count Mirbach, said: "The position of the Moscow government has no doubt become insecure of late. . . . We have received news from reliable sources that a great many influential members of the government have already, as a precaution, secured for themselves foreign passports with visas from foreign consulates." He also expressed concern that the success of the Czech-SR forces would "bring a group friendly to the Entente, that is to say, the Socialist Revolutionaries and the Mensheviks, to the helm." Two weeks later the ambassador reported a conversation with a highly placed "friend of Germany" who had told him that a Red Army commander's report to Moscow had described the situation at the Czech front as "unfavorable."[72]

Count Mirbach's successor, Karl Helfferich, later recalled that he had reported to his government early in August that "the Bolsheviks' power was so weak that one could not help reckoning with the possibility of a change, and soon." The defection in July of a Red Army commander, Muraviev, to the Komuch side created panic in Moscow, and "the Bolsheviks were saying openly that their last days were coming."[73] The territory under Komuch control expanded during July and early August until it abutted on that controlled by the Siberian regional anti-Bolshevik government. With the defeat of the Bolshevik forces near Kazan on August 7, many high-ranking Bolsheviks believed Nizhnii Novgorod would fall next, opening the way to Moscow.[74]

With every passing week, the Bolsheviks' repressions against their opponents intensified. The upolnomochennye movement had already been crushed; the Mensheviks and SRs had been ejected from the trade unions and factory committees; and in July the final onslaught against the opposition press had taken place.[75] By the end of August, it seemed almost inconceivable that the Mensheviks and SRs had been campaigning in the elections to the Petrograd soviet only two months before.

---

istorii grazhdanskoi voiny, document no. 330, p. 343; I. I. Vatsetis, "Grazhdanskaia voina: 1918 god," *Pamiat': Istoricheskii sbornik,* col. no. 2 (Moscow, 1977; Paris, 1979), p. 27.

72. Bothmer, *Mit Graf Mirbach,* pp. 62, 69.

73. Karl Helfferich, "Moia Moskovskaia missiia," Nik. Col. no. 128, box 1, file 9, p. 17. Helfferich's description of specific facts and situations in this (unpublished) article is identical with another source on Helfferich's mission in Moscow, which quotes him extensively: Joost, *Botschafter,* pp. 66–99. For the Bolsheviks' own description of how Muraviev's action might have ended, see "Chto gotovil Murav'ev," *Izvestiia,* 13 July 1918, p. 2.

74. For the SRs' description of the battle for Kazan, see V. Arkhangel'skii, "Kazan' vo vremia bor'by s bol'shevizmom, 7 avgusta–9 sentiabria 1918 goda," *Volia Rossii,* nos. 8–9 (1928), pp. 267–85.

75. For a discussion of the Bolshevik measures against the opposition press in June and July 1918, see Dumas, *La Vérité sur les Bolcheviki,* pp. 78–79.

After the closing of its newspaper *Vpered* (Forward) in May, the Menshevik CC was still able to launch a new one, *Nash golos* (Our Voice), although without identifying it as its publication. *Nash golos* lasted only a few weeks before it was closed. Its successor, *Iskra* (Spark), which appeared at the end of June, did not survive more than a few days. When the Menshevik faction in the Moscow soviet applied to the Commissariat of the Press for a permit to publish a new newspaper, *Zaria* (Dawn), they received this reply: "No permits will be issued to pogrom instigators and counterrevolutionaries."[76] In Petrograd, the Commissariat for the Press was ordered in early July to refuse registration to newspapers "whose titles contained the words 'Workers' or 'Social Democratic.' . . . The employees of the commissariat explain this [order] by the fact that such titles suggest that what's involved is Menshevik newspapers, and the publication of the newspapers of this party will under no circumstances be allowed."[77] Early in July, the Printers' Union newspaper reported that "military censorship" had been imposed on periodical publications in Petrograd.[78]

Immediately after the Left SR uprising on July 6, all non-Bolshevik papers in Moscow were shut down. Several days later, some papers resumed publication; no one expected that the ban would be final, since so many times in the past publication permits had once again been issued once a crisis was over. This time, however, the Cheka raided printing shops and editorial offices and, on July 15, confiscated previously issued publication permits.[79] Only the Printers' Union newspaper and a couple of other nonparty publications survived. Numerous printing presses were confiscated, premises sealed, and editors arrested and declared enemies of the people.[80]

On August 14, 1918, a detachment of Red Guards arrived at the offices of the Menshevik CC. The secretary protested, but in vain: the premises were searched and everything was confiscated—piles of newspapers, party documents, even furniture. The CC's sign was smashed and a Red Guard sentry was placed at the entrance.[81] Several CC members had by then been arrested and jailed. Martov and Dan went into hiding. Without declaring the Menshevik party outlawed, the Cheka had made its existence impossible by mid-August 1918.

At about the same time there appeared what must be one of the first

---

76. "Protiv pechati," *Novyi vechernii chas*, 27 June 1918, p. 2.

77. "Polozhenie pechati," *Utro Petrograda*, 8 July 1918.

78. "Voennaia tsenzura," *Novyi vechernii chas*, 5 July 1918, p. 2.

79. "Moskva bez gazet," *Era*, 18 July 1918.

80. Krasnikova, *Na zare sovetskoi vlasti*, p. 199; "Delo gazety Vpered v Revoliutsionnom tribunale," *Novaia Petrogradskaia gazeta* (nonparty newspaper), 10 August 1918, p. 3.

81. "V Rossii: Iz zhizni RSDRP," *Bor'ba*, 22 September 1918, p. 3.

references to concentration camps (*kontsentratsionnye lageria*), in an announcement by the military commander for Petrograd that orders had been given "for the creation of concentration camps in Murom, Arzamas, and Sviiazhsk, where suspicious agitators, counterrevolutionary officers, saboteurs, parasites, and speculators will be placed, except those who will be shot on the spot."[82] After the fall of Kazan, Lenin sent a telegram to the chairman of the Nizhnii Novgorod provincial soviet: "It is necessary to act without restraint: mass searches, executions for keeping firearms, *mass deportations of Mensheviks* and unreliables."[83] When the SR leader Vladimir Zenzinov arrived in Kazan early in August, his party comrades told him that the Bolsheviks were executing several dozen people every night. The SR organization went underground, and Zenzinov himself escaped arrest only by pure chance.[84]

The military threat posed to the Bolsheviks by the Komuch forces intensified but did not create the Bolshevik repressions. The Bolsheviks were no longer exacting retribution for specific actions but launching systematic terror against entire social groups that they considered likely to join or assist the anti-Bolshevik forces. This kind of prophylactic terror against politically "unreliable" groups reached its apogee in September and October 1918.

The Erosion of Central Party Authority

The successes of the Komuch forces put the issue of relations with the SRs at the top of the Menshevik agenda. It is difficult to judge how strongly the Right Menshevik stand was affecting local Menshevik organizations in August 1918. It is certain, however, that the Volga and Urals organizations were in virtual rebellion against the CC. The Mensheviks in those areas had long and firmly established ties with the SRs. To deny support to their long-time ally in a crucial moment was morally and politically impossible. The CC resolution against participation in anti-Bolshevik uprisings still envisioned the possibility of crushing the Bolshevik regime by "the forces of democracy." The Menshevik organizations in the Volga-Urals area interpreted this as giving them the right to support the SRs, an interpretation they believed was justified by a vague reference in a CC resolution of August 2 to "suggestions

---

82. "Prikaz Narkoma po voennym delam," *Izvestiia Petrogradskogo gorodskogo obshchestvennogo samoupravleniia*, 17 August 1918, p. 1.

83. Lenin, *Polnoe sobranie*, 50:142 (emphasis added).

84. Vladimir Zenzinov, *Iz zhizni revoliutsionera*, p. 105.

that individual members of local organizations receive freedom of action in cases of local uprisings for the overthrow of Soviet power or in connection with the advance of the Allied or Czech troops."[85] The CC was faced with a choice: it could either condone the action of Volga-Urals Mensheviks in joining hands with the SRs or take one more step toward a complete and final break with the SRs and the Right Mensheviks. The resolution of August 2 forbade party members to take part not only in uprisings led by the "counterrevolutionary" officers' organizations but also in those that broke out on the approach of the Czech-SR troops. This decision generated a storm of protest from the Right Mensheviks. Despite the prohibitions, individual Mensheviks and whole provincial organizations joined the SR forces in an attempt to overthrow the Bolshevik regime by force. The Menshevik CC was powerless to stop them.[86]

In late July, the Right Menshevik Maiskii acted on the convictions he had expressed previously within the CC. He crossed the front line, went to Samara, and accepted the post of minister of labor in the Komuch government—an act of great political significance. The Komuch government thus became a "coalition" government, its orders signed by a member of the Menshevik CC.[87] A controversy erupted over whether Maiskii's actions were in accord with Menshevik party resolutions. Martov later declared that Maiskii not only had taken the position without the knowledge or approval of the CC but had actually obtained a travel permit by saying that his work for the cooperatives required a trip to Perm; his going to Samara instead was therefore illegal.[88] The Menshevik CC promptly disavowed him and expelled him from the CC (but not yet from the party).[89] The Menshevik CC was obviously distancing itself from the SRs and their government in Samara as well as from Maiskii.

Soviet historians and emigre Right Mensheviks—though for different reasons, of course—have gathered evidence to show that Maiskii's actions were both legal and fully in accord with Menshevik party resolu-

85. "Rezoliutsiia TsK," (2 August 1918), *Rabochii internatsional*, no. 10 (7 August 1918), p. 4.
86. The CC did reprimand the Volga-Urals party organizations at the December 1918 party conference; see *Partiinoe soveshchanie RSDRP 27 dekabria 1918–1ianvaria 1919* (rezoliutsii), Nik. Col. no. 6, box 3, file 32, pp. 26–27.
87. Footman, *Civil War in Russia*, esp. pp. 101–4.
88. Martov, "Vospominaniia renegata," *Sotsialisticheskii vestnik* (Berlin), nos. 23–24 (9 December 1922), pp. 15–16. This article was Martov's response to Maiskii's memoirs, published in Soviet Russia after Maiskii's conversion to Bolshevism. Concerning this conversion, see Martov, "Po povodu odnogo prevrashcheniia," *Sotsialisticheskii vestnik*, no. 11 (8 July 1921), p. 8.
89. The Menshevik resolution concerning Maiskii was printed in *Utro Moskvy*, 9 September 1918.

tions.[90] They point out that the resolutions of the May 1918 Menshevik party conference clearly stated that in the territories of Russia cut off from the center by the front lines, the supreme authority in the party passed from the CC to the congress of local organizations in the region. Such a congress of the Menshevik organizations of eleven provinces in the territory of the Constituent Assembly had been convened, and it had passed a resolution stating that

> in these conditions the duty and obligation of Social Democracy is to render support to the Committee of Members of the Constituent Assembly [Komuch] for the realization of the great . . . state tasks confronting it—the Regional Committee of the RSDWP of the territory of the All-Russian Constituent Assembly has resolved to sanction Comrade Maiskii's acceptance of Komuch's offer of the post of director of the Department of Labor.[91]

Maiskii was also backed in a resolution adopted by nearly one hundred delegates from Menshevik organizations in the Komuch territory meeting in a party conference at the end of September.[92] Thus, for many Mensheviks, Maiskii remained a CC member, and they protested his expulsion.[93] Moreover, on all major issues, the Volga-Urals conference resolutions rejected the policies of the CC. The delegates welcomed the "military accord of the Komuch government with the Allies" and were in favor of continuing armed struggle against the Bolsheviks.[94] The conferences of the Volga-Urals organizations were legitimate party gatherings representing thousands of party members in a dozen provinces. Indeed, their decisions posed a more serious problem for the CC than the formation of the Activists' committee.

The conflict between the CC and the Volga-Urals regional committee was intensified over the state conference in Ufa in September. In the territories where the Bolsheviks had been overthrown, a number of regional governments emerged, ranging in political composition from monarchist and pro-German to socialist and pro-Allied. The Ufa conference was an attempt by these regional governments to come to terms with each other and to form a national Russian government that could

90. Aronson, *K istorii pravogo techeniia*, p. 62; Mints, *Men'sheviki v interventsii*, p. 85.

91. Mints, *Men'sheviki v interventsii*, p. 87, reprinting the full text of the resolution as it appeared in *Rabochaia zhizn'* (a Menshevik paper published in Tyumen), 16 September 1918. Though Soviet publications about the Mensheviks in 1930–31 may be unreliable, this document does seem authentic.

92. Mints, *Men'sheviki v interventsii*, p. 91.

93. Martov acknowledged this in his "Otvet kritikam," *Sotsialisticheskii vestnik* (Berlin), no. 2 (17 January 1923), pp. 10–13.

94. Mints, *Men'sheviki v interventsii*, p. 91.

coordinate efforts to drive the Bolsheviks out of the remaining central provinces. The composition of the new government, known as the Directory, and its political program were unacceptable to the Menshevik leadership. In a letter to local organizations, the CC explained that on such matters as the agrarian question, labor relations, and the eight-hour day, the newly created government, which ostensibly recognized the legitimacy of the Constituent Assembly, failed to conform to the laws that had been passed by the assembly at its first and only session on January 5. Even the reference to a republic had been dropped and the word "state" used instead. The CC also criticized the Volga-Urals committee for speaking on behalf of the entire party at the Ufa conference. A regional organization had no such right, especially on such issues as the composition and program of an all-Russian government. The CC admitted that it was powerless to do anything about the "conduct of the Volga-Urals comrades," but said that it must nevertheless "decisively protest against the use of the name of our party as a whole to sanction the act at Ufa."[95]

This confrontation reveals the depth of the discord within the Menshevik party. The divisions had gone beyond mere differences of opinion and even beyond the formation of a factional group; now two legitimate representatives, the CC and the Volga-Urals committee, were speaking on behalf of the party, and they publicly defended irreconcilable policies. On the basis of the Mensheviks' record in the Volga-Urals region and Siberia, a Soviet historian has argued that more than half of the provincial Menshevik organizations favored armed struggle against Bolshevism and backed anti-Soviet governments.[96]

Such an interpretation, however, oversimplifies or even distorts Menshevik attitudes and policies. Despite proclamations of support for the Komuch government, which indeed were plentiful, the relations of the Menshevik party organizations with the Komuch authorities were not particularly smooth. Both Right Menshevik authors and Soviet historians tend to glide over the difficulties and present a picture of a united front of Mensheviks and SRs against the Bolsheviks. In fact, the local Mensheviks for the most part were less interested than the SRs in fighting the Bolsheviks or in taking power. What they seem to have

95. "Ko vsem partiinym organizatsiiam: Taktika SD na vostoke" (16 October 1918), Nik. Col. no. 6, box 1, file 4, document 1. The Ufa resolution was also opposed by Chernov and his supporters in the SR party. See, for example, a document that came to be known as the "Chernov Manifesto," Nik. Col. no. 7, box 3 (printed in *Narodnoe delo*, 24 October 1918). For documents concerning the Ufa conference and Komuch's negotiations with the Siberian government, see S. A. Piontkovskii, ed., "Ufimskoe soveshchanie i Sibirskoe pravitel'stvo," *Krasnyi arkhiv* (Moscow, 1933), 6:58–81. For the SR account, see Vishniak, *Vserossiiskoe uchreditel'noe sobranie*, pp. 170–88.

96. Mints, *Men'sheviki v interventsii*, p. 78.

been most concerned with, in the areas where the Bolsheviks had been ousted, was the reestablishment of strong, independent workers' organizations. Such organizations, the soviets and the trade unions, invariably led by Mensheviks, frequently clashed with entrepreneurs and even with the Komuch authorities.[97] Despite general public backing for the Committee of the Constituent Assembly, the Menshevik-led workers' organizations did not balk at criticizing the Komuch government's policies or even at protesting against the arrests of some suspected Bolsheviks.[98] Most of the workers' organizations in Komuch territory expressed pacifist attitudes and objected especially to the escalation of the "civil war within the ranks of the proletariat."[99] Their statements echoed Martov's and were sometimes in defiance of the Komuch authorities.

As in the case of anti-Bolshevik uprisings in Tambov, Yaroslavl, and elsewhere, officers' organizations often surfaced and began to act on their own in cities taken by the Komuch forces. They claimed to recognize the legitimacy of the Constituent Assembly, but they also displayed undisguised contempt for the Komuch's red flag, the soviets, and anything that smacked of the overthrown regime. The supposedly victorious SRs were for the most part powerless to prevent mob rule in the streets and summary executions of suspected Bolsheviks by White bands. A Menshevik newspaper published details of what had happened in Kazan on the day after the Bolsheviks' overthrow there:

What was striking . . . was the abundance of armed men in uniforms with white bands on their arms. Their separate detachments were seizing people on the streets and in their apartments on the basis of some lists and "tips" and were finishing them off in front of the mob with a shot or two. A mere shout from the crowd—"That's a commissar!" "That's a Bolshevik!"—was enough to seal the fate of the one pointed at.[100]

The Kazan Mensheviks themselves were in an awkward situation. On the one hand, they supported Komuch, but on the other, they were repelled by the acts of terror for which the Komuch government had to bear responsibility. When their representatives, together with those of other groups, went to the military commandant of the city to register a

97. Relatively little is known about the Menshevik organizations' activity in the Komuch territory, but some relevant documents have been printed in Lelevich, *V dni Samarskoi uchredilki.*

98. One resolution, for example, protested "energetically" against "the nonstop arrests of members of the workers' assembly without even informing the executive committee about them" (ibid., p. 24 [first published in *Samarskie vedomosti,* 5 July 1918]).

99. Dallin, "Outbreak," in *Mensheviks,* p. 172.

100. "Pravda o Kazani," *Golos rabochego,* 10 September 1918, reprinted in Lelevich, *V dni samarskoi uchredilki,* p. 19.

protest, they were met with the response "Now you're sticking up for the Bolsheviks, but where were you when they were seizing and executing the officers?" The representatives said they had "protested then as well, just as we do now," but the commandant simply insisted that "to stop what was going on in the streets was not in his . . . power and was beyond his authority."[101]

The division within the Menshevik party was therefore not clear-cut. The Volga-Urals organizations supported armed struggle against the Bolsheviks—the Right Mensheviks' position; but they had reservations about it because of the Whites' participation, and this was the center-left position. A given organization at different times may have followed the Right Mensheviks' policy of uncompromising anti-Bolshevism and the center-left's pacifist, neutralist position. Thus there was a division not only between the CC and the local organizations, and not only within the CC itself, but also within local organizations, both in the "right" Volga-Urals area and in the "center-left" central provinces. The front line of the civil war ran through the Menshevik party organizations and through the minds of many Mensheviks. CC members, provincial organizations, individual party members acted as they saw fit. For all practical purposes, the Martov-led CC had lost control over the party by the end of August. Harassed by the Cheka and separated from the provincial organizations by the civil war, the CC did not even know for weeks on end about political developments in various regions. The party ceased to exist as a whole; each regional organization pursued its own policy. The Volga-Urals organization supported the Komuch government, whereas the CC did not; the Arkhangelsk organization welcomed the landing of the Allied troops, whereas the CC objected to it. Only in the central region were the provincial organizations, or at least the majority of them, in accord with the CC.

The chaos in the Menshevik party, however, should be seen as part of the general chaos in the country as a whole. In August, the north was controlled by Anglo-American forces; the western provinces, the Baltic area, Belorussia, and the Ukraine, by the German occupation force; the Don, by the pro-German general Krasnov; the Kuban, by the pro-Allied general Alekseev. Georgia had a Menshevik government, the Volga-Urals basin an SR one, the central provinces a Bolshevik one, Siberia an SR-Kadet one, and the Far East was held by the Allies. In each region, local Menshevik organizations attuned their policy to their own regional priorities. Mensheviks of all persuasions could justify their

101. Ibid. It is noteworthy that an independent account of the officers' conduct in Kazan also spoke of the Whites' "debauchery" (Stewart, *White Armies*, p. 116). Resolutions of the Kazan Mensheviks in support of Komuch are cited in Maiskii, *Demokraticheskaia kontrrevoliutsiia*, p. 27.

course by reference to resolutions of the May party conference. The carefully worded compromise resolutions designed to secure peace within the party turned out to have legitimated division within the party instead.

Terror as Policy

Following the attempted assassination of Lenin on August 30, the application of terror against the enemies of soviet power was instituted as an official state policy. To be sure, mass terror against certain groups had already been unleashed in early August in the provinces along the front line.[102] Executions of counterrevolutionaries were reported from some cities as early as April. Mass terror against officers began immediately after the October overturn. In January and February 1918, 2,500 victims of Bolshevik terror were reported in Kiev, 3,400 in Rostov, 2,000 in Novocherkassk.[103] Yet the changes in the Bolsheviks' application of terror during 1918 should not be overlooked.

Perhaps the most prominent of these changes was the gradual widening of the net to cover new categories of enemies of soviet power. By June 1918, the list of Bolshevik enemies included not only former gendarmes, officers, property owners, and Kadets but also rich peasants, petty traders, and workers who supported the Mensheviks and SRs. At that time Feliks Dzerzhinskii described quite frankly the nature of Bolshevik repressive policy in an interview published in a Menshevik newspaper:

> Society and the press do not understand correctly the tasks and character of our [Extraordinary] Commission. They conceive of struggle with counterrevolution in terms of normal state policy, and that is why they scream about [legal] guarantees, courts, about inquiries, investigations, etc. We have nothing in common with military revolutionary tribunals. We represent organized terror. This must be said straightforwardly—terror is absolutely necessary in current circumstances. Our task is to struggle with the enemies of soviet power. We terrorize enemies of soviet power in order to nip crime in the bud.[104]

Nipping crime in the bud meant, in practical terms, the use of terror against individuals or groups who had committed no crime but were

---

102. A. Ia. Gutman-Gan, "Izhevskoe vosstanie," in Bernshtam, ed., Ural i Prikam'e, p. 373.

103. Dioneo, Russia under the Bolsheviks, p. 32. On Kiev, see "K sobytiiam v Kieve v ianvare 1918 goda," Nik. Col. no. 100, file 15.

104. B. Rossov, "Dzerzhinskii i Zaks o rasstrelakh," Novaia zhizn', 19 June 1918, p. 4.

thought to be likely to do so. Thus the new element in Bolshevik terror in the summer of 1918 was its application against *potential* enemies. Executions on the spot for bearing arms and mass deportations of Mensheviks (as Lenin recommended to his comrades in Nizhnii Novgorod) were among the measures to be employed.

In September and October 1918, arrests, internments in concentration camps, and executions were carried out not for specific offenses but as a matter of state policy. On September 2, 1918, the CEC passed a resolution that proclaimed the beginning of "mass terror against the bourgeoisie and its agents."[105] The CPC's resolution of September 5 ordered that "all persons who are connected with White Guards organizations, conspiracies, and rebellions are to be executed."[106] As the nature of such "connections" was not specified, enormous authority was being given to local Cheka units. They could label any village "a nest of White Guards" and any group of striking workers "counter-revolutionary Menshevik-SR conspirators."

The instructions of the Commissar of Internal Affairs (NKVD) in September to take hostages expanded the terror further. Upon "any attempt at resistance, mass shootings [of hostages] must be unconditionally applied."[107] It was common practice for the Cheka to seize the wives and children of officers as hostages; if the officers did not surrender, their families would be executed.[108] The terms *burzhui* (a derogatory form of *bourgeois*), *class enemy*, and *enemy of the people* became convenient labels that could be attached to those marked for elimination. Lists of victims published in the provincial press suggest that the "class enemies" included peasants, workers, and even Red Army soldiers, in addition to officers, priests, merchants, and intelligentsia. In Nizhnii Novgorod, the local Cheka announced that it had executed 41 enemies to avenge the attempt on Lenin's life; in Yaroslavl, suspected counter-revolutionaries were interned in a concentration camp and members of the bourgeoisie were subjected to compulsory labor.[109] In Tver, the local Cheka took 130 hostages, among them officers and members of the Kadet and SR parties; in Ivanovo-Voznesensk, 184 hostages were taken; in Perm, 50 victims were executed.[110] Detailed accounts of the Red Terror were found in areas where the Bolsheviks were overthrown in

105. Mel'gunov, *Krasnyi terror*, p. 41.

106. *Bolshevism in Russia*, p. 98. This document has been reprinted in Baynac, *Terror sous Lenine*, p. 57.

107. "Tsirkuliarnaia telegramma," *Vestnik Narodnogo kommissariata vnutrennikh del*, nos. 21–22 (26 September 1918), p. 1.

108. *Bolshevism in Russia*, p. 14.

109. Mel'gunov, *Krasnyi terror*, p. 24.

110. *Bolshevism in Russia*, pp. 98–99.

1918. The newspaper of the North Caucasus soviet, for example, informed its readers that, in compliance with orders from Moscow, the local Cheka had taken 32 hostages; on October 21, 59 counterrevolutionaries were shot, and on October 31, 47 more were executed. The last entry in the published list read, "Polonskaia, Elda—writer [litera-tor]; shot for belonging to a counterrevolutionary organization."[111] The Cheka in Tsaritsyn reported that it had arrested 3,000 soldiers of the Vol'skaia division for abandoning the front line. Another 2,500 soldiers were arrested for armed rebellion against soviet power.[112] When the Bolsheviks took Izhevsk, they publicly machine-gunned 800 workers in the main city square.[113] When workers' military detachments, part of the White army, then took Izhevsk again in March 1919, it was determined that 7,983 people had been executed during the period of Bolshevik rule.[114] In Votkinsk, 5,000 victims were counted.[115]

In October, Martov wrote to a colleague abroad that "the reports about the 'Red Terror'" that had appeared in the German newspapers "are less than the reality, because they do not give a detailed picture of what has taken place in Petrograd and in the provinces."

> For it may be said that this wave of terror has nowhere arisen from any tangible pressure from the masses, nor was it a result of mob rule. The most the Bolsheviks can say in their own defense is that fringe elements of their party threatened to take the law into their own hands if the center did not order them to do it. Ostensibly under the influence of this threat, Zinoviev began to incite murder in the districts [of Petrograd] and directly ordered the Kronstadt sailors to execute 300 officers kept there (a most innocent bunch). According to the statement of the Petrograd Cheka itself, they executed 800 people. Then followed [Commissar of Internal Affairs] Pokrovskii's order about the obligatory taking of hostages, and executions rolled across the provinces. The overall number undoubtedly exceeds 10,000.

He gave the specific instance of a Menshevik worker, Krakovskii, who had been a member of the Petrograd delegation of upolnomochennye to

111. "Chrezvychainym kommissiiam Severnogo Kavkaza po bor'be s kontrrevoliutsiei i sabotazhem: Prikaz No. 73," Izvestiia TsIK Severo-Kavkazskoi Sovetskoi Sotsiali-sticheskoi Respubliki i Piatigorskogo soveta (Piatigorsk), 8 October 1918, p. 1. This order was brought to light by the Commission for Investigation of Crimes of the Bolsheviks (Kommissiia po rassledovaniiu zlodeianii Bol'shevikov) and is cited in the report of its findings, Akt rassledovaniia po delu ob areste i ubiistve zalozhnikov v oktiabre 1918 goda (Rostov, 1919), pp. 10, 18. This commission, under General Denikin's forces, had Allied observers, and collected much documentary evidence on the Bolshevik terror. Some published reports of its findings are in Nik. Col.
112. "Gruzoles," Izvestiia Tsaritsinskoi Cheka po bor'be s kontrrevoliutsiei i prestu-pleniiami po dolzhnosti, Nik. Col. no. 89, file 9.
113. Fedichkin, "Izhevskoe vosstanie," in Bernshtam, ed., Ural i Prikam'e, p. 356.
114. Bernshtam, ed., Ural i Prikam'e, p. 421.
115. S. N. Lotkov, "Kamsko-Votkinskii zavod i ego rabochie," in ibid., p. 436.

the Moscow workers. He had been arrested on June 9 but then "released from the Moscow prison at the demand of the entire plant. . . . A local Cheka fellow seized him on the street and immediately shot him, before the city Bolsheviks had a chance to interfere."[116] In another case, Semen Gorbatov, who had also been a workers' representative, was arrested near Moscow in July during the strikes; despite persistent Menshevik pleas in the CEC and assurances from high-ranking Bolsheviks that the matter would be resolved without bloodshed, Gorbatov was executed.[117] The secretary of the Menshevik organization in Nizhnii Novgorod, Rydnek, was also killed by the local Cheka. Executions of Mensheviks were reported in Rybinsk, Vologda, Vitebsk, and other cities.[118] According to a British intelligence report, "the worst crimes of the Bolsheviks have been against their Socialist opponents. Of the countless executions which the Bolsheviks have carried out, a large percentage has fallen on the heads of Socialists."[119] But among the socialists, as the report noted, the SRs suffered even more than the Mensheviks. The order of the Commissariat of Internal Affairs said flatly, "All SRs known to local soviets must be arrested immediately."[120] In February 1919, an SR party conference in Moscow attempted to count the number of SR victims of the Red Terror. A list of more than 70 names was published by a Menshevik newspaper, but it was impossible in the chaotic conditions of the time to calculate even an approximate total.[121]

Perhaps one of the most significant effects of the Red Terror on the Bolshevik party was that it encouraged the habit of dealing with political opponents in the framework of civil war. By the fall of 1918, struggle with political opponents became equivalent to struggle at the front line—the "internal" front. The Bolsheviks became accustomed to thinking in terms of categorical imperatives: either one is for soviet power, and should then unquestioningly obey all orders of the local administration, or one is against soviet power, and then no mercy need be shown. Menshevik workers' demands for independent organizations were seen now as nothing less than attempts to launch an antisoviet conspiracy. Strikes were perceived as sabotage organized by the agents

116. Iu. Martov to A. Stein, 25 October 1918, Nik. Col. no. 17, box 1, file 3.
117. For this and other cases of executions of Mensheviks at this time, see TsK Ital'ianskoi delegatsii (Moscow, July 1920), Nik. Col. no. 6, box 1, file 17, pp. 10–11.
118. L. Martov, "Krovavoe bezumie," Volia Rossii, 29 December 1920, pp. 1–2.
119. R. H. B. Lockhart, 10 November 1918, document no. 10 in Bolshevism in Russia, p. 14. For a general discussion of terror against the socialists in Russia, see Wally Zepler, "Sozialistische Bewegung: Bolschewismus," Sozialistische Monatshefte, 52 (1919), pt. 1:650–52.
120. "Tsirkuliarnaia telegramma," Vestnik Narodnogo kommissariata vnutrennikh del, nos. 21–22 (26 September 1918), p. 1.
121. "Getakomby," Vsegda vpered, 16 February 1919, p. 2.

of world imperialism—the Mensheviks, who should be unmasked and shot.

This was apparently the attitude of the Bolsheviks in Perm province at the end of 1918, when protests and strikes broke out again in this troubled region. Workers at the Motovilikha state gun plant protested against the allotment of food rations on the basis of social origin, the so-called class ration. On December 5 they struck for the abolition of class rations, grain requisitioning, and the death penalty; for free speech and freedom to trade; and for immediate new and free elections to the soviet. The Bolsheviks responded as though they faced a military rather than a political challenge. The plant was declared to be under siege and the town was occupied by Red forces. There were to be no negotiations with the strikers. All workers were fired. A search for the instigators and troublemakers began. After numerous interrogations and intimidation, most workers were allowed to return to work. Up to this point, the Bolsheviks' actions were like those undertaken by the Petrograd Bolsheviks against the Obukhov workers in June. But in December 1918, the Bolsheviks at Motovilikha went further: they executed 100 workers.[122]

Not only had policies and attitudes changed by the fall of 1918, but—perhaps even more important for the fate of the socialist parties in Soviet Russia—so had the structure of local government. The local Cheka units acquired unlimited power to dispose of people's lives with no formal judicial procedures; anyone could be shot on their orders. As one Bolshevik explained, "some guarantee of personal security is enjoyed only by members of the government, of the CEC, and of the ECs. We see that with the exception of these few individuals, all others, including members of local [Bolshevik] party committees, can be shot at any time, with a report 'afterwards' by any district [uezd] Cheka. . . ."[123] As many Bolsheviks admitted on the pages of the party press, the local Chekas got out of control. From Tambov, the agent of the Commissariat of Internal Affairs reported a series of abuses of power by the Cheka, whose cadres included many "undesirable elements." The local Cheka detachment was glutted with soldiers, machine guns, and armored cars.[124] Another report said that "in the provinces, the Chekas took a place above the Executive Committees and are not controlled by them"; they assumed a "dominant position," and their actions were particularly provocative if they had an armed detachment.[125] Some Bolsheviks demanded drastic

122. Bernshtam, ed., Ural i Prikam'e, p. 129.

123. S. Dukhovskii, "'Chrezvychaiki' i 'ispolkomy,'" Vestnik Narodnogo kommissariata vnutrennikh del, no. 24 (28 October 1918), p. 30.

124. "Doklad po obsledovaniiu Tambovskoi gubernii instruktora-revizora tovarishcha Valentina Kefadili," Vlast' sovetov, no. 27 (1 December 1918), p. 22.

125. "Prilazhivanie apparata," Vestnik Narodnogo kommissariata vnutrennikh del, no. 23 (20 October 1918), p. 23.

curtailment of the Cheka's power or even supported a Menshevik proposal to abolish the Cheka altogether.[126] Perhaps out of institutional rivalry, the Commissariat of Internal Affairs was particularly outspoken in its criticism of the Cheka. Its journal asked who should be exercising power in local communities—"the soviets, as represented by their ECs, or the Chekas?"[127] The author did not mention, of course, that the ECs' claim to represent the soviets was itself dubious. By July 1918, the popularly elected soviet assemblies had almost everywhere been disbanded and replaced by appointed ECs. The period of election politics had given way to a period of anti-Bolshevik uprisings and civil-war skirmishes, with a corresponding strengthening of the apparatus of coercion. In the end, the ECs found themselves powerless vis-à-vis the Chekas. The transformation of the political and administrative role of the soviets which had been unfolding throughout 1918 was now completed.

In comparison with the terror in the fall of 1918, the period of soviet elections in the spring looked to the Mensheviks almost like a working democracy. Now, faced with a new reality, they had to redefine their goals once again, to adjust them to what it seemed feasible to achieve.

The Mensheviks' "New Course"

During September and October 1918, the Menshevik CC took further steps to dissociate itself from the Right Mensheviks. It drew up a statement about the Activists' committee titled "The New Party" and delivered it to, among others, the office of *Izvestiia*.[128] The very title suggested that the CC regarded the split as definitive. If in the preceding months the CC had seemed to be trying to paper over the differences, it now accentuated them. Indeed, it put the matter in stark terms to the local organizations: "Do you support the Activists' committee or the Central Committee?" This effort to force a choice may have been based on a belief that the Activists' cause was becoming less and less attractive. The conservative forces in the east and the south wanted no coalition with any socialists. With Kolchak's coup d'état and the arrests of socialists that followed, the Activists' idea of a national anti-Bolshevik front was finished. As a result, the Right Mensheviks' influence in the local organizations was considerably diminished.

---

126. For a discussion of this effort, see Boris Nikolaevsky, "Pervaia popytka istorii mashiny sovetskogo terrora," *Sotsialisticheskii vestnik* (New York), no. 1 (1958), pp. 54–56.

127. Dukhovskii, " 'Chrezvychaiki'i 'ispolkomy,' " p. 30.

128. "Zhalkie uvertki," *Izvestiia*, 20 September 1918, p. 1.

At the end of December, the Mensheviks assembled for a conference, the "first since the destruction of the RSDWP organizations by the Bolshevik dictatorship," as the preamble to the published resolutions put it. The majority was solidly behind Martov and Dan. The conference reprimanded the Volga-Urals organizations for systematic violation of the CC's decisions and condemned factional groups that pursued their own policies: "These attempts, made possible by the shattered state of the country and by the regime under whose oppression a part of the party was living, had a most disorganizing influence on party life and threatened to undermine its prestige completely in the eyes of the proletarian masses."[129] Though it had no wish to impose iron discipline or turn the party into a "monastic order," the CC could not, "without becoming a laughingstock," allow regional organizations to define party policies and factional committees to challenge the CC's leadership. Diversity of opinion could continue to exist, but not to the point where policies diametrically opposed to those of the CC would be adopted. Other documents make it clear that the measures against the rightists went as far as the expulsion of individual party members and in some cases of entire local organizations.[130] The conference banned the Activists' committee from the Menshevik party.[131] Some Right Mensheviks (Kolokol'nikov, for example) remained in the party and reluctantly accepted Martov's policies, but continued to oppose them. Others (Liber, for example) wanted to have nothing more to do with Martov's leadership. This group went underground and managed to continue its activities in Petrograd well into 1921.[132] Although its members had severed their ties with the Menshevik party, they continued to consider themselves Mensheviks, and for years afterward they criticized what they called "Martov's official Menshevism."[133]

In the late fall, opposition from the Right Mensheviks was perhaps less important than the left-wing pressure on the CC. As Martov explained in a letter:

> Another part of the party, by way of reaction against this "activism," has begun to "wobble," especially under the influence of reports of the Bolsheviks' growing popularity in Europe. There is talk that the socialist world revolution is evidently "bypassing democracy" and taking the Bolshevik road . . . one must look for some kind of "bridge" to Bolshevism.[134]

129. *Partiinoe soveshchanie*, Nik. Col. no. 6, pp. 1, 6.
130. See, for example, L. Isaev, "Pis'ma o taktike: Otshchepentsy i partiinoe bol'shinstvo," *Zaria* (Right Menshevik journal, Berlin), no. 4 (19 June 1922), pp. 107–11.
131. *Partiinoe soveshchanie*, p. 27.
132. See a document dated August 1920, "K protsessu nad Rozanovym," Nik. Col. no. 6, box 1, file 9, and "Iz bumag Portugeisa, 1919–1921," Nik. Col. no. 154.
133. Potresov, *V plenu u illiuzii* (subtitled *Moi spor s ofitsial'nym men'shevizmom*).
134. Martov to Stein, 25 October 1918, Nik. Col. no. 17, box 1, file 3.

These ideas acquired particular credence with the outbreak of revolution in Germany in November 1918.[135] The emergence there of workers' and soldiers' councils tended to reinforce, at least for the moment, the impression that social revolutions in Europe were taking a Bolshevik turn. In the same letter, Martov wrote that the Menshevik party experienced more defections to the Bolsheviks in the fall of 1918 than ever before.

The Mensheviks were undergoing a profound crisis of identity, which stemmed not only from German enthusiasm for Bolshevism but from the painful realization that their hopes that the socialists could topple the Bolshevik dictatorship had come to nothing. Worse, their efforts had led to the consolidation of "reactionary forces" that had only used the socialist-led protest movements for their own advantage. The battle of the summer resulted in frustration among the Mensheviks, mixed with not a little resentment toward the SRs. These views were well expressed in a letter that one Menshevik wrote to his wife at the end of 1918:

> The SRs are adventurists of the first water. They didn't understand that the Bolsheviks were able to hold on to power only because of the civil war. If it hadn't been for the Czechoslovaks and the uprising in Siberia, the Bolsheviks would have been wiped off the face of the earth by the working class itself. (This is a historical fact.) And when the rumors started to reach the workers that they had begun [in the Komuch territory] to lower wages and lengthen the workday . . . they immediately rushed off and all our efforts of the summer of 1918, entirely Menshevik ones—assemblies of upolnomochennye, workers' conferences, strikes—everything went to rack and ruin. At all the plants, the workers were saying: "We're against the Bolsheviks, but when they fall, power will pass not to the Mensheviks and not to the SRs but to the Black Hundreds. . . . I repeat: the SRs have ruined us, just as they ruined the first eight months of the revolution.[136]

The Mensheviks who shared these views, fearing a monarchist restoration, argued that the overthrow of the Bolshevik regime in the conditions of late 1918 would mean victory for the Kolchak regime, which had begun its rule by overthrowing the SR-Kadet government and arresting prominent socialists. To avert such an outcome, the left wing was pressing for an accommodation with the Bolsheviks. But how far could the Mensheviks go in that direction?

135. Martov's own enthusiasm about the German revolution can be seen in his "Letter to Our German Comrades," reprinted in Ascher, ed., *Mensheviks in the Russian Revolution*, p. 117. For a discussion of the impact of the German revolution on Bolshevik policy, see Abraham Ascher, "Russian Marxists and the German Revolution, 1917–1920," *Archiv für Sozialgeschichte*, nos. 6–7 (1966–67), pp. 415–22.

136. S. D. Shchupak to his wife, Nik. Col. no. 53, file 3.

In the resolutions of the December conference and in a series of pronouncements issued two months earlier,[137] the Mensheviks defined what might be called their own "new course." In its essentials, it consisted of recognition of soviet power; withdrawal of the demand for reconvocation of the Constituent Assembly from the immediate practical agenda; condemnation of the foreign intervention and of "restorationist" governments; and a revision of the concept of the bourgeois revolution. Bit by bit, this new course crystallized into a doctrine of loyal, legal opposition to the Bolshevik regime within the system of soviets.[138]

How is one to explain the fact that at the height of the Red Terror, when thousands of "class enemies" were being executed, socialists among them, the Mensheviks sought an accommodation with the Bolshevik regime? Was it a capitulation to Bolshevism, as one Western historian has implied?[139] Was it a betrayal of Social Democratic ideals, as the Right Menshevik critics asserted?[140] Was it a sign of repentance over mistakes committed in the past, or perhaps a masking of their true intentions by the agents of the bourgeoisie, as the Bolshevik press conjectured?[141]

A letter of Martov's sheds some light on at least his own attitudes:

> Our party's position has become unbearable. All outward manifestations of its existence have been erased in Soviet Russia; everything is destroyed: the press, organizations, and so on. Unlike [the situation] in tsarist times, it is impossible even to "go underground" for work that is at all fruitful, because now not only the gendarmes, street sweepers, and the like are keeping an eye out for unreliability, but also a segment of the ordinary citizens themselves (Communists and those with a vested interest in the soviet regime) regard denunciation, surveillance, and shadowing not only as proper but as the fulfillment of a supreme duty. Therefore, thinking about at least somewhat regular functioning of underground organizations is out of the question. A lot of Mensheviks have been arrested.

At the same time, Martov had few illusions about the chances for a loyal, legal opposition under the Bolshevik regime:

> Actually, of course, no "bridge" [to the Bolsheviks] is possible except outright surrender, since Bolshevism does not admit the idea of an opposi-

---

137. "Tezisy i rezoliutsii TsK po tekushchemu momentu ot 17–21 oktiabria 1918 goda," Nik. Col. 6, box 1, file 4.

138. For a Soviet historian's comment on the Mensheviks' new position, see E. Gimpel'son, "Iz istorii obrazovaniia odnopartiinoi sistemy v SSSR," Voprosy istorii, no. 11 (1965), p. 21.

139. Haimson, "Mensheviks after the October Revolution," pt. 2, pp. 206–7.

140. See, for example, the Right Mensheviks' report to the West European socialists, "O polozhenii v Sovetskoi Rossii v 1919 godu," Nik. Col. no. 6, box 1, file 13.

141. "Gorbatogo mogila ispravit," Izvestiia, 30 October 1918, p. 1.

tion party, even if it is ultraloyal and accepts the soviet principle. The only "reconciliation" they admit is for members of this or that opposition party to join them as individual guests.[142]

Despite this privately expressed pessimism, Martov kept trying in public to persuade the Bolsheviks to accede to the existence of a legal opposition party. The choice was clear: either the Menshevik party had to find an accommodation with the Boleshevik regime or, like all the others, it would be obliterated, its activities banned, and its members arrested. In order to determine the price they had to pay for their legalization under a Bolshevik regime, we must see just how their positions had changed.

Menshevik public pronouncements on key issues of the time can be grouped into three major categories: the civil war and foreign intervention, economic policies, and—the most explosive issue—Russia's constitutional order. The new Menshevik platform condemned the Allied intervention in even stronger terms than it had used in August. Before, the Allied intervention had been seen as merely a lesser evil than the German occupation; now the Germans were gone but the Allies remained, and as supporters not of the SRs but of the White armies. Now the Mensheviks saw the Allies as a reactionary force exerting pressure on revolutionary Germany and openly aiding reaction in revolutionary Russia. As long as the SRs were at the helm of the armed struggle, the Mensheviks could remain neutral, despite their suspicions of the SRs' allies on the right. Now that Kolchak had taken over, the Mensheviks had to support a struggle against the White armies and foreign intervention. "The party still decisively rejects all plans for a forcible overthrow of the soviet power, which in the given historical situation would unavoidably lead either to stirring up an internecine war among the laboring classes or to directly assisting the forces of the landlords and capitalists and imperialist reaction."[143] In one sense, this resolution was an extension of the course taken by the CC in the summer, but there was a crucial difference: the Mensheviks had now given up the idea of overthrowing the Bolshevik dictatorship, whereas earlier they had considered this project possible if it could be carried out by the forces of democracy.

Nevertheless, the Mensheviks demanded that the Bolsheviks rule out any attempt at forcible subjugation and incorporation into Soviet Russia of the detached territories where democratic governments were in

---

142. L. Martov to Stein, 25 October 1918, Nik. Col. no. 17, box 1, file 3.
143. *Partiinoe soveshchanie*, p. 14. For the Bolsheviks' reaction to the Mensheviks' stand on foreign intervention, see "Martov uvodiashchii inostrannye voiska," *Vechernie izvestiia Mossoveta*, 8 October 1918.

power[144] (probably a reference to Georgia). The Mensheviks wanted negotiations and agreement between Moscow and socialist governments in these outlying areas. As far as armed struggle against the White armies was concerned, the Mensheviks were willing to support it, but they expected the Bolsheviks to guarantee unobstructed political freedom for the socialist parties in Soviet Russia in return. The Menshevik and SR contribution to the struggle against the Whites acquired great importance later in the civil war, at the height of the Whites' offensives, which represented a grave threat to the Bolshevik regime. The Menshevik-SR underground also played a crucial role in the uprisings against the Kolchak regime in Siberia, which aided the Red Army's offensive. This role has remained a neglected subject, because all parties concerned have wanted it so. The Bolsheviks prefer to belittle the Menshevik and SR contribution to their victory, the emigre Mensheviks and SRs do not particularly wish to call attention to the fact that they helped the Red Army, and the Whites do not like to admit that there were popular uprisings against them. In any event, the Bolsheviks did not keep their part of the bargain. They used the socialists in the effort against the Whites and then, when they no longer needed them, discarded them.

As we have seen, the Mensheviks had criticized Bolshevik economic policies ever since the October revolution, and on this score the new platform showed relatively little change. The Mensheviks still regarded the early policies of reckless nationalizations and confiscations as fundamentally wrong, utopian, and destructive, premature attempts to introduce socialism before a foundation had been laid. A long period of industrial development was needed before socialist methods of production could take root. The Mensheviks continued to advocate partial denationalization of industry, especially of enterprises that private entrepreneurs could manage more productively than the state.[145] A combination of state regulation of industry with a revival of private entrepreneurship could eventually restore production. The new platform also reiterated that workers' rights could be defended only by independent organizations.

On the issue of food-supply policy, the Mensheviks also repeated, almost word for word, their proposals of May 1918. They condemned grain requisitioning and the committees of the poor. Agrarian legislation had to recognize the peasants' right to own land. Any acts of coercion against the peasants would backfire against the new regime, as they had done in the summer. The state had to readjust the prices it

144. *Partiinoe soveshchanie*, p. 15.
145. Ibid., pp. 17–21.

paid to the peasants frequently in order to encourage production. Private trade had to take its competitive place alongside the state food agencies.[146] The only difference between these positions and those taken in the spring was that criticism of the Bolsheviks was now expressed in less categorical terms.

As we have seen, the new platform recognized soviet power and acknowledged that reconvocation of the Constituent Assembly was not immediately practical.[147] However, the idea that it would be reconvened at some time in the future was retained. The resolutions on this subject explained that in the conditions of late 1918 the defense of the Constituent Assembly was inevitably associated with the Directory and its successor, the Kolchak regime. In other words, it was necessary to put the Constituent Assembly aside and work for the eventual restoration of universal suffrage and parliamentary democracy. "The Social Democratic Party," read the December resolution, "will continue to defend, in all its public statements and campaigning, the idea of democracy, universal suffrage, and the Constituent Assembly."[148] The party could achieve this goal only by working within the soviet system, eventually widening the limited soviet franchise to universal suffrage. It was necessary to "step back in order to leap."[149] Meanwhile, soviet power was recognized "as a factual reality and not as a principle."[150] Martov pointed out that this de facto acceptance of soviet power was similar to the Mensheviks' recognition of the tsarist duma after the first Russian revolution in 1905.[151] Democracy based on universal suffrage remained the party's ultimate goal, but this did not mean that the Social Democrats could not take part in limited-franchise institutions before the goal was reached. Instead of philosophizing about the advantages of the Constituent Assembly over the soviets, the Social Democrats had resolved to stay in the soviets, explaining to the workers that their interests could be best secured not by a "terrorist minority dictatorship but only by sound and consistent democracy in the framework of a democratic republic, based on equal and universal suffrage and direct and secret ballot."[152]

Martov hammered away at the point that, in the Russia of 1918, restoration of democratically elected soviets would already be a giant step toward democracy. He urged his associates to give up the illusion

146. Ibid., p. 20.
147. Ibid., p. 23–25.
148. Ibid., p. 24.
149. Ibid., p. 5.
150. Ibid., p. 24.
151. "Men'sheviki i sovetskaia vlast' (Beseda s L. Martovym)," *Utro Moskvy*, 8 October 1918, p. 4.
152. *Partiinoe soveshchanie*, p. 15.

that they had a choice between soviet democracy and parliamentary democracy. The real choice was between the rule of the Cheka and the rule of soviets properly elected, however limited the franchise. According to the Soviet constitution, all power had to belong to the soviets, not to the Cheka, and government officials were responsible to the electorate. The role of the Social Democrats in these conditions was to press for strict implementation of these laws and provisions. The Bolsheviks themselves liked to pay lip service to the "most democratic procedures in the soviets," which reflected the wishes of the masses. It would be difficult for them to accuse the Mensheviks of subversion if the Mensheviks were defending the democratic provisions of Soviet laws. Specifically, the Mensheviks demanded

> free elections and reelections of the soviets in conditions of complete freedom of printed and oral campaigns for all parties; reestablishment of freedom of the press, assembly, unions, and strikes; inviolability of domicile; unconditional abolition of the death penalty, either with or without trial; and repudiation of all summary executions and of terroristic methods of suppressing peasant uprisings; denial to any party whatsoever of the status of a government institution and of the right to special privileges in comparison with other parties of Revolutionary Democracy.[153]

In all, there was a remarkable degree of continuity in the new Menshevik platform. Support for soviet power against the Whites had been foreshadowed by the ban on Menshevik participation in the anti-Bolshevik uprisings of July and the condemnation of the Allied intervention in August. The economic proposals and critique of Bolshevik economic policy remained virtually unchanged. On political issues, it may be recalled that the May party conference criticized the soviets for what they actually were under the Bolshevik dictatorship and praised them for what they could be in theory. Thus the Mensheviks' new positions represented extensions of Martov's center-left brand of Menshevism. While step by step distancing the party from the more militant anti-Bolsheviks, Martov had been steering it throughout 1918 toward basic acceptance of the system of soviets, at the same time opposing the Bolshevik party dictatorship. The new element in the Menshevik position was that it no longer favored the overthrow of the Bolsheviks. After the split with the Right Mensheviks, Martov set forth what he believed to be the task for Social Democrats in Soviet Russia: competition with Bolshevism, not civil war. The Menshevik opposition would henceforth be a legal one, in the sense that its aim would be to uphold soviet

---

153. Ibid., pp. 15–16. See also "Vserossiiskoe soveshchanie RSDRP," *Gazeta pechatnikov*, 2 January 1919, p. 1.

laws, and a loyal one, in the sense that the party would repudiate any underground activity. In the following years, the Mensheviks pursued their goals as a loyal, legal opposition, in an attempt, as Martov put it, to "straighten out the course of the Russian Revolution."[154]

154. For Martov's reflections on Menshevik policy after October, see "Liniia Sotsial Demokratii," in Martov, ed., *Voprosy Sotsial Demokraticheskoi politiki: Oborona revoliutsii i Sotsial Demokratiia,* pp. 1–8.

Conclusions

The history of the Menshevik opposition during the year after October 1917 reveals the close relationship between the Bolsheviks' struggle against their socialist opponents and the development of the Soviet system. The political system underwent constant change throughout the period; so did the views, attitudes, political objectives, platforms, and influence of the parties that vied for power.

Following the October Revolution, both the Bolsheviks and the Mensheviks were faced with a choice between one-party dictatorship and some form of democracy, but the choice was posed in different terms for the two parties. For the Bolsheviks, the question was whether they, as the ruling party, were going to tolerate opposition parties, especially if the latter gained a majority. For the Mensheviks, the question was whether to accept as legitimate the rule of the soviets, based on a limited franchise and often forcibly dominated by the Bolsheviks, or to continue to strive for their ideal of a parliamentary republic based on universal suffrage—in effect, whether to oppose the government through electoral competition or through insurrection. The answers to these questions had a profound impact on the development of Soviet politics in 1918.

The transfer of power to the soviets in October 1917 was not immediately followed by establishment of a one-party dictatorship. To be sure, Lenin wanted as much power for his party as possible and tried to derail the interparty negotiations, even though the Bolshevik CC had initially voted for a multiparty CEC. The inability of the Mensheviks and SRs to counter Lenin's policy, primarily because of their internal disputes, allowed Lenin to silence his Bolshevik opponents, secure control of the CEC, and prepare for the disbandment of the Constituent Assembly, despite the fact that the Bolsheviks had a very narrow margin over their opponents in the soviets (and no majority at all in the Constituent Assembly). Indeed, it is possible to posit that the die was cast the moment the Vikzhel negotiations broke down: the Bolshevik party was determined to establish its dictatorship.

Even after disbanding the Constituent Assembly in the name of soviet power, however, the Bolsheviks explicitly recognized the right of the opposition socialist parties to compete with the Bolsheviks for popular support within the system of soviets. In early March, the Mensheviks ended their boycott of the CEC and worked to regain the majorities in the soviets which they had lost to the Bolsheviks in October, and thus legally to force the Bolshevik government to resign.

Bolshevik-Menshevik interaction in the CEC, the courts, the local soviets, and the workers' organizations led to the breakdown of multiparty competition. No one factor can be singled out as the cause of this change. Unemployment and the breakdown of the food-supply system, combined with a shift in loyalties among Bolshevik supporters, produced electoral victories for the Bolsheviks' opponents. A chain reaction was set in motion: the Mensheviks' electoral victories provoked the Bolsheviks to disband soviets and expel their opponents; these actions led in turn to new efforts to enlist workers in Menshevik-led organizations, which then led to new clashes between protesting workers and Bolsheviks, which led finally to the imposition of martial law. The Bolsheviks in the provinces outdid their Moscow comrades in repression of political opponents.

From the Bolsheviks' point of view, the periodic elections of government officials were unnecessary and even harmful, because they disrupted the normal functioning of the party apparatus; the opposition press had to be shut down because it discredited the government's policy; and the opposition's questioning in the CEC had to be stopped because it compromised the government. Menshevik agitation confused the workers and undermined their confidence in the proletarian vanguard, the Communist party. It was hard for the Bolsheviks to admit that the party of the proletarian revolution, the party of Red October, was losing popular support. It was much easier to destroy the evidence that testified to that effect and to do away with the party that was providing that evidence. The Mensheviks were dangerous because they belied the Bolsheviks' image of themselves. The dissenters had to be driven out—from the soviets, from the trade unions, from the councils of upolnomochennye. With each passing month the Bolsheviks became more accustomed to wielding power and acquired a greater taste for it; they then developed doctrines to justify their retention of power. Holding on to power was ideologically defined as defending the dictatorship of the proletariat, which in the summer of 1918 meant, in practical terms, fighting the Mensheviks and SRs. Changing attitudes shaped policy and made the assault on the opposition inevitable.

What Lenin and the Bolsheviks did not fully take into account was that their apparatus of coercion, the Cheka, given a free hand against the Mensheviks, the SRs, the Kadets, and the bourgeoisie, would become a powerful institution in its own right—one that would be more difficult to bring into line in the provinces than the Mensheviks and SRs had been in their day. The Bolsheviks won a Pyrrhic victory: they defeated the Mensheviks and SRs, but in the process they created a monster they themselves did not know how to deal with for years to come.

The contrast between the political situation in early June and that at the end of July was enormous. In early June, the Mensheviks and SRs constituted a formidable opposition in the soviets, trade unions, and other organizations. Persecution and expulsions notwithstanding, these parties had reason to believe that they had a good chance of winning a majority against the Bolsheviks at the upcoming Fifth Congress of Soviets. The expulsions from the CEC, the rigging of the Petrograd elections, and the arrests of the upolnomochennye marked the three stages in the unfolding of the Bolshevik attack on the Mensheviks and SRs. By the end of July, the opposition-controlled soviets had been disbanded and replaced by Bolshevik ECs or revolutionary committees, or simply by Cheka detachments; the peasants' soviets were abolished altogether and replaced by the Committees of the Poor; the opposition parties were expelled from the institutions of government, the trade unions, and all other organizations, even nonpolitical ones. Strikes were banned and independent workers' organizations outlawed, the opposition press was shut down, Menshevik and SR leaders were arrested and some were executed. The dictatorship of the Bolshevik party had been established and was being maintained by force.

The establishment of the Bolshevik dictatorship has traditionally been seen as stemming from Lenin's vision of Marxist ideology. That vision was not the Mensheviks', though they, and even Lenin's critics within the Bolshevik party, also claimed to be following Marxist precepts. Marxist ideology did not preclude Kamenev's acceptance of a multiparty system of soviets or the Mensheviks' defense of the Constituent Assembly. It was not a case of Marxist ideology corrupting Russia; rather, it was the age-old story of power transforming the power-holders.

It is frequently argued that the transformation of the Soviet political system and the establishment of the Bolshevik dictatorship can be attributed at least in part to foreign intervention and the civil war between the Bolsheviks and the Whites. The Whites were of course active during this period. After the defeat of General Kaledin's troops in December 1917, however, their forces were numerically insignificant and relegated to the outlying borderlands. The first stage of a civil war on a national rather than regional scale began in June 1918 between the Bolsheviks and the Komuch government. This armed struggle must be seen as an outgrowth of the preceding electoral battles. It was only after the demise of electoral politics—after numerous soviets had been disbanded, strikers had routinely been arrested, and martial law had been imposed—that the Right Mensheviks, the SRs, the peasants, and the workers in many cities turned to armed struggle against the Bolshevik dictatorship.

The Menshevik party could not withstand the pressures of the civil war. The evidence on Menshevik party life and factional struggle suggests that its decisions were invariably compromises. Party factions and local organizations enjoyed broad autonomy. The Right Mensheviks went so far as to challenge the CC's authority. The diversity of political opinion within the Menshevik party was damaging; the political face of the party was at times obscured when its two factions advocated irreconcilable policies. In the end, the party split. The Right Mensheviks joined the SRs; the center-Left Mensheviks continued to oppose the Bolshevik dictatorship, but their fear of the Whites kept them from taking up arms against it. After intense debate, the center-Left Mensheviks rejected armed struggle as a means of restoring democracy.

Once interparty competition was abolished from the political arena and was transformed into armed struggle, the chances for success were determined by military strength. The Bolsheviks, holding state power and acting from the industrial center of the country, clearly had an advantage. The crisis in the Menshevik-SR alliance further weakened the position of the Komuch government, until it was finally defeated by the combined blows of the Bolsheviks on the front line and the tsarist officers within. The SRs' defeat in the fall of 1918 ended the most concerted effort to provide a political alternative to both the Communist dictatorship and a restoration of the monarchy.

The center-Left Mensheviks were committed to nonviolent resistance to the establishment of a one-party dictatorship. Their strongest argument was that in theory the country was supposed to be ruled by popularly elected soviets, whereas in practice it was ruled by the Communist party apparatus. By late 1918 the Mensheviks came to the conclusion that, in comparison with the lawlessness of Cheka terror, simple observance of soviet laws would represent a step toward the restoration of democracy.

The evidence suggests that the defeat of the Mensheviks can be attributed to three factors. The first was the brutal suppression of opposition by the Bolsheviks. The second was the withering away of the working class, at least temporarily, as workers fled to the countryside to escape the famine and upheaval in the cities. The third was the split among the socialists themselves. The moderate Mensheviks could not offer meaningful political alternatives in the face of the mounting Bolshevik attack. Their entire approach to politics and their goal of exerting pressure on the Bolshevik government presupposed continued political coexistence and competition with the Bolsheviks. In other words, the moderate Mensheviks could have put their program into practice only if the Bolsheviks had remained true to the principle of multiparty competition.

The Mensheviks attempted to lead a workers' protest movement. The outcome only emphasized the workers' weakness against the coercive powers of the state. Martov's efforts to "straighten out the course of the Russian Revolution" by persevering in the leadership of a loyal, legal opposition have been seen in retrospect as naive. Indeed, Martov himself was not sure his method would yield results. In view of the Bolsheviks' treatment of opposition parties in 1918, it would seem hard to make a case for their readiness to tolerate opposition, no matter how loyal and legal. One may be tempted to conclude that few center-Left Mensheviks, at least at that time, understood the nature of the Bolshevik dictatorship. The Mensheviks' frame of reference was limited to what they themselves had lived through—the tsarist autocracy, the Bolshevik dictatorship, and the brutalities of the White bands. Although most of them believed that the Bolshevik dictatorship was worse than the tsarist autocracy, the center-Left Mensheviks believed that a victory for the Whites would be worse yet. These Mensheviks were paralyzed by the specter of counterrevolution. Victory for the Whites would signify for them the destruction not only of Bolshevism but of all they thought had been achieved in February 1917, after so many years of struggle against the tsarist autocracy. In short, the Bolsheviks were perceived as a lesser evil. They were a dictatorial party, but nevertheless one that recruited its supporters from the masses. The Mensheviks, at least those in the center-left wing of the party, believed that after a period of turmoil and the brief ascendancy of extremist policies, the laws of the soviets would be observed; and with their observance, democracy would eventually emerge.

When the White offensive threatened the survival of the Bolshevik regime in the summer of 1919, the Bolsheviks sought and obtained an agreement with the Mensheviks and SRs for a common struggle against the monarchists. Thus the civil war with the Whites loosened the one-party dictatorship for a time and restored some characteristics of the multiparty soviet system. The Mensheviks and SRs did make a significant contribution to victory over the Whites—in the Far East their contribution was crucial—but the Bolsheviks then turned against their socialist rivals once again. They did not expel the Mensheviks from the soviets as they had done in 1918; until the fall of 1922 they maintained the fiction that the popular will was expressed through elections to the soviets and that the opposition could offer its candidates to the voters. In practice, however, the Cheka arrested any candidate whose name was publicly announced.

The Mensheviks were the first to point to the duplicity that has since confused many students of Bolshevism. The Bolsheviks appeared to be heirs to European traditions of socialism, Marxism, and proletarian revolution. They presented themselves as champions of liberty and socialist democracy. But in turning Marxism into Marxism-Leninism, they created a party apparatus that Marx would not recognize. Menshevik opposition and Menshevik testimony represent the initial attempts to dispel these claims and to reveal the antidemocratic nature of Bolshevism. Although the Mensheviks were defeated in their own day, the historical argument between Communists and Social Democrats over democracy, socialism, and the role of workers' parties continues. From this perspective, the Mensheviks' critique of Bolshevism in 1918 and their struggle for democratic socialism have not lost their timeliness today.

Members of the Central Committee of the Russian Social Democratic Workers' Party

Party Congress of August 1917

Elected unanimously by all factions

Aksel'rod, P.

Defensists and Revolutionary Defensists

Baturskii, B.
Chkeidze, N.
Chkhenkeli, A.
Dan, F. [Gurvich]
Ermolaev, K.
Garvi, P.
Gol'dman, D.
Gorev, B.

Isuv, I.
Iudin, F. [I. Aizenshtadt]
Khinchuk, L.
Kolokol'nikov, P.
Liber, M. [M. Gol'dman]
Smirnov, A.
Tsereteli, I.
Zaretskaia, S.

Internationalists

Abramovitch, R. [Rein]
Broido, E.
Ezhov, V. [S. Tsederbaum]
Iakhontov, V.

Martov, L. [Iu. Tsederbaum]
Martynov, A. [Piker]
Rozhkov, N.
Semkovskii, S. [S. Bronshtein]

Party Congress of December 1917

Abramovitch, R.
Akhmatov, I.
Astrov, I. [I. Poves]
Aksel'rod, P.
Ber, B. [B. Gurevich]
Broido, E.
Cherevanin, N. [F. Lipkin]
Dan, F.
Erlikh, G.
Ezhov, V.

Gogua, K. G.
Gorev, B.
Maiskii, I.
Martov, Iu.
Martynov, A.
Iugov [A. Frumson]
Pinkevich
Semkovskii, S.
Volkov, I.

Party Conference of May 1918[1]

Abramovitch, R.
Akhmatov, I.
Astrov, I.
Broido, E.
Cherevanin, N.
Dallin, D.
Dan, F.
Erlikh, G.
Ermanskii, O. [O. Kogan]
Gorev, B.

Iakhontov, V.
Iugov, A.
Kuchin, G.
Liber, M.
Maiskii, I.
Martov, Iu.
Martynov, A.
Trifonov, E.
Troianovskii, A.

---

1. This list includes only those CC members who were present at the conference in Moscow.

Sources: Party congress of August 1917—V. L. L'vov-Rogachevskii, ed., *Sotsialisty o tekushchem momente* (Moscow: Delo, 1917), p. 263; party congress of December 1917— "Iz zhizni RSDRP," *Luch'*, 19 November 1917, p. 4; party conference of May 1918— "Sostav TsK RSDRP," *Partiinye Izvestiia*, no. 8 (10 June 1918), p. 13.

Selected Bibliography

Primary Sources

Archives, Hoover Institution on War, Revolution, and Peace, Stanford, California

1. Boris I. Nikolaevsky Collection

The Nikolaevsky Collection contains more than 200 collections, each consisting of one or several boxes of materials concerning an individual, organization, or geographical area. Only the most important of the collections and documents are listed here.

> Collection no. 6. Official documents of the Menshevik Central Committee— statements, resolutions, declarations, leaflets, and appeals

M. Gurevich, "O polozhenii v Rossii i o RSDRP," box 1.
Letter of the Menshevik Central Committee to the Italian delegation, "TsK ital'ianskoi delegatsii," box 1.
Letters of the Menshevik Central Committee to local organizations, "Ko vsem partiinym organizatsiiam," box 1.
Letters of local organizations to the Menshevik Central Committee, box 1.
A. Lokerman, "74 dnia sovetskoi vlasti (Iz istorii diktatury bol'shevikov na Donu)," box 2
Partiinoe soveshchanie 27 dekabria 1918–1 ianvaria 1919 goda (rezoliutsii), box 3.
Report of the Menshevik Central Committee to the Second International, "Rabochii klass pod bol'shevistskoi diktaturoi: Doklad Vtoromu Internatsionalu," box 1.
Report of the Right Mensheviks, "O polozhenii v Rossii i o RSDRP," box 1.

Collection no. 7. Official documents of the Party of Socialist Revolutionaries

Viktor Chernov, "Kommentarii k protokolam TsK PSR (sentiabr' 1917–fevral' 1918)," box 3.
The Chernov Manifesto, box 3.
"Polozhenie Partii SR v Rossii (sekretno)," box 2.
Protokoly TsK PSR, September 1917–February 1918, box 3.
Tezisy dokladov i rezoliutsii, box 3.
V. M. Zenzinov, "Bor'ba russkoi demokratii s bol'shevikami v 1918 godu," box 1.

Collection no. 16. Pavel Aksel'rod papers

Letters of and correspondence with key Mensheviks: Iu. O. Martov, F. Dan. R. Abramovitch, S. Zaretskaia, A. Martynov, G. O. Binshtok, V. Levitskii, K. M. Ermolaev, G. Erlikh, and others.
File 119: Documents on the movement of upolnomochennye, compiled by Aksel'rod.

Collection no. 17. Iu. O. Martov papers

Articles, brochures, and correspondence with Russian and West European Social Democrats, the most important of whom were A. N. Stein, P. Aksel'rod, S. D. Shchupak, and Karl Kautsky.

Smaller collections and separate documents

Collection no. 53. S. D. Shchupak papers.
Collection no. 95. Burtsev papers: *Materialy k istorii grazhdanskoi voiny v Rossii.*
Collection no. 100. "K sobytiiam v Kieve v ianvare 1918 goda."
Collection no. 200. Documents of the Yaroslavl Committee of the RSDRP.
Collection of Petr Garvi. Typescripts, memoirs, clippings.
Kommissiia po rassledovaniiu zlodeianii bol'shevikov: Several published documents on the Red Terror.
Krasnaia kniga Vecheka (Moscow, 1920).
Boris Nikolaevsky, "RSDRP (men'shevikov) v period s oktiabria 1917 po iiul' 1918 goda," unpublished manuscript.

2. S. P. Mel'gunov Archive
Seventeen boxes of newspaper clippings, writings, correspondence, and reports on the activities of the Cheka and on the Red Terror.

3. Alexander Kerensky papers
Newspaper clippings on the October 1917 crisis.

4. Press, Archangel, Russia
Translations of articles and extracts, 1918–19.

5. Russia, History, Revolution
Miscellaneous photographs and posters.

6. T. S. Russia Collection
Newspaper clippings and separate issues of Russian newspapers.

Archives of Russian and East European History and Culture, Columbia University

Raphael Abramovitch papers.
Especially important are Abramovitch's newspaper clippings on the movement of upolnomochennye, as well as the research notes for his book *The Soviet Revolution, 1917–1939.*

Newspapers and Journals

The newspapers and journals listed here are to be found in the collections of one or more of the following institutions: Columbia University; Harvard University; the Hoover Institution on War, Revolution, and Peace; the Library of Congress; Princeton University. Most of the newspapers were of very short duration, sometimes only one or two days. Abbreviations: B = Bolshevik (including state agencies); K = Kadet (Constitutional Democrat); LSR = Left Socialist Revolutionary; M = Menshevik; N = nonparty; SR = Socialist Revolutionary.

Newspapers

Bor'ba. Tiflis, 1918 (M).
Delo naroda. Petrograd, Moscow, 1917–18 (SR).
Delo svobody. Novonikolaevsk, 1918 (SR).
Den'. Petrograd, 1917–18 (M).
Den' za dnem. Petrograd, 1918 (M).
Edinstvo. Petrograd, 1917–18 (M).
Era. Petrograd, 1918 (N).
ESER. Vladivostok, 1918 (SR).
Ezhenedel'nik Vecheka. Moscow, 1918 (B).
Fakel. Petrograd, 1917 (M).
Gazeta pechatnikov. Moscow, 1918 (M; Printers' Union).
Golos iuga. Donetsk, Kharkov, 1918 (M).
Golos Kieva. Kiev, 1918 (N).
Golos Rossii. Berlin, 1922 (SR).
Golos Sotsial Demokrata. Petrograd, 1917 (M).
Iskra. Moscow, 1918 (M).
Iskra. Petrograd, 1917 (M).
Izvestiia. Moscow, 1918 (B).
Izvestiia Omskogo oblastnogo ispolnitel'nogo komiteta. Omsk, 1918 (B).
Izvestiia Petrogradskogo gorodskogo obshchestvennogo samoupravleniia. Petrograd, 1918 (N).
Izvestiia Saratovskogo soveta. Saratov, 1918 (B).
Izvestiia Tverskogo soveta. Tver, 1918 (B).
Klich'. Petrograd, 1917 (M).
Luch'. Petrograd, 1917 (M).
Mira khleba svobody. Petrograd, 1917 (M-SR).
Molva. Petrograd, 1918 (N).
Nachalo. Moscow, 1918 (M).
Narod. Petrograd, 1917 (SR).

Nashe edinstvo. Petrograd, 1918 (M).
Nashe slovo. Moscow, 1918 (M).
Nash vek. Petrograd, Moscow, 1917–18 (K).
Novaia petrogradskaia gazeta. Petrograd, 1918 (N).
Novaia zhizn'. Petrograd, 1917–18 (M).
Novoe delo naroda. Moscow, 1918 (SR).
Novyi den'. Petrograd, 1918 (M).
Novyi luch'. Petrograd, 1917–18 (M).
Novyi vechernii chas. Petrograd, 1918 (N).
Petrogradskii golos. Petrograd, 1918 (N).
Petrogradskoe ekho. Petrograd, 1918 (N).
Pravda. Moscow, 1918 (B).
Rabochaia gazeta. Petrograd, 1917 (M).
Rabochii mir. Moscow, 1918 (?).
Rannee utro. Moscow, 1918 (N).
Rossiia. Petrograd, 1918 (SR).
Severnaia kommuna. Petrograd, 1918 (B).
Severnaia zaria. Vologda, 1918 (M).
Shchit. Petrograd, 1917 (M).
Sovremennoe slovo. Petrograd, 1918 (N).
Strana. Petrograd, 1918 (SR).
Tekushchii moment. Petrograd, 1917 (M-SR).
Utrenniaia molva. Petrograd, 1918 (N).
Utro Moskvy. Moscow, 1918 (M; Printers' Union).
Utro Petrograda. Petrograd, 1918 (M: Printers' Union).
Vecherniaia zvezda. Petrograd, 1918 (M).
Vechernie izvestiia Mossoveta. Moscow, 1918 (B).
Vechernie ogni. Moscow, 1918 (N).
Vechernii chas. Petrograd, 1918 (N).
Vestnik anarkhii. Briansk, 1918 (anarchist).
Volia strany. Petrograd, 1918 (SR).
Vozrozhdenie. Moscow, 1918 (SR).
Vpered. Moscow, 1917–18 (M).
Vsegda vpered. Moscow, 1919 (M).
Zaria. Petrograd, 1917–18 (M).
Zaria Rossii. Moscow, 1918 (N).
Znamia bor'by. Petrograd, 1918 (LSR).
Znamia revoliutsii. Saratov, 1918 (Left SR).
Znamia truda. Moscow, Petrograd, 1918 (SR).

Journals

Biulleten' Narodnogo Kommissariata Truda. Moscow, 1918 (B).
Delo. Petrograd, 1917–18 (M).
Les Echos de Russie. Stockholm, 1918 (M-SR).
Edinstvo. Petrograd, 1918 (M).
Ekho bor'by. Paris, 1936 (M).
Le Journal de Russie. Petrograd, 1917–18 (N).
Kommunist. Moscow, 1918 (B).
Mysl'. Kharkov, 1919 (M).

Narodovlastie. Ekaterinodar, 1918–19 (SR).
Narodovlastie. Moscow, 1919 (SR).
Nash golos. Moscow, 1918 (M).
Novaia zaria. Moscow, 1918 (M).
Partiinye izvestiia. Moscow, Petrograd, 1918 (M).
Rabochii internatsional. Moscow, 1918 (M).
Sotsialisticheskii vestnik. Berlin, 1921– (M).
Sotsialist revoliutsioner. Moscow, 1918 (SR).
Stimmen aus Russland. Stockholm, 1918 (M-SR).
Vestnik Kommissariata Vnutrennikh Del. Moscow, 1918 (B).
Vlast' Sovetov. Moscow, 1918 (B).
Volia Rossii. Prague, 1928 (SR).
Zaria. Berlin, 1922–23 (M).
Za rodinu. Petrograd, 1918 (SR).
Zemskii rabotnik. Moscow, 1918 (M-SR).

Political Pamphlets, Memoirs, and Contemporary Accounts

Abramovitch, Raphael R. *The Soviet Revolution, 1917–1939.* New York: International Universities Press, 1962.

Aksel'rod, Pavel B. *Kto izmenil sotsializmu?* New York: Narodopravstvo, 1918.

Aronson, Grigorii. *K istorii pravogo techeniia sredi Men'shevikov.* Inter-University Project on the History of the Menshevik Movement, paper no. 4. New York, 1960.

——. *Na zare krasnogo terrora.* Berlin: Hirschbaum, 1929.

——. *Rossiia v epokhu revoliutsii.* New York: Walden, 1966.

Axelrod, Paul. *Die russische Revolution und die Sozialistische Internationale: Aus dem literarischen Nachlass von Paul Axelrod.* Jena: Karl Zwing, 1932.

Benario, Miguel S. *Von der Demokratie zur Diktatur.* Munich: Drei Masken, 1920.

Braun, M. J. *Zur Geschichte und Taetigkeit der Sowjets in Russland.* Berlin, 1919.

Bronski, M. G. *Ein Jahr proletarischer Diktatur.* Berlin: Junge Garde, 1919.

C. E. B. *Facts about the Bolsheviks.* London: Macmillan, 1919.

Chavichvily, Khariton. *Lettre ouverte au camarade Jean Longuet. . . : Les Bolchevikis d'après les journaux des partis socialistes russes.* Berne: Freie Verlag, 1919

Cherevanin, Fedor A. *Organizatsionnyi vopros.* Geneva: Izdanie RSDRP, 1904.

Chernov, V. M. *Rozhdenie revoliutsionnoi Rossii: Fevral'skaia revoliutsiia.* Paris, Prague, New York: Komitet po izdaniiu trudov V. M. Chernova, 1934.

Chessin, Serge de. *L'Apocalypse russe: La Revolution bolchevique, 1918–1921.* Paris: Plon-Nourrit, 1921.

Dallin, David. *Posle voin i revoliutsii.* Berlin: Grani, 1922.

Dan, Fedor. *Dva goda skitanii, 1919–1921.* Berlin, 1922.

——. *K istorii poslednikh dnei Vremennogo pravitel'stva.* Berlin: Letopis' Revoliutsii, 1923.

Dioneo [I. V. Shklovskii]. *Russia under the Bolsheviks.* London: Wilkinson, 1919.

Dvinov, Boris. *Moskovskii sovet rabochikh deputatov, 1917–1922: Vospominaniia*. New York, 1962.

——. *Pervaia mirovaia voina i Rossiiskaia Sotsial Demokratiia*. Inter-University Project on the History of the Menshevik Movement, paper no. 10. New York, 1961.

Ermanskii, O. A. *Iz perezhitogo*. Moscow: Gosizdat, 1927.

Garvi, Peter A. *Zapiski Sotsial Demokrata (1906–1921)*. Newtonville, Mass.: Oriental Research Partners, 1982.

Gawronsky, Dimitri. *Die Bilanz des russischen Bolshewismus*. Berlin: Cassirer, 1919.

Hirschberg, Max. *Bolschewismus: Eine kritische Untersuchung ueber die amtlichen Veroeffentlichungen der Russischen Sowjetrepublik*. Munich: Duncker & Humblot, 1919.

Kamkov, Boris. *Respublika sovetov*. Berlin, 1920.

Kaplun, Kogan. *Russisches Wirtschaftsleben seit der Herrschaft der Bolschewiki (nach Russischen Zeitungen)*. Berlin, 1919.

Keeling, H. V. *Bolshevism*. London: Hodder & Stoughton, 1919.

Kreml' za reshetkoi (Vospominaniia levykh eserov). Berlin: Skify, 1922.

Lenin, V. I. *Collected Works*. Moscow: Progress, 1978–80.

——. *Polnoe sobranie sochinenii*. Moscow: Gosizdat, 1967–70.

——. *Sochineniia*. 4th ed. Moscow: Gosizdat, 1947–67.

Lokerman, A. *74 dnia sovetskoi vlasti (Iz istorii diktatury Bol'shevikov na Donu)*. Rostov, 1918. Published in French *Les Bolcheviks à l'oeuvre*. Paris: Rivière, 1920.

Maiskii, I. M. *Demokraticheskaia kontrrevoliutsiia*. Moscow: Gosizdat, 1923.

Makhno, Nestor. *Pod udarami kontrrevoliutsii*. Paris: Izdanie komiteta N. Makhno, 1936.

Martov, Iu. O.* *A bas la peine de mort*. Paris: Editions du Parti Social Democrate de Russie, 1919.

Martov, L. *Bor'ba s osadnym polozheniem v Rossiiskoi Sotsialdemokraticheskoi partii (Otvet na pis'mo N. Lenina)*. Geneva, 1904.

Martov, Iu. O. *Melkoburzhuaznaia stikhiia v russkoi revoliutsii*. Moscow: TsK RSDRP, 1918.

——. *Mirovoi Bol'shevizm*. Berlin: Sotsialisticheskii Vestnik, 1923.

Martov, L. *Proletariat i natsional'naia oborona*. Petrograd: Kniga, 1917.

——. *Rabochii klass v Rossii i ego trebovaniia*. Moscow, 1917.

Martov, Iu. O. *The State and the Socialist Revolution*. New York: International Review, 1938.

Martov, J., ed. *La Dictature du proletariat*. Paris: Editions de la Liberté, 1947.

Martov, Iu. O., ed. *Voprosy Sotsial Demokraticheskoi politiki: Oborona revoliutsii i Sotsial Demokratiia*. Moscow: Kniga, 1920.

Martov, L., ed. *Za god*. Petrograd: Kniga, 1918.

Martov i ego blizkie: Sbornik. New York, 1959.

Nikolaevsky, B. N. *A. N. Potresov: Posmertnyi sbornik proizvedenii*. Paris: Navarre, 1937.

---

*Martov's first name and patronymic were Iulii Osipovich, but he sometimes used the transliterated first name Julius or Jules (J.) and sometimes the initial L.

Oehme, Walter. *Sozialismus und Bolschewismus (Streitfragen Revolution-saera)*. N.s., vol. 4. Berlin, 1919.

Paustovskii, K. G. *Povest' o zhizni*. 2 vols. Moscow: Sovetskaia Rossiia, 1966. Vol. 1.

Plekhanov, G. V. *God na rodine: Stat'i i rechi, 1917–1918 g*. Paris: J. Povolozky, 1921.

Portugeis, S. O. [St. Ivanovich, pseud.] *Piat' let bol'shevizma: Nachala i kontsy*. Berlin: Izdatel'stvo zhurnala *Zaria*, 1922.

———. *Sumerki russkoi Sotsial Demokratii*. Berlin: Zaria, 1921.

Potresov, A. N. *V plenu u illiuzii: Moi spor s ofitsial'nym men'shevizmom*. Paris: Société Nouvelle d'Editions Franco-Slaves, 1927.

Price, M. Philips. *Das räte System in Russland*. Berlin, 1919.

Robien, Lous de. *Russisches Tagebuch, 1917–1918: Aufzeichnungen eines französischen Diplomaten in Petersburg*. Stuttgart: Dr. Riederen, 1967.

Semenov, Grigorii [Vasil'ev, pseud.]. *Voennaia i boevaia rabota partii SR za 1917–1918 gody*. Berlin: G. German, 1922.

Spiridonova, Maria. *Otkrytoe pis'mo TseKu partii Bol'shevikov*. Moscow: Izdatel'stvo TsK Partii Levykh SRov, 1919.

Sukhanov, N. N. *Zapiski o revoliutsii*. 7 vols. Berlin: Z. I. Grzhebin, 1922.

Traut, Johanes Ch. *Russland zwischen Revolution und Kontrrevolution: Berichte 1917–1921*. Vol. 2. Munich: Willing, 1975.

Tsereteli, I. G. *Vospominaniia o fevral'skoi revoliutsii*. Vol. 1. Paris: Mouton, 1963.

Ustinov, G. *Men'sheviki, pravye esery, i kontrrevoliutsiia*. Moscow: VTsIK, 1919.

Vatsetis, I. I. "Grazhdanskaia voina, 1918 god." In *Pamiat' istoricheskii sbornik*. Vol. 2. Moscow, 1977; Paris: YMCA, 1979.

Vishniak, M. V. *Vserossiiskoe uchreditel'noe sobranie*. Paris: Sovremennye zapiski, 1932.

Wolin, S. *Deiatel'nost' Men'shevikov v profsoiuzakh pri sovetskoi vlasti*. Inter-University Project on the History of the Menshevik Movement, paper no. 13. New York, 1962.

Zagorskii, Semen. *La République des soviets*. Paris: Payot, 1921.

Zenzinov, V. M. *Iz zhizni revoliutsionera*. Paris, 1919.

———, ed. *Gosudarstvennyi perevorot Admirala Kolchaka v Omske 18 noiabria*. Paris: I. Rurakhovskii, 1919.

Zhordaniia, N. N. *Bol'shevizm*. Berlin: TsK RSDRP, 1922.

———. *Za dva goda: S 1 marta 1917 po 1 marta 1919*. Tiflis: IK Soveta, 1919.

Zinov'ev, Grigorii. *Dve rechi*. Petrograd: Petrogradskii Sovet, 1918.

———. *Kontrrevoliutsiia i zadachi rabochikh: Rech na zasedanii Petrogradskogo soveta 15 iiunia 1918 goda*. Moscow: TsIK, 1918.

Documents

Akademiia Nauk SSSR, Institut Istorii. *Sovety v pervyi god proletarskoi diktatury, oktiabr' 1917–noiabr' 1918*. Moscow: Nauka, 1967.

Antonov-Saratovsky, V. P. *Sovety v epokhu voennogo kommunizma, 1918–1921*. Vol. 1. Moscow: Kommunisticheskaia Akademiia, 1928–29.

Arkhivnoe upravlenie Kalininskogo oblispolkoma and Partiinyi arkhiv Kalininskogo obkoma KPSS. *Podgotovka i provedenie velikoi oktiabr'skoi so-tsialisticheskoi revoliutsii v Tverskoi gubernii.* Kalinin: Knizhnoe Izdatel'stvo, 1960.

Arkhivnyi otdel Upravleniia vnutrennikh del Kostromskogo oblastnogo is-polkoma. *Ustanovlenie sovetskoi vlasti v Kostrome i Kostromskoi gubernii: Sbornik dokumentov i materialov, mart 1917–sentiabr' 1918.* Kostroma: Kostromskoe Knizhnoe Izdatel'stvo, 1957.

Arkhivnyi otdel UVD Gor'kovskogo oblispolkoma. *Pobeda Oktiabr'skoi So-tsialisticheskoi Revoliutsii v Nizhegorodskoi gubernii,* ed. A. I. Velikorechin and K. G. Seleznev. Gorki: Knizhnoe Izdatel'stvo, 1957.

Arkhivnyi otdel UVD Tul'skoi oblasti. *Oktiabr' v Tule: Sbornik dokumentov i materialov o bor'be za vlast' v Tule i gubernii v 1917 godu.* Tula, 1957.

Arkhivnyi otdel UVD Tul'skoi oblasti. *Uprochenie sovetskoi vlasti v Tul'skoi gubernii: Sbornik dokumentov i materialov, god 1918.* Tula, 1961.

Arkhivnyi otdel Vladimirskogo oblispolkoma. *Sovety Vladimirskoi gubernii v period podgotovki i razvitiia Velikoi Oktiabr'skoi Sotsialisticheskoi Re-voliutsii, 1917–1918.* Vladimir, 1969.

Arkhivnyi otdel Riazanskogo oblispolkoma. *Bor'ba za ustanovlenie i ukre-plenie sovetskoi vlasti v Riazanskoi gubernii, 1917–1920.* Riazan: Izdatel'stvo Gazety Priokskaia pravda, 1957.

Ascher, Abraham, ed. *The Mensheviks in the Russian Revolution.* Ithaca: Cor-nell University Press, 1976.

Baynac, Jacques. *La Terror sous Lenine, 1917–1924.* Paris: Sagittaire, 1975.

Belov, G. A., ed. *Iz istorii Vserossiiskoi chrezvychainoi kommissii, 1917–1921: Sbornik dokumentov.* Moscow: Gospolitizdat, 1958.

Bernshtam, M. S., ed. *Nezavisimoe rabochee dvizhenie v 1918 godu: Doku-menty i materialy.* Paris: YMCA Press, 1981.

——, ed. *Ural i Prikam'e, noiabr' 1917–ianvar' 1919: Dokumenty i materialy.* Paris: YMCA Press, 1982.

Bor'ba za Kazan': Sbornik materialov o Chekho-uchredilovskoi interventsii v 1918 godu. Kazan: Vostok, 1924.

Bor'ba za ustanovlenie i uprochenie sovetskoi vlasti v Kurskoi gubernii. Kursk, 1957.

Bor'ba za ustanovlenie i uprochenie sovetskoi vlasti v Simbirskoi gubernii, mart 1917–iiun' 1918. Ulianovsk, 1957.

Bothmer, Karl von. *Mit Graf Mirbach in Moskau: Tagebuch, Aufzeichnungen, und Aktenstuecke vom 19 April bis 24 August 1918.* Tübingen: Osiandersche Buchhandlung, 1922.

Buisson, Etienne. *Les Bolcheviki, 1917–1919: Faits, documents, commen-taires.* Paris: Fischbacher, 1919.

Bunyan, J., and H. H. Fisher, eds. *The Bolshevik Revolution, 1917–1918: Docu-ments and Materials.* Stanford: Stanford University Press, 1934.

The Case of Russian Labor against Bolshevism. New York: Russian Information Service, 1919.

Chugaev, D. A., ed. *Rabochii klass sovetskoi Rossii v pervyi god diktatury proletariata: Sbornik dokumentov i materialov.* Moscow: Nauka, 1964.

A Collection of Reports on Bolshevism in Russia: Abridged Edition of Parlia-mentary Paper, Russia, No. 1. London: His Majesty's Stationery Office, 1919.

Dekrety sovetskoi vlasti. Vol. 2. Moscow: Gospolitizdat, 1959.

Drobizhev, V. Z., ed. *Rabochii klass Sovetskoi Rossii v pervyi god proletarskoi diktatury*. Moscow: Moskovskii Gosudarstvennyi Universitet, 1975.

Dumas, Charles. *La Vérité sur les Bolcheviki: Documents et notes d'un temoin*. Paris: Editions Franco-Slaves, 1919.

Iz istorii grazhdanskoi voiny v SSSR, mai 1918–mart 1919. Vol. 1. Moscow: Sovetskaia Rossiia, 1960.

Keep, John L. H., ed. *The Debate on Soviet Power: Minutes of the All-Russian Central Executive Committee of Soviets, Second Convocation, October 1917–January 1918*. Oxford: Clarendon, 1979.

Kritchewsky, Boris. *Vers la catastrophe russe: Lettres de Petrograd au journal "L'Humanité" (octobre 1917–fevrier 1918)*. Paris: F. Alcan, 1919.

Kurskaia guberniia v gody inostrannoi voennoi interventsii i grazhdanskoi voiny, 1918–1920. Voronezh: Tsentral'no-Chernozemnoe Knizhnoe Izdatel'stvo, 1967.

Lelevich, G. [L. Mogilevskii, pseud.]. *V dni Samarskoi uchredilki*. Moscow: Gosizdat, 1921.

L'vov-Rogachevskii, V. L., ed. *Sotsialisty o tekushchem momente*. Moscow: Delo, 1917.

Narodnyi Kommissariat Vnutrennikh Del. *God raboty, 1918–1919*. Moscow, 1920.

Nikolaevsky, Boris. *Men'sheviki v dni oktiabr' skogo perevota*. Inter-University Project on the History of the Menshevik Movement, paper no. 8. New York, 1962.

Odessa Menshevik Committee. *Protsess "Iuzhnogo Rabochego" v revoliutsionnom tribunale (Stenograficheskii otchet)*. Odessa: Komitet RSDRP, 1918.

Oldenbourg, S. S., ed. *Le Coup d'état bolcheviste*. Paris: Payot, 1929.

Partiia Sotsialistov Revoliutsionerov. *Che-Ka: Materialy po deiatel'nosti*. Berlin: Izdanie Biuro Partii SR, 1922.

Partiinyi Arkhiv Kaluzhskogo Obkoma KPSS i Gosudarstvennyi Arkhiv Kaluzhskoi Oblasti. *Ustanovlenie sovetskoi vlasti v Kaluzhskoi gubernii: Dokumenty i materialy, mart 1917–iiul' 1918*. Kaluga: Izdatel'stvo gazety Znamia, 1957.

Partiinyi Arkhiv Obkoma KPSS i Arkhivnyi Otdel UVD Tambovskoi Oblasti. *Bor'ba rabochikh i krest'ian pod rukovodstvom Bol'shevistskoi partii za ustanovlenie i uprochenie sovetskoi vlasti v Tambovskoi gubernii (1917–1918): Sbornik dokumentov*. Tambov, 1957.

Partiinyi Arkhiv Orlovskogo Obkoma KPSS i Arkhivnyi Otdel UVD Orlovskogo Oblispolkoma. *Bor'ba trudiashchikhsia Orlovskoi gubernii za ustanovlenie sovetskoi vlasti v 1917–1918 godakh (sbornik dokumentov)*. Orel: Orlovskaia Pravda, 1957.

Partiinyi Arkhiv pri Iaroslavskom Oblastnom Komitete KPSS. *Ustanovlenie sovetskoi vlasti v Iaroslavskoi gubernii: Sbornik dokumentov i materialov*. Yaroslavl: Knizhnoe Izdatel'stvo, 1957.

Partiinyi Arkhiv Voronezhskogo Obkoma KPSS i Arkhivnyi Otdel UVD Voronezhskogo Oblispolkoma. *Bor'ba za sovetskuiu vlast' v Voronezhskoi gubernii, 1917–1918*. Voronezh: Knizhnoe Izdatel'stvo, 1957.

Perepiska Sekretariata TsK RSDRP(b)-RKP(b) s mestnymi organizatsiiami: Sbornik dokumentov i materialov. Vols. 1–3. Moscow: Gospolitizdat, 1967.

Podgotovka i provedenie Velikoi Oktiabr'skoi Revoliutsii v Tverskoi gubernii. Kalinin: Knizhnoe Izdatel'stvo, 1960.

Polgunov, N. G., and A. I. Rozanova. Shestnadtsat' dnei: Materialy po istorii Iaroslavskogo belogvardeiskogo miatezha (6–21 iiulia 1918 goda). Yaroslavl, 1924.

Popov, A. L., ed. Oktiabr'skii perevorot: Fakty i dokumenty. Petrograd: Novaia epokha, 1918.

"Protokoly soveshchanii TsIK pervogo sozyva." Krasnyi arkhiv 3, no. 10 (Moscow, 1925): 95–137.

Protokoly TsK RSDRP (b), avgust 1917–fevral' 1918. Moscow, 1958.

Protokoly zasedanii Vserossiiskogo Tsentral'nogo Ispolnitel'nogo Komiteta, chetvertogo sozyva: Stenograficheskii otchet. Moscow: Gosizdat, 1920.

Sobranie uzakonenii i rasporiazhenii rabochego i krest'ianskogo pravitel'stva: Sbornik dekretov. Moscow: Narkom Iustitsii, 1920.

Texte der Menschewiki zur Russischen Revolution und zum Sowjetstaat aus den Jahren 1903–1937. Hamburg: Junius, 1981.

Trotsky, Lev, ed. Stalinskaia shkola fal'sifikatsii. Berlin: Granat, 1932.

TsK RSDRP. Sbornik rezoliutsii i tezisov Tsentral'nogo Komiteta RSDRP i partiinykh soveshchanii. Vladivostok, 1921.

Uprochenie sovetskoi vlasti v Moskve i Moskovskoi gubernii. Moscow: Institut Istorii, Moskovskii Rabochii, 1958.

Vtoroi Vserossiiskii s''ezd sovetov. Kronstadt: Izdanie Kronshtadtskogo Soveta, 1917.

Secondary Sources

Antonov-Ovseenko, Anton. Portret Tirana. New York: Khronika, 1980.

Anweiler, Oskar. The Soviets: The Russian Workers', Peasants', and Soldiers' Councils. New York: Pantheon, 1974.

Ascher, Abraham. Pavel Axelrod and the Development of Menshevism. Cambridge: Harvard University Press, 1972.

Astrakhan, Kh. M. Bol'sheviki i ikh politicheskie protivniki v 1917 godu. Leningrad: Lenizdat, 1973.

Avrich, Paul. Kronstadt 1921. Princeton: Princeton University Press, 1970.

Bankrotstvo melkoburzhuaznykh partii v Rossii, 1917–1922. Moscow, 1977.

Baron, S. H. Plekhanov, the Father of Russian Marxism. Stanford: Stanford University Press, 1963.

Basil, John D. The Mensheviks in the Revolution of 1917. Columbus, Ohio: Slavica, 1984.

Berk, Stephen. "The 'Class Tragedy' of Izhevsk: Working Class Opposition to Bolshevism in 1918." Russian History 2, pt. 2. (1975): 176–90.

Bonnell, Victoria. Roots of Rebellion: Workers' Politics and Organizations in St. Petersburg and Moscow, 1900–1914. Berkeley: University of California Press, 1983.

Bourguina, A. M. Russian Social Democracy. The Menshevik Movement: A Bibliography. Stanford: Hoover Institution Press, 1968.

Bradley, John. Allied Intervention in Russia. London: Weidenfeld & Nicolson, 1968.

Bushnell, John. *Mutiny and Repression: Russian Soldiers in the Revolution of 1905–1906.* Bloomington: Indiana University Press, 1985.

Bystrianskii, V. *Men'sheviki i SRy v Russkoi Revoliutsii.* Petrograd, 1921.

Carley, Michael J. *Revolution and Intervention: The French Government and the Russian Civil War, 1917–1919.* Kingston, Ont.: McGill-Queens University Press, 1983.

Carr, E. H. *The Bolshevik Revolution, 1917–1923.* 3 vols. Baltimore: Penguin, 1966.

Carrère d'Encausse, Hélène. *Lenin, Revolution, and Power.* New York: Longman, 1982.

Cohen, Stephen. *Bukharin and the Bolshevik Revolution: A Political Biography.* New York: Knopf, 1973.

——. *Rethinking the Soviet Experience: Politics and History since 1917.* New York: Oxford University Press, 1985.

Daniels, Robert V. *Red October: The Bolshevik Revolution of 1917.* New York: Scribner's, 1967.

Davydov, M. I. *Bor'ba za khleb: Prodovol'stvennaia politika kommunisticheskoi partii i sovetskogo gosudarstva v gody grazhdanskoi voiny.* Moscow: Mysl', 1971.

Debo, Richard K. *Revolution and Survival: The Foreign Policy of Soviet Russia, 1917–1918.* Toronto: University of Toronto Press, 1979.

Deutscher, Isaac. *The Prophet Armed: Trotsky, 1879–1921.* New York: Oxford University Press, 1954.

Elufimova, N. A. "Pervye meropriiatiia bol'shevikov po sotsialisticheskomu preobrazovaniiu promyshlennosti (noiabr' 1917–1918) po materialam Riazanskoi gubernii." In *KPSS v period fevral'skoi i oktiabr'skoi revoliutsii i v pervye gody sovetskoi vlasti.* Riazan, 1975.

Elwood, Ralph Carter. *Russian Social Democracy in the Underground: A Study of the RSDRP in the Ukraine, 1907–1914.* Assen: Van Gorcum, 1974.

Emmons, Terence. *The Formation of Political Parties and the First National Elections in Russia.* Cambridge: Harvard University Press, 1983.

Erde, D. I. *Men'sheviki.* Kharkov: Proletarii, 1930.

Fainsod, Merle. *How Russia Is Ruled.* Cambridge: Harvard University Press, 1970.

Farbman, Michael S. *Bolshevism in Retreat.* London: Collins, 1923.

Fedorov, K. G. *VTsIK v pervye gody sovetskoi vlasti, 1917–1920.* Moscow: Gosiurizdat, 1957.

Fel'shtinskii, Iu. G. *Bol'sheviki i Levye SR, oktiabr' 1917–iiul' 1918: Na puti k odnopartiinoi diktature.* Paris: YMCA Press, 1985.

Ferro, Marc. *La Révolution de 1917: Octobre, naissance d'une société.* Aubier: Montaigne, 1976.

Fitzpatrick, Sheila, *The Russian Revolution.* New York: Oxford University Press, 1983.

Footman, David. *Civil War in Russia.* London: Faber & Faber, 1961.

Frenkin, Mikhail, *Zakhvat vlasti Bol'shevikami v Rossii i rol' tylovykh garnizonov armii: Podgotovka i provedenie oktiabr'skogo miatezha, 1917–1918.* Jerusalem: Stav, 1982.

Fuller, C. *Civil-Military Conflict in Imperial Russia, 1881–1914.* Princeton: Princeton University Press, 1985.

Galili, Ziva. "The Menshevik Revolutionary Defensists and the Workers in the Russian Revolution of 1917." Ph.D. diss., Columbia University, 1978.

——. "Workers, Industrialists, and Mensheviks: Labor Relations and the Question of Power in the Early Stages of the Russian Revolution." *Russian Review* 44 (1985): 239–69.

Gelbard, Arye. *Der Judische Arbeiter-Bund Russlands im Revolutionsjahr 1917*. Vienna: Ludwig Boltzman Institut für Geschichte der Arbeiterbewegung, 1982.

Gerasimenko, G. A. *Khronika revoliutsionnykh sobytii v Saratovskom povolzh'e*. Saratov: privolzhskoe knizhnoe izdatel'stvo, 1968

Gerson, Lennard D. *The Secret Police in Lenin's Russia*. Philadelphia: Temple University Press, 1976.

Getzler, Israel. *Kronstadt: The Fate of a Soviet Democracy*. Cambridge: Cambridge University Press, 1983.

——. *Martov: A Political Biography of a Russian Social Democrat*. Melbourne: Melbourne University Press, 1967.

——. "The Mensheviks." *Problems of Communism* 16 (November–December 1967): 15–29.

Geyer, Dietrich. *Kautskys russisches Dossier: Deutsche Sozialdemokraten als Treuhänder des russischen Parteivermögens, 1910–1915*. Frankfurt: Campus, 1981.

——. *Lenin in der russischen Sozialdemokratie: Die Arbeiterbewegung im Zarenreich als Organisationsproblem der revolutionären Intelligenz, 1890–1903*. Cologne: Böhlau, 1962.

——. *Die russische Revolution: Historische Probleme und Perspektiven*. Göttingen: Vandenhoeck & Ruprecht, 1977.

Gimpel'son, E. G. *Iz istorii stroitel'stva sovetov, noiabr' 1917–iiul' 1918*. Moscow: Gosizdat, 1958.

Gleason, Abbott, Peter Kenez, and Richard Stites, eds. *Bolshevik Culture*. Bloomington: Indiana University Press, 1985.

Gogolevskii, A. V. *Petrogradskii sovet v gody grazhdanskoi voiny*. Leningrad: Nauka, 1982.

Golikov, G. N. *Velikii oktiabr'*. Moscow: Molodaia gvardiia, 1982.

Golinkov, D. L. *Krushenie antisovetskogo podpol'ia v SSSR*. Moscow: Politizdat, 1978.

Golub, P. A. *Revoliutsiia zashchishchaetsia*. Moscow: Politizdat, 1982.

Grishin, P. P. *Men'sheviki i oktiabr'skaia revoliutsiia*. Moscow, 1923.

Gusev, K. V. *Krakh partii levykh EsErov*. Moscow: Izdatel'stvo Sotsial'no-Ekonomicheskoi Literatury, 1963.

Gusev, K. V., and Kh. Eritian. *Ot soglashatel'stva k kontrrevoliutsii (ocherk istorii politicheskogo bankrotstva i gibeli partii Sotsialistov Revoliutsionerov)*. Moscow: Mysl', 1968.

Haimson, Leopold. "The Mensheviks after the October Revolution," pts. 1 and 2, *Russian Review* 38 (1979): 454–73, and 39 (1980): 181–207.

——. *The Politics of Rural Russia, 1904–1914*. Bloomington: Indiana University Press, 1979.

——. "The Problem of Social Stability in Urban Russia, 1904–1917." *Slavic Review* 23 (1964): 619–42.

——. *The Russian Marxists and the Origins of Bolshevism.* Cambridge: Harvard University Press, 1955.

——, ed. *The Mensheviks: From the Revolution of 1917 to the Second World War.* Trans. Gertrude Vakar. Chicago: University of Chicago Press, 1974.

Helgesen, Malvin M. *The Origins of the Party-State Monolith in Soviet Russia: Relations between the Soviets and Party Committees in the Central Provinces, October 1917–March 1921.* Ann Arbor, Mich.: University Microfilms International, 1980.

Heller, Michael. "Lenin and the Cheka: The Real Lenin." *Survey* 24 (Spring 1979): 175–92.

Hildermeier, Manfred. *Die Sozialrevolutionäre Partei Russlands: Agrarsozialismus und Modernisierung im Zarenreich (1900–1914).* Cologne: Böhlau, 1978.

Hough, Jerry E., and Merle Fainsod. *How the Soviet Union Is Governed.* Cambridge: Harvard University Press, 1979.

Husband, William. "The Nationalization of the Textile Industry of Soviet Russia, 1917–1920." Ph.D. diss., Princeton University, 1984.

Jones, M. Ellen, "The Uses and Abuses of Article 87: A Study of the Development of Russian Constitutionalism, 1906–1917." Ph.D. diss., Syracuse University, 1975.

Joost, Wilhelm. *Botschafter bei den roten Zaren: Die deutschen Missionschefs in Moskau, 1918 bis 1941, nach geheimakten·und persönlichen Aufzeichnungen.* Vienna: Fritz, 1967.

Keep, J. L. H. "October in the Provinces." In *Revolutionary Russia,* ed. Richard Pipes. Cambridge: Harvard University Press, 1968.

——. *The Rise of Social Democracy in Russia.* Oxford: Clarendon, 1963.

——. *The Russian Revolution: A Study in Mass Mobilization.* London: Weidenfeld & Nicolson, 1976.

Kenez, Peter. *Civil War in South Russia, 1918: The First Year of the Volunteer Army.* Berkeley: University of California Press, 1971.

Khesin, S. S. *Stanovlenie proletarskoi diktatury v Rossii.* Moscow: Nauka, 1975.

Koenker, Diane. *Moscow Workers and the 1917 Revolution.* Princeton: Princeton University Press, 1981.

——. "Urbanization and Deurbanization in the Russian Revolution and Civil War." *Journal of Modern History* 57 (1985): 424–50.

Komin, V. V. *Bankrotstvo burzhuaznykh i melkoburzhuaznykh partii Rossii v period podgotovki i pobedy Velikoi Oktiabr' skoi Sotsialisticheskoi Revoliutsii.* Moscow: Moskovskii Rabochii, 1965.

——. *Bol'sheviki i neproletarskie partii v period oktiabr'skoi revoliutsii i grazhdanskoi voiny.* Moscow, 1982.

——, ed. *Simpozium: Krakh neproletarskikh partii Rossii.* Kalinin, 1981.

Kramář, Karel. *Die russische Krisis: Geschichte und Kritik des Bolschewismus.* Munich: Duncker & Humbolt, 1925.

Krasnikova, A. V. *Na zare sovetskoi vlasti: Bol'sheviki Petrograda v pervye mesiatsy proletarskoi diktatury, noiabr' 1917–iiul' 1918.* Leningrad: Lenizdat, 1963.

Lane, David. *The Roots of Russian Communism: A Social and Historical Study of Social Democracy, 1898–1907.* Assen: Van Gorcum, 1975.

Leggett, George. *The Cheka: Lenin's Political Police*. New York: Oxford University Press, 1981.

Lehovich, Dimitry V. *White against Red: The Life of General Anton Denikin*. New York: Norton, 1974.

Liebich, André. *Les Mencheviks en exil face à l'Union soviétique*. Montreal: Cahiers de Recherche du CIEE/ICES, 1982.

Lih, Lars. "Bread and Authority: Food Supply and Revolutionary Politics in Russia, 1914–1921." Ph.D. diss., Princeton University, 1984.

Lisovskii, P. A. *Na sluzhbe kapitala: SRo-men'shevistskaia kontrrevoliutsiia*. Leningrad: Priboi, 1928.

Lorenz, Richard. *Anfänge der bolschevistischen Industriepolitik*. Cologne: Wissenschaft & Politik, 1965.

Malashko, A. M. *K voprosu ob oformlenii odnopartiinoi diktatury v SSSR*. Minsk: Belorusskii Gosudarstvennyi Universitet, 1969.

Malia, Martin. *Comprendre la révolution russe*. Paris: Seuil, 1980.

Malle, Silvana. *The War Communism Economic Organization, 1918–1921*. Ann Arbor, Mich.: University Microfilms International, 1979.

Mandel, David. *The Petrograd Workers and the Fall of the Old Regime*. New York: St. Martin's Press, 1983.

——. *The Petrograd Workers and the Soviet Seizure of Power: From the July Days 1917 to July 1918*. New York: St. Martin's Press, 1984.

Mandel'shtam, M. N. *So stupen'ku na stupen'ku. K istorii rossiiskogo Men'shevizma*. Moscow, 1926.

Melancon, Michael. "The Socialist Revolutionaries from 1902 to February 1917: A Party of the Workers, Peasants, and Soldiers." Ph.D. diss., Indiana University, 1984.

Mel'gunov, S. P. *Krasnyi terror v Rossii*. New York: Brandy, 1979.

Mgeladze, I. V. *Protiv men'shevizma*. Moscow: Gosizdat, 1921.

——. *Revoliutsiia i men'shevizm*. Moscow: Gosizdat, 1925.

Miliukov, Pavel. *Rossiia na perelome: Bol'shevistskii period Russkoi Revoliutsii*. Paris: Source, 1927.

Millard, Michael. "Russian Revolutionary Emigration: Terrorism and the Political Struggle." Ph.D. diss., University of Rochester, 1973.

Mints, I. I. *God 1918*. Moscow: Nauka, 1982.

——. *Istoriia velikogo oktiabria*, vol. 3, *Triumfal'noe shestvie sovetskoi vlasti*. Moscow: Nauka, 1972.

——. *Men'sheviki v interventsii*. Moscow, 1931.

——, ed. *Oktiabr'skoe vooruzhennoe vosstanie v Petrograde*. Moscow: Nauka, 1980.

Okorokov, A. Z. *Oktiabr' i krakh russkoi burzhuaznoi pressy*. Moscow: Mysl', 1970.

Osipova, T. V. "Razvitie sotsialisticheskoi revoliutsii v derevne v pervyi god diktatury proletariata." In *Oktiabr' i sovetskoe krestianstvo, 1917–1927*, ed. I. M. Volkov. Moscow: Nauka, 1977.

Podbolotnikov, P. A. *Krakh SRo-men'shevistskoi kontrrevoliutsii*. Leningrad, 1975.

Popov, N. N. *Melkoburzhuaznye i antisovetskie partii*. Moscow: Krasnaia nov', 1924.

Potekhin, M. N. *Pervyi sovet proletarskoi diktatury.* Leningrad: Lenizdat, 1966.

Rabinovich, Alexander. *The Bolsheviks Come to Power: The Revolution in Petrograd.* New York: Norton, 1976.

Rabochie Leningrada v bor'be za pobedu sotsializma. Moscow: Akademiia Nauk, 1963.

Radkey, Oliver. *The Elections to the Russian Constituent Assembly.* Cambridge: Harvard University Press, 1950.

——. *The Sickle under the Hammer: The Russian Socialist Revolutionaries in the Early Months of Soviet Rule.* New York: Columbia University Press, 1963.

Razgon, A. I. *VTsIK sovetov v pervye mesiatsy diktatury proletariata.* Moscow: Nauka, 1971.

Reisser, Claus Thomas. "Menschewismus und Revolution, 1917: Probleme einer sozialdemokratischen Standortbestimmung." Ph.D. diss., University of Tübingen, 1981.

Remington, Thomas F. "Democracy and Development in Bolshevik Socialism." Ph.D. diss., Yale University, 1978.

Rigby, T. H. *Lenin's Government: Sovnarkom (1917–1922).* Cambridge: Cambridge University Press, 1979.

Rogger, Hans. *Russia in the Age of Modernisation and Revolution, 1881–1917.* London: Longman, 1983.

Roobol, W. H. *Tsereteli, a Democrat in the Russian Revolution: A Political Biography.* The Hague: Nijhoff, 1976.

Rosenberg, William. *Liberals in the Russian Revolution: The Constitutional Democratic Party, 1917–1921.* Princeton: Princeton University Press, 1974.

——. "Russian Labor and Bolshevik Power after October." *Slavic Review* 44 (Summer 1985): 213–38.

Ruban, N. V. *Oktiabr'skaia revoliutsiia i krakh men'shevizma, mart 1917–1918.* Moscow: Gospolitizdat, 1968.

Saul, Norman. *Sailors in Revolt: The Russian Baltic Fleet in 1917.* Lawrence: Regents Press of Kansas, 1978.

Schapiro, Leonard. *The Communist Party of the Soviet Union.* 2d ed. New York: Vintage, 1970.

——. *The Origin of the Communist Autocracy: Political Opposition in the Soviet State, 1917–1922.* New York: Praeger, 1965.

——. *The Russian Revolution of 1917: The Origins of Modern Communism.* New York: Basic Books, 1984.

Scheibert, Peter. *Lenin an der Macht: Das russische Volk in der Revolution, 1918–1922.* Weinheim: Acta Humaniora, 1984.

Schwartz, S. M. *The Russian Revolution of 1905: The Workers' Movement and the Formation of Bolshevism and Menshevism.* Chicago: University of Chicago Press, 1967.

Serge, Victor. *Year One of the Russian Revolution.* Chicago, 1972. First published in French as *L'An premier de la révolution russe.* Paris, 1930.

Service, Robert. *The Bolshevik Party in Revolution: A Study in Organisational Change, 1917–1923.* New York: Barnes & Noble, 1979.

——. *Lenin: A Political Life.* Vol. 1, *The Strengths of Contradiction.* Bloomington: Indiana University Press, 1985.

Sirianni, Carmen. Workers' Control and Socialist Democracy: The Soviet Experience. London: Verso, 1982.

Sivokhina, T. A. Krakh melkoburzhuaznoi oppozitsii. Moscow: Gospolitizdat, 1973.

Slobodin, Henry. Questions on the Bolsheviks and the Soviets Which Albert Rhys Williams Failed to Answer. New York, 1918.

Smith, Edward E. The Young Stalin: The Early Years of an Elusive Revolutionary. New York: Farrar, Straus & Giroux, 1967.

Smith, S. A. Red Petrograd: Revolution in the Factories, 1917–1918. Cambridge: Cambridge University Press, 1983.

Sobolev, P. N., ed. The Great October Socialist Revolution. Moscow: Progress, 1977.

Soboleva, P. I. Bor'ba Bol'shevikov protiv SRov i Men'shevikov v period ukrepleniia sovetskoi vlasti. Moscow: Moskovskii Gosudarstvennyi Universitet, 1961.

———. Bor'ba Bol'shevikov protiv Men'shevikov i SRov za Leninskuiu politiku mira (noiabr' 1917–1918). Moscow: Moskovskii Gosudarstvennyi Universitet, 1965.

———. Oktiabr'skaia revoliutsiia i krakh sotsial soglashatelei. Moscow: Moskovskii Gosudarstvennyi Universitet, 1968.

Sofinov, P. G. Ocherki istorii Vecheka. Moscow: Gospolitizdat, 1960.

Sokolov, S. A. Revoliutsiia i khleb. Saratov, 1967.

Solov'ev, O. F. Velikii oktiabr' i ego protivniki. Moscow: Mysl', 1963.

Spirin, L. M. Klassy i partii v grazhdanskoi voine v Rossii. Moscow: Mysl', 1968.

Stewart, George. The White Armies of Russia: A Chronicle of Counterrevolution and Armed Intervention. New York: Russell & Russell, 1970 (1933).

Strizhkov, Iu. K. Prodovol'stvennye otriady v gody grazhdanskoi voiny i interventsii, 1917–1921. Moscow: Nauka, 1973.

Suvorov, K. I. Istoricheskii opyt bor'by KPSS protiv men'shevizma. Moscow: Mysl', 1979.

Swain, Geoffrey. Russian Social Democracy and the Legal Labour Movement, 1906–1914. London: Macmillan, 1983.

Tucker, Robert. Stalin as Revolutionary, 1879–1929: A Study in History and Personality. New York: Norton, 1974.

Ullman, Richard. Anglo-Soviet Relations: Intervention and Civil War. Vol. 1. Princeton: Princeton University Press, 1961.

V. I. Lenin i Novgorodskaia guberniia. Leningrad, 1970.

Vladimirova, Vera. God sluzhby sotsialistov kapitalistam. Moscow: Gosizdat, 1927.

Vompe, P. Dni Oktiabr'skoi Revoliutsii i zheleznodorozhniki. Moscow: Gosizdat, 1924.

Wade, Rex. Red Guards and Workers' Militias in the Russian Revolution. Stanford: Stanford University Press, 1984.

———. The Russian Search for Peace, February–October 1917. Stanford: Stanford University Press, 1969.

Wildman, Allan K. The End of the Russian Imperial Army: The Old Army and the Soldiers' Revolt, March–April 1917. Princeton: Princeton University Press, 1980.

———. *The Making of a Workers' Revolution: Russian Social Democracy, 1891–1903*. Chicago: University of Chicago Press, 1967.

Wolf, B. D. *Three Who Made the Revolution: A Biographical History*. New York: Dial, 1948.

Znamenskii, O. N. *Vserossiiskoe Uchreditel'noe Sobranie: Istoria sozyva i politicheskogo krusheniia*. Leningrad, 1976.

Index

Abramov, A., 134

Abramovitch, Raphael, 30, 89, 114, 115–17, 148

Activists (Committee for an Active Struggle for the Regeneration of Russia), 270–71, 285, 286

Akhmatov, I. I., 137

Aksel'rod, Pavel, 36–37, 39, 46, 48, 54, 166, 211–12, 268

Aleksandrovskii railworks, 61, 221

Allied intervention, 217–19, 270–71, 276, 289–92, 297

All-Russian Congress of Workers' Assemblies of Upolnomochennye, 173, 221, 244–45, 247

Anti-Bolshevik uprisings: and army/sailors, 257, 260–62; and Civil War, 257–74; and Mensheviks, 257, 261–65; and peasants, 257, 258–60, 263, 264; and SRs, 260–62, 266–71; and Whites, 257, 262, 264–65.

Antiprofiteering detachments, 92, 98, 99, 190

Antonov, V., 70, 148, 156, 150

Anweiler, Oskar, 16, 128

Arkhangelsk, 147, 252, 279

Army: and anti-Bolshevik uprisings, 257, 260–62; discontent of, 249; and Mensheviks, 5–8; obligatory enlistments in, 263, 266; in Petrograd, 239; as robbers, 157; and soviets, 30–31, 136–37, 146, 160; and terrorism, 280, 281

Arsenal plant, 173, 178, 180, 236–37

Arzamas, 274

Avilov, Boris, 62

Avksent'ev, N. D., 20, 35, 213

Bagmen (meshochniki), 92, 95–96, 99, 178

Baltic Fleet, 183–84, 260

Baltic plant, 167, 183

Banks, 50–51, 53–54, 86–91, 103, 104

Baturskii, G., 163–64, 173

Bazarov, Vladimir, 83

Beloretsk, 155

Belyi, 259

Berezovskii plant, 155

Berg, Efrem, 173

Berzin, R. I., 263–64

Billiuten' chrezvychainogo sobraniia u-polnomochennykh, 173

Black Earth Region, 41, 141–47

Bogdanov, B. O., 163–64, 168, 263

Bogorodsk, 259

Bolsheviks: and CEC, 232; and crisis of 1918, 159–60; economic policies of, 50–54, 71, 77–78, 95, 103–4; factions in, 16–17, 24–30, 73, 103–4, 185; foreign policy of, 63–73; goals/image of, 1–2, 50, 299; leadership/membership of, 16–17, 159, 234; and Marxism, 2, 77, 299; and negotiated settlement with Mensheviks, 15–35, 295–96; and one-party dictatorship, 295–99; soviet elections policy of, 146, 295–96, 299; and state budget, 86–91; and state capitalism, 79–86, 104. See also Communists; Lenin, V. I.; New Course; specific name or topic

Borisenko, N. K., 173

Library of Congress Cataloging-in-Publication Data

Brovkin, Vladimir N.
  The Mensheviks after October.

  Bibliography: p.
  Includes index.
  1. Soviet Union—History—Revolution, 1917–1921. 2. Mensheviks. 3. Rossiiskaia sot-
sial-demokraticheskaia rabochaia partiia—History. I. Title.
DK265.9.M45B76 1987   947.084'1   87–47592
ISBN 0–8014–1858–5